Reality Television

Reality Television

Oddities of Culture

Edited by Alison F. Slade, Amber J. Narro, and
Burton P. Buchanan

LEXINGTON BOOKS
Lanham • Boulder • New York • Toronto • Plymouth, UK

Published by Lexington Books
A wholly owned subsidiary of Rowman & Littlefield
4501 Forbes Boulevard, Suite 200, Lanham, Maryland 20706
www.rowman.com

10 Thornbury Road, Plymouth PL6 7PP, United Kingdom

British Library Cataloguing in Publication Information Available

Library of Congress Cataloging-in-Publication Data

Reality television : oddities of culture / edited by Alison F. Slade, Amber J. Narro, and Burton P.
Buchanan.
p. cm.
ISBN 978-0-7391-8564-3 (cloth : alk. paper) -- ISBN 978-0-7391-8565-0 (electronic)
1. Reality television programs--United States--History and criticism. I. Slade, Alison, 1977- editor of
compilation. II. Narro, Amber J., editor of compilation. III. Buchanan, Burton P., 1963- editor of
compilation.
PN1992.8.R43R425 2014
791.45'655--dc23
2013045901

∞™ The paper used in this publication meets the minimum requirements of American
National Standard for Information Sciences Permanence of Paper for Printed Library
Materials, ANSI/NISO Z39.48-1992.

Printed in the United States of America

Contents

Introduction

Alison F. Slade

Although most viewers believe reality television began its history with the 1990 debut of MTV's *The Real World,* reality television firmly has its roots in the early days of television. From *Queen for a Day* to *I'd Like to See* or Alan Funt's *Candid Camera*, viewers have long been interested in watching the real, the normal, pictures of everyday life displayed on the small screen.

In the modern era of reality television, programming has run the gamut from crime, celebrity, dating and relationship shows to extreme physical makeovers of persons and homes. No topic or cultural group is exempt from the reality show formula. However, within the last decade, reality programming has shifted from only a few absurdities here and there (e.g., *Who Wants to Marry a Millionaire?*) to an entire line-up of odd and unique programs. As a television viewing culture, we have become more obsessed with instant gratification and the bigger and weirder, the better. Who knew television audiences would be completely enthralled with a Southern family acting out every stereotype of "redneck" on *Here Comes Honey Boo Boo*, or obsess over a backwoods Christian family from Louisiana who make duck calls on *Duck Dynasty?* This anthology seeks to explore not the mundane reality programs, but rather those reality programs that illustrate the odd, unique or peculiar aspects of our society. This anthology will explore these reality television programs across the categories of culture, gender and celebrity.

This anthology offers a critical look at odd reality programs from a variety of lenses. In chapter 1, Burton Buchanan examines the portrayals of masculinity in The Discovery Channel's *Deadliest Catch.* Buchanan conducts a contextual analysis of the themes represented in this series, seeking to analyze the extent that reality television is reinforcing or destroying long held cultural and sociological constructs such as what constitutes masculinity. In chapter 2, Leandra Hernandez also investigates masculinity from a Southern perspective in her analysis of A&E's *Duck Dynasty*. Hernandez examines how Southern masculinity is performed and produced in *Duck Dynasty* by exploring the consumption practices that "make Willie a man," albeit a new type of Southern swamp man who is refined and transformed by his material possessions, and also the discourse of gender relations and gender roles that are both discussed in the show amongst various characters and also put forth by the series as a whole.

Andre Cavalcante takes on the discourses of realness, social defiance, and happiness in an examination of *Here Comes Honey Boo Boo*. By focusing on fan interactions on Facebook with the program, Cavalcante performs a textual analysis of the commentary on social media to discover why *Here Comes Honey Boo Boo* is so compelling and how the fans perceive realness and happiness. In contrast to the happiness seen on *Here Comes Honey Boo Boo*, Elizabeth Christian delves in the underworld of prison reality programs to look at the narrative of shame found within the program *Louisiana Lockdown*. Christian seeks to explore and begin discussion on whether prison reality shows are based in documentary and realism or simply a vehicle to exploit the downtrodden prisoners.

Chapter 5 takes on *The Real Housewives* and the reflections of class and capitalism seen within the program. Nicole Cox utilizes ideological and textual analysis to examine the portrayal of class and capitalism in contrast with viewers' perceptions in online fan communities. Do the fans have a sense of their own class and capitalistic tendencies in comparison with those presented in the program? Rebecca Curnalia also tackles consumerism and consumption in her examination of TLC's *Extreme Couponing*. In chapter 6, Curnalia uses directed content analysis to determine how identification and normalization of the practice of extreme couponing is presented in the program, as well as how viewers might use this information in the Great Recession.

In chapter 7, Gordon Alley-Young investigates the unique and odd lives of gypsies along the lines of gender spectacles and culture in the program *My Big Fat American Gypsy Wedding*. Alley-Young's essay compares the American and Romani/Traveler cultures as they relate to gender (the body) and weddings. Does this program exploit the Romani/Traveler culture simply for the celebrity spectacle?

Pamela Morris and Charissa Niedzwiecki also explore culture and family by conducting a social comparison of real and reality families. In chapter 8, Morris and Niedzwiecki survey participants on perceptions of family using two reality programs centered on family: *Sister Wives* and *17 and Counting/ 18 and Counting*. Leandra Hernandez also looks at the family relationships between mothers and daughters in the chapter 9 feminist analysis of *Toddlers and Tiaras*. Hernandez seeks to understand the portrayal of ideal femininity on *Toddlers and Tiaras*, in addition to exploring the Lolita spectacle and how mothers live vicariously through these odd exploitations of their young daughters. William Trapani and Laura Winn take readers to the frontier in an exploration of masculinity and family on The Discovery Channel's *Gold Rush*. Trapani and Winn compare the "man" of the frontier with the hyper representation of man in more recent programming. Can discovering gold reconcile these ideas of what masculinity and maleness mean in our culture?

In chapter 11, Christopher Mapp delves into the celebrity and narcissistic culture of *Celebrity Rehab with Dr. Drew*. Mapp explores the program to determine if the show contributes to the demise of the participants, simply furthers their and Dr. Drew's celebrity status, or a wicked combination of both.

Matthew Ferrari takes readers back to the wild in an exploration of masculinity and survivor type programs such as *Survivorman*, *Mountain Men*, and *Man vs. Wild*. Ferrari's chapter 12 analyzes the regeneration of primitive maleness in these odd programs pitting man against a variety of forms of nature.

In chapter 13, Leslie Rasmussen explores viewers' perceptions of online relationships in an analysis of the MTV program *Catfish: The TV Show*. How do online and Internet relationships transfer to television and how do fans react to those images? Finally, Julie Haynes offers an in-depth look at the Southern United States and displays of Southern horror in an analysis of *Swamp People*. Cajun and Southern culture are linked to the authenticity of reality television and the realism of horror in chapter 14.

There is a long list of odd and unique reality programs, some of which have yet to be produced. While this anthology only touches the tip of the iceberg where these odd and unique reality programs are concerned, this edited volume provides a beginning look at those programs which fascinate and enthrall audiences throughout the United States. It will remain to be seen how long reality television producers will continue to push the boundaries of the odd and extraordinary in television programming.

Chapter One

Portrayals of Masculinity in The Discovery Channel's *Deadliest Catch*

Burton P. Buchanan

Reality television programs have enjoyed widespread popularity among American television audiences for the last several decades. The genre encompasses a wide range of subject matter and themes. Of particular interest to national audiences has been a specific subgenre; the reality program that showcases and documents the efforts of American workers doing their jobs. Programs such as these have included *Airline*, *Dirty Jobs*, *Parking Wars*, *Cops*, *Dog the Bounty Hunter*, *Family Plots*, *Ice Road Truckers*, and *Deadliest Catch*. Reality television has offered the viewer a realistic insight into the work that goes along with the execution of the duties while on these various jobs.

Television programming has consistently reflected a fairly rigorous depiction of male and female gender roles with not a large amount of variation. Men are continuously portrayed as the breadwinners of the family. Women are often relegated to matters concerning home and family, with exceptions. Decades of episodic television have established these norms. One reality program in particular, *Deadliest Catch*, which airs on The Discovery Channel, serves to perpetuate many of the traditional notions concerning such gender portrayals. The program which premiered in 2005 has remained quite popular among male adult audiences as it continues into its ninth season. [1]

The Western male patriarchal hegemony can be seen playing out in the episodes of *Deadliest Catch* as the men go about their duties on board the various vessels as they navigate the waters of the Bering Sea on their quest to harvest crab for profit. Men value and judge their very masculinity on their work output, stamina and attitudes toward their work. The heroes are the men who have proven themselves over numerous successful harvests. The work itself is among the most dangerous jobs in existence.[2] Weakness and failure are often portrayed as feminine attributes and those not able to withstand the rigor of the labor are ultimately forced to leave the job. Often the men engage in struggles over power, respect and status while harvesting crabs. The men bond over the work and form cohesive work groups. New workers, or "greenhorns," are often ridiculed, tested and are subject to practical jokes, and other forms of ritual hazing.

The Discovery Channel's *Deadliest Catch* has become a very popular television program showcasing the treacherous work involved in crab fishing on the Bering Sea. The boats and crews race against other in search of Alaskan king crab, seeking the best fishing locations and attempting to haul in as much of the crab as possible in a specified amount of time. The characters, the action, danger, harsh environment and hegemonic themes strike a chord with audiences. *Deadliest Catch* has received continually good ratings, with the highest ratings ever during the 2010 season. In 2010, during its sixth season opener, 4.6 million viewers tuned in to follow the death of Captain Phil Harris. The show had garnered its highest ratings ever and was the most viewed program on cable for that Tuesday evening.[3]

In the post-feminist, post-metrosexual culture, *Deadliest Catch* reinforces long held concepts on traditional masculinity. The traditional Western male, patriarchal hegemony has suffered many onslaughts by new cultural constructs. Moreover, white male power has endured encroachment as women, gays and minorities have gained social power in recent decades. *Deadliest Catch* serves as a fine example of a reality television program that demonstrates an environment where traditional masculinity is exercised, a place where white males can perform masculine rituals, compete with one another in an adverse environment and reassert their position in the social and cultural hierarchies.

HEGEMONIC MASCULINITY AND TELEVISION GENDER PORTRAYALS

Television is one of society's primary modes of perpetuating a particular value or concept. The role of television in society is that of a storyteller, common to everyone. Acting as a cultural bard like those in the middle Ages, television is the primary purveyor of today's popular culture. People are told about such topics as the mysteries of life, far off places, power, fate, and strivings. It is a powerful agent of socialization for the American people.[4] Americans spend a great deal of their leisure time viewing television. It is the primary and most omnipresent mass medium in American culture.[5]

Television therefore is a powerful source of information with respect to the concept of gender and gender stereotyping. In fact, television does an excellent job of depicting men and women in established and accepted ways.[6] Adults on average tend to watch four hours of television per day. Moreover, gender norms are then cultivated by viewers and even strengthened due to the volume of television consumption.[7] Within these gendered structures of American television, men are almost always portrayed as possessing positions of power and authority.[8] Television aids in creating a specific "categorization" of its viewers and characters as masculine and feminine subjects.[9]

For decades, scripted episodic television has created this structure of men and women as masculine and feminine characters to reflect the accepted and established norms in society. This idea is central to a television program's success. Producers of television programming have a principal focus and that is profit. As part of the "culture industry," these cultural texts must resonate with the viewers in such a way that they maintain a desire to keep viewing the program.[10] This profit motive prompts producers to create characters that are relatable to viewers. Likeable and relatable characters that audiences can engage with will ensure repeat audiences week after week.[11] Reality television is no different even though the programs are not traditionally scripted, cheaper to produce and feature "real" people instead of celebrities.

Television has succeeded in perpetuating traditional gender roles and stereotypes that reinforce accepted notions of femininity and masculinity. The accepted concept of "male supremacy" is assumed.[12] Since television first programmed its daily schedules, men have consistently been seen as the primary breadwinner and the head of the household. Men assert their dominance and expend much energy to protect their families from potential harm. As a mirror of society, male characters were depicted in this domineering role since in reality men have fought wars, exclusively held jobs and were financially secure. This masculinity is therefore portrayed as white, heterosexual, financially independent and often middle class.[13]

The dominant form of masculinity within a culture, even though not the most prevalent form, tends to be the hegemonic masculinity. This form helps explain the power of men over women and the hierarchy involved in men's power over men and others in society.[14] White men are understood as a force that subordinates women and others (gays, women, minorities and the foreign born).[15] A plurality of masculinities has arisen in recent times. All types of men are expressing all types of masculinity in new and different ways.[16]

The white masculine hegemony takes for granted that there is a fundamental difference between men and women. It assumes that heterosexuality is normal. The hegemony accepts without question the sexual division of labor and it sanctions the political and dominant role of men in the public and private sphere.[17] For decades, this hegemony has been played out over and over across countless television programs, series and genres. Programming has consistently depicted male characters in the dominant and powerful role while the female roles have been relegated to society's traditional sphere for women; that of homemaker, caretaker and mother of children.

Reality television programs since their explosion onto the television landscape in the late 1990s have been very popular among television audiences. This new genre has produced a wide variety of programming. Much of it has been a challenge to the societal status quo while much of it still tends to reinforce standard thinking along gender lines. Meanwhile, over the past several decades, other groups such as women, gays, and minorities have made inroads in society gaining both economic and political power. Cultural events such as women's rights, gay rights and civil rights have begun to create a perceived loss of masculine authority.[18] These groups or "others" have moved into the workplace and into politics, further encroaching upon the traditional masculine hegemony.[19]

MASCULINITY IN CRISIS

Even men and their roles on reality television have given acceptance in society to alternative masculinities. Images of new masculinities have been seen in mainstream media now with depictions of gay, Latino, African-American masculinities. Various programs have begun to depict masculinity and sexuality as belonging to others rather than only to the white, male heterosexual. Other "types" of men are depicted as well such as the "sensitive" heterosexual and the metrosexual.[20] This metrosexual is a prime example of the new man. He is typically an urban male, who is enthusiastic about displaying his feminine side, adopts accoutrements such as expensive hairstyles, suits by famous designers and the use of expensive grooming products. This of course is in direct opposition to the traditional masculine concepts of low-key dress, minimal grooming and stoicism.[21] Male portrayals in this new era of television are being depicted as less macho, less sexist, more feeling and more sensitive to the needs of their significant others. Feminized masculinity is seen for the first time in direct opposition to the traditional white masculine hegemony.[22] Even mainstream television has featured gay men offering makeovers for heterosexual men on Bravo's *Queer Eye for the Straight Guy*.

With the encroachment of other forms of masculinity and other groups asserting themselves in modern society, part of the white male hegemony harken back to the time when "men were men." In other words, they long for an era when their hegemonic paradigm was in full force. The various "others" in society were therefore much weaker and possessed less power over society as a whole.[23] Men, they fear, have a great deal to lose from gender equality since men collectively have received a "patriarchal dividend."[24]

They feel an assault upon the very foundation of their social structure. Men feel a palpable sense of loss on many fronts: the workplace, the political arena and the social structure. The traditional white, male hegemony has been under a series of attacks and many have felt a loss of privilege and power.[25] Traditional television programming as well as that of the reality genre has started to depict this change, a shift in the dominant male paradigm.

MEN AT WORK

Media scholars have delineated five primary features of hegemonic masculinity in American culture: (1) physical force and control, (2) occupational achievement, (3) familial patriarchy, (4) frontiersmanship and (5) heterosexuality.[26] In addition to these features, scholars add that men are depicted as unconcerned with their appearance, indulgent in alcohol use, involved in dangerous situations as a matter of routine and willing to expose themselves to situations that could cause them physical harm (health issues).[27] Researchers have sought to explain much about hegemonic masculinity through this five-part concept and argue that this concept serves to clarify the American hegemonic male ideal. With respect to *Deadliest Catch*, the men of the Bering Sea in the business of catching Alaskan king crab embody and exemplify these concepts very well. The program, in its ninth season, serves to play out a great many aspects of these concepts regarding American masculinity.

Deadliest Catch follows the lives of a group of Alaskan crab fishermen as they work to catch as many Alaskan king crabs as they can during the short crab-fishing season on Alaska's Bering Sea. The boat captains as well as the deckhands work together to garner as many crab as they can to earn as much money as possible. They divide the profits among themselves at the season's end. A somewhat patriarchal hierarchy is played out each week as each boat's captain is featured as the unequivocal leader of the group and the others adhere to a somewhat rigorous hierarchy often established through the tough and treacherous experiences lived through by the deckhands. New crew members are known as "greenhorns." These men are working on the boats for the first time. It is a time of trial for the new worker. He must prove himself not only to the other deckhands as worthy, but to the captain as well.

PHYSICAL FORCE AND CONTROL

Physical ability and control are integral parts of the hegemonic masculinity.[28] For men, power often originates from physical capabilities. Physical strength, stamina, and facility with the work at hand are all prized characteristics for a man. Central to many themes in masculinity are those of meeting challenges, physical risk and mastery of such risks and challenges.[29] Deckhands on *Deadliest Catch* are constantly attempting to assert their physical prowess, their strength and fortitude against the brute forces thrown at them by their natural environment and the work at hand. Men who cannot live up to the challenge of the physical work involved are ostracized and even forced to leave their jobs onboard. Monte Colburn of the "Wizard" once said of one of the "greenhorns" during their trial period; "you've just basically admitted you're a quitter and you're not man enough to step up to the plate and do the task."[30]

The men must endure long hours of being out on the deck, facing rogue waves crashing over the deck, getting tangled up in the gear, and keeping up with the rapid pace of the duties as the men bring in the crab pots from the icy sea. The men are pitted against nature in a constant battle. They must use their physical abilities to harvest the crab in the wake of the deadly physical danger. Physical toughness is a trait that the men must possess to be successful in any of the jobs depicted in the program. Facility with the duties must be accomplished quickly and tasks mastered quickly to be successful in the harvest as well as to prevent accidents and mishaps. The display of speed and agility in the execution of these duties on board proves the men's' physical ability and their right to be on the boat. Speed and skill in the work increases the likelihood of a larger harvest. Captain Henry Blake said of skill on deck, "Hesitation could mean somebody's life."[31]

The mastery of the duties involved translates into an actual language of the male body, as a holder of male domination and power. The superiority of men is manifested in the successful execution of the duties of crabbing where a profit was secured and no injuries were sustained. Captain Keith Colburn said, "nobody's lost any body parts on this boat and we're not about to start now."[32] Skillful performance of the work involved symbolizes this first masculine ideal in that the superiority of men is proven in evidence of a successful harvest. Characteristics such as physical strength, application of controlled force, rapid execution of the jobs, as well as toughness and domination of the physical environment serve to exemplify the program's representation of the masculine hegemony.[33]

OCCUPATIONAL ACHIEVEMENT

A second component of these distinguishing characteristics of hegemonic masculinity seen in *Deadliest Catch* is the idea of occupational achievement.[34] America is a capitalist society. For men to be successful as men and participate fully in the hegemony, they must display economic and entrepreneurial competency. Men must prove themselves as good providers and seize the opportunity to earn a bounty in the marketplace. Hegemonic masculinity dictates too that labor be divided along gender lines. The jobs themselves become delineated according to appropriateness for each gender. Tasks and jobs are either "men's work" or "women's work."[35] Some work is largely conceptualized as more masculine than other jobs. Substantial manual labor therefore is considered to be more masculine.[36]

As the episodes of *Deadliest Catch* unfold, such manifestations of this idea of occupational achievement are seen at work. The world of the crab fishermen is a male-dominated realm where these men engage in work that is often too tough, too strenuous for many men. Captain Greg Moncrief once reminded his crew, "You're an employee now. It's not 'The Love Boat.'"[37] Men must prove themselves worthy of the job and keep proving this harvest, after harvest demonstrating they are capable of the work at hand. Those who achieve the most are rewarded and lauded the most.

Fraught with constant danger, crab fishing is a perilous, even often deadly, endeavor. Elements of the job such as the frigid temperatures, slippery decks, the potential of getting hurt by the loading and offloading of the crab pots, and the treacherous weather all prove that the occupation is one worthy of a man's time and effort. The danger is directly proportionate to the reward that is possible in the duties of the crab fishermen. Even in this highly mechanized, service-oriented world, the world of the crab fishermen and their life on the boats as they traverse the Bering Sea exists as a splendid example of men executing this concept of engaging in simple, strenuous manual labor and profiting from the "sweat of their brow."

The work involved in crab fishing aids the men in proving their masculinity. This environment is not an appropriate place for women. They attempted to prove this during one episode in which they invited captain Greg Moncrief's wife Ragnhild on board as the boat's new greenhorn, cook and "den mother."[38] Ultimately she felt as if the boat was not an appropriate place for women even though she had made notable contributions to the overall success of the season. Moncrieff noted that there simply were very few jobs on board women could do and felt as if she oftentimes "wasted space."[39] This episode's theme serves to prove the hegemonic standard that the work on board these boats is not appropriate for women. The primary attributes that men value in women in the world away from the job (gentility, vulnerability, fragility) are held as prime reasons they do not belong on crab boats.[40]

New deckhands, the greenhorns are responsible for very specific job tasks as rites of passage on their way to becoming seasoned and capable deckhands. The job is most assuredly entry level. Everyone on board started as a greenhorn, learning the job through trial and error and proving themselves worthy for more responsible jobs on board the crab vessels. The pay for the job is close to one half that of the more experienced men.[41]

The greenhorn's area of responsibility is accomplishment of all the "grunt work" on board the boats. They clean the vessels and knock ice from the boat railing using a sledgehammer. Another entry-level task left to the greenhorn is acting as the processor of the bait. Thousands of pounds of fish must be cut up by hand and attached to the individual crab pots. This work is executed in extremely cold temperatures and in winds as high as sixty miles per hour and on icy decks. This job aids the greenhorn in demonstrating his value to the boat and earning the trust and respect of his superiors. Captain Sig Hansen, captain of the "Northwestern," is seen early on refusing to talk to or otherwise acknowledge greenhorn Bradford Davis until an appropriate amount of time has passed and Hansen can then see how Davis is working out on board. [42]

For a man to begin work as a greenhorn, no fishing experience is required. However, due to the preparation of bait, salmon and crab processing experience is a desired skill for the greenhorn. The successful candidate must possess a very high endurance, a willingness to accomplish menial tasks, work without question, and receive much less pay than anyone else on board. Skills with handling a sledgehammer and fillet knife are very desirable as well. [43] The job is accomplished in a very hazardous environment and once the candidate is on board, there is no turning back due to second thoughts.

The life of a greenhorn is made to be miserable. The job is a test of a man's mettle, to see whether he will work out and be suitable for more responsible jobs on the boat in the future. Upward mobility does exist for the greenhorn, but he must prove himself worthy. Such occupational achievement ensures the greenhorn of being able to climb up the ranks on the boat to gain more responsible work and with that a much larger portion of the overall boat profits at season's end.

Life on board a crab boat embodies this second feature of the hegemonic masculinity, occupational achievement. The tenets underscore the importance of a man being able to make a way for himself in the world. To achieve financial success is a strong measure of a man's hegemonic masculinity quotient. Success in so-called "men's work," jobs that are labeled and established as uniquely masculine, brings success and fulfillment to the man. He is a success in the marketplace and therefore can successfully provide for his family as the primary breadwinner. [44]

FAMILIAL PATRIARCHY

Men in the masculine hegemony are seen as being members of the "dominant classes," holding power over women and other men. Others are "subordinated. The "social ascendancy" claimed by the masculine hegemony has given men the ability to maintain the subordination of these "others." Moreover, men maintain their willingness to be acknowledged leaders within the capitalist patriarchy.[45] In their quest to maintain dominance, and earn and provide for their family, men also accept a responsibility to act as "father figures," "family protectors," and "breadwinners."[46]

Media depictions of men over the decades have been consistent in reinforcing this patriarchal and familial head of the family. The images have predominantly portrayed these patriarchs as white, secular, heterosexual, North American, masculine men.[47] Men therefore must embrace the role of breadwinner and provider. He early on in his formative years must take a path toward adulthood that prepares him to accept the ascribed responsibilities. Men embracing the hegemony accept this role of caretaker and protector willingly.

Many television programs in recent memory have often portrayed new versions of masculinity. As part of this new iteration of masculine structure, men are many times portrayed as rejecting adulthood and the duties and responsibilities that go with that traditional masculine role. Modern characters are often selfish, dependent, and flawed in many ways.[48] Many of these men would be considered unfit for the role of a hegemonic patriarch.

Character Tim Taylor of ABC's *Home Improvement* is an example of such male characters. He, although a patriarchal figure, has rejected a traditional masculine vocation and works as a television personality as part of his character. In addition, his wife must often ride herd on his overzealousness to add "more power" to the tools and appliances found around the family home.[49] Jerry Seinfeld in NBC's *Seinfeld* portrays a man who has rejected the indications of traditional male adulthood and responsibility. He is not married, holds no steady job and carries on sexual relationships with multiple partners.[50]

In opposition to such nonhegemonic depictions, *Deadliest Catch* sometimes shows the private and personal sides of the men on the crab boats, as traditional masculine male characters who have committed ongoing relationships with wives or girlfriends. They are often dedicated fathers. Family is stressed on the program as very important to all the men. They take their vocation very seriously and want to do the best job they possibly can in order to earn a livelihood for their families. These men reinforce the traditional masculine concept of patriarch, caretaker and provider.

Women are rarely portrayed at all but the wives and girlfriends are referenced and at times are depicted as calling the boat to deliver some type of news. In season five, episode one, the wife of Captain Keith Colburn calls to tell him that their bank account has been depleted due to repairs made to the boat during the off season.[51] Colburn then must push onward to catch enough of a harvest to make up for such losses. In one episode in season five Captain Hansen's wife calls in to warn her husband of bad weather.[52] Another instance when viewers are shown the personal and familial side of the men on board took place when the wife of deckhand Nick Mavar, Jr. calls. She calls to tell Greenhorn Jake Anderson that his sister had passed away. Jake then is allowed to transfer to another boat in order to go to his family. Also, Deck Boss Edgar Hansen, in an act of patriarchal privilege, assures Jake that his place on board will remain until he can return to his duties.[53]

Deadliest Catch captains many times have taken on the paternal characteristics as father figures for the crewmen on the boats. The crews look to the captains for guidance, leadership and management of the boats during their fishing expeditions. The crews also have grown to respect and admire the captains. For some crew members, they aspire themselves to be captains one day. Therefore the captains often act as parental figures for their crewmen. For example, aboard the "Wizard" in season nine, episode six, Crewman Freddy made the announcement that he and his fiancée were going to have a baby. Freddy then asked Captain Keith Colburn to be the baby's godfather. Captain Keith was visibly moved and expressed how honored he was to have been asked.[54]

The feature of familial patriarchy is evident in the episodes of *Deadliest Catch*. The white, male hegemonic concept of being caretaker, provider and patriarch is echoed many times during the course of the series' episodes. The notions, although contemporary, nonetheless reinforce the traditional ideas of the male hegemony. Viewers see this theme acted out in the episodes and it resonates with viewers as they watch the episodes.

FRONTIERSMANSHIP

This fourth feature of hegemonic masculinity is embodied by the daring, rugged outdoorsman very much like the images of those men who "tamed the American frontier." As Frederick Jackson Turner put forth, the frontiersmen were those rugged individuals, daring and romantic who helped build up the American continent and left a lasting image that remains symbolic of America.[55] One such enduring symbol of this uniquely American imagery is that of the cowboy. This archetypal image is utilized in American media and is used to construct the image and spirit of America's independence, freedom, and self-sufficient nature.

The cowboy spirit is seen in *Deadliest Catch* fairly often. The men set off in search of crab to seek their fortune in their own untamed and wild frontier. Not so much the range, but the open sea, this frontier is representative is the place the men are beckoned in order to seek their livelihoods. Henry Blake is quoted in season five as saying, "The thing about the Aleutians . . . it's almost . . . it's almost like the last frontier."[56] Harry Lewis said of being out on the open sea, "It just goes on and on. Mother Nature's in control here. We do what we can with the weather we're dealt."[57] The narrator Mike Rowe says in the very first season of the fishermen's resolve, "These are Alaskan crab fishermen, and that means never giving up."[58] This seems to symbolize the essence of independence and self-reliance so prevalent in the concept of frontiersmanship.

The men have a limited amount of time to fish for crab, a limited time to get the crabs to the processor and a grueling schedule in which to accomplish it all. The lifestyle of the men on the crab boats is very reminiscent of the lifestyle of the American cowboy as he makes his way with his herd during one of the many cattle drives he endures. He too has a limited schedule, faces natural calamities that damage his herd and is out of the normal environment for most people. The corollary between the crab fisherman and the American cowboy is seen in action in the episodes of *Deadliest Catch*. The program serves to reinforce the masculine notions of free spiritedness, independence, self-sufficiency and efficiency.

A lack of concern for one's outward appearance is yet another tenet of the hegemonic masculinity code since narcissism and vanity can be construed as traits associated with femininity and homosexuality.[59] As in the frontier of the old west, the crab fishermen have a minimal of personal space where they work. They cannot carry a great deal of personal effects along with them. They use only what is essential to them. Many of the men have somewhat long hair and an abundance of facial hair. Long hair, beards and mustaches are sometimes synonymous with antiestablishment behavior. These men do not have a great deal of time and would not care to spend their time on personal grooming. The indifference to appearance stands to reinforce the frontier aspects of life aboard a crab boat. Again, such comparisons reinforce the hegemonic themes of frontiersmanship, rugged independence and self-reliance.

HETEROSEXUALITY

The white male masculine hegemony presumes that heterosexuality is the "natural order of things," and that one sex, the female, exists as a sexual object for the male. [60] This type of sexuality is "normal, natural and good."[61] Sexuality must be heterosexual, monogamous, marital and reproductive. Men must behave in a manly way, not have relationships with men that are sexual or overtly intimate and should always be successful in their relationships with women.[62] Heterosexuality and homophobia are a big part of the foundation of hegemonic masculinity and are predicated upon the idea that men's relationships with women are oppressive. Women provide heterosexual men with sexual validation and therefore men compete with one another for this validation. [63]

The hegemonic masculinity feature of heterosexuality is the accepted norm in *Deadliest Catch*. Men on the show respect and involve themselves in long-term, heterosexual relationships. As a corollary to the feature of familial patriarchy, heterosexuality keeps the men at the top of the paradigm. The women they left at home validate them, give them a reason to do the job and act as beneficiaries of the bounty for which the men are searching.

The men are exercising their heterosexuality constantly as they hold up to the pressures, the rigors of crab fishing. The men who stand up to the adverse conditions and difficult work are revered by the other men and respected as one of the elite group of men who are seasoned experienced fishermen. Within this heterosexual dimension, men must never appear to be weak or effeminate, lest they risk appearing homosexual. Dislike of homosexual men often may be utilized in defining their heterosexuality.[64] Men who do not hold up to the challenges of the job on board the boats can be compared to women, therefore neither masculine nor heterosexual.

Heterosexual hegemonic themes are seen played out in the episodes of *Deadliest Catch*. The men aboard the boats are close knit, but keep enough of a distance from one another both physically and emotionally so as not to be thought of as homosexual or deviant. Their work output is indirectly tied to their sexual prowess; the more a man can handle the conditions of the job, the more of a complete and successful man he is thought to be. Therefore he could be thought of as a good provider and caretaker, therefore a successful man, who never exhibits any indication of anything but heterosexual behavior.

DANGERS AND HEALTH ISSUES

Life aboard any of the crab boats is very difficult and the specter of possible injury is always near. The Bureau of Labor Statistics ranks crab fishing as the most dangerous job in existence.[65] Work on the boats is extremely dangerous and risks are omnipresent: high winds, heavy seas and the inherent dangers of operating heavy gear on the lurching, ice-covered deck of a boat on rough seas. The work schedules take a toll on the men, sometimes lasting a marathon pace where twenty hour work shifts are commonplace.[66] Incidents have occurred ranging from relatively minor mishaps to loss of life.

Men due to their masculine nature take pleasure in taking unnecessary risks. Men of *Deadliest Catch* risk their lives often. They have chosen jobs that allow them to live their lives by other sets of rules where engaging in "death-defying" labor is a daily part of the job. One particular episode from season four, episode twelve, entitled, "Mortal Men" characterizes how such work is part of the job. With a backdrop of subfreezing temperatures, high unpredictable waves, and random pieces of equipment smashing onto the boat decks and deckhands, the crew had to stay awake, on duty and focused for long stretches of time. The crews must often endure work shifts sometimes as long as thirty-six hours. They stay awake crediting a combination of Red Bull, nicotine and adrenaline.[67] As viewers watch the episodes, the inherent dangers become obvious. Such risks contribute to the hegemonic theme of the male's embrace of danger. After crewman Travis Lofland gets slammed by an enormous wave over the deck he says, "Nothing like a little wash around the deck to make you feel alive."[68]

Perhaps the dangers and risks to the men's mortality are one more way the program derives resonance from its male viewers. Other shows in the reality television landscape characterize all sorts of jobs, but few are depicted such as these of the fisherman where such strenuous work takes place in such a dangerous environment. The male bodies begin to show the rough treatment they have received since the series first aired.[69] These men embrace this work. They have obviously rejected "safer" jobs perhaps like those found in the service-oriented economy, such as those that might be held by women. In fact, men who embrace the male hegemony depicted in *Deadliest Catch* are much more like to engage in behavior that is categorized as unhealthy and risky.[70]

Membership in this dangerous, all-male realm brings along with the perils a sense of pride, self-satisfaction and control. The men conduct the work in an environment where men constantly must prove their worth, where simple mistakes and the unpredictable nature of the work could cause them great harm. The work is not depicted as feminine. The environment represents one where the men working in it are approved by one another as being fit for such difficult duties. Moreover, the men must constantly work together in order to secure the rewards offered by the harsh, unforgiving environment.[71] Deckhand Josh Harris said of work on the Bering Sea, "There's something about coming up here and risking your life. Sounds weird but it makes you feel alive."[72]

Dangers inherent in the work alleviate any notion about the work being feminized. The men perform the work in an "otherworld" type of environment where they only work with other qualified and approved men. The men take a certain amount of self-satisfaction knowing that they can successfully manage the dangers and execute the duties with precision and rapidity. With the reduction in less dangerous, though no less masculine jobs in the economy (manufacturing, construction) the fishermen are able to perform masculine jobs in an all-male environment where no threats to the masculine hegemony are present.[73] *Deadliest Catch* again appears to reinforce and to some extent glorify many hegemonic ideals. Captain Phil Harris offered a bit of philosophy, "Well, you just hope it isn't your time. Every day you're out there it's just more risk and more risk."[74]

Accepting the life of a crab fisherman and subsequently embracing the hegemonic masculine ideal brings with it a toll of human suffering. In fact, conforming to these masculine ideals can be deadly. The reward is public status while the costs of conformance can be high. Men embracing this lifestyle often are faced with shorter life expectancies, poorer health, and reduced time spent with loved ones. [75] Execution of the ideals of the hegemony in everyday life can exact a toll on the men who opt to do so. Deckhand Matt Bradley expressed his view of things, "We're replaceable. The crabs are not replaceable." [76]

Typically men are less apt to visit doctors and seek regular and systematic medical care than women. They will not make appointments for [77] medical treatments for what they perceive to be "minor" aches and pains. Men are conditioned to "work through" pain and simply endure the discomfort until it subsides. Men often take more risks with their health, indulging in unhealthy and unsafe activities on a more regular schedule than women. Captain Phil Harris commented on the measure of manhood, "You're not a man until you've pulled a tooth out with a pair of pliers." [78]

Other issues men deal with regularly are suicide, homicide, accidents, and higher incidences of abuse of drugs and alcohol as well as occupational injuries. [79] On *Deadliest Catch*, injuries have ranged from minor cuts to severed limbs and broken ribs. Deaths from falling overboard into the icy Bering Sea have taken place as well. Crab fishermen face such dangers routinely as part of the territory. They affirm the masculine ideal by facing these dangers and accepting them as a man would do, in stride and as part of his regular realm.

The crab boat captain Phil Harris of the "Cornelia Marie" exemplified the masculine hegemonic male tenets described here. Harris started his career working on crab boats from age eight. At twenty-one, he had become one of the youngest boat captains on the Bering Sea. At the time of his death, he had been at the helm of the "Cornelia Marie" for over twenty years. Harris had been a regular part of *Deadliest Catch* and was quite popular with viewers.

Beginning in 2008 on an episode, Harris had been thrown from his bunk during a storm. He thought he had broken his ribs. After several hours of coughing up blood was convinced by his sons to seek medical attention. He received news that he had experienced a pulmonary embolism. His subsequent medical treatment kept him off his boat for nearly an entire year. He however did return to fishing in January 2009. While back on the job, he suffered a massive stroke on January 29, 2010, while at St. Paul Island Harbor, Alaska. He received emergency treatment and surgery in Anchorage soon after. He regained consciousness and had begun to show signs of improvement only to succumb to a brain hemorrhage days later on February 9, 2010. [80]

Famous for his rough and tumble lifestyle, Harris himself acknowledged his lack of attention to his own personal health. "You go through a couple marriages, smoke cigarettes like it's going out of style, your body aches from the time you get up to the time you go to bed, and you wake up in the middle of the night thinking about where you're going to put the next pot. It's a great lifestyle."[81] Harris admitted to engaging in a great deal of unhealthy and risky behaviors throughout his life. The stroke was most likely directly related to the blood clots he had suffered from and received treatment for two years prior. Harris had received a great number of injuries over the years due to his experience on crab boats.[82] His lifestyle undoubtedly contributed to his early demise.

With the death of Captain Harris, viewers see a very possible end result of living the lifestyle exalted by the masculine hegemony. Men pay little or no attention to issues of health and personal safety. They often think of injuries and health troubles sustained as badges of honor, examples of living the life so to speak. However, the ultimate consequences are, as seen with Harris's untimely death. Viewers see this in the episodes of *Deadliest Catch* and the themes and images that typify the masculine hegemony resonate and reinforce the program's popularity with audiences.

VIEWERSHIP AND POPULARITY

Reality television programs have enjoyed a great deal of commercial success as a genre over the past several decades. A wide variety of themes and topics exist to satisfy a myriad of niche markets. Narrowcasting in recent times has targeted specific types of programs to a specific audience. Other reality programs however enjoy a broad viewer base. The so-called occupational reality television shows depict Americans engaged in a variety of specialized jobs or occupational fields. Programs feature many types of job from pawn brokers, airline workers and mechanics, to tattoo artists, memorabilia collectors, and parking meter attendants. Even in a "classless" society such as the United States, programming that showcases those working in this style of jobs resonates with the viewers and therefore receives a loyal and substantial following.

Even in subsequent seasons, *Deadliest Catch* has proven to be a strong ratings contender. During the 2011 season, the April 26th episode, "Old Age and Treachery" received 3.6 million viewers and was the number one rated cable show in its timeslot and had been for two weeks prior.[83] Ratings for the reality fishing program continued strongly into its eighth season as the season opener and 100th episode caught 3.14 million viewers making it the number one non-sports primetime cable program among men 25-54 and male and female viewers 18-49.[84] The program is a regular ratings stronghold, proving its popularity and viewer response to the content and themes.

Aside from the labor aspects, the program also does an excellent job of exemplifying some other well-established social norms found in the United States social structure. A very compelling reason for the program's popularity is in its adherence to the themes and concepts associated with the white, male North American masculine hegemony. *Deadliest Catch* maintains the male-female dichotomy fairly consistently throughout the series. Men are seen as primary breadwinners of the family unit. Women on the other hand are still seen as nurturers, caretakers of children and possessing subservient roles in the social structure. Men originate and maintain all social power. Traditional gender roles are acted out and perpetuated through the episodes, season after season.

Viewers see the men executing the difficult tasks involved in crab fishing in the icy cold waters of the Bering Sea. Hard work comes with the job. Men must prove themselves and earn their place in the hierarchy. They must be strong, willing to work hard and perform in the prescribed style in line with the male hegemonic paradigm. Men form deep bonds in the heterosexual superstructure of their male-dominated world. Anyone not worthy of the job is deemed not worthy, feminine and otherwise unsuited to the job and environment.

Even in this post-feminist, post-metrosexual world, *Deadliest Catch* still serves to reinforce long-held notions of traditional hegemonic masculinity. Men have had to begin sharing their societal power with other groups such as women, minorities and the LGBT communities. Alternative masculinities have begun to appear alongside the traditional masculinity. Yet, the program still manages to uphold and at times exalt the traditional masculine hegemony. *Deadliest Catch* serves as a retreat where the viewer can tune in and be reminded of a traditional social structure, where the dominant males within the society have determined the rules and work to maintain order according to the rules they have set in place based on these traditional ideas and norms. Their world tends to contain a great many constants where things appear in an unequivocal way, being "either black or white." Men are men and women are women. The captain is in charge and the crew does as it is told. Men catch crab or they do not. They are working or they are not. They either are injured or they are not. The absolutes mirror the rigid structure of the male hegemony and exist to maintain order in their traditional male world.

REFERENCES

Brittan, Arthur. *Masculinity and Power*. Oxford, England: Blackwell, 1989
Carrigan, Tim, Connell, Bob, and Lee, John. "Toward a New Sociology of Masculinity." *Theory and Society*, 1985: 551-604.

Coneliamarie.com. Captain and Owner Phil Harris. n.d. http://www.corneliamarie.com/phil-harris/ (accessed March 4, 2013).

Connell, Raewyn W. "Change Among the Gatekeepers: Men, Masculinities and Gender Equality in the Global Arena." *Signs*, 2005: 1801-1825.

corporate.discovery.com. Deadliest Catch Ratings Contine Strong: Series is #1 Primetime Cable Program Third week in a Row. April 27, 2011. http://corporate.discovery.com/discover-news/deadliest-catch-ratings-continue-strong-series-is-/ (accessed April 18, 2013).

Craig, Steve. *Men, Masculinity and the Media*. Newbury Park, CA: Sage Publications, 1992.

De Visser, Richard. O., Smith, Johnathan A., and McDonnell, Elizabeth J. "That's Not Masculine: Masculine Capital and Health-related Behavior." *Journal of Health Psychology*, 2009: 1047-1058.

Deadliest Catch, The. "No Season for Old Men" *Deadliest Catch*. May 27 2008.

Discovery Channel. "A Fist to the Face." *Deadliest Catch*. May 6, 2013.

———. "A Frozen Finish." *Deadliest Catch*. June 19, 2007.

———. "A Tragic Beginning" *Deadliest Catch*. April 3, 2007.

———. "Bering Sea Salvation." *Deadliest Catch*. May 1, 2007.

———. "Bitter Tears." *Deadliest Catch*. July 14, 2009.

———. "Ends of the Earch." *Deadliest Catch*. July 7, 2009.

———. "Everything on the Line." *Deadliest Catch*. April 14, 2009.

———. "Greenhorns." *Deadliest Catch*. April 12, 2005.

———. "Mortal Men." *Deadliest Catch*. June 4, 2008.

———. "On the Edge." *Deadliest Catch*. May 23, 2006.

———. "Pain and Paybacks." *Deadliest Catch*. April 3, 2007.

———. "Red Skies in the Morning." *Deadliest Catch*. April 21, 2009.

———. "Stay Focused or Die." *Deadliest Catch*. April 28, 2009.

———. "The Unforgiving Sea." *Deadliest Catch*. April 10, 2007.

———. "Trial of the Greenhorns." *Deadliest Catch*. June 5, 2007.

———. Crab Boat Greenhorn. n.d. http://dsc.discovery.com/tv-shows/deadliest-catch/about-this-show/hsw-crab-boat-greenhorn/htm (accessed March 13, 2013).

———. *Deadliest Catch*. 2010. 29 June .

Donaldson, Mike. "What is Hegemonic Masculinity." *Theory and Society*, 1993: 643-657.

Fleras, Augie and Dixon, Michael. "Cutting, Driving, Digging and Harvesting; Re Masculinizing the Working Class Heroic." *Canadian Journal of Communication*, 2011: 580-598

Gitlin, Todd. *Inside Prime Time*. Berkeley, CA: University of California Press, 2000.

hollywoodreporter.com. Discovery's Deadliest Catch Still Catching Viewers in Season 9. April 17, 2013. (accessed April 18, 2013).

Jackson, Peter. "The Cultural Politics of Masculinity: Towards a Social Geography." *Transactions of the Institue of British Geography*, 1991: 199-213.

Leistyna, Pepi. "Working Hard to Entertain You: The Discovery Channel Looks at Labor; Dirtiest Jobs, Miami Ink, American Chopper and Deadliest Catch." *New Labor Forum*, 2008: 148-154.

Messner, Michael A. *Politics of Masculinity: Men in Movements*. University of Southern California: Sage Publications, 1997.

Miller, Diana. "Masculinity in Popular Sitcoms." *Culture, Society and Masculinities*, 2011: 141-159.

press.discover.com. Ahoy Ratings! Deadliest Catch Season Premiere Scores Number One, Delivering Three Million Viewers. April 11, 2012. http://press.discovery.com/us/dsc/press-releases/2012/ahoy-ratings/deadliest-catch-season-press-releases (accessed April 24, 2013).

Rann, Jennifer A., and Calvert, Sandra L. "The Relation Between Gender Schemas and Adults' Recall of Stereotyped and Counterstereotyped Televised Information." *Sex Role*, 1993: 449-459.

Signorielli, Nancy. "Aging on Television: Messages Relating to Gender, Race and Occupation in Prime Time." *Journal of Broadcasting and Electronic Media*, 2004: 279-301.

Tragos, Peter. "Monster Masculinity: Honey I'll Be in the Garage Reasserting My Manhood." *Journal of Popular Culture*, 2009: 541-553.

Trujillo, Nick. "Hegemonic Masculinity on the Mound: Media Representations of Nolan Ryan and American Sports Culture." *Critical Studies in Mass Communication*, 1991: 290-308

NOTES

1. Pepi Leistyna, "Working Hard to Entertain You: The Discovery Channel Looks at Labor; Dirtiest Jobs, Miami Ink, American Chopper and Deadliest Catch," *New Labor Forum* 17, no. 1 (2008) : 150.

2. Leistyna, p. 150.

3. "Deadliest Catch Gets Highest Ratings Ever," Live Feed, accessed March 16, 2013. http://www.hollywoodreporter.com/blogs/live-feed/deadliest-catch-highest-ratings-53451

4. Nancy Signorielli, "Aging on Television: Messages Relating to Gender, Race and Occupation in Prime Time," *Journal of Broadcasting and Electronic Media* 48, no. 2 (2004) : 279.

5. Signorielli, p. 2709.

6. Craig, Steve, *Men, Masculinity and the Media* (Newbury Park, CA: Sage Publications, 1992), 26.

7. Jennifer A. Rann and Sandra L. Calvert, "The Relation Between Gender Schemas and Adults' Recall of Stereotyped and Counterstereotyped Televised Information," *Sex Role* 28, no. 8 (1993) 450.

8. Craig, p. 26.

9. Craig, p. 188.

10. Diana Miller, "Masculinity in Popular Sitcoms, 1955-1960 and 200-2005," *Culture, Society and Masculinities* 3, no, 2 (2011) : 143.

11. Todd Gitlin, *Inside Prime Time* (Berkely, CA: University of California Press, 2000), 25.

12. Raewyn W. Connell, "Change Among the Gatekeepers: Men, Masculinities and Gender Equality in the Global Area," *Signs* 30, no. 3, (2005) : 1808.

13. Craig, p. 12.

14. Raewyn Connell, *Masculinities* (Los Angeles: Polity Press, 1995), 181.

15. Craig, p. 190.

16. Peter Jackson, "The Cultural Politics of Masculinity: Towards a Social Geography," *Transactions of the Institute of British Geography* 16, no. 2 (1991) : 200.

17. Arthur Brittan, *Masculinity and Power* (Oxford: Blackwell, 1989), 4.

18. Craig, p. 191.

19. Miller, p. 150.

20. Miller, p. 151.

21. Peter Tragos, "Monster Masculinity: Honey, I'll Be in the Garage Reasserting my Manhood," *Journal of Popular Culture* 42, no. 3 (2009) : 545.

22. Craig, p. 196.

23. Tragos, p. 545.

24. Connel, p. 1808.

25. Craig, p. 191.

26. Nick Trujillo, "Hegemonic Masculinity on the Mound: Media Representations of Nolan Ryan and American Sports Culture," *Critical Studies in Mass Communication* 8, no. 3 (1991) : 290.

27. Richard O. De Visser, Jonathan A. Smith and Elizabeth J. McDonnell, "That's Not Masculine: Masculine Capital and Health-related Behavior," *Journal of Health Psychology* 14, no. 7 (2009) : 1049.

28. Trujillo, p. 290.

29. Craig, p.82.

30. "Trials of the Greenhorns," *Deadliest Catch*, The Discovery Channel (Season 3, episode 10, June5, 2007).

31. Henry Blake, "Stay Focused or Die," *Deadliest Catch,* The Discovery Channel (Season 5, episode 3, April 28, 2009).

32. Keith Colburn, "Pain and Paybacks," *Deadliest Catch,* The Discovery Channel (Season 3, episode 3, April 3, 2007).

33. Trujillo, p. 290.

34. Trujillo, p. 290.

35. Tim Carrigan, Bob Connell, and John Lee, "Toward a New Sociology of Masculinity," *Theory and Society* 14, no. 5 (1985) : 594.

36. Trujillo, p. 290.

37. Greg Moncrief,"The Unforgiving Sea," *Deadliest Catch,* The Discovery Channel (Season 3, episode 2, April 10, 2007).

38. "A Frozen Finish," *Deadliest Catch,* The Discovery Channel (Season 3, episode 12, June 19, 2007).

39. "A Frozen Finish," *Deadliest Catch,* The Discovery Channel (Season 3, episode 12, June 19, 2007).

40. Jackson, p.202.

41. "Crab Boat Greenhorn," *Discovery Channel's Deadliest Catch—About the Show.* accessed March 5, 2013, http://dsc.discovery.com/tv-shows/deadliest-catch/about-this-show/hsw-crab-boat-greenhorn.htm

42. "Greenhorns," *Deadliest Catch,* The Discovery Channel (Season 1, episode 1, April 12, 2005).

43. Crab Boat Greenhorn," *Discovery Channel's Deadliest Catch—About the Show.* accessed March 5, 2013, http://dsc.discovery.com/tv-shows/deadliest-catch/about-this-show/hsw-crab-boat-greenhorn.htm

44. Trujillo, p. 290.

45. Craig, p. 190.

46. Trujillo, p. 291.

47. Miller, p. 145.

48. Miller, p. 141.

49. Miller, p. 146.

50. Miller, p. 147.

51. "Everything on the Line," *Deadliest Catch,* The Discovery Channel (Season 5, episode1, April 14, 2009).

52. "Red Skies in the Morning," *Deadliest Catch,* The Discovery Channel (Season 5, episode 2, April 21, 2009).

53. "Bitter Tears," *Deadliest Catch,* The Discovery Channel (Season 5, episode, episode 14, July 14, 2009).

54. "A Fist to the Face," *Deadliest Catch,* The Discovery Channel (Season 9, episode 6, May 21, 2013).

55. Trujillo, p. 291.

56. Henry Blake, "Stay Focused or Die," *Deadliest Catch,* The Discovery Channel (Season 5, episode 3, April 28, 2009).

57. Harry Lewis, "Ends of the Earth," *Deadliest Catch,* The Discovery Channel (Season 5, episode 13, (July 7, 2009).

58. Mike Rowe, "Beat the Clock," *Deadliest Catch,* The Discovery Channel (Season 1, episode 4 May 3, 2005).

59. De Visser, et. al, p. 1049.

60. Carrigan, et. al, p. 586.

61. Trujillo, p. 291.

62. Trujillo, p. 291.

63. Mike Donaldson, "What is Hegemonic Masculinity?," *Theory and Society* 22 no. 5 (1993) : 645.

64. De Visser, et. al, p. 1049.

65. Leistyna, p. 150.

66. "No Season for Old Men," *Deadliest Catch,* The Discovery Channel (Season 4, episode 8, May 27, 2008).

67. "Mortal Men," *Deadliest Catch,* The Discovery Channel (Season 4, episode 12, June 24, 2008).

68. Travis Lofland, "Stay Focused or Die," *Deadliest Catch.* The Discovery Channel (Season 5, episode 3, (April 28, 2009).

69. Kirby, p. 114.

70. De Vissser et. al, p. 1056.

71. Augie Fleras and Michael Dixon, "Cutting, Driving, Digging and Harvesting: Re-masculinizing the Working Class Heroic," *Canadian Journal of Communication,* 36, no 4 (2011) : 591.

72. Josh Harris,"A Tragic Beginning," *Deadliest Catch,* The Discovery Channel (Season 3, episode 1, April 3, 2007).

73. Fleras and Dixon, p. 592.

74. Phil Harris,"A Tragic Beginning," *Deadliest Catch,* The Discovery Channel (Season 3, episode 1, April 3, 2007).

75. Michael A. Messner, *Politics of Masculinities: Men in Movements* (University of Southern California: Sage Publications, 1997), 6.

76. Matt Bradley,"Stay Focused or Die," *Deadliest Catch.* The Discovery Channel (Season 5, episode 3, (April 28, 2009).

77. "Bering Sea Salvation," *Deadliest Catch* , The Discovery Channel (Season 3, episode5, May 1, 2007).

78. Phil Harris,"Bering Sea Salvation," *Deadliest Catch* , The Discovery Channel (Season 3, episode 5, May 1, 2007).

79. Connell, p. 1813.

80. "Empty Throne," *Deadliest Catch,* The Discovery Channel (Season 6, episode 6, June 29, 2010).

81. "On the Edge," *Deadliest Catch,* The Discovery Channel (Season 2, episode 9, May 23, 2006).

82. "Captain and Owner Phil Harris," Corneliamarie.com, accessed March 4, 2013. http://www.corneliamarie.com/phil-harris/

83. "Deadliest Catch Ratings Continue Strong: Series is #1 Primetime Cable Program Third Week in a Row," Discovery News, accessed April 18, 2013. http://corporate.discovery.com/discovery-news/deadliest-catch-ratings-continue-strong-series-is-/

84. "Ahoy Ratings! Deadliest Catch Season Premiere Scores Number One, Delivering Three Million Viewers," Discovery Communications, accessed April 24, 2013. http://press.discovery.com/us/dsc/press-releases/2012/ahoy-ratings-deadliest-catch-season-press-releases

Chapter Two

"I Was Born This Way": The Performance and Production of Southern Masculinity in A&E's *Duck Dynasty*

Leandra H. Hernandez

As we embark upon a new century of broadcasting, it is clear that no genre form or type of programming has been as actively marketed by producers, or more enthusiastically embraced by viewers, than reality-based TV. —James Friedman[1]

White southern masculinities, like other southern identities, often seem to contain contradictions and dualities . . . White manhood in the recent South is widely viewed as both natural *and* learned. Most white men in the South believe that they are "that way," as my hometown businessman put it, in some natural, irreducible sense, but they also firmly believe that manhood must be learned through rites of initiation and passage, and must be lived and displayed to one's peers and others in order to be fully realized.[2]

Reality television has become one of the most popular television genres in the last decade.[3] Shows ranging from MTV's *Jersey Shore* to TLC's *Toddlers & Tiaras* and Bravo's *Queer Eye for the Straight Guy* all present and produce various types of masculinities and femininities that are consumed by reality television viewers every day. One such series that has recently won the hearts of many Americans is A&E's *Duck Dynasty*. Having premiered in 2012, *Duck Dynasty* chronicles the rags-to-riches story of the Robertson clan, which made its millions from the family patriarch's infamous duck call contraption first created over 25 years ago. Now, the Robertsons' third son, Willie, has taken over the corporation entitled "Duck Commander" and, as

CEO, has earned the family millions and transformed their Southern way of living to a new bourgeoisie, Southern-chic way of life that still holds on to its hunting, outdoorsy family values.[4] As the series progresses, viewers are drawn into the Robertson boys' adventures as they try to run the company, create duck calls, and hunt ducks, all with their long beards—the true signifier of a certain type of Southern masculinity—complete with bandanas and flannel shirts.

This essay, however, specifically observes Southern masculinity that is portrayed in *Duck Dynasty*. It asks the question: How is Southern masculinity performed and produced in *Duck Dynasty*? It examines the performance and production of Southern masculinity by exploring the consumption practices that "make Willie a man," albeit a new type of Southern swamp man who is refined and transformed by his material possessions. This essay argues that the Southern masculinity performed and produced in *Duck Dynasty* is characterized by contradictions, as evidenced in the masculine performances brought forth by Phil, the patriarch, and Jase, the oldest brother, and how these performances are in constant conflict with the new, refined Southern swamp man masculinity performed by Willie. Furthermore, Willie's performance of masculinity is rife with contradictions, as he struggles to reconcile his outdoorsy, swamp boy roots with his newfound riches and material possessions.

It is important to examine the masculine performances in *Duck Dynasty* and the discourse of gender relations and gender roles in the series because "popular culture is the bedrock upon which ideas of gender crystallize."[5] Anoop Nayak and Mary Jane Kehily posit that cultural studies analyses of popular culture texts "may have a great deal to say about the changing world in which we live and the types of gender identities that are being envisioned."[6] Furthermore, *Duck Dynasty* has the potential to shape audiences' perceptions of Southern culture in both national and global contexts. Karen Cox argues that industries that spread Southern popular culture and are located outside of Dixie exert more influence over the concepts that Americans readily accept about the South, as opposed to native Southerners themselves, and examines how the South is constructed in reality television and other forms of popular culture can help scholars understand how the South is constructed in both national and global contexts.[7] Thus, this essay attempts to understand *Duck Dynasty*'s implications for the region in a national context, both implications for understanding and representing Southern masculinity and also Southern gender roles and relations. The first part of this essay will explore the literature surrounding Southern manhood and masculinity. Then, the second part of this essay will explore the Southern masculinity performed and produced in *Duck Dynasty*, as well as the class relations that contribute to and construct the competing masculinities in the television series. Finally, the essay will conclude with implications about how the

South and Southern men are constructed and represented in the American consciousness.

SOUTHERN MASCULINITY & SOUTHERN MANHOOD

The American "South," Southerners, and Southern living have recently occupied and, some might argue, dominated American imaginary and contemporary popular culture. In a *New York Times* article about the American "South," Karen Cox notes that "series purporting to show a slice of Southern life are huge, and getting bigger: more than a dozen new programs have been introduced so far this year, while others have been renewed for second or even third seasons."[8] Examples of this surge in movies about Southern life and Southern living include *Sweet Home Alabama, Dukes of Hazzard,* and *Junebug,* in addition to reality television shows, including A&E's *Storage Wars Texas*, The History Channel's *Swamp People,* ABC's *Good Christian Bitches*, Lifetime's *Glamour Belles,* CMT's *Sweet Home Alabama*, and truTV's *Lizard Lick Towing,* to name a few. Karen Cox argues that shows and movies about Southern life promise to provide new insights into Southern culture and "what it's like to be a Southerner," but "what they really represent is a typecast South: a mythically rural, white, poorly educated and thickly accented region that has yet to join the 21st century. If you listen closely, you may even hear banjos." Furthermore, these shows and movies focus on what it means to be a "Southern man" and a "Southern woman," or, rather, to perform a "Southern man" and a "Southern woman." However, before one can explore contemporary versions of Southern masculinities and femininities, it is necessary to explore how Southern masculinity and Southern manhood have traditionally been defined.

Many scholars use the Civil War as the genesis of the initiation of historical studies about Southern manhood and Southern masculinity. Research on Southern masculinity and Southern manhood dates back to the Civil War, when the shadow of the Civil War began to shape Southern manhood and masculinity.[9] National conflict and the emancipation of slaves created new opportunities for both white and black men to (re)define and (re)shape manliness and manhood. Moreover, black manliness was strengthened simultaneously as white manliness was destabilized. Craig Thompson Friend notes that "former Confederates had to find new ways to frame white manhood without the mastery that slavery had offered or the honor that victory would have provided."[10] Michael Kimmel discusses various types of Southern men and ways of performing Southern manhood, including the men of the Ku Klux Klan who worked to reclaim Southern manhood, the Populists who worked to restore the commonwealth from a position of noble manhood, and the stereotypical portrayal of the drunken, brawling Southern men who found solace over their lost manhood in alcohol and their debacles. [11] Craig Thompson Friend shows that "honor and mastery had been the dominant idealized masculine traits among antebellum southern whites, but gone with the wind was the world of plantations, slaves, and the exclusivity of the gentlemanly class," and honor and mastery soon transformed into new structures and types of masculinity that would come to characterize white Southern men. [12]

THE CHRISTIAN GENTLEMAN & THE MASCULINE MARTIAL IDEAL

The transformation of white manliness, according to Craig Thompson Friend, [13] included two distinct forms of manhood that emerged directly out of the Civil War: the Christian gentleman and the masculine martial ideal. The first masculinity, the Christian gentleman, was modeled upon Robert E. Lee and in reaction to the emasculation that occurred as a result of losing the Civil War. The Southern Christian gentleman was demonstrated through self-esteem, self-control, and respect for war. Lee embodied the "intractability of southern civilization," despite being defeated in the Civil War, and white Southerners "made him a model for their own form of the Christian gentleman—honorable, master of his household, humble, self-restrained, and above all, pious and faithful." [14] The Southern Christian gentleman was a God-fearing man who was dedicated to his family and to his household and also honored war and his civic duties. Masculinity for the Southern Christian gentleman was situated in terms of civic and religious dedication, and was further carried out in the family sphere by being faithful and dedicated to the family structure.

The masculine martial ideal bore similarities to the Southern Christian gentleman in that this ideal also exemplified honor and mastery, yet masculinity was derived via participation in war. According to Craig Thompson Friend, the masculine martial ideal was warrior-like and heroic, and "violence had to contain a broader and more ideological purpose, specifically to demonstrate honor and protection of one's self, family, and region." [15] Although it might seem on the surface as if the two masculine ideals comprise the parts of the Southern masculinity dichotomy, they are actually very similar. Both the Southern Christian gentleman and the masculine martial ideal were based upon the same values of honor, mastery, and dedication to family, yet the masculine martial ideal performed his masculinity via violence and war, whereas the Southern Christian gentleman performed his masculinity via religious and civic dedication. However, Karen Taylor shows in her analysis of Reconstruction-era masculinity that Southern Christian gentlemen often utilized various forms of violence in order to defend and protect their honor, land, and family, thus showing yet another link between the

Southern Christian gentleman and the masculine martial ideal.[16] Thus, in concluding his discussion of Southern Christian gentlemen and the masculine martial ideal, Craig Thompson Friend notes:

> In many regards, all postbellum Southerners had remained committed to the communal manhood of an earlier era, in which their identities were inseparable from their familial and communal responsibilities and from their public worth. For a variety of economic, political, and social reasons, few Southerners turned to self-made manhood, although it tempted many. Instead, they viewed themselves in opposition to what they described as urban, industrial, liberal, corrupt, effeminate men of the North. Even as the nineteenth century drew to a close, they remained entangled in codes of honor and virility that characterized communal manhood.[17]

Therefore, two types of masculinity performances that characterized much of post-Civil War times included the Southern Christian gentleman and the masculine martial ideal, which both exemplified honor and mastery, just via different performative manners.

THE HUNTER

An additional construction of Southern manhood/masculinity includes the hunter/gatherer, also known as the Southern man who excels at being one with the wilderness in terms of hunting and killing.[18] Scholars have noted that the hunter/gatherer ideal has been used to signify true Southern manhood, and has also been viewed as a leisurely activity.[19] For example, Adam Watts chronicled the experiences of Southern boys and men at a deer camp in southwest Mississippi and found that "the deep baying of a pack of hounds, the reverberating concussion of a shotgun, and the pursuit of whitetail deer" are essential and natural, even necessary, activities for white Southern men.[20] He argues that hunting, especially at a deer camp, is a legitimate cultural institution of Southern masculinity that preserves Southern masculine values and passes them on to Southern boys so that they can become good Southern men. Additionally, Adam Watts discusses the importance of friendships in perpetuating hunting and deer camps as an institution:

> There is more, too, than the friendship of the members or their enthusiasm for the sport—indeed, some members rarely hunt. What makes this institution special (even sacred, some might say, considering the number of hunters to be found sitting around a fire on any given Sunday morning) seems to be something like a collective sense of place where the roots of its members—and, some might say, of a particular caste of white Southern masculinity—remain firmly planted.[21]

Thus, hunting is an important male-dominated space and institution for Southern masculinity because it both preserves and passes down Southern masculine values.

An important part of this construction of hunting as signifier of Southern masculinity is the individual pleasures that Southern men engage in when hunting. Ted Ownby discusses how various scholars have conceptualized Southern masculine hunting as a leisurely activity that both signifies and constructs antebellum Southern culture.[22] Hunting is important for Southern men and Southern masculinity because it allows them to "enjoy the individual pleasures of the frontier."[23] Wilbur Joseph Cash argues that hunting for white men was not a continuation of English tradition, but rather a hedonistic pursuit of individualistic, intense excitement.[24] It represents a type of sportsmanship that has no boundaries, no limits, and even resists authority by ignoring family and work responsibilities temporarily to hunt and enjoy brotherly fraternization with fellow Southern men. Adam Watts notes how the men in his study intentionally remove themselves from a world containing a controlled work environment and women to a place where social rules of engagement and their masculine performances are fundamentally altered. This place, he argues, could be problematic because it sets up a masculine versus feminine dichotomy in which men (the masculine) are pitted against nature (the feminine), and that this construction, entrenched with misogyny, further locates hunting as a hypermasculine activity and performance where "what appears on the surface to be the relatively harmless pursuit of an escapist fantasy of a wild, idealized past of masculine control, then, may have more sinister implications in its encouragement of subjugation and control, of violence toward nature and the feminine."[25] Thus, hunting for Southern men is a natural and essential cultural institution, a sport, a means of strengthening brotherhood, proving one's manhood, and also passing values and rituals of Southern masculinity to the up and coming Southern masculinity torchbearers.

THE WHITE-TRASH REDNECK

The third and final construction of Southern manhood/masculinity is the stereotypical redneck/white-trash man. American popular culture purveyors have constructed negative images of poor Southern whites and stereotyped them for profit.[26] White-trash rednecks have been depicted as rural white men who are poor, stupid, lazy, racist drunks who are perpetually unemployed, violent, and uneducated.[27] In the hierarchy of white masculinities, the white-trash redneck has been othered, placed at the bottom of the masculinity hierarchy. Othering this masculinity takes the form of labeling this masculinity with pejorative terms including redneck, white trash, and hillbilly, which originated as both class and racial slurs.[28] Pre-Civil War, upper-class Southern elites referred to lower-class whites as "poor white trash," and this demarcation automatically assumed that whites should not be poor and culturally inferior and implies that only blacks and other minorities can occupy that end of the impoverished, othered spectrum.[29]

It might seem a bit out of place to list the white-trash redneck as a type of masculinity, considering that it has been constructed as "a problematic whiteness polluted by poverty and rural culture."[30] However, it is still a performance of manhood and masculinity, despite how it is positioned by other hegemonic masculinities. For example, some men have reclaimed the pejoratives "white trash" and "redneck" and used them as terms of empowerment, such as Southern rock musicians and Southern wrestlers. Eastman and Schrock interviewed Southern rock musicians and found that, instead of defending themselves from the negativity surrounding the stereotypical term "white trash," they celebrated being called white-trash, redneck hillbillies and even incorporated aspects of these stereotypes into their band names and their lyrics.[31] They defined themselves as the "cultural ambassadors of poor rural whites, and they proudly painted themselves, their music, and their fans as authentically trashy."[32] Furthermore, they also emphasize positive aspects of living in rural, poverty-stricken areas; they reject middle-class, materialistic values and the notion of upward economic mobility; and they also engage in masculine normative behavior that glorifies drinking and aggression as quintessential characteristics of white trash, redneck manhood. Combined, these acts of white-trash, redneck manhood embrace white trashiness and are utilized to mark boundaries between them and the white, upper-class outsiders. These performances are acts of resistance that white-trash, redneck Southern men use to empower themselves and resist white Southern hegemonic masculinity by positioning white, upper-class Southern men as the other.

Kyriakoudes and Coclanis explored how Southern cultural stereotypes shaped professional wrestling in the South and found that wrestling was the South's first spectator sport.[33] It is still an integral part of Southern manhood, considering that Southern athletes make up a disproportionate percentage of professional wrestlers, and the sport has many of the same characteristics as does hunting, including being free from restraints and rules.[34] Furthermore, wrestling is an important signifier of Southern manhood and masculinity because it draws upon Southern stereotypes to create identities that will attract and maintain fan interest. Some of these stereotypes include hillbillies, rednecks, and "good ol' boys," and "the role of Southern cultural stereotypes in wrestling tells us not only a great deal about sport in the South, but also about how Southern identity has been constructed in American popular culture."[35] Thus, similar to how Southern rock musicians reclaimed Southern stereotypes as part of their identities, Southern wrestlers also embraced and reclaimed Southern stereotypes and integrated them as part of their wrestling identities. These reclamations, stereotype-based identities, and performances not only have empowered the rockers and wrestlers and created new conceptualizations of what it means to be a hillbilly, redneck, Southern rocker and wrestler in the American imagination, but they also enabled Southern rockers and wrestlers to commoditize themselves. The Southern rockers and wrestlers also need to market themselves in order to be considered manly and successful—in their cases, masculine performances with no profit have the potential to label their performances of Southern masculinity as failed and unsuccessful. It also opens the possibility for those who perform Southern hegemonic masculinities to label the Southern rocker/wrestler "white trash," "redneck," or "hillbilly" in a pejorative manner. What results is a perpetuation of marginalized Southern masculinity that is deemed as failed and unsuccessful, thus perpetuating the cycle that this type of marginalized masculinity has been trying to break out of and distance itself from.

COMPLEMENTARY & CONTRADICTORY SOUTHERN MASCULINITIES & MANHOOD ACTS

Thus, taken together, Southern masculinities and manhood have been represented and performed in various ways. Historically, after the Civil War, the Southern man was characterized by the Southern Christian gentleman and the masculine martial ideal. Two sides of the same coin, the Southern Christian gentleman and the masculine martial ideal both embodied honor and mastery, although they performed honor and mastery in different ways. Both the Southern Christian gentleman and the masculine martial ideal valued family and dedication to their civic duties, except the Southern Christian gentleman's manhood acts were rooted in religious and civic duties, whereas the masculine martial ideal's manhood acts had foundations in violence and war.

In addition to the Southern Christian gentleman and the masculine martial ideal, another type of Southern masculine performance is that of the hunter. This performance is probably one of the most popular contemporary representations of Southern masculinity in American popular culture, which is exemplified in reality television shows such as A&E's *Swamp People* and *Duck Dynasty*. The Southern hunter both displays and reaffirms his masculinity by becoming one with the outdoors and by showing his mastery of weapons in killing various types of hunting game. Furthermore, the Southern hunter preserves and perpetuates hunting as a cultural institution by bonding with fellow Southern men and by introducing young Southern boys to the ritual.

Lastly, another type of Southern masculinity is the Southern white-trash, redneck man. Although it might seem a bit unusual that this masculinity type is listed as a Southern masculine performance, white-trash, redneck Southern men have reclaimed the pejoratives "white trash," "redneck," and "hillbilly" and are now using them as forms of empowerment, as identity performances, as ways to commodify themselves in an effort to both be rewarded for a successful Southern masculine performance and also as a way of resisting hegemonic Southern masculinities. Taken together, it is evident that there are multiple manifestations of Southern manhood and Southern masculinities, each with its distinct manhood acts and masculine performative acts. These Southern masculinities are not only evident via historical artifacts and writings, but they are also evident in the American psyche, particularly in reality television shows. As many scholars have noted, the South has occupied a dominant space in American popular culture lately,[36] and one exemplar reality television show that explicates this is A&E's *Duck Dynasty*. A&E's *Duck Dynasty* chronicles the daily adventures of the Robertson clan, a rags-to-riches Louisiana family torn between maintaining Southern ideals of family, tradition, and being one with the land, and their duck call company's newfound riches that bring with it materialistic pressures and an entrance to a new bourgeoisie culture.

Duck Dynasty presents interesting new portrayals of performances of Southern masculinity, contradictory gender roles, and Southern masculine identity crises. Jason Eastman said it best when he noted that "Southern men occupy a contradictory place in U.S. culture as the rest of the country stereotypes them as backwards and deviant, yet simultaneously celebrates Southern males as quintessential exemplars of American manhood."[37] So, one must ask: How is Southern masculinity performed and produced in *Duck Dynasty*? Does the Southern masculinity in *Duck Dynasty* reinforce and/or contradict earlier ideals and representations of Southern masculinity? Necessary is the exploration of these contradictions evident in the masculine performances in the reality television series, as well as how the Robertson men reconcile their masculinity crises and negotiate both their newfound riches and gender relations with their wives and children. Karen Cox argues that industries that spread Southern popular culture are located outside of Dixie and actually exert more influence over the concepts that Americans accept about the South than native Southerners themselves, and that examining how the South is constructed in reality television and other forms of popular culture—particularly *Duck Dynasty*—can help scholars understand how the South is constructed in national and global contexts.[38] Thus, effort is needed to take Southern popular culture seriously as a topic of investigation and to understand further its implications for the region in a broader context. Representations of masculinity in *Duck Dynasty* have larger implications for how the American psyche understands Southern femininities, masculinities, and gender roles and relations.

THE PRODUCTION AND PERFORMANCE OF MASCULINITY IN *DUCK DYNASTY*

The hegemonic masculinity performed and produced in *Duck Dynasty* is a self-proclaimed and self-identified redneck masculinity that is carried out successfully by all of the males in the Robertson clan, except for Willie. Willie, the third Robertson son and the CEO of Duck Commander (the family's duck call manufacturing company), faces a Southern masculinity identity crisis as he struggles between performing both his Southern redneck masculine acts and his newfound Southern upper-class masculine acts.

SELF-PROCLAIMED REDNECK MASCULINITY

The masculinity performed and produced in *Duck Dynasty* is, for most of the Robertson men, a self-identified redneck masculinity that is produced and performed via hunting, killing, skinning, and engaging in humorous, childish acts. Southern masculinity in this show is redneck, and being a redneck man is being a *real* man. What constitutes being a real man in *Duck Dynasty* are the Robertson men's abilities to shoot ducks; make good duck calls to further their business; hunt, capture, and skin frogs; appreciate their land and live off of it; and be dedicated to their work and to their family. All of the Robertson men and their teenage sons go hunting together to strengthen their relationships, prove their successful masculine performances to each other, and also to introduce hunting and masculine brotherhood and camaraderie to the young boys in the family. In reliving the characteristics of the Southern Christian gentleman, the masculine martial ideal, and the hunter, the Robertson men engage in hunting ducks and frogs (violence against animals and nature—the feminine) for both sport and for (both masculine *and* nurturing) sustenance. In an interesting turn, each episode ends with a shot of the entire Robertson clan eating a dinner cooked by Miss Kay, wife of the family patriarch, Phil, with Willie telling the moral of the story and stressing the importance of Southern family values. As Jack Temple Kirby argues about old Southern Winston cigarette advertisements, a theme that can definitely be extended to this television series, "The message about the region is clear: the white South represents home, family, good old values."[39]

Returning to the idea of redneck masculinity, the men in the Robertson clan have, on numerous occasions, said on the show that they are rednecks and proud of it. To the men of the Robertson clan, the term "redneck" is not a pejorative; rather, it signifies honor, love of one's family, and dedication to their land and to hunting. When discussing his "redneckness," Jase, the oldest Robertson son, says, "I was born this way." Moreover, Jase notes that, "You ain't a redneck unless you're off the road and in the swamps." Thus, being a man—a masculine, redneck Southern man—is all about being in the swamps, killing and hunting animals. Moreover, the clothing worn by the Robertson men signifies their redneck status. They wear camouflage outfits and apply hunting paint to their faces. Furthermore, each of the Robertson men display the characteristic Southern swamp man's excessively long beard and long hair, which is always decorated with a bandana. Hence lies the first contradiction of the Southern masculinity performed in *Duck Dynasty*—although most might assume (incorrectly) that the Robertson men are poor, rural, and uneducated due to their love of hunting and their brusque appearances, almost all of the Robertson men are college-educated and even performed the quintessential American man's masculine act while in college: they were the college quarterbacks. Phil, the Robertson patriarch, Jase, the oldest son, and Willie, the third son and CEO of the company, all attended state universities in Louisiana and played quarterbacks on their football teams. In an interesting twist of events, Phil decided to give up a career as a football coach, let his hair and beard grow, and decided to dedicate his life to creating duck calls. Jase and Willie, although once considered "preppy," followed in their father's footsteps, let their hair and beards grow, donned camouflage outfits, and dedicated their careers to the family empire. Thus, the hegemonic masculinity that emerges from *Duck Dynasty* is the redneck masculinity that emphasizes characteristics of all three types of Southern masculinity previously detailed: the Southern Christian gentleman, the hunter, and the white-trash redneck. The redneck masculinity in *Duck Dynasty* emphasizes hunting, donning the correct attire, being one with the land, and being dedicated to one's family. This is an interesting change from the concept of the Christian gentleman who typically dominated the Southern masculinity hierarchy. The white-trash redneck masculinity becomes the gender performance in the show that is most performed and most valued. However, as the first season unfolds, it becomes apparent that Willie is experiencing a masculinity crisis as he struggles to navigate his redneck masculinity and his newfound bourgeoisie, upper-class masculinity.

MASCULINITY CRISES: THE REDNECK SWAMP MASCULINITY VS. THE BOURGEOISIE MATERIALISTIC MASCULINITY

The hegemonic masculinity in *Duck Dynasty* emphasizes traditional Southern manhood acts such as hunting, living off of the land, and being dedicated to and providing for one's family. While Willie excels at providing for his family, he is less successful at hunting and maintaining the family's premodern values of living off of the land. As a result, his family members, mostly Phil and Jase, criticize him for his unsuccessful redneck masculine performance and, instead, his embrace of a newfound bourgeoisie masculinity. For example, in many episodes Willie stresses his riches, his success, and all the things his money can buy. In one episode, he takes his mom, Miss Kay, to look at goats. When she decides to buy them, Willie screams, "Miss Kay, you're NOT putting those goats in my $70,000 Escalade!" Furthermore, Willie prides himself on his privileged access to the country club where he can leisurely play golf and enjoy all of the luxuries that his country club membership has to offer. When asked about Willie's country club, Jase notes, "Willie's going through an identity crisis. If you're not gonna be a redneck, shave your beard and wear a three-piece suit." Additionally, Willie drags some of his family members to an art show where he hoped to "diversify his [business] portfolio." This art show does not sit well with Jase, and Willie tells the cameraman, "I like the finer things in life. I didn't get the finer genes in this family—I started them." Thus, as opposed to Jase's notion of Southern redneck masculinity as being inherent and natural because he was born with it, Willie partially resists the Southern redneck masculinity by engaging in "the finer things in life," despite the cost. Lastly, in the exemplar performance of the new Southern bourgeoisie masculinity, Willie buys a vineyard, which eventually fails because it had no grapes. When the family puts grapes in the vineyard, the wine tastes terrible, and the entire business venture withers away. Willie says he bought the vineyard because, "I'm a businessman. I can see the potential." The vineyard, a business endeavor, represented a means of advancing the family corporation and expanding the business. However, Jase retorts with, "It's like someone gave me backstage passes to a disaster." Thus, it is evident that Jase was waiting for Willie's performance of refined Southern bourgeoisie masculinity to fail, which it eventually does.

As the series progresses, it becomes apparent that two masculinities are seen competing in *Duck Dynasty*: the redneck masculinity, exemplified through Jase and Phil's performances and manhood acts, and the refined bourgeoisie masculinity, through Willie's performances and manhood acts. Willie's masculinity is derived via high amounts of consumption to express his masculinity. He buys high-dollar items, including a Cadillac Escalade and vineyard, making it very clear to his family members and to America that his purchases are, indeed, very pricey. Furthermore, Willie's bourgeoisie masculinity is expressed through his CEO status. As CEO of Duck Commander, the family's duck call business, Willie makes all of the business decisions and spends most of his time at the Duck Commander warehouse. When Jase, Phil, and the rest of the Robertson men spend less time at work and more time hunting because "it's what real men do," Willie criticizes them for negating their work duties. Willie says, "These guys know how to duck hunt, but they don't know how to run a company. They don't appreciate hard work and dedication." Phil, Jase, and the rest of the Robertson men argue that Willie's CEO status has "gone to his brain," and they are angered because, in their eyes, Willie is both not letting them have any fun and negating their bonding/hunting time. Thus, Willie exhibits a masculinity crisis in *Duck Dynasty* by trying to reconcile his redneck masculinity performances and his newfound bourgeoisie masculinity. Although he dresses in the expected manner by having long hair and beard and by wearing camouflage attire, he also resists the hegemonic redneck masculinity by partaking in the "finer things in life," thus producing a more refined bourgeoisie masculinity.

DISCUSSION

An analysis of A&E's *Duck Dynasty* indicates that the reality television series represents a type of masculinity that combines many characteristics of historical Southern masculinities, including dedication to one's family, honoring war and violence, being a successful hunter in a male-dominated space, and also reclaiming the term "redneck" and using it as an identity performance, a form of empowerment, and a method of resistance. The hegemonic masculinity performed and produced in *Duck Dynasty* is characterized as redneck masculinity, one that the Robertson men claim proudly. Being a masculine redneck Southern man means occupying the swamps and successful manhood acts, such as hunting ducks and creating duck calls, in addition to being able to provide for one's family and also dressing the part with long hair, long beards, and camouflage outfits. Being a real man in *Duck Dynasty* also means holding on to pre-modern values, including dismissing technology (cell phones) and highly respecting the land. For example, Phil mentions, "Part of being a Robertson is learning to live off the land."

Willie, the CEO of Duck Commander, represents a rupture in this hegemonic masculinity as he navigates between his redneck masculine performances and his newfound bourgeoisie masculinity. Willie hangs on to certain redneck masculine acts of manhood, including his attire and his attempts at hunting, although he is ridiculed by the men in his family when he fails at hunting (one of the most important signifiers of Southern masculinity) and when his cell phone constantly interrupts the brotherhood and the bonding of the Robertson men's duck hunting trips. Furthermore, Willie's family, particularly Phil and Jase, ridicule him because of his business endeavors and his new, "refined" and "sophisticated" bourgeoisie acts including taking the family to an art show to "diversify his portfolio" and buying a failing vineyard. Willie's marginalized masculinity is met with resistance from his family members because it is not, in their eyes, a true performance of redneck Southern masculinity. Instead, Willie symbolizes the modern world, with his expensive SUVs, his cell phone, his mansion, and his "redneck millions." It does not resonate with the hegemonic redneck masculinity accepted and performed by the Robertson men, especially by Phil, the Robertson patriarch.

What becomes the most important factor in Willie's masculinity crisis is his class status. Willie's newfound upper-class status and his family's riches are precisely what enable him to perform his newfound bourgeoisie masculinity with his expensive cars and new business ventures. While the typology of white Southern masculinities does not necessarily focus on class (except for the Christian gentleman, to a certain extent), Willie's masculinity crisis creates a dichotomy between the Christian gentleman and the white trash redneck. The white trash redneck masculinity ultimately works to reject middle-class materialism, and this is one of Willie's main struggles throughout the series. Willie traverses the boundaries between the Christian gentleman masculinity performance and the white-trash redneck masculinity performance as he works to construct his own type of Southern masculinity. His is a masculinity that attempts to reconcile the Southern beard, Southern camouflage, and duck hunt with the country club membership, expensive cars, and businessman persona. His family's love of the land and hunting excellence are masculine characteristics that are inherent to Willie, while his business persona and upper-class status construct new masculine performances that he still struggles to carry out successfully. As Trent Watts notes, "White southern masculinities, like other southern identities, often seem to contain such contradictions, or dualities. White masculinity in the recent South is widely viewed as both natural *and* learned. Most white men in the South believe that they are "that way," in some natural, irreducible sense, but they also firmly believe that manhood must be learned through rites of initiation and passage, and must be lived and displayed to one's peers and others in order to be fully realized."[40] The fact that Willie has signed on to do a reality television series about his family's company is no coincidence. His display of dual masculine performances could perhaps represent one way that he makes sense of being both a Christian gentleman with upper-class status and a redneck with a beard, bandana, camouflage outfit, and family hunting outings.

Taken together, the images of masculinity portrayed in *Duck Dynasty* reflect not only what good, Southern masculine men should be and how they should act, but these images also seem to speak more broadly to the culture in which they are produced.[41] The production of this reality television show, which is at least partially scripted, reflects how A&E and other media industries portray and perceive the South—still slightly backwards, pre-modern, and redneck, except now with an upper-class status and entry into a new bourgeoisie culture. However, slightly backwards, pre-modern, and redneck are not seen as pejorative terms by the Robertson clan. Rather, they embrace these terms and utilize them to define their identity performances. Trent Watts notes that post-World War II, the American South has exhibited a variety of models of white manhood, and print and electronic media have worked to both disseminate and shape models of Southern masculinity for both Southerners and the rest of America.[42] Television shows and country music show how Southern men resist, embrace, and navigate their cultural ideals, including country music singer George Jones, comedians Jeff Foxworthy and Larry the Cable Guy, and now Willie Robertson of *Duck Dynasty*. These performances of the hunting, white-trash, redneck, good ol' boy are not only more accepted now than they were decades ago, but now they are also consumed eagerly by national audiences. Moreover, he argues that the redneck, good' ol boy Southern hunter is now a national favorite,[43] and this is evidenced in *Duck Dynasty,* as it has become one of the most popular reality television shows in the past few years. In the end, being a redneck Southerner is an honor for the Robertson clan characterized by hunting ducks and bonding with the other men in the family; occupying the swamps; making duck calls; having long hair, beards, and dressing in camouflage; and honoring their family. As Willie says, "We just invite the cameras and say 'this is how we do it—like it or not!'" Furthermore, Korie, Willie's wife, notes, "In the end, it's all about love, family, and putting family first."[44]

REFERENCES

Cash, Wilbur Joseph. *The Mind of the South.* New York: Vintage Books, 1941.

Cox, Karen. "The South ain't just Whistlin' Dixie." New York Times, September 17, 2011. http://www.nytimes.com/2011/09/18/opinion/sunday/the-south-aint-just-whistlin-dixie.html?pagewanted=all&_r=0 (accessed).

Cox, Karen. *Dreaming of Dixie: How the South was Created in American Popular Culture.* Chapel Hill: The University of North Carolina Press, 2011.

Eastman, Jason, and Douglas Schrock. "Southern rock musicians' construction of white trash." *Race, Gender, & Class*, 15, no. 1 (2008): 205-19.

Eastman, Jason. "Rebel manhood: The hegemonic masculinity of the Southern rock music revival." *Journal of Contemporary Ethnography*, 41, no. 2 (2012): 189-219.

Friedman, James. *Reality Squared: Televisual Discourse on the Real.* New Brunswick: Rutgers University Press, 2002.

Hartigan, John. "Unpopular culture: The case of white trash." Cultural Studies, 11, no. 2 (1997): 316-43.

Hartigan, John. "Who are these white people? 'Rednecks,' 'hillbillies,' and 'white trash' as marked racial subjects." In *White Out: The Continuing Significance of Racism*, edited by Ashley W. Doane and Eduardo Bonilla-Silva, 95-111. New York: Routledge, 2003.

Kimmel, Michael. *Manhood in America: A Cultural History.* New York: Free Press, 1996.

Kyriakoudes, Louis, and Peter Coclanis. The Tennessee Test of Manhood: Professional Wrestling and Southern Cultural Stereotypes." *Southern Cultures*, 3, no. 3 (1997): 8-27.

Malin, Brenton. "Viral manhood: Niche marketing, hard-boiled detectives and the economics of masculinity." *Media, Culture & Society*, 32, no. 3 (2010): 373-89.

Nayak, Anoop, and Mary Jane Kehily. *Gender, Youth, and Culture: Young Masculinities and Femininities.* Houndmills: Palgrave, 2008.

Orbe, Mark. "Representations of Race in Reality TV: Watch and Discuss." *Critical Studies in Media Communication*, 25, no. 4 (2008): 345-52.

Owens, Ryan, and Jim Scholz. "Redneck Millionaires Built 'Duck Dynasty' in Duck Call Business." *ABC News*, March 20, 2012. http://abcnews.go.com/Entertainment/redneck-millionaires-built-duck-dynasty-duck-call-business/story?id=15961955.

Ownby, Ted. "Manhood, Memory, and White Men's Sports in the Recent American South." *The International Journal of the History of Sport*, 15, no. 2 (1998): 103-18.

Schroeder, E. R. "Sexual racism" and reality television: Privileging the white male prerogative on MTV's *The Real World.*" In *Readings in Intercultural Communication: Experiences & Contexts,* edited by Judith N. Martin, Thomas K. Nakayama, and Lisa A. Flores, 219-26. Boston: McGraw-Hill. 2006.

Smith, D. "Cultural Studies' Misfit: White Trash Studies." *The Mississippi Quarterly,* 57, (2004): 369-388.

Taylor, Karen. "Reconstructing men in Savannah, Georgia, 1865-1876." In *Southern Masculinity: Perspectives on Manhood in the South since Reconstruction,* edited by Craig Thompson Friend, 1-24. Athens: The University of Georgia Press, 2009.

Temple Kirby, Jack. *Media-made Dixie: The South in the American Imagination.* Athens: The University of Georgia Press, 1986.

Thompson Friend, Craig. "From Southern Manhood to Southern Masculinities: An Introduction." In *Southern Masculinity: Perspectives on Manhood in the South since Reconstruction,* edited by Craig Thompson Friend, vii-xxvi. Athens: The University of Georgia Press, 2009.

Watts, Adam. "A Real Man's place: Attitudes and Environment at a Southern Deer Camp." In *White Masculinity in the Recent South,* edited by Trent Watts, 86-97. Baton Rouge: Louisiana State University Press, 2008.

Watts, Trent. "Telling White Men's Stories." In *White Masculinity in the Recent South*, edited by Trent Watts. Baton Rouge: Louisiana State University Press, 2008.

Williams, Randall. "Tonight the Hulk vs. Ox Baker." *Southern Exposure,* 7, (1979): 30-35.

NOTES

1. James Friedman, *Reality Squared: Televisual Discourse on the Real,* (New Brunswick: Rutgers University Press, 2002), p. 6.

2. Trent Watts, "Telling White Men's Stories," in *White Masculinity in the Recent South,* ed. Trent Watts. (Baton Rouge: Louisiana State University Press, 2008), 2.

3. Mark Orbe, "Representations of Race in Reality TV: Watch and Discuss," *Critical Studies in Media Communication,* 25, no. 4 (2008): 345-52. E. R. Schroeder, "Sexual racism" and reality television: Privileging the white male prerogative on MTV's *The Real World,*" in *Readings in Intercultural Communication: Experiences and Contexts,* ed. Judith N. Martin et al. (Boston: McGraw-Hill, 2006), 219-26.

4. Ryan Owens and Jim Scholz, "Redneck Millionaires Built 'Duck Dynasty' in Duck Call Business." *ABC News,* March 20, 2012. http://abcnews.go.com/Entertainment/redneck-millionaires-built-duck-dynasty-duck-call-business/story?id=15961955.

5. Anoop Nayak, and Mary Jane Kehily, *Gender, Youth, and Culture: Young Masculinities and Femininities*, (Houndmills: Palgrave, 2008), p. 35.

6. Ibid, p. 34.

7. Karen Cox, *Dreaming of Dixie: How the South was Created in American Popular Culture,* (Chapel Hill: The University of North Carolina Press, 2011).

8. Karen Cox, "The South ain't just Whistlin' Dixie." *New York Times.* Retrieved from http://www.nytimes.com/2011/09/18/opinion/sunday/the-south-aint-just-whistlin-dixie.html?pagewanted=all&_r=0 (accessed).

9. Craig Thompson Friend, "From Southern Manhood to Southern Masculinities: An Introduction," in *Southern Masculinity: Perspectives on Manhood in the South since Reconstruction*, ed. Craig Thompson Friend. (Athens: The University of Georgia Press, 2009), vii-xxvi.

10. Ibid, vii-viii.

11. Michael Kimmel, *Manhood in America: A Cultural History*, (New York: Free Press, 1996).

12. Craig Thompson Friend, "From Southern Manhood to Southern Masculinities," viii.

13. Ibid.

14. Ibid., xi.

15. Ibid., xii.

16. Karen Taylor, "Reconstructing men in Savannah, Georgia, 1865-1876," in *Southern Masculinity: Perspectives on Manhood in the South since Reconstruction*, ed. Craig Thompson Friend. (Athens: The University of Georgia Press, 2009), 1-24.

17. Craig Thompson Friend, "From Southern Manhood to Southern Masculinities," x.

18. Ted Ownby, "Manhood, Memory, and White Men's Sports in the Recent American South." *The International Journal of the History of Sport*, 15, no. 2 (1998): 103-18. Adam Watts, "A Real Man's Place: Attitudes and Environment at a Southern Deer Camp," in *White Masculinity in the Recent South*, ed. Trent Watts. (Baton Rouge: Louisiana State University Press, 2008,) 86-97.

19. Ownby, "Manhood, Memory, and White Men's Sports," 103-18.

20. Watts, "A Real Man's Place," 86-97.

21. Ibid., 88.

22. Ownby, "Manhood, Memory, and White Men's Sports," 103-18.

23. Ibid, p. 105.

24. Wilbur Joseph Cash, *The Mind of the South*, (New York: Vintage Books, 1941).

25. Watts, "A Real Man's Place," 90.

26. Jason Eastman and Douglas Schrock, "Southern rock musicians' construction of white trash," *Race, Gender, & Class*, 15, no. 1 (2008): 205-19. John Hartigan, "Unpopular culture: The case of white trash," *Cultural Studies*, 11, no. 2 (1997): 316-43. D. Smith, "Cultural Studies' Misfit: White Trash Studies," *The Mississippi Quarterly*, 57 (2004): 369-388.

27. Jason Eastman and Douglas Schrock, "Southern rock musicians' construction of white trash," *Race, Gender, & Class*, 15, no. 1 (2008): 205-19.

28. Ibid.

29. Eastman and Schrock, "Southern rock musicians' construction of white trash," 205-19.

30. John Hartigan, "Who are these white people? 'Rednecks,' 'hillbillies,' and 'white trash' as marked racial subjects," in *White Out: The Continuing Significance of Racism,* edited by Ashley W. Doane and Eduardo Bonilla-Silva. (New York: Routledge, 2003), pp. 95-111.

31. Eastman and Schrock, "Southern rock musicians' construction of white trash," 205-19.

32. Ibid, 209.

33. Louis Kyriakoudes, and Peter Coclanis, "The Tennessee Test of Manhood: Professional Wrestling and Southern Cultural Stereotypes," *Southern Cultures*, 3, no. 3 (1997): 8-27

34. Kyriakoudes, and Coclanis, "The Tennessee Test of Manhood," 8-27. Randall Williams, "Tonight the Hulk vs. Ox Baker," *Southern Exposure,* 7. (1979): 30-35.

35. Kyriakoudes, and Coclanis, "The Tennessee Test of Manhood," p. 10.

36. Cox, *Dreaming of Dixie.* Jack Temple Kirby, *Media-made Dixie: The South in the American Imagination*, (Athens: The University of Georgia Press, 1986).

37. Jason Eastman, "Rebel manhood: The hegemonic masculinity of the Southern rock music revival," *Journal of Contemporary Ethnography*, 41, no. 2 (2012): 189-219, p. 189.

38. Cox, *Dreaming of Dixie.*

39. Jack Temple Kirby, *Media-made Dixie*, 134.

40. Watts, "Telling White Men's Stories," 2-3.

41. Brenton Malin, "Viral manhood: Niche marketing, hard-boiled detectives and the economics of masculinity," *Media, Culture & Society*, 32, no. 3 (2010): 373-89.

42. Watts, "Telling White Men's Stories."

43. Ibid.

44. Owens and Scholz, "Redneck Millionaires." http://abcnews.go.com/Entertainment/redneck-millionaires-built-duck-dynasty-duck-call-business/story?id=15961955.

Chapter Three

You Better "Redneckognize"!: Deploying the Discourses of Realness, Social Defiance, and Happiness to Defend *Here Comes Honey Boo Boo* on Facebook

Andre Cavalcante

"This show is poison . . . society doesn't need to see some bumpkins that act like idiots and hype their kids up on energy drinks . . . you people supporting it are morons." —Comment from Facebook user (posted on the Official *Here Comes Honey Boo Boo* Facebook page, September 26, 2012)."

"They may not be ur "typical" family (whatever that may be now a days!), but they r loving and happy."—Comment from Facebook user (posted on the Official *Here Comes Honey Boo Boo* Facebook page, October 17, 2012)."

Since its premiere in August 2012, cable network TLC's reality television show *Here Comes Honey Boo Boo* (*HCHBB*) has become a controversial pop cultural phenomenon, causing a stir in the popular press, on social media, and with viewers. The show follows the life of Alana Thompson, a dynamic and headstrong six-year-old child beauty pageant contestant (who never wins), her mother "Mama" June, and their boisterous working-class family, a tight-knit group of self-proclaimed "rednecks" from rural Georgia. Even for reality television, the family is unique and displays a distinctive lifestyle and aesthetic. Their bodies are unrestrained. Much of the family is overweight to some degree, and when addressing the camera, they are often smudged by dirt, spotted with sweat, and swatting flies from their face. Apart from Alana's pageant regalia, their clothes are second-hand and tattered. Their diet, which seemingly lacks the fundamentals of proper nutrition, includes "go-to" staples such as cheese balls, Mountain Dew, grilled "roadkill," and something called "sketti" (a dish consisting of spaghetti, margarine, and ketchup). Alana's sister Ana is seventeen years old and pregnant, and in the season one finale, gives birth to a baby girl with an extra thumb. For recreation, the family goes four-wheeling, plays in the mud, and collects home furnishings from the local dumpster. As a text displaying a family who proudly and loudly violates the dictates of a white, cosmopolitan, middle-class propriety, the show has invited significant criticism. Critics, bloggers, journalists, and pundits alike highlight the problematic nature of the show, raising questions concerning the ethics of children on television, the exploitation of the economically disadvantaged, and the perpetuation of "redneck" stereotypes. Tim Goodman of *The Hollywood Reporter* denounces the show as "horrifying," guilty of "selling and promoting trash" and of "the dehumanization and incremental tearing down of the social fabric."[1] Likewise, David Brooks in the *New York Times* defines the Thompsons as "a train wreck working-class family" who evidence "how social dysfunction can ruin lives."[2]

At the same time, averaging 2.4 million viewers, the series is a ratings powerhouse and appreciates a devoted and passionate fan base.[3] Its September 26th (2012) episode earned the highest Nielsen Ratings of any cable show among 18-to-49-year-olds, and its August 29th (2012) episode attracted more adults than coverage of the Republican National Convention by Fox News.[4] In addition to audience ratings, popular interest in (and disgust for) the show is evidenced on the official *HCHBB* Facebook page. As a lively and well-populated virtual space, fans and critics alike flock to the page to engage in spirited and contentious conversations about the show, the Thompson family, and the socio-cultural messages the program potentially circulates. Some Facebook users criticize and condemn the show as hazardous, exploitative, and vulgar. Yet this discourse is met with an equal proportion of users who defend the value of the show, and its family. As a vehement defender of the show, one user posts, *"Haters will hate but i LOVE this show & this Family . . . they know what's important in life . . . JUNE rocks and Honey boo boo is the sweetest thing . . . I Will watch as long as they keep making this show!!!!"*[5] In responding to the myriad discussions populating the *HCHBB* Facebook page, another user wonders: *"What the heck is all the talk on this family? I do not understand."*[6]

Echoing the user's query about "all the talk on this family," this chapter seeks critical insight into what makes *HCHBB* such a compelling text for audiences. What kinds of discourses do fans mobilize in defending the Thompson family on Facebook? A textual analysis of the show's first season and the fan discourse posted on its official Facebook page is conducted because, when compared to purely textual investigations of media, it provides a more complex and variable account of media texts, their meanings and cultural relevance. Although limited by the technological and communicative affordances of the social network, the *HCHBB* Facebook page serves as a digital archive of audience discourse. Screening their thoughts, opinions and interactions with others, Facebook allows researchers to analyze viewers' social engagement with media texts. In analyzing just over 5,300 Facebook comments, this study reveals that fans' regard for *HCHBB* centers around three dimensions: the Thompson family's perceived "realness," its defiance of middle-class cultural sensibilities, and the performance of happiness the family expresses through articulations of self and togetherness. *HCHBB* presents a modality of happiness that fans find particularly attractive, identified in this study as the "happiness of the disenfranchised." This modality of happiness locates beauty within the ugly, embraces the likeable in an unlikeable fashion, and celebrates the joy of outwardly violating white, middle-class standards of propriety.

AUDIENCE INVESTMENT IN REALITY TELEVISION

Reality television is a particularly provocative and personal media form, and scholarship on reality TV offers insight into why audiences make serious investments in its representations and may take to social media to share their thoughts and opinions. Rooted in the experience of real people, Skeggs and Wood argue that reality television is "a curious space between documentary and home video," and its textual conventions and technological affordances have the ability to screen "recognizable lifeworlds" steeped in intimacy and immediacy for viewers.[7] Reality television invites viewers into the everyday, domestic, and backstage regions of ordinary individuals' lives. Accordingly, it "invests the minutiae of everyday life with dramatic importance."[8] Coupled with the production of intimacy and the quotidian, the reality genre constructs a televised morality play for it "relies upon attaching signs of value, making good and bad behaviour specific to practices, bodies and people."[9] Reality TV personalities are fundamentally "value loaded," represented as inhabiting either good or bad subject positions.[10] The reality television program becomes a cultural field upon which the behavioral codes that govern social life are disputed and consolidated, a mass mediated resource for "*enacting* and *shaping* (constituting) spaces and populations . . . for establishing the rules and standards (constitutions) of belonging and participation."[11] As a result, the reality genre encourages a form of hyper-discriminating viewership, in which audiences engage in practices of comparison, criticism and evaluation.[12]

These dynamics of judgment and social comparison play out on social media, for it affords a platform where audiences can "talk back" to media texts and to other audience members, staking claims and engaging in semi-public conversation under varying levels of anonymity. In the case of *HCHBB*, audiences migrate to Facebook engaging in discursive practices of devaluation or praise, using the Thompson family and their show as reasons to debate the "proper" and moral parameters of self, family, society and nation. In this chapter, the ways fans specifically mobilize and deploy the cultural codes of realness, social defiance and happiness are investigated as discursive ammunition in defending the show and the Thompson family.

REALNESS: "THEY ARE JUST A REAL FAMILY NOT PUTTING ON AIRS."

"Mutants," "scumbags," "idiots," "morons," and *"fat-asses."* In castigating the Thompson family, these are just a few examples of the kind of language Facebook users employed in comment threads on the official *HCHBB* page. In analyzing the tenor of user comments, an apparent "us" versus "them" divide emerges. The fans ("us") write positive and celebratory comments, and respond to those they designate as "the haters" ("them"), or users who post negative and derogatory comments (like the above). These outright expressions of contempt motivate *HCHBB* fans to defend and justify the Thompson family's character and lifestyle. For example, one Facebook user asserted, *"If people do not like the show then they shouldn't watch it. They are just a real family not putting on airs and not trying to impress anyone. I think June is doing a great job"*.[13] Categorizing the Thompson family in terms of the "real" and the "authentic" was a common strategy deployed by fans on Facebook in countering aspersion from the "haters." Realness was offered as a justification for why viewers were attracted to the show and valued the family. It was associated with positive affect and veracity, as one user posted, *"I like the show because they are REAL, they don't act while on camera, they are their true selves and that is the best kind of reality tv."*[14]

It is not surprising that fans mobilize the discourse of the "real" in defending the Thompson family, for realness and "real life" are the currency of reality television. As rare and precious resources, audiences seek out "authenticity" and "realness" in reality TV's settings, contexts, and its personalities, their emotions and performances of self.[15] The reality genre's production conventions and incorporation of aesthetic realism synergistically contribute to the Thompson family's perceived "realness." As a form of "observational realism," the reality television genre is structured by a set of editorial practices and stylistic choices that attempt to indicate that what is presented on screen, while mediated, still approximates the "real."[16] For example, *Here Comes Honey Boo Boo* is situated primarily within a domestic frame, and most of the show's action is shot inside the family's house and in their backyard. The camera follows the family throughout mundane, everyday tasks such as food shopping. A sense of intimacy is generated through the now standard "first person confessional," whereby family members address the camera (and at home audience) directly as if speaking a personal diary.

Showrunners' intentional and strategic display of the intersecting symbols of white, rural, working class life and the American South cultivated a sense of "working class realness" for fans on Facebook. Often, comments about the family's realness were coupled with a description or mention of their class position, as one user posted *"I love the whole family — working class real people who ain't afraid to just be themselves!"*[17] The sonic landscape of the show often consists of a rapid, "twangy" acoustic guitar or banjo-style music that punctuates the scene. Accompanying this musical structure are establishing shots featuring traditional cultural markers of a working-class, rural American South. After commercial breaks, scenes are introduced with images of emaciated stray cats, local dogs lying in dirt, crows pecking on roadkill, broken down pick-up trucks abandoned in fields, and storefronts of small, local businesses called the "Kuntry Stoe." The family inhabits this land. They are *of* this land, and the intimate relationship the show constructs between the Thompsons, the Georgian countryside, and working class realness strongly resonates with Facebook users, as one exclaims, *"I Love this family!!! They are the real thing, and PURE COUNTRY TO THE BONE!!!!"*[18] Perhaps the most frequently employed symbolic reminder of the family's social position is the roaring freight train that runs next to the family's house. Shots of the train, its blaringly loud whistle, the railroad tracks and crossing signs are routinely and prominently displayed in every episode. These images generated a strong sense of nostalgia and identification for one user, who wrote, *"I love it that the train is always passing. When I was a kid we lived right at the tracks, I mean 'right' . . . Precious memories!"*[19]

Working in tandem with reality television's aesthetics and narrative conventions are the ways in which audiences seek "realism" in television, and often employ it as a benchmark in determining the value of a text.[20] With respect to reality television, audiences generally bring to the viewing experience an expectation it will in some way convey "visual evidence of real life."[21] Consequently, Bauwel contends that while reality TV programs "explore authenticity and celebrate 'real' people, the reality of everyday life," the genre's realness equally derives from the "merger of strong professional intervention in the way that reality is mediated and constructed, and the desire for unmediated access to reality, authenticity and ordinariness."[22] Thus, the "realness" of *Here Comes Honey Boo Boo* is a synergy of the production practices of the showrunners working within the conventions and aesthetics of reality TV, the audiences' desire for "authenticity," and finally the Thompson family's actual personalities, worldviews, and life situation (their "down-to-earthness").

Importantly, the Thompson family's "real" life situation does convey a sense of working-class realness. Alana's father works seven days a week performing demanding blue-collar labor as a chalk miner. The six-person family shares a small house with one bathroom, a living situation making it necessary for family members to share bedrooms and wash their hair in the kitchen sink. Money is tight and to save, the Thompson family routinely cuts coupons for groceries. They purchase nearly expired food at a local "food auction," and visit the town dump to go "shopping." The Thompsons' visits to the town dump resonated with one Facebook user, *"Back in the '50's we too went shopping at the landfill."*[23] Importantly, for viewers, the family's rural, working-class lifestyle exhibits a rejection of the extravagant, the new, and the trendy. Another user posted, *" So many people are so used to seeing blingy things and over the top lifestyle that they forget what ' real ' everyday people look like in an everyday true life. Love the show."*[24] While one user feels favorably about the family because they are *"not completely materialistic,"*[25] another praises the family for being *"real and down home,"*[26] and a third explains, *"They are ordinary people . . . they don't show off like most people in this world do."*[27]

In Facebook comment threads, the "realness" of the Thompsons is often co-constructed alongside the "fakeness" of other reality TV families and personalities. One user admits, *"I would feel comfy talking & hanging out w/ mama June & honey boo boo than Kardashians. They r real people!"*[28] As J. L. Austin (1964) notes about the "real," "there are no criteria to be laid down *in general* for distinguishing the real from the not real."[29] According to Austin, the "real" is "substantive hungry," and as a context specific construct, it relies on comparison and contrast for its determination.[30] In this way, viewers come to legitimate the "realness" of the Thompson family by accentuating their difference from the now archetypical privileged, wealthy reality TV families depicted in shows such as the *Real Housewives* franchise, *Big Rich Texas*, and *Keeping up with the Kardashians*. A Facebook user articulates the realness of *Here Comes Honey Boo Boo* in the following way: *"It's real sh*t. That's why I love them, not everybody can be as classy as the Kardashians (sarcasm)."*[31]

SOCIAL DEFIANCE: "YOU LIKE US OR YOU DON'T LIKE US. WE JUST DON'T CARE."

According to fans, the perception of the Thompson family's "realness" is bolstered and reinforced by their defiant attitude toward middle-class norms and standards of propriety. As with their realness, the Thompsons' defiance is textually reproduced through the interpenetration of the family's actual worldview and behaviors with the strategic production and editing choices of the *HCHBB* showrunners. At the start of the first episode in season one, June ("Mama") introduces her family to the show's viewers, foreshadowing what they can expect from the series: "Our family is crazy. We like to be ourselves. You like us or you don't like us. We just don't care." Further anchoring these sentiments, each episode of the series opens with the same scene: the Thompson family gathers together for a family portrait, yet this moment of order is quickly interrupted and punctuated by an ear-splitting fart, courtesy of "Mama" June. In fact, the Thompson family consistently performs culturally unbecoming "backstage" behaviors, or those privatized actions typically executed outside of a public gaze, unashamedly for the camera.[32] Scenes of the family burping, farting, sneezing, sniffling, and nose picking are intentionally and frequently woven into the show's narrative, for their bodies are depicted as leaky and uncontrolled.

Although fans interpret this behavior as "real," the *HCHBB* Facebook page is also populated with comments that strongly judge, castigate and reproach the show and its personalities. For example, one Facebook user framed the family in terms of severe cultural corrosion, *"Honey boo boo and her family represent the decay of western civilization, and should be watched by no one."*[33] This viewer discourse confirms that reality television stages and encourages what Skeggs identifies as a "moral economy of person production," in which positive and negative moral values are associated with specific performances of self.[34] In contemporary Western culture, Joffe and Staerkle argue that good subject positions are generally characterized by a "self-control ethos," or "maintaining active control over one's desires, emotions and actions."[35] Defined by discipline, self-regulation and careful management, the self-control ethos is a highly valued and dominant standard that serves in the assessment of self and others. As a result, "social representations concerning lacking self-control over body, mind and destiny underpin many of the contents of stereotypes and prejudice."[36] Typically, the self-control ethos lies within the domain of the middle and privileged classes.[37] Moreover, the importance of the self-control ethos may be legitimated and circulated through dominant social institutions and media culture. In particular, popular media images of the self-disciplined person are "associated with moral rectitude and civility," whereas cultural portrayals of bodies 'out-of-control' are "linked to their converse."[38]

On television, working-class people often bear the burden of bad subject positions characterized by the absence of a "self-control ethos." Specifically, reality television facilitates a "middle-class gaze," or "a mode of production (symbolic as well as material) which is underpinned by an anxiety about the working classes that has historically entailed the (mis)recognition of the working class."[39] This misrecognition casts the working as less valuable, abject and in need of restoration and rehabilitation.[40] Specifically, reality TV turns its focus toward female identity as a subject position warranting cultural surveillance, scrutiny, and repair. Shows such as *Wife Swap* and *What Not to Wear*, for example, operate as correctives meant to ameliorate an impoverished modality of contemporary femininity. Through reality television shows such as these and similar others, middle class values are imposed onto working-class women and reasserted as "morally good and right and as the embodiment of propriety and good taste."[41]

As working class and primarily female, the Thompson family bears a considerably heavy burden of representation, and as an American family on television they are held accountable to the dictates of the self-control ethos. For in Facebook comment threads, they are routinely criticized for failing to live up to white, middle-class norms of propriety, subjectivity, appearance, behavior, and health. In commenting on a picture of the Thompson family gathered for Thanksgiving, a Facebook user admonishes, " *I think this TV show is so disgusting . . . The whole family should join weight watchers. And take some cleaning lessons.*"[42] Similarly, another user remarks, "*I find the glorification of ignorance to be revolting. These ppl need to be educated in how to speak and act with some dignity.*"[43] Facebook comments also point to the Thompson family as a tragically flawed symbol of specifically American values. In commenting on Alana and "Mama" June, one user posted, "*She's horrible . . . Her manners are not for 7-year-old girl. And her mom should hide herself somewhere for " better " times. National shame!.*"[44] In this way, the white, working-class family, and particularly women, are constituted as "the national constitutive limit to propriety," and their bodies, behaviors, and lifestyles become symbolic indicators of national virtue, integrity and progress.[45] This kind of moral scrutiny in the name of nationalism did not go uncontested on Facebook in that fans rallied to defend the family and articulate alternative ideas regarding the state of America. A user posted: "*To me - the negative responses that people have to this show is what is wrong with America, to hate and insult people (including Kids!) based on their appearance, upbringing, poverty, weight, or where in the country they are from.*"[46]

While televised representations of American female identity and worth are often tied to a mythic notion of the middle-class woman, Press notes that working-class shows (such as *HCHBB*) are capable of evading these class and gender conventions, celebrating alternative forms of lifestyle and femininity.[47] For example, the character Roseanne, from the network TV show *Roseanne* (which ran on ABC from 1988-1997), "thwarts our expectations of proper female behavior."[48] As a sharp-witted, blue-collar, and confident matriarch, Roseanne Connor, and her working-class family became (controversial) national treasures during the show's time on air. The Connor family was proudly steeped in American working-class culture and iconography: motorcycles, cheap beer, construction work, "junk food," penny pinching, and a healthy portion of disdain for bourgeoisie conduct and decorum. Notably, *Roseanne* celebrated non-normative femininity as embodied by the show's protagonist Roseanne, an over-weight, outspoken, and brash personality, and her daughter, Darlene, a "tomboyish" and artistic intellectual who preferred black t-shirts, ripped jeans and sneakers to dresses and heels.

In the tradition of *Roseanne*, *HCHBB* continues this rare representational tradition of disobedience toward gendered and classed cultural norms, presenting an overweight, junk-food-eating, crass and outspoken family, unkempt and disheveled in appearance. The Thompson family's difference from middle-class modes of lifestyle and propriety are clearly brought into relief in the second episode. "Mama" June invites an etiquette coach to the house in hopes that the cultivation of "appropriate" manners will help her daughter Lauryn become more "refined" and Alana become more competitive in beauty pageants. The episode presents two contrasting representations of whiteness. "Tasteful," neatly dressed, and hyper-restrained, the etiquette coach is the fulfillment of a white self-control ethos, highly skilled and concerned with the presentation of the bourgeoisie self. By contrast, the Thompsons are whiteness in excess: unbounded, obstinate, and rambunctious. Before the session begins, Lauryn is resistant to the thought of being "cultivated," explaining, "Mama thinks I need etiquette classes. Look at me. I don't need no etiquette classes. I don't need to be married or anything. What you see is what you get." Throughout their time together around the family's kitchen table, the etiquette coach, as a representative of middle-class taste and behavior, struggles to discipline the two. Unable to be contained by either the coach or the structure of the kitchen table, Alana and Lauryn resist sitting still and become distracted. Noticeably flustered, the coach subsequently fails to convince the girls about the social importance of "good manners." In summing up the etiquette experience, Alana criticizes, "In etiquette class I learned nothing . . . etiquette class is for stupid people." After she leaves, "Mama" June refers to the coach as a "square" and a "tight ass," maintaining that, "no one can be proper and etiquettely all the time." Rather than being sources of shame, these "deficiencies" of decorum and violations of the self-control ethos are embraced by the family. Although the show frames the Thompsons in terms of working-class failure, as "noisy, out of place, ungovernable," they recode these behaviors and attitudes as affirmative resources for identity, and as sources of pride and personality. [49]

On Facebook, the Thompsons' self-assured attitude, rooted in distance from middle-class privilege and propriety, is praised by *HCHBB* fans. They often cite the family's class position when defending them against comments from "the haters." One fan on Facebook maintains, *"You should never judge someone by where they live, or what they drive. Some people weren't born with a silver spoon in their mouth, they get by the best way they can."* [50] Likewise, another explains, *"This world is full of snobs and people judging. We need more laughs and to respect each other regardless of looks, race, size, and the size of our bank accounts!"* [51] In addition to the family's distance from the middle and privileged classes, fans on Facebook commended the family's outward defiance of dominant cultural norms and standards. Users praised the Thompson family's *"bravery"* for not conforming to *"the norm within uppity society values."*[52] Offering an explanation of why she enjoys the show, one user posted: *"Luv 'em. Much better than watching a bunch of regimented, politically-correct tight @*##'s."*[53] By referring to the idea of "regimentation," this post celebrates the family's disregard for the self-control ethos. In enthusiastically communicating their admiration for the Thompson family, Facebook users often referenced the language of disregard (such as "not caring" and "don't care") to describe why they applaud family. As one user acknowledges, the family *"don't live to please others!"*[54] Another expressed, *"They are who they are and don't care what anyone thinks! Love it!"*[55] Similarly, in reacting to "the haters," a fan on Facebook offers, *"They* [the Thompson family] *are amazing, not ashamed of who they are, how they live, how they are perceived by others . . . how many of you are that comfortable?"*[56]

The Thompson family's defiance is not only communicated via a rejection of middle-class sensibility, but also expressed through an approving, warm acceptance of Southern "Redneck" culture. During the series' first episode, the family participates in the "Redneck Games," an annual event held in Southern Georgia that raises money for local charities. For the 2012 games, activities included bobbing for pig's feet, mud-pit belly flopping, watermelon seed spitting, and hubcap hurling contests. Clothes soiled, dripping with sweat and giggling from the joy of playing in the mud, the family happily participated in many of them. In delineating the games, "Mama" June explains, "It's all about Southern pride, similar to the Olympics but with a lot of missing teeth and a lot of butt cracks showing." The family's embrace of Redneck culture continued with the choice of family pet. In the series' second episode, rather than opting for the more traditional cat or dog, "Mama" June adopts a teacup pig for Alana. As a loud, frenetic, and undisciplined presence, the farm animal mirrors the family's collective energy and personality. Yet, in breaking with stereotypes that link Southern "Redneck" culture with social conservatism and intolerance, Alana decides to name her male pig "Glitzy," describing him as "the pageant gay pig." Alana is insistent on the pig's homosexuality, asserting to her family, "it can if it wants to. You can't tell that pig what to do." Responding favorably to the show and the Thompson family's distinctive embrace of Redneck culture, fans of *HCHBB* post affirming comments, such as one user's offering, *"cool azz rednecks."*[57] Another fan on Facebook shared, *"Just watched all your shows tonight. Made me so homesick for my redneck family in Oklahoma."*[58] Moreover, the Thompson family's catch phrase, "You better redneckognize!," a boastful affirmation of Southern "Redneck" culture, has become a fan favorite. The expression is frequently articulated in the textual content of fan Facebook posts. Employing capital letters and exclamation points for emphasis, as one user professed to fellow Facebook users, *"You better REDNECKOG-NIZE!!!!"*[59]

THE HAPPINESS OF THE DISENFRANCHISED

In posting about why she approves of the Thompson family, a fan on Facebook testified, *"Gotta love them! I wish them nothing but the Best because they are already happier than most*!!"[60] In addition to supporting the Thompson's realness, social defiance and embrace of themselves as "Rednecks," fans flock to Facebook to discuss and defend the family's distinct articulation of happiness, identified in this study as the "happiness of the disenfranchised." In short, the happiness of the disenfranchised is the ability to uncover joy from economic hardship, as one Facebook user, commented, *"I love June. She makes lemonade out of lemons in life."*[61] Likewise, another affirmed, *"This family takes what life gives them and turns it into love & laughter."*[62] Alongside portrayals of working-class disadvantage and struggle, each episode of *HCHBB* is replete with shots of laughter, humor, smiles and a lightness of spirit. One Facebook user notices, *"They may not have much, but that family is close, happy and always smiling."*[63] From the first episode, "Mama" June, in speaking on behalf of the family, accentuates their happiness as a defining characteristic, "We love our little life, and we're having fun doing it."

In the spirit of working-class television, including shows such as *Roseanne, Married with Children,*[64] and more recently Showtime's *Shameless,*[65] *Here Comes Honey Boo Boo* is part of a media tradition that displays and legitimates the happiness of the disenfranchised. In the media studies literature, however, scholars often conceptualize the happiness of the disenfranchised as impossibility, a false illusion that works to mask economic inequality and sustain class relations. Scholars have argued that mass-mediated representations of the working and disenfranchised classes overemphasize and glorify their felicity, goodness and fortitude. Pasqualino maintains that within popular media the myth of the "happy poor" is a durable cultural trope that "endures and outlives eras and ideologies."[66] When circulated within media culture, Thomas and Callahan argue that the "myth of the happy poor" plays an essential role in "limiting social mobility (or social change in general) so as to preserve the status quo."[67] Specifically, the myth "teaches the poor that being rich does not mean being happy and that harmonious interpersonal relations are a "priceless" possession."[68] Likewise, Press points out working class shows like *Roseanne* generally uncritically celebrate family and domestic life, depicting an idealized contentment and an almost unrealistically supportive familial unit.[69]

In presenting a highly edited and stylized caricature of a happy, close-knit and quirky working-class family, *HCHBB* has the potential to romanticize the Thompsons' domestic life, trivialize class struggle, and reinforce the social and economic status quo by showing that the economically disenfranchised are after all (mindlessly) happy in their situation. As Kompare cautions, "even though the genre is reality, and the actions of the subjects are real, the production and promotion of reality TV programs ensure that its subjects function in the end as *characters*: attractive constructions of personalities." [70] However, while the Thompson family's televised lives and articulations of happiness are heavily edited, and their personalities are condensed into characters through the industry routines of reality television, the family nonetheless escapes pure caricature. Importantly, the family's happiness is depicted alongside the actual economic hardships they encounter, including but not limited to noticeable health problems, the challenges of living in a small and cramped living space, the necessity of hand-me-down clothes and dumpster diving, and a reliance on the unhealthy kinds of mass produced bulk food items that can cheaply feed a large family. Although it is often located in the background, the show bears witness to working-class struggle and "real," everyday experiences of austerity. Moreover, while there is no way to discern whether the Thompsons' happiness is "real," the joy they perform for the cameras is not mindless and uncritical. In their own way, they question the social status quo and access happiness on their own terms, a happiness fueled by the joy in disregarding the self-control ethos and in rejecting bourgeoisie manners and standards (to be further discussed later in this section).

Although the show's encoding carries the potential to trivialize and romanticize the Thompsons and their happiness, viewers ultimately decode the show in alternative and resistant ways. Practices of audience viewing are critical, and social media comment threads reveal that fans of *HCHBB* are aware the show is a media representation. On Facebook, they call out TLC for production choices that trivialize the family. In commenting on how TLC promoted the show, one user posted, "*Shame on you TLC- always trying to make fun of this family.*" [71] Along these lines, Bricklin notes, "TLC is trying its hardest to portray Alana's family as a horde of lice-picking, lard-eating, nose-thumbing hooligans south of the Mason-Dixon line, but it's not working. It falls flat, because there's no true dysfunction here, save for the beauty pageant stuff." [72]

Importantly, rather than as illusion, fans encounter the family and their joy as genuine, socially relevant and commendable. Facebook comments disclose that fans support and revel in the family's portrayal of happiness. For one user, happiness is one of *HCHBB*'s defining attributes. Notably, a form of the word happy appears four times in her brief post: "*This family is totally happy with who they are . . . Totally happy family and a happy man in their lives too. She* ['Mama' June] *can't be doing much wrong to have so much happiness in her family.*"[73] Similarly, another user perceives the family's happiness as genuine, writing, "*They don't have much, but they are happy . . . Alana enjoys her childhood and you can see it on how she acts and talks. You can't fake happy.*"[74]

As with the Thompson family's realness, their happiness is also brought into relief through comparison with other reality television families. According to Facebook users, whereas the *Desperate Housewives* or *Kardashian* clans, for example, seek and engage in mindless pleasure, the Thompsons cultivate and deliver happiness. Underscoring this difference, one viewer on Facebook posted "[I'd] *rather watch this then those stupid brainless fake plastic Hollywood wives who are drunk drinking all day long.*"[75] Throughout season one, the show routinely depicts the Thompsons engaged in inexpensive practices of leisure not reliant on conspicuous consumption: assembling and swimming in an above-ground pool, having grass fights in the backyard, making a lemonade stand, and playing games together such as "Guess whose breath?"—wherein one family member breathes on another who identifies to whom that breath belongs. On the Facebook site, fans cheer the Thompsons facility in creating joy outside of conspicuous consumption and their ability to locate happiness outside of bourgeoisie entertainments. One user celebrates the show because the family "*doesn't need a lot of money or electronics to have fun,*"[76] whereas another opines, "*A family full of love and not worried about material things! . . . How many of you spend this much time together without tv or video games?*"[77]

On Facebook, fans articulate the Thompson family's happiness in accord with Haybron's conceptualization of the term, as representing something more than a temporary "particular emotion or mood."[78] Rather, Haybron theorizes happiness as an "overall emotional state or condition," not an episodic feeling of pleasure, but a long-term experience of contentment.[79] Accordingly, happiness "is not something that happens to a person. It is rather a state of the individual."[80] Happiness is "forward-looking," and it is "having a certain attitude toward one's life. Experiencing pleasure is not."[81] In particular, Haybron argues that the crucial dimensions of happiness include such things as feeling confident and not "small spirited,"[82] being engaged with the immediate world, and experiencing "exhuberance"[83] and "cheerfulness."[84] Notably, viewers posting on Facebook perceive exactly these attributes within the family, echoing a conception of happiness as a life condition, a total way of living and approaching the world. A fan on Facebook posted, "*As far as I am concerned this family seems happy and they know how to have fun, live life and not take themselves too seriously.*"[85] In commenting on "Mama" June's approach to parenting, one user wrote, "*I like that she lets her kids be themselves, they seem happy and confident people!*"[86] For fans on social media, the Thompson family is happy and their happiness is durable. According to Facebook users, the durability of the Thompson family's happiness is a result of its location outside of "fake" pleasures and conspicuous consumption. Specifically, their happiness is humanist, springing from a gazing inward toward the family unit, from its embeddedness in social relationships, and from being engaged with others. Fans on Facebook appreciate the Thompson's togetherness and sense of humor, as a user notes: *"Love that this family is happy, does things as a family, they appear to find humor in their lives."*[87] Likewise, another applauds the family's closeness and value system: *"I think they are a very loving family. They do everything together. They have fun. How many 7 year olds would say "I like my sister's gift because it came from the heart."*[88]

In addition to being uncommodified and humanist, the happiness of the disenfranchised is also informed by finding delight in an oppositional stance toward middle class standards of value, embodiment, and comportment. The Thompson family locates beauty within the ugly, presents the likeable in an unlikeable fashion, and celebrates the joy of outwardly violating middle-class standards of propriety. For example, in *HCHBB*, negatively codified substances such as dirt and mud are re-signified. Rather than portrayed as polluted and undesirable, dirt and mud are reworked as an expedient, accessible resource for fun and entertainment. According to Douglas, dirt represents "matter out of place," and results from a "systematic ordering and classification of matter, insofar as ordering involves rejecting inappropriate elements."[89] It is the culturally abject. As Grosz argues, dirt signals vulnerability and indicates a "site of possible danger to social and individual systems."[90] By contrast, Grosz suggests the clean body is a normative representation of propriety, lawfulness, and discipline.[91] West shows how reality television in particular has a strong and intimate connection with dirt, highlighting the ways in which shows on home improvement and domestic advice privilege cleanliness and the elimination of filth.[92] As reality television engages with the "real" world often on a low, common and near level, "dirt," as West maintains, "is key to the reality TV project; intimate, spectacular, human, visceral and incontrovertibly real."[93] In particular, reality television reproduces social classifications, favorably connecting cleanliness and tidiness with "an implied cache of middle-class values: discretion, moderation, conformity, sobriety, privacy."[94]

In embracing the mud, the Thomspon family repudiates these values in favor of the happiness of the disenfranchised—a dirty happiness, one that undermines the self-control ethos. As West maintains, dirt is a potential "site of cultural subversion."[95] Rather than being "out of place," dirt and mud are narratively in place within the diegetic flow of the first season of *HCHBB*. Members of the family embrace the mud, going swimming, tubing and four-wheeling in the brown muck, and their bodies are often covered in it. In episode three, mud played a central role in facilitating the family's leisure time together. During the peak of a hot summer's day, "Mama" June constructs what she identifies as a "Redneck waterslide" in the yard for her children. Smothering a plastic tarp with baby oil, soap, and water, she instructs her children to "have fun with it." Inevitably, a pool of mud forms at the end of the slide, into which the family gleefully slides. Covered in mud, the sisters wrestle and chase each other around the grass, as one asserts through her hurried breathing, "God made dirt, and dirt don't hurt." In summarizing the experience, "Mama" June offers, "If you're not having fun and making memories, then it's not worth the experience . . . We are who we are. We like having fun." Users on Facebook respond to these kinds of dirty activities that disregard the self-control ethos with approval and appreciation. One posted, *"WOOP! That's what I'm talking about! FOLKS! let your girls get dirty if they want to! its good for um. they gotta take a shower anyways b4 they go to bed . . . *applauds.*"*[96] In explaining the Thompson family's choice of leisure activities to "haters" and "snobs," some users connect their experiences as Southerners to the show's representation of mud: *"For you who think this isn't the life Americans should be celebrating you must be very cut off from the South . . . Here in Texas people do go mudding in jeeps, pickups and four wheelers. What irks some people is they can't stand to know about others who don't live just like them and turn their noses up at them. Where I come from thats called being a snob!!!. They are a wonderful family who plays together and a lot more of you should be as committed to your children's happiness and well being as they are."*[97] Similarly, another user explains, *"Love this show! A real family! I love How June loves her family! I love the South!. . . We can go to a Ball one day and the next we can go mudding! . . . Life is so simple!"*[98] In painting vivid portraits of everyday leisure, these comments seek to legitimate a specifically Southern manifestation of the happiness of the disenfranchised.

Notably, for fans on Facebook, the Thompsons' embrace of the mud represents everything they like about *HCHBB*: its realness, audaciousness, and the simple happiness it affords the family. In wanting to stand up and affirm these values and the Thompsons' lifestyle, fans convene on Facebook and praise the family's ability to embrace themselves as is and commend their penchant for locating treasure in trash. Fans deploy discourses centered on realness, disobedience, and happiness to justify what one user called their *"rough around the edges"* "Redneck," working-class lifestyle.[99] In this way, Facebook offers an accessible avenue for fans to "redneckognize," and to "talk back" to those in the popular press and the "haters" on Facebook who view the family as a depiction of ethical inadequacy, social decline and moral decay. Through social media discourse, fans also talk back to the Thompson family, celebrating, protecting, and supporting their lifestyle, values and distinct articulation of happiness.

REFERENCES

Ang, Ien. *Watching Dallas: Soap Opera and the Melodramatic Imagination*. London: Methuen & Co., 1985.

Austin, J.L.. *Sense and Sensibilia*. Oxford: Oxford University Press, 1964.

Bauwel, Sofie Van. "A Short Introduction to Trans-Reality." In *Trans-Reality Television: The Transgression of Reality, Genre, Politics, and Audience*, 21-22. Edited by Sofie Van Bauwel and Nico Carpentier. Lanham: Lexington Books, 2010.

Bricklin, Julia. "TLC's 'Here Comes Honey Boo Boo' Isn't All That Bad." *Forbes Magazine*, August 12, 2012, http://www.forbes.com/sites/juliabricklin/2012/08/12/tlcs-here-comes-honey-boo-boo-isnt-all-that-bad/

Brooks, David. "The Psych Approach." *New York Times*, September 27, 2012, http://www.nytimes.com/2012/09/28/opinion/brooks-the-psych-approach.html?_r=0

Douglas, Mary. *Purity and Danger: An Analysis of the Concepts of Pollution and Taboo*. London: Routledge and Kegan Paul, 1966.

Goffman, Erving. *The Presentation of Self in Everyday Life*. New York: Anchor Books, 1959.

Goodman, Tim. "'Honey Boo Boo': That Joke Isn't Funny Anymore." *The Hollywood Reporter*, August 22, 2012, http://www.hollywoodreporter.com/bastard-machine/here-comes-honey-boo-boo-alana-mama-364933

Grosz, Elizabeth. *Volatile Bodies: Towards a Corporeal Feminism*. Bloomington: Indiana University Press, 1994.

Haybron, Daniel. M.. *The Pursuit of Unhappiness: The Elusive Psychology of Well-Being*. New York: Oxford University Press, 2008.

Hill, Annette. *Reality TV: Audiences and Popular Factual Television*. New York: Routledge, 2005.

Hill, Annette. *Restyling Factual TV: Audiences and News, Documentary and Reality Genres*. New York: Routledge, 2007.

Joffe, Helene and Staerkle, Christian. "The Centrality of the Self-Control Ethos in Western Aspersions Regarding Outgroups: A Social Representational Approach to Stereotype Content." *Culture & Psychology* 13, no. 4 (2007): 395-418.

Kepler, Adam. "'Honey Boo Boo' Has the Ratings, if Not the Critics." *New York Times*, September 28, 2012, http://artsbeat.blogs.nytimes.com/2012/09/28/honey-boo-boo-has-the-ratings-if-not-the-critics/

Kompare, Derek. "Extraordinarily Ordinary: The Osbournes as '*An American Family.*'" In *Reality TV: Remaking Television Culture*, 97-112. Edited by Susan Murray and Laurie Ouellette. New York: NYU Press, 2004.

Lyle, Samantha A. "(Mis)recognition and the Middle-Class/Bourgeois Gaze: A Case Study of Wife Swap." *Critical Discourse Studies* 5, no.4 (2008): 319–330.

Ouellette, Laurie and Hay, James. *Better Living Through Reality TV: Television and Post-welfare Citizenship*. Malden, MA and Oxford, UK: Blackwell Publishing, 2008.

Pasqualino, Caterina. "The Gypsies, Poor but Happy." *Third Text* 22, no.3 (2008): 337-345.

Press, Andrea. *Women Watching Television: Gender, Class, and Generation in the American Television Experience*. Philadelphia: University of Pennsylvania Press, 1991.

Skeggs, Beverly. "The Making of Class and Gender through Visualizing Moral Subject Formation." *Sociology* 39, no. 5 (2005): 965-982.

Skeggs, Beverly. "The Moral Economy of Person Production: The Class Relations of Self-Performance on 'Reality' Television." *The Sociological Review* 57, no. 4 (2009): 626-644.

Skeggs, Beverley and Wood, Helen. "The labour of transformation and circuits of value 'around' reality television." *Continuum: Journal of Media & Cultural Studies* 22, no. 4 (2008): 559–572.

Thomas, Sari and Callahan, Brian P. "Allocating Happiness: TV Families and Social Class." *Journal of Communication*, Summer (1982): 184-190.

West, Amy. "Reality Television and the Power of Dirt: Metaphor and Matter." *Screen* 52, no. 1 (2011): 63-77.

Woodruff, Betsy. "Much Ado About Honey Boo Boo." *The National Review*, October 15, 2012, http://www.nationalreview.com/articles/330365/much-ado-about-honey-boo-boo-betsy-woodruff

NOTES

1. Tim Goodman, "'Honey Boo Boo': That Joke Isn't Funny Anymore," *The Hollywood Reporter*, August 22, 2012, http://www.hollywoodreporter.com/bastard-machine/here-comes-honey-boo-boo-alana-mama-364933
2. David Brooks, "The Psych Approach," *New York Times*, September 27, 2012, http://www.nytimes.com/2012/09/28/opinion/brooks-the-psych-approach.html?_r=0
3. Adam Kepler, "'Honey Boo Boo' Has the Ratings, if Not the Critics," *New York Times*, September 28, 2012, http://artsbeat.blogs.nytimes.com/2012/09/28/honey-boo-boo-has-the-ratings-if-not-the-critics/
4. Kepler, "'Honey Boo Boo' Has the Ratings, if Not the Critics."
5. Official *Here Comes Honey Boo Boo Facebook* Page, Facebook, posted January 11, 2013, http://www.facebook.com/HereComesHoneyBooBoo?fref=ts
6. Official *Here Comes Honey Boo Boo* Facebook Page, Facebook, posted February 7, 2013, http://www.facebook.com/HereComesHoneyBooBoo?fref=ts
7. Beverley Skeggs and Helen Wood, "The labour of transformation and circuits of value 'around' reality television," *Continuum: Journal of Media & Cultural Studies* 22, no. 4 (2008): 569 and 565.
8. Laurie Ouellette and James Hay, *Better Living Through Reality TV: Television and Postwelfare Citizenship* (Malden, MA and Oxford, UK: Blackwell Publishing, 2008), 4.
9. Ouellette and Hay, *Better Living Through Reality TV*, 560.
10. Beverly Skeggs, "The Moral Economy of Person Production: The Class Relations of Self-Performance on 'Reality' Television," *The Sociological Review* 57, no. 4 (2009): 639.
11. Ouellette and Hay, *Better Living Through Reality TV*, 170-171.
12. Ouellette and Hay, *Better Living Through Reality TV*.
13. Official *Here Comes Honey Boo Boo* Facebook Page, Facebook, posted February 7, 2013, http://www.facebook.com/HereComesHoneyBooBoo?fref=ts
14. Official *Here Comes Honey Boo Boo* Facebook Page, Facebook, posted October 15, 2012, http://www.facebook.com/HereComesHoneyBooBoo?fref=ts
15. Annette Hill, *Restyling Factual TV: Audiences and News, Documentary and Reality Genres* (New York: Routledge, 2007).
16. Annette Hill, *Reality TV: Audiences and Popular Factual Television* (New York, USA and Milton Park, Canada: Routledge, 2005).
17. Official *Here Comes Honey Boo Boo* Facebook Page, Facebook, posted October 4, 2012, http://www.facebook.com/HereComesHoneyBooBoo?fref=ts
18. Official *Here Comes Honey Boo Boo* Facebook Page, Facebook, posted March 11, 2013, http://www.facebook.com/HereComesHoneyBooBoo?fref=ts
19. Official *Here Comes Honey Boo Boo* Facebook Page, Facebook, posted February 8, 2013, http://www.facebook.com/HereComesHoneyBooBoo?fref=ts
20. Ien Ang, *Watching Dallas: Soap Opera and the Melodramatic Imagination*, (London: Methuen & Co, 1985).
21. Hill, *Reality TV*, p. 59.
22. Sofie Van Bauwel, "A Short Introduction to Trans-Reality," in *Trans-Reality Television: The Transgression of Reality, Genre, Politics, and Audience,* ed. S. Bauwel and N. Carpentier (Lanham, MD: Lexington Books, 2010), 21.
23. Official *Here Comes Honey Boo Boo* Facebook Page, Facebook, posted December 11, 2012, http://www.facebook.com/HereComesHoneyBooBoo?fref=ts
24. Official *Here Comes Honey Boo Boo* Facebook Page, Facebook, posted October 17, 2012, http://www.facebook.com/HereComesHoneyBooBoo?fref=ts
25. Official *Here Comes Honey Boo Boo* Facebook Page, Facebook, posted October 16, 2012, http://www.facebook.com/HereComesHoneyBooBoo?fref=ts

26. Official *Here Comes Honey Boo Boo* Facebook Page, Facebook, posted October 2, 2012, http://www.facebook.com/HereComesHoneyBooBoo?fref=ts

27. Official *Here Comes Honey Boo Boo* Facebook Page, Facebook, posted October 15, 2012, http://www.facebook.com/HereComesHoneyBooBoo?fref=ts

28. Official *Here Comes Honey Boo Boo* Facebook Page, Facebook, posted February 5, 2013, http://www.facebook.com/HereComesHoneyBooBoo?fref=ts

29. J. L. Austin, *Sense and Sensibilia* (Oxford, UK: Oxford University Press, 1964), 76.

30. Austin, *Sense,* 69.

31. Official *Here Comes Honey Boo Boo* Facebook Page, Facebook, posted March 11, 2013, http://www.facebook.com/HereComesHoneyBooBoo?fref=ts

32. Erving Goffman, *The Presentation of self in everyday life* (New York, NY: Anchor Books, 1959).

33. Official *Here Comes Honey Boo Boo* Facebook Page, Facebook, posted January 12, 2013, http://www.facebook.com/HereComesHoneyBooBoo?fref=ts

34. Skeggs, "The Moral Economy of Person Production."

35. Helene Joffe and Christian Staerkle, "The centrality of the self-control ethos in Western aspersions regarding outgroups: A social representational approach to stereotype content," *Culture & Psychology*, 13(4) (2007): 402.

36. Joffe and Staerkle, 404.

37. Ibid.

38. Ibid.

39. Samantha A. Lyle, "(Mis)recognition and the middle-class/bourgeois gaze: A case study of Wife Swap," *Critical Discourse Studies*, 5(4) (2008): 320.

40. Lyle, "(Mis)recognition."

41. Lyle, 320.

42. Official *Here Comes Honey Boo Boo* Facebook Page, Facebook, posted January 28, 2013, http://www.facebook.com/HereComesHoneyBooBoo?fref=ts

43. Official *Here Comes Honey Boo Boo* Facebook Page, Facebook, posted January 12, 2013, http://www.facebook.com/HereComesHoneyBooBoo?fref=ts

44. Official *Here Comes Honey Boo Boo* Facebook Page, Facebook, posted October 18, 2012, http://www.facebook.com/HereComesHoneyBooBoo?fref=ts

45. Beverly Skeggs, "The Making of Class and Gender through Visualizing Moral Subject Formation," *Sociology*, 39(5) (2005): 968.

46. Official *Here Comes Honey Boo Boo* Facebook Page, Facebook, posted December 25, 2012, http://www.facebook.com/HereComesHoneyBooBoo?fref=ts

47. Andrea Press, *Women Watching Television: Gender, Class, and Generation in the American Television Experience* (Philadelphia, PA: University of Pennsylvania Press, 1991).

48. Press, *Women Watching Television*, 42.

49. Skeggs, "The Making of Class and Gender," 966.

50. Official *Here Comes Honey Boo Boo* Facebook Page, Facebook, posted October 2, 2012, http://www.facebook.com/HereComesHoneyBooBoo?fref=ts

51. Official *Here Comes Honey Boo Boo* Facebook Page, Facebook, posted February 7, 2013, http://www.facebook.com/HereComesHoneyBooBoo?fref=ts

52. Official *Here Comes Honey Boo Boo Facebook* Page, *Facebook*, posted January 12, 2013, http://www.facebook.com/HereComesHoneyBooBoo?fref=ts

53. Official *Here Comes Honey Boo Boo* Facebook Page, Facebook, posted March 6, 2013, http://www.facebook.com/HereComesHoneyBooBoo?fref=ts

54. Official *Here Comes Honey Boo Boo* Facebook Page, Facebook, posted December 26, 2012, http://www.facebook.com/HereComesHoneyBooBoo?fref=ts

55. Official *Here Comes Honey Boo Boo* Facebook Page, Facebook, posted October 15, 2012, http://www.facebook.com/HereComesHoneyBooBoo?fref=ts

56. Official *Here Comes Honey Boo Boo* Facebook Page, Facebook, posted February 8, 2013, http://www.facebook.com/HereComesHoneyBooBoo?fref=ts

57. Official *Here Comes Honey Boo Boo* Facebook Page, Facebook, posted October 17, 2012, http://www.facebook.com/HereComesHoneyBooBoo?fref=ts

58. Official *Here Comes Honey Boo Boo* Facebook Page, Facebook, posted October 1, 2012, http://www.facebook.com/HereComesHoneyBooBoo?fref=ts

59. Official *Here Comes Honey Boo Boo* Facebook Page, Facebook, posted October 17, 2012, http://www.facebook.com/HereComesHoneyBooBoo?fref=ts

60. Official *Here Comes Honey Boo Boo* Facebook Page, Facebook, posted October 2, 2012, http://www.facebook.com/HereComesHoneyBooBoo?fref=ts

61. Official *Here Comes Honey Boo Boo* Facebook Page, Facebook, posted February 4, 2013, http://www.facebook.com/HereComesHoneyBooBoo?fref=ts

62. Official *Here Comes Honey Boo Boo* Facebook Page, Facebook, posted September 26, 2012, http://www.facebook.com/HereComesHoneyBooBoo?fref=ts

63. Official *Here Comes Honey Boo Boo* Facebook Page, Facebook, posted March 15, 2013, http://www.facebook.com/HereComesHoneyBooBoo?fref=ts

64. *Married with Children* (1987-1997) was a sitcom featuring a dysfunctional working class family with a shoe salesman father, an out of work, couch potato mother, and two directionless and unmotivated children.

65. *Shameless* (2011-present) is a dramedy following the mischievous Gallagher family struggling to survive in Chicago's working-class South Side. The show airs on the cable network *Showtime*.

66. Caterina Pasqualino, "The Gypsies, Poor but Happy," *Third Text*, 22(3) (2008): 345.

67. Sari Thomas and Brian P. Callahan, "Allocating Happiness: TV Families and Social Class," *Journal of Communication*, Summer (1982): 184.

68. Thomas and Callahan, 184.

69. Ibid.

70. Derek Kompare, "Extraordinarily Ordinary: The Osbournes as *"An American Family"*," in *Reality TV: Remaking Television Culture,* ed S. Murray and L. Ouellette. (New York: NYU Press, 2004), 111.

71. Official *Here Comes Honey Boo Boo* Facebook Page, Facebook, posted March 31, 2013, http://www.facebook.com/HereComesHoneyBooBoo?fref=ts

72. Julia Bricklin, "TLC's 'Here Comes Honey Boo Boo' Isn't All That Bad," *Forbes Magazine*, August 12, 2012, http://www.forbes.com/sites/juliabricklin/2012/08/12/tlcs-here-comes-honey-boo-boo-isnt-all-that-bad/

73. Official *Here Comes Honey Boo Boo* Facebook Page, Facebook, posted October 18, 2012, http://www.facebook.com/HereComesHoneyBooBoo?fref=ts

74. Official *Here Comes Honey Boo Boo* Facebook Page, Facebook, posted September 27, 2012, http://www.facebook.com/HereComesHoneyBooBoo?fref=ts

75. Official *Here Comes Honey Boo Boo* Facebook Page, Facebook, posted October 2, 2012, http://www.facebook.com/HereComesHoneyBooBoo?fref=ts

76. Official *Here Comes Honey Boo Boo* Facebook Page, Facebook, posted October 17, 2012, http://www.facebook.com/HereComesHoneyBooBoo?fref=ts

77. Official *Here Comes Honey Boo Boo* Facebook Page, Facebook, posted October 2, 2012, http://www.facebook.com/HereComesHoneyBooBoo?fref=ts

78. Daniel. M. Haybron, *The Pursuit of Unhappiness: The Elusive Psychology of Well-Being* (New York, NY: Oxford University Press, 2008), 66.

79. Haybron, *The Pursuit of Unhappiness*, 66.

80. Haybron, *The Pursuit of Unhappiness*, 69.

81. Ibid.

82. Haybron, *The Pursuit of Unhappiness*, 119.

83. Haybron, *The Pursuit of Unhappiness*, 121.

84. Ibid.

85. Official *Here Comes Honey Boo Boo* Facebook Page, Facebook, posted January 12, 2013, http://www.facebook.com/HereComesHoneyBooBoo?fref=ts

86. Official *Here Comes Honey Boo Boo* Facebook Page, Facebook, posted December 15, 2012, http://www.facebook.com/HereComesHoneyBooBoo?fref=ts

87. Official *Here Comes Honey Boo Boo* Facebook Page, Facebook, posted October 2, 2012, http://www.facebook.com/HereComesHoneyBooBoo?fref=ts

88. Official *Here Comes Honey Boo Boo* Facebook Page, Facebook, posted September 27, 2012, http://www.facebook.com/HereComesHoneyBooBoo?fref=ts

89. Mary Douglas, *Purity and danger: An analysis of the concepts of pollution and taboo* (London: Routledge and Kegan Paul, 1966), 35.

90. Elizabeth Grosz, *Volatile Bodies: Towards a Corporeal Feminism* (Bloomington: Indiana University Press, 1994), 192.

91. Ibid.

92. Amy West, "Reality Television and the Power of Dirt: Metaphor and Matter," *Screen*, 52(1) (2011): 63-77.

93. West, "Reality Television and the Power of Dirt," 77.

94. West, "Reality Television and the Power of Dirt," 73.

95. West, "Reality Television and the Power of Dirt," 77.

96. Official *Here Comes Honey Boo Boo* Facebook Page, Facebook, posted January 16, 2013, http://www.facebook.com/HereComesHoneyBooBoo?fref=ts

97. Official *Here Comes Honey Boo Boo* Facebook Page, Facebook, posted October 7, 2012, http://www.facebook.com/HereComesHoneyBooBoo?fref=ts

98. Official *Here Comes Honey Boo Boo* Facebook Page, Facebook, posted October 16, 2012, http://www.facebook.com/HereComesHoneyBooBoo?fref=ts

99. Official *Here Comes Honey Boo Boo* Facebook Page, Facebook, posted January 13, 2012, http://www.facebook.com/HereComesHoneyBooBoo?fref=ts

Chapter Four

Are you ready for your 15 minutes of shame? *Louisiana Lockdown* and Narrative in Prison Reality Television

Elizabeth Barfoot Christian

" Reality television is a euphemism. " [1]

Critics and scholars, as well as regular viewers, of reality television have been skeptical about the authenticity of the genre since it began overtaking television programming in the late 1990s. Reality television is a hybrid version of more traditional types of television program, and while not a new development, it has never before in television history been so prevalent. In this age of reality programs it offers a cheap and popular solution to filling time slots.

RISE IN INFOTAINMENT

Much reality television belongs to programming that combines traditional journalism or documentary information with traditional popular entertainment forms. This marriage of entertainment and information is now commonly referred to as "infotainment" and has become a "dominant style of postmodern journalism." [2]

This chapter seeks to shed light on and start a discussion on whether prison reality shows are immersion journalism or exploitative entertainment on a vulnerable population. Do they have the power to influence society's view of prisoners and prisons in a positive way or do they simply reinforce society's fears of those locked behind bars? Are they helping or hurting, and do the producers have an obligation to do either or is this simply the latest fad in television entertainment in America.

Crime reality programming, popularized by programs like *Cops* and *America's Most Wanted*, *Dateline's To Catch a Predator* and MSNBC's *Lockup*, is now one of the most popular areas of reality TV. This chapter will examine existing literature on the above-mentioned shows and the reality genre and the subgenre of prison reality programming, at the same time addressing the rise in infotainment as journalism to suggest the possible implications on the greater culture.

A qualitative textual analysis of the first season of Animal Planet's series *Louisiana Lockdown* will illustrate that in addition to the continual blurring of the line between fact and fiction that reality television (and news media as a whole) has experienced in recent years that the subgenre of prison documentary-style shows further blurs the line between punishment and entertainment.

HUMILIATION AND SHAME

Critical scholars studying punishment have found that since the 1970s sentencing has become harsher and more emotive with chain gangs and mandatory three strikes sentencing.[3] According to Canadian scholar Steven Kohm, shame and ridicule re-emerged in the last decade of the twentieth century as a form of punishment in the criminal justice system[4] itself, so it's no surprise that reality television imagery of incarcerated populations mirrors that narrative. Even at the local level, numerous stories appeared of judges sentencing some petty offender to stand on a street corner wearing a sandwich board sign declaring his crime.[5]

As the same time, the reality programming genre has been on the rise. One need only look at the most popular and longest running of reality television programs to see the narrative of shame clearly running through them. *American Idol* and *America's Funniest Videos* both represent popular reality programs that have stood the test of time and have spawned numerous copycat shows both in America and abroad. While the programs represent two distinct types of reality subgenres, one message the shows clearly share is that of the shame narrative. In fact in recent years, some contestants familiar with the way *AI* operates have gone on stating the desire not to be included in any outtakes or blooper reel in which they will be mocked.

One of the earliest reality television shaming rituals began with *Dateline NBC: To Catch a Predator*, a tabloid magazine type format hosted by journalist Chris Hanson "organized around the spectacle of humiliating putative pedophiles on network television in partnership with local police agencies and a rag-tag band of internet vigilantes known as Perverted Justice.[6] *To*

Catch a Predator was one of the earliest reality programs that married the idea of criminal justice and humiliation as a form of entertainment. The constructed narrative was that the "bad guys" in each week's episode deserved it, so to speak, and to emotionally connect the audience to the victims or survivors. *America's Most Wanted*, one of the longest running shows of any kind in history, made the emotional appeal even more important by suggesting to viewers the entire community was under attack by the criminal element, and it was up to every viewer to be on the lookout for the evil.

Cops further separates the "us" from the "them." Images of law enforcement officials manhandling the "bad guys" over oftentimes relatively insignificant infractions desensitizes viewers further to the humiliation of people portrayed in a negative light. The only images offered are when these people are engaged in a confrontation with law enforcement—shown as the good guys nearly without exception in the program. This, like the above-mentioned tell the continuing story of serving the public interest. The burgeoning subgenre of prison reality shows includes programs that follow the criminal justice system post-arrest and conviction. Numerous shows have been developed to showcase the criminal offenders—murderers, rapists, armed robbers, drug lords—and their keepers—prison guards, wardens and officers.

"While humiliation has emerged in recent years as a viable and symbolically rich vehicle for social control, when commodified and refracted through the lens of popular culture the outcomes are unpredictable and may contain seeds of discontent," according to Canadian scholar Steven Kohm in 2009. The end result may, in fact, bring about the opposite of intentions in the long run. Viewers, he suggests, will eventually tire of this mediated form of bullying. This remains to be seen as all forms of reality shows continue to dominate programming.

The reasons for appearing on a reality program and watching them are different. Every subgenre of reality TV comes with a form of shame or humiliation from *American Idol* and talent competitions to *The Biggest Loser* or *Celebrity Rehab with Dr. Drew*, now highly criticized following the untimely death of the fifth of its contestants. Reasons include career move for celebrities, or people trying to break into show business, according to Dr. Stuart Fischoff, senior editor of *The Journal of Media Psychology*.[7]

The reasons for watching differ. Paul Mason suggests people watch out of a sense of connectivity, that average citizens would want to see someone punished and/or shamed if he hurt one of their loved ones. This type of program allows us to live our own vengeful feelings for people who we perceive as having wronged us personally. Punishments, he contends, become crueler in times of political and economic uncertainty, as well. So it stands to reason that televised imagery of punishment would follow the same pattern.[8] Most people would say they don't enjoy seeing others shamed, but American culture is shaped by media content and media by culture. It would be hard not to acknowledge this debasement present in much of media programming. Dr. Geoffrey White, a psychologist and consultant to reality program producers, said shame TV is part of our "current zeitgeist" because Americans are experiencing a growing economic and philosophical angst, which is lessened by seeing others in states of suffering because we can identify with those feelings without being the cause of them. And when it's a group of people with whom we don't identify, the pleasure in watching the humiliation may be even stronger. Dr. Elliot Arson, a psychologist and professor emeritus from University of Calfiornia, Santa Cruz, agrees that we constantly evaluate ourselves by the actions of others. When "real" people, rather than actors playing a role, do something ridiculous or self-debasing, it raises our own self-esteem and moral superiority.[9]

According to Arlid Fetveit in 2002, one of the problems is that reality TV, not unlike works of documentary film or journalism, comes with an unwritten contract with the consumer to provide a glimpse into real life from a safe distance.[10] However, in the subgenre of docudrama programs, just how much of the narrative that we receive remains any kind of representation of reality? If days of footage are reduced to 22 to 45 minutes, for 30 or 60 minute programming, does the edited version offer a look at the reality or is it a representation that has created a new reality?

Do prisoners ever have the complete freedom on whether or not to appear in a televised reality series or documentary of prison life? And as wards of the state, who are not paid for their appearances, what would be the motivation to appear?

In May 2013 HuffPost Live held a roundtable discussion on this topic.[11] Rasha Drachkovitch, executive producer of MSNBC's *Lockup* series, which has filmed in more than 50 prison and jail facilities in the United States and boasts more than 200 episodes, said the primary purpose of his show is to give people a "rare peek into the world of corrections." Drachkovitch said his crews spend up to four months at each facility getting to know the staff and the inmates. "First and foremost we are a real show," he said. "There are no second takes on *Lockup*."[12] Still, he admitted that 95 percent of what goes on inside the prison walls was mundane.

It's because of that, Mansfield Frazier, executive director of Neighborhood Solutions, Inc., argued that prison reality shows are anything but reality. Frazier said they show what happens one percent of the time as 99 percent of their shows, which is disingenuous and purports a lie to the viewing public. In addition, prisoners don't have the capacity to consent because they don't have a free choice. Outside of the camera's lens, the viewers nor the producers do not know what kinds of incentives or threats are given to prisoners for their participation on these shows.[13]

"When you put a camera in front of anyone it changes the dynamics," according to Seth Kaufman, former *TV Guide* editor and author of *The King of Pain*, a novel about the reality of reality television.[14] "None of these shows is real."

Prison reality drama is especially grim and the effects may be greater than other shows of this genre because the population participating have a motivation that can't be quantified like shows that offer prize money, contracts or exposure that could translate into positive career enhancements. The one thing that seems clearly gained from prisoner participation is their fifteen minutes of shame.

Shameful isn't a harsh enough word to describe this kind of programming. Frazier likens it to "caging animals and then poking them with sticks for the amusement of the audience."[15] It strips whatever "remaining shreds of dignity" these people have from them and is done in the public sphere, greenlighted by elected officials, who have an obligation to serve for the good of the community.

Addressing the show *Lockup* specifically, Frazier takes great issue with the statement that it's true TV. "They take the worst of the worst and put it on the screen because that's what sells," he said. Frazier said the positive programs done inside prisons go ignored. "This hurts re-entry in the long run." Frazier goes so far as to suggest that the television crews may do things to create situations to serve to instigate drama for better TV.

Prisoners have become a commodity, Frazier said. The producers, however, believe they are coercing no one to appear. And those who agree go through rigorous screening processes, sign releases, and the Department of Corrections must approve. While *Lockup* has been on for 200 episodes this year, this study will focus on a show filmed at America's largest maximum security prison.

ANGOLA AND LOUISIANA LOCKDOWN

This study focuses on the entire first season of the Animal Planet cable reality docudrama *Louisiana Lockdown*. Louisiana State Prison, known as Angola, sits on 18,000 acres that were previously a slave plantation, twenty miles from the closest town of St. Francisville. All offenders work forty-hour-per-week jobs, and the first several years for nearly all inmates is working the fields in sweltering 100+ degree temperatures for two cents per hour.

Louisiana Lockdown appeared on Animal Planet channel and remains available through Amazon.com. The introduction to the program hypes the violence and "bad guy" images that viewers will see while showcasing Warden Burl Cain and several of his assistant wardens as stars of the program—or "Warden Cain's World" as it is defined. Cain defines the prison, one of America's most notorious, as "the land of new beginnings."[16] Yet, it's the beginning of the end for most incarcerated at Angola. As Louisiana's only maximum security prison, most of the more than 5,000 prisoners are serving life sentences.[17] In Louisiana, that means mandatory life without parole. Louisiana holds the distinction of being the incarceration capital of the world,[18] locking up people at five times the rate of Iran and thirteen times the rate of China. One of every eighty-six Louisiana residents is locked up—double the national average. Louisiana may be near the bottom on many lists, but it takes No. 1 spot every year in incarceration rates. Interestingly, however, Louisiana's percentage of people locked up who are violent offenders is lower than average—just one-third.[19] Louisiana's prison population has exploded in the last decade. Eighty-five percent of the Angola population will die in prison.

Criminals have long been cultural commodities. The names Jesse James, Ted Bundy and Bonnie and Clyde are just a few examples of famous felons who are more likely to evoke folk hero worship as disdain when mentioned in conversation. However, this has brought about even greater interest in the stories behind the criminals. As such, television became a perfect vehicle to further commodify the crimes that made the criminals. Unfortunately, felons like those noted are the rarity. Hence to commodify the narrative of a killer lurking behind ever corner, liberties must be taken with the truth.

Prisoners, who have largely always been a commodity, at least in the plantation prison model in the South, have now become a hot entertainment television commodity, as well. Prisoners, now referred to as offenders in Louisiana, behave as "chattel" planting and picking crops at a working plantation.[20] Even though this isn't the narrative storyline, these images are often used as bridges between the bad guy (offender), good guy (prison staffer) drama. Prior to the abolition of slavery, the prison system leased out its convicts to work on the large Southern plantations,[21] and showcasing prisoners toiling in the fields on cable television once again makes them a profitable commodity.

If every person locked behind bars is to be feared and hated, it cultivates a public that believes itself dependent upon the state for its protection. This ensures support for taxation and policies that are beneficial to the growth of political and economic policy people will support. Once we believe the state has our best interest at heart, we buy into the narrative that these people are less than those of us on the outside and become hardened bit by bit to their suffering and humiliation. The more we encounter "mass-mediated spectacles of shame and humiliation" the more we separate ourselves from those on the receiving end of that treatment.

Prison scholar Bill Yousman explored key themes in news stories about prison. Among the most often recurring messages he found that prisoners are dangerous; prisoners deserve whatever punishment they receive; prisoners drain our economic resources.[22]

The question now, do prison reality docudramas consciously or subconsciously construct situations and storylines that exploit prisoners for entertainment purposes and profit? *Louisiana Lockdown*, while using symbols of shame, at the same time continues the romanticizing of the bad boy in pop culture. The inmates get their "15 minutes," not realizing it's actually shame. Textual analysis of the episodes of the first season will repeatedly demonstrate this.

EPISODE ONE, "KILLER ROADTRIP"

It is clear from the show's intro that the "stars" of the show are the prison administration. In addition to Warden Cain, the program regularly features Assistant Warden Cathy Fontenot, Major Ronnie Fruje, and Lt. Col. Harvey Slater.

The episode introduces Cain as "commander-in-chief of the micro-nation that is Angola" presiding over "5,300 men who wake up to serve penance for heinous crimes, locked far away from the free world." The introduction to Cain includes his zero-tolerance policy for rule-breaking that was developed from his career as a high school teacher before he came to Angola two decades earlier. He articulates clearly what his purpose is from the beginning: "We have to change the perception that a prison is a place of torture and torment." Yet, this episode is perhaps one of the most bittersweet for the inmates, as they get a small taste of life on the outside. Continually the viewers are reminded of Cain's benevolent dictatorship by Cain himself. "Criminals are selfish, like teenagers. I have to discipline them positively to make them a better person," he says during a close-up.[23] Immediately, images of dozens of inmates working in the fields flashes before the viewers.

Newcomers arrive at the prison Monday morning, and it is Major Fruge's job to make dorm assignments. Fruge has worked at Angola for 40 years. Fruge refers to one newcomer convicted of killing his bed-ridden mother, as "a weak little white individual," and says "I'm saving his life. That's what I do, putting him in the right place."[24] Fruge puts him in a solitary cell for his own protection, he says.

The drama of this episode is the potential catastrophic flooding of the prison and the never-before evacuation of nearly half the inmates. Thirteen buses take 2,000 of Angola's "most troublesome" to other facilities outside the flood zone some seven hours away. Travis Johnson, who has been incarcerated at Angola for ten years is highlighted. He is serving a life sentence for second-degree murder. The pleasure Johnson gets in seeing the outside world from the confines of the bus is visible, and he acknowledges what he has lost and will probably never see again. Upon returning to Angola, he smiles and sings "Sweet home Angola."[25]

EPISODE TWO, "PRISON SUICIDE"

As Travis Johnson and about 100 other inmates begin preparations for the rodeo, the prison marks the self-inflicted death of another. An inmate has hanged himself, according to Fontenot. The narrative background: "Stay out of trouble. If you did it right, God's going to bless you,"[26] and following the path of rehabilitation to earn privileges clearly serves as an indictment of the dead offender's actions. Cain repeats his mantra of punishment and reward.

The suicide narrative is juxtaposed against that of Joseph Ward, Angola's youngest trustee affectionately called "Redneck," illustrating Cain's path to redemption. Ward is housed in a 90-man open dormitory rather than a cell. Ward, arrested at 17, was convicted of the manslaughter of a teacher and given a 100-year sentence. Ward sings Cain's praises and says he has turned his life of drugs and alcohol around and now has "one of the best jobs" at Angola, training horses.

The drama revisits Camp J, where the suicide occurred, and we learn it is the lowest tier in Cain's system. Men housed here, unlike Ward and other trustees who have followed the rules, spend twenty-three hours a day in stifling, solitary cells.

An offender, identified as Jones by Fontenot, has hanged himself. Fontenot reads from his records about his long, troubled history that has included suicide attempts. Fontenot goes to Camp J where the suicide happens and is escorted to the cell while talking to the camera about the "very calm, very quiet" mood of the other inmates in that tier. The guard who found him goes into graphic detail to Fontenot and within earshot of the other offenders, with the camera noting each spot in the deceased's cell. "It's our job to protect them from themselves," Fontenot says. "This is failure."[27] As Fontenot drives back to her office in the main prison, she says, "It's not supposed to happen like that." Yet, it isn't remorse that someone has died. She adds, "It's like one who got away. He's not going to serve his time. We give 'em a life sentence, but they find a life here."[28]

One who isn't so hopeless, we are told, is Travis Johnson. Onscreen the viewer watches Johnson and other inmates happily picking vegetables. We don't see complaining, but we do see a young white, male guard armed with a rifle on horseback overseeing a nearly all-minority inmate work crew in the fields. Johnson tells us he is hopeful to get off the hard labor crew soon so that he can participate in the rodeo, and since he has not gotten any disciplinary write-ups he thinks he is in good shape with Cain to get back in the general population.

The episode ends as the first rodeo events begin. Johnson's family is there to watch him compete in "something that's totally good," Johnson tells the viewers.[29] The narrator says Johnson seeks to prove to his family he is on the right track. The imagery is complete with the patriotic imagery of the

American flag and national anthem. And the rodeo events begin right after church services are over.

Johnson takes first place in his event and moves on to next week's rodeo, while Ward is stomped by a horse and taken to receive medical attention. In this instance he pokes fun at his own on-screen humiliation. "It's about as bad as getting drunk and waking up with an ugly girl the next day." If the shaming imagery hasn't been clear enough, Slater calls the injured, who have been beaten up and pummeled by horses and bulls "titty babies."[30]

EPISODE THREE, "DRUG BUST"

In Episode Three the audience meets trustee Todd "Tiger" Plaisance, who has been serving a life sentence for second-degree murder since 2000. A newspaper article about the crime flashes on-screen. Plaisance has had no contact with his son for ten years, and he is now awaiting a letter from him on whether or not he will attend the rodeo. Plaisance is competing for the coveted title of convict cowboy of the year, and since he broke his promise to be there for his son this is the best he can do.

Plaisance's story is juxtaposed with Fontenot's, who is celebrating twenty years at Angola. Cain remarks that she was working at Burger King while in college when they met, and he took her under his tutelage where she has risen to the rank of assistant warden.

"I can't really remember myself before I was here," Fontenot says. "Warden Cain was that person who gave me a chance."[31] Her words are near echoes of several of the offenders shown throughout the *Louisiana Lockdown* season.

We return to Plaisance who admits his own poor judgment kept him from enjoying Cain's privileges his first few years inside the prison, until he decided to change and begin competing in the rodeo. He says he has earned "more than an elite job."[32] And he is hopeful that his son, whom he last saw at age 8, will attend this year's rodeo.

In this episode, the viewers also meet Jerry Johnson, who is incarcerated in Camp J. His purpose in the story seems only to provide more humiliation for the viewer to enjoy. Johnson has requested a transfer to another prison closer to home, and Fontenot pays him a visit to let him know that she talked to his mother and let her know that he is not eligible for a transfer. He reiterates to her his dislike of Angola. Fontenot, speaking to the man through the bars he sits behind twenty-three hours every day, tells him, "I can tell and that's why I left my office and got out in the cold to come and see you."[33] Johnson tells her he appreciates it very much, to which Fontenot replies she will call and tell his mother that she visited with him. He smiles and shakes her hand through the bars.

The narrative returns to Tiger, and we learn that his son Tony Sprouse, will attend the rodeo this year. Sprouse is now an adult and recently learned that his father had written over the years, but his mother had not forwarded any of the letters to him. The reunion, although done in front of the cameras, brings genuine tears and apologies, and Plaisance tells his son, who has brought his fiancée with him to meet dad, not to follow in his footsteps. He gives his son the buckle he won at last year's rodeo.

Fontenot serves as warden for this weekend's rodeo and oversees the other guards as they search for any contraband being snuck into the prison. In this episode, they find what they are looking for—marijuana hidden in the nastiest of places. "From his buttocks to his mouth," Cain iterates, while the punishment of never attending another rodeo seems the more damning.[34]

EPISODE FOUR, "HUNGER STRIKE"

Lt. Col. Harvey Slater is the star of Episode Four, and what he shares with viewers seems quite similar to many of the inmates' own stories. Slater was born and raised on the B-line, an area on Angola grounds where dozens of staff families live. He and his wife, whom he separates from in a later episode, have four children. "I'm armed and dangerous,"[35] Slater jokes, while waving around a loaded handgun while his smiling wife, a narcotics officer in Mississippi, holds their baby girl.

"I didn't always walk a straight line," Slater says. "I was a bad boy once. I smoked dope, growed dope, and sold dope. Just got by by the skin of my teeth. The difference in them and me is I didn't get caught. I'm guilty of everything they're guilty of except murder and rape."[36] The insinuation is that all inmates at Angola are in for violent felonies like murder and rape, but that is not the case. Less than half are serving life sentences for murder; twenty percent were convicted of robbery, and just sixteen percent for rape. The remaining are serving hard time for drug offenses, theft, assault, burglary and kidnapping.[37]

Slater lucked out. Lenny "Six" Nicolas, who has spent thirty years at Angola, serving a second-degree murder life sentence, wasn't so lucky. He didn't have the good fortune to straighten out pre-prison. Still, he counts himself fortunate—at least for the camera—considering it a blessing to now be a trustee working on the horse late because he "always wanted a horse and looks forward to going to work every day," adding "there's no limits to the heights you can achieve in prison."[38]

Cain takes the screen to remind us this is his world and he is the "benevolent dictator," whose rules must be obeyed. "I'm going to ask you to do what we say, but if you don't do it, I'm going to do something to you."[39] Reaching trustee status and earning coveted positions like those working with the horses take more than a decade to earn and can be lost with one minor infraction.

Nicolas, Cain tells the audience, has been the "poster child of success and now is the poster child of failure and stupidity."[40] Slater says Cain is the same with his staff. Cain will give you a break, but if you mess up it's very hard to earn back his trust. Nicolas talked back to a guard and has fallen from trustee status to a punishment unit, where he works in the fields picking peas. (A white guard is shown yelling while overseeing Nicolas and dozens of other predominantly black inmates in the fields). Nicolas, known as "Angola's horse whisperer" tells the viewers again that working with the horses is the best job he ever had.

Months pass and we revisit Nicolas, who is smiling because he has earned back his position with the horses. "I'd rather be a broken, gentle horse," Nicolas says. "It's a lot less trouble than to be a bad horse."[41] The Animal Planet program reminds us how we are to think of the men housed at Angola.

EPISODE FIVE, "BONES"

Episode Five juxtaposes Major Ronnie Fruje, who has lived and worked at Angola for forty years, with Lloyd Bone, who has also spent the last four decades at Angola. Bone is serving life for a New Orleans murder. This episode, in which he meets his grandson for the first time, seems especially humiliating for Bone, though he seems happily unaware of it as he smiles and tells the camera, "Every morning I wake up feeling good."[42] This day Lloyd's grandson, Eric Bone, will begin the rest of his life inside Angola's walls.

Eric is 23. "It's my first time in jail ever, and I have a life sentence," he says to the camera.[43] Eric was the driver in a drive-by shooting. Fruge acknowledges the sadness of the meeting of Lloyd and Eric, who is shown with feet shackled and hands cuffed. Three days later, we see Eric on the yard getting reacquainted with many of his old friends from New Orleans. The voice-over says: "For a shocking number of young men from Louisiana, Angola is a rite of passage."[44]

Eric may not have accepted his fate, saying he won't be here long. But the storyline reminds us that he will die here—along with 90 percent of his fellow inmates. Images of his grandfather in a top hat and tuxedo driving the inmate-made stagecoach hearse for an Angola funeral and burial serve as the backdrop for his initiation into the prison. Lloyd was given the responsibility of being the hearse driver, and he takes it very seriously.

Eric talks to his father and his six-year-old son via phone. Ashamed of his absence, he tells his father, "Don't tell him I'm in jail. Tell him I'm on vacation." Then he turns to the camera, "He ain't nothing but six years old. I don't want him to know that."[45] Lloyd says he hopes Eric doesn't dwell on getting out for years like he did but accepts his fate. Now, Lloyd says he thinks about a cup of coffee and cigarettes rather than freedom.

EPISODE SIX, "ESCAPE!"

Viewers are introduced to Teddy, one of a small group of elite trustees, who live in the only air-conditioned dormitory at Angola. They raise Angola's dogs. Teddy, serving life for a double murder, has been at Angola since he was 17. "When I was a little kid, I wanted my mother to be proud of me, but it just didn't work out like that," he tells the viewers. "Dogs give uncondi-tional love. Some better than family. Most of us want to make a good name for ourselves, even if it's just in prison."[46] We are reminded, again, though, that one infraction could send Teddy or any offender all the way back to Camp J.

Assistant Warden Chad Mezzina, the narrator tells the viewers, oversees the "motley crew"[47] of Camp J inmates, as an image of an overweight black inmate in an orange jumpsuit in what looks like an over-sized dog run fills the screen. These completely fenced-in spaces are the only outdoor areas Camp J offenders ever see.

Teddy prepares dogs for a fake manhunt, which serves to train the dogs in the event of an inmate escape. Real offenders are given a twenty-minute headstart in the exercise that tests the dogs' skills and the inmates' loyalty. All ends well with no escape attempt on the part of the offenders, yet when Teddy arrives back to his home he learns that his dog Chloe has died and must be buried. Circumstances remind the viewer and Teddy of his fate. "You're definitely a forgotten man here," Teddy says. "I'm condemned for the rest of my life."[48] No parole exists in this prison state. No matter how much you do to improve yourself, you're still just an inmate and in Louisiana life means life.

Even Oliver Howard, a trustee fourteen years into a fifty-year sentence, who has been granted the rare privilege to marry by Warden Cain, realizes there will be no wedding night celebration. Howard and fiancée Leona John-son, who appears going through the prison metal detector donned in her wedding gown, marry in one of Angola's many chapels. One wonders if the decision to televise the event was the couple's or Cain's. Viewers are re-minded that the marriage is taking place solely at the discretion of the war-den, who is in attendance and allows Howard to kiss his bride. The pair will live apart the next three decades, and conjugal visits are barred by law in Louisiana. Yet, the silver lining voiced by Cain, chuckling, is that, "she knows he won't run around on her. That's a good thing."[49]

EPISODE SEVEN, "DEATH RIDE"

Episode Seven highlights the fourth rodeo of the October 2011 season. Cain responds on camera to a letter in the local newspaper calling for a boycott of the rodeo on humanitarian grounds. "Gladiators didn't have a choice. Inmates have a choice," he contends.[50] It seems clear that Cain truly believes the rodeo builds morale inside the prison and is a benefit for all. Of course, it also is an economic boon for the prison itself through tickets sales and a percentage of hobbycrafts sold by inmates. Speaking directly to the audience in response to rodeo criticism, Cain states,

> I would like the public to understand that prisons are to correct deviant behavior, not to torture, torment and get even for what they did in the past but to prevent them from doing it again in the future. This day right here does so much to encourage and inspire the inmates that are here to be remorseful for the horrible things they have done and then maybe if they ever get out, they won't ever do it again and we won't have a future victim. It's worth everything we do.[51]

Cain is shown from his box presiding over the "wildest show on earth"[52] before a record crowd of 15,000. A bloodied black inmate is shown leaving the arena with a medic attending to him.

The Angola Rodeo, probably the most well-known thing about the prison that previously claimed the title of the bloodiest prison in America, is held twice a year in April and October. The narrative throughout *Louisiana Lockdown* is that the rodeo itself is part of the rehabilitation for inmates. Clearly, the danger of the events takes a back seat to the understanding that participation and winning the rodeo carries Warden Cain's favor. That favor includes privileges not available to other inmates. The rodeo, which has taken place since 1965 and began as a spectacle for prison employees and locals has grown into a tourist destination for tens of thousands each year.[53] It has expanded into a full-blown carnival with amusement rides, concession stands with cotton candy, chicken-on-a-stick, funnel cakes and Cajun treats, and an arts and crafts show (called hobbycrafts) featuring all kinds of inmate-created arts, woodworks, jewelry, and trinkets.

Rodeo participants have little or no training in riding bucking broncos or fighting off raging bulls. Yet, Cain firmly believes this event or spectacle builds character. Cain says repeatedly that inmates behave all year for the rodeo.[54] Rodeo participants don black and white prison stripes even though the stigmatizing prison uniforms were abandoned decades ago.

Scholar Schrift specifically asked about the voyeuristic nature of the rodeo, and participants echoed the same thing, that "the benefits of the rodeo override its voyeuristic and exploitative aspects."[55] They believed they made their own choice whether or not to participate, and it was a welcome break for many from the mundane prison experience as well as the possibility to make money. To viewers, the warden's favor seems even more invaluable than the relatively miniscule amount of money up for grabs. Cain presides over the arena from his special perch. It is impossible not to think of Roman gladiators fighting to the death, prisoners doing the king's bidding.

Israel Ducree, twenty-three years into a life sentence for second-degree murder, readies for his rodeo appearance. His nephew Danny Richardson, who grew up visiting him in prison, has landed the same fate, devastating Israel. Israel convinces Danny, who has a life sentence for murder, to attend daily church services and participate in the rodeo in order to move up inside the prison. "I want to be a winner, not a loser," Danny says to the camera. Cain criticizes Danny's short ride and three falls from his bucking horse. "That was awful."[56] The narrator underscores the danger by telling the audience that a former winner has been removed from competition because of his previous loss of a kidney due to a rodeo injury. Another is shown bleeding from the head.

Still, Danny perseveres to win the warden's favor, and in his next competition he and his partner flip the bull. Danny is now hooked on the rodeo, and he has made a positive impression on Cain.

EPISODE EIGHT, "AFTER MIDNIGHT"

The final episode of the season highlights the final rodeo of 2011 and opens with the narrator reminding the viewers that Angola is "a place of lost hopes and unfulfilled dreams, and 90 percent of these men will die here."[57] Cain offers a chant," Somebody's gonna get bloody; somebody's gonna get banged; somebody's gonna get swung, almost from here to Kingdom Come." Cain acknowledges to the participants their year of hard work getting to the event. "It's a big deal to get to be a cowboy," he said. "The public has the chance to see how well-behaved the inmates are, how successful we've been."[58]

The title of All-Around Cowboy is given to the contender who wins the most events over the five Sundays. (October 2011 had five Sundays). Myron Smith, the 2010 All-Around Cowboy, competes again for the title against rookie Aubrey Sikes, an Iraq war combat veteran. Both are serving life sentences for murder.

Smith talks smack about having the proof of how good he is, pointing to his 2010 belt. Images then show him being gored in the behind by a bull during the convict poker competition. He is tossed and thrown to the ground, breaking an arm, and ending his dream of a repeat win and his "dream of sending prize money home to his kids."[59] Aubrey sticks the bull and becomes 2011's All-Around Cowboy, and he acknowledges he almost forgot for a while he was two years into a life sentence.

The All-Around Cowboy, known as the Big Buckle, is worth $380. Cain tells the audience, "The rodeo is great incentive because of the dignity it gives them." Offenders earn two cents per hour after two years, so Aubrey, bloody faced and bruised, is "a billionaire in prison terms," Cain adds.[60]

SHAMING THE STAFF

The staff did not escape unscathed from the shame narrative. Both Fontenot and Harvey's personal failings served as a source of shame. Throughout the entire season of *Louisiana Lockdown*, Judeo-Christian imagery and dialogue are pervasive. Chapels of varying denominations, offenders prayers, crosses on walls, the white crosses in the inmate cemetery, and conversations about church services are woven into every episode. Christian faith teaches against divorce. Yet, the failures of both Fontenot and Harvey's marriages are major storylines in two different episodes. Fontenot's recent divorce has left her a single mother to raise three children, and one of her children is already getting into trouble at school. The message is clear—her career has upended her family. Harvey's wife has left him to care for four children, including his children from a previous marriage, whose mother recently committed suicide. Again, his divorces have had lasting and shameful repercussions.

CONCLUSION

Louisiana Lockdown is not unique in its shaming of incarcerated men, and no research was done to place blame on the prison administration. However, many more positive programs go on behind Angola gates that were not featured in this season of episodes.[61]

However, several studies have shown the severe and deadly repercussions of shameful televised imagery of both felons and criminal suspects, as well as victims of shock documentary TV. In 1995, a guest, Jonathan Schmitz, on *The Jenny Jones Show* was lured to the show to meet a secret admirer. Unbeknownst to him the admirer was a gay neighbor, Scott Amedure. Schmitz, who suffered from mental illness, felt such humiliation that he snapped and killed Amedure. Likewise in 2006, Louis William Conradt, a Dallas attorney, committed suicide after being targeted as part of a pedophile ring. The sting was arranged by *Dateline NBC*. Conrad's sister sued and was awarded $105 million for wrongful death. The irony of *Louisiana Lockdown* focusing one episode around a suicide, which presumably had nothing to do with the filming but was a boon for production, was not lost on this viewer.

As long as the prison reality genre continues to garner a healthy viewership, programs like *Louisiana Lockdown* will continue the shame narrative. Time and studies will tell if society is better or worse for the emotional wear. The bottom line for the producers of these shows is economic. It won't be a direct effect on criminal activity that is felt from these subtle or in some cases, outright, displays of humiliation. It will be the effect on American criminal justice policies. The cumulative effect of this television genre will be an increasing dehumanization in our punishment of all those accused and convicted of crimes.

REFERENCES

Alderman, Tom. "Shame TV: Why Humiliation Sells on American Idol and Others." Feb. 13, 2008. Huffingtonpost.com.
Blow, Charles M. "Plantations, Prisons and Profits." *New York Times*. May 25, 2012.
Chang, Cindy. "Louisiana is the world's prison capital." May 13, 2012. nola.com. Fetveit, Arlid.
"Reality TV in the Digital Era: A Paradox in Visual Culture?" In *Reality Squared: Televisual Discourse on the Real*. New Brunswick, N.J.: Rutgers University Press, 2002.
Frazier, Mansfield. "The Saddest Reality Stars of All: Prisoners," May 19, 2013. hedailybeast.com.
Jewkes, Yvonne. *Media and Crime*. Thousand Oaks, California: SAGE, 2004.
Karp, David. "The Judicial and Judicious Use of Shame Penalties," *Crime & Delinquency*. 44, no. 2 (1998): 277-294.
Kohm, Steven A. "Naming, shaming and criminal justice: Mass-mediated humiliation as entertainment and punishment." *Crime, Media, Culture* 5, no. 189 (2009): 188-205.
Louisiana Lockdown. First season, all episodes, 2008.
Mason, Paul, ed. *Captured by the Media*. Portland, Oregon: Willan Publishing, 2005.
McGaughy, Lauren. "Death row inmates sue Angola Prison over 'extreme temperatures." June 10, 2013. nola.com.
Pratt, John. "Emotive and Ostentatious Punishment: Its Decline and Resurgence in Modern Construction of Virtual Victimhood." *Punishment & Society*. 2, no. 4, (October 2000): 417-439.
"Prisoners: The Saddest Reality Stars," May 22, 2013. Live.huffingtonpost.com.
Rennett, Michael. "Baudrillard and The Joe Schmo Show." *International Journal of Baudrillard*.
Studies 6, no. 1 (January 2009). http://www.ubishops.ca/baudrillardstudies/vol-6_1/v6-1-rennett.html.
Schrift, Melissa. "The Angola Prison Rodeo: Inmate Cowboys and Institutional Tourism" *Ethnology* 43, no. 4 (autumn 2004): 331-344.
Yousman, Bill. *Prime Time Prisons on U.S. TV*. New York: Peter Lang, 2009.

NOTES

1. Michael Rennett, "Baudrillard and The Joe Schmo Show," *International Journal of Baudrillard Studies*. Vol. 6, No. 1, Jan. 2009).

2. Jewkes, Yvonne. *Media and Crime*. Thousand Oaks, California: SAGE, 2004.

3. Pratt, John. "Emotive and Ostentatious Punishment: Its Decline and Resurgence in Modern Construction of Virtual Victimhood," *Punishment & Society*. 2 (4), 417-439.

4. Kohm, Steven A. "Naming, shaming and criminal justice: Mass-mediated humiliation as entertainment and punishment," *Crime, Media, Culture*. (2009) 5:189 (188-205).

5. Karp, David. "The Judicial and Judicious Use of Shame Penalties," *Crime & Delinquency*. 1998. 44(2): 277-294.

6. Kohm, 189.

7. Alderman, Tom. "Shame TV: Why Humiliation Sells on American Idol and Others," Huffingtonpost.com, Feb. 13, 2008.

8. Mason, Paul, ed. *Captured by the Media*. Portland, Oregon: Willan Publishing, 2005, 1.

9. Alderman.

10. Arlid Fetveit, "Reality TV in the Digital Era: A Paradox in Visual Culture?" in *Reality Squared: Televisual Discourse on the Real*. New Brunswick, N.J.: Rutgers University Press, 2002.

11. "Prisoners: The Saddest Reality Stars," May 22, 2013, HuffPostLive.

12. Ibid.

13. "Prisoners: The Saddest Reality Stars."

14. Ibid.

15. Frazier, Mansfield. "The Saddest Reality Stars of All: Prisoners," thedailybeast.com, May 19, 2013.

16. Introductory monologue in *Louisiana Lockdown*.

17. McGaughy, Lauren. "Death row inmates sue Angola Prison over 'extreme temperatures," nola.com, June 10, 2013.

18. Chang, Cindy. "Louisiana is the world's prison capital." Nola.com, May 13, 2012.

19. Kohm, 195.

20. Blow, Charles M. "Plantations, Prisons and Profits," New York Times, May 25, 2012.

21. Blow.

22. Yousman, Bill. (2009) *Prime Time Prisons on U.S. TV*. New York: Peter Lang, 81.

23. Cain, Burl. *Louisiana Lockdown*, Episode 1, June 1, 2012.

24. Fruje, Ronnie. *Louisiana Lockdown*, Season 1, Episode 1, June 1, 2012.

25. Johnson, Travis. *Louisiana Lockdown*, Season 1, Episode 2, June 8, 2012.

26. Heard over radio station KLSP during Episode 2.

27. Fontenot, Cathy. *Louisiana Lockdown*, Season 1, Episode 2, June 8, 2012.

28. Fontenot. *Louisiana Lockdown*, Season 1, Episode 2, June 8, 2012.

29. Johnson. *Louisiana Lockdown*, Season 1, Episode 2, June 8, 2012.

30. Johnson, and Harvey Slater. *Louisiana Lockdown*, Episode 2, June 8, 2012.

31. Fontenot. *Louisiana Lockdown*, Season 1, Episode 3, June 15, 2012.

32. Plaisance, Todd. *Louisiana Lockdown*, Season 1, Episode 3, June 15, 2012.

33. Fontenot. *Louisiana Lockdown*, Season 1, Episode 3, June 15, 2012.

34. Cain. *Louisiana Lockdown*, Season 1, Episode 3, June 15, 2012.

35. Slater. *Louisiana Lockdown*, Season 1, Episode 4, June 22, 2012.

36. Slater. *Louisiana Lockdown*, Season 1, Episode 4, June 22, 2012.

37. Schrift, 334.

38. Nicolas, Lenny. *Louisiana Lockdown*, Season 1, Episode 4, June 22, 2012.

39. Cain. *Louisiana Lockdown*, Season 1, Episode 4, June 22, 2012.

40. Cain. *Louisiana Lockdown*, Season 1, Episode 4, June 22, 2012.

41. Nicolas. *Louisiana Lockdown*, Season 1, Episode 4, June 22, 2012.

42. Bone, Lloyd. *Louisiana Lockdown*, Season 1, Episode 5, June 29, 2012.

43. Bone, Eric. *Louisiana Lockdown*, Season 1, Episode 5, June 29, 2012.

44. Narrator. *Louisiana Lockdown*, Season 1, Episode 5, June 29, 2012.

45. Bone, Eric. Louisiana Lockdown, Season 1, Episode 5, June 29, 2012.

46. *Louisiana Lockdown*, Season 1, Episode 6, July 6, 2012.

47. Narrator. *Louisiana Lockdown*, Season 1, Episode 6, July 6, 2012.

48. Houser, Teddy, *Louisiana Lockdown*, Season 1, Episode 6, July 6, 2012. (spelling on last name is not given on-screen)

49. Cain. *Louisiana Lockdown*, Season 1, Episode 6, July 6, 2012.

50. Cain. *Louisiana Lockdown*, Season 1, Episode 7, July 13, 2012.

51. Cain, *Louisiana Lockdown*, Season 1, Episode 7, July 13, 2012.

52. Loudspeaker announcement, *Louisiana Lockdown*, Season 1, Episode 7, July 13, 2012. This statement appears on the prison website, on T-shirts and in numerous articles about Angola's rodeo, as well.

53. Melissa Schrift, "The Angola Prison Rodeo: Inmate Cowboys and Institutional Tourism," *Ethnology*, Vol. 43, No. 4 (autumn 2004) 331-344 (334)

54. *Louisiana Lockdown*, Season 1, Episodes 7 and 8, July 13 and 20, 2012.

55. Schrift, 335.

56. Richardson, Danny. *Louisiana Lockdown*, Season 1, Episode 7, July 13, 2012.

57. Narrator. *Louisiana Lockdown*, Season 1, Episode 8, July 20, 2012.

58. Cain. *Louisiana Lockdown*, Season 1, Episode 8, July 20, 2012.

59. Narrator. *Louisiana Lockdown*, Season 1, Episode 8, July 20, 2012.

60. Cain. *Louisiana Lockdown*, Season 1, Episode 8, July 20, 2012.

61. Author's note: Angola has been the site of multiple documentaries and news articles on its inmate-run hospice program, its seminary training, its inmate-run radio station and award-winning magazine, *The Angolite*. Mentions of these appeared very briefly. None were the focus of any episodes.

Chapter Five

Bravo's "The Real Housewives": Living the (Capitalist) American Dream?

Nicole B. Cox

In March of 2006, the United States' cable-viewing audience was introduced to a group of women who would— as it turned out—provide the foundation for a reality programming powerhouse. As the gates of Coto de Caza swung open for an all-access pass to watch the "lives of the rich," *The Real Housewives* (*TRHW*) *of Orange County* hit the small screen as it followed a group of wealthy women balancing martinis, shopping sprees, Botox injections and exotic vacations.

Documenting the trials and tribulations of the women's personal lives, Bravo had discovered a proverbial goldmine. While *TRHW of Orange County* averaged 977,000 total viewers for its first season finale, and by season five's finale the series garnered roughly 2.45 million viewers.[1] Noting *Orange County's* success, Bravo quickly created six spin-off locations for its *TRHW* franchise: *Atlanta, New York City, New Jersey, D.C., Beverly Hills,* and *Miami.* As popularity continued to grow, *Beverly Hills* set records with its season one finale that brought in 4.2 million viewers,[2] although that record was soon beat out by *Atlanta*'s season three finale that attracted 4.4 million viewers total.[3] Thus in the seven years since its inception, *TRHW* has grown to include seven series locations and roughly 350 episodes, with millions of viewers routinely tuning in.

In light of this success, *TRHW* have received ample attention by mainstream press, and have emerged as a hot topic of debate in the academic realm.[4] While multiple scholars have examined the reality TV genre and specific programs for portrayals of individuals and culture,[5] this research adds to existing literature by exploring *TRHW* with specific regard to class. As a reality series *predicated* on luxurious living, this research examines 172 episodes and 71,000 message board threads from Bravo's official website,[6] applying feminist political economy to interrogate how such reality fare perpetuates hegemonic ideologies regarding class, and how audiences make sense of those messages online. Because mass media play a significant role in structuring our social and personal relationships,[7] critical explorations into class are necessary if we are to better understand how social and power relations are upheld via mass media portrayals.[8]

FEMINIST POLITICAL ECONOMY

How gender enters into commercial arrangements and functions as a commodity in the media market is the crux of feminist political economy.[9] Emerging from the political economy of communication, feminist political economy incorporates feminist concerns into studies of media ownership and control,[10] explicating the ways in which capitalism and patriarchy are enmeshed in media and the daily lives of women.

In this sense, feminist political economy elucidates the ways in which social and power relations are perpetuated by media corporations, and how females interact and reproduce those social and power relations themselves.[11] "Feminist political economy analyzes how power and social class intersect with gender, making gender a variable of analysis in its own right. It is concerned with structures that guide media content and the ways in which these structures create and perpetuate gendered ideals."[12] As communication systems are "a means of circulation of capital reproducing power relations based on class and gender,"[13] understanding the intersections between gender and political economy are integral to changing (if not improving) the system.

"I'M GONNA DIE WEARING DIOR": CLASS AND THE "AMERICAN DREAM" ON-SCREEN

Throughout *TRHW*, even the most casual viewer is aware that programming centers on wealth and the American Dream. By creating an entire franchise centered on living lavishly, Bravo suggests that *this* version of living (i.e., capitalist class lux) is worth watching, envying, and—if possible—emulating via consumption. And when these portrayals are combined with *TRHW*'s propensity to include and target female audiences, the on-screen messages designate a version of female identity bound by consumerism, image, and status.

In this vein, the good life on-screen is largely based in conspicuous consumption. The capitalist class is marked by never-ending shopping sprees, exotic vacations and fine dining events. It is illustrated through extravagant parties, owning multiple cars and multiple homes, and the ability to demand the finer things in life. Class is conveyed via material goods and brandname items that immediately connote expensive taste (i.e., Prada, Rolex, Maybach). As Kim Zolciak states,[14] "I'm gonna die wearing Dior." One's taste in material goods is indicative of belonging to—or aspiring to achieve—a certain class,[15] perpetuating the hierarchical social relations in the United States.

On *TRHW,* those in the capitalist class embrace consumerism and treat all of life's occasions—good or bad—as an excuse to shop. Audiences are encouraged to view consumption as exciting, fun, empowering, and a solution to all of life's problems. Consumerism is framed as something to be envied, but is also a distinctly *female* activity. It is a female bonding experience.[16] Positive connotations of consumerism are conveyed both discursively and visually, via countless shopping trips accompanied by upbeat music, close-ups of brand name items, and bright lighting/exposure suggestive of a fun and happy experience. And this consumerism runs rampant: of the 172 episodes examined, there were more than 650 visual and discursive references to consumption.

In this regard, *TRHW* suggests that one has made it in life only when she can parade around in Prada and die in Dior. The series also suggests that if one is *able* to buy such things, she *should.* Capitalist class status is proven via material goods and is simultaneously *deserving* of them. As in the case of the former, Jeana's husband explains, "guys who are wearing big earrings on TV, they've accomplished a lot,"[17] while Vicki equates downsizing with "failure."[18] In the latter, Shereé buys herself an Aston Martin sports car (between $120,000-$280,000) for working hard, and Tamra celebrates her husband's business success with a shopping trip *for herself.* In all of this, linking happiness and female identity with consumerism services Bravo's commercial goals of appealing to advertisers and, in turn, creates an environment that promotes sales.

And while capitalist class membership is marked by having the best and newest material goods, there is also an expectation of budget-free shopping and little concern for price. As Taylor states, "I don't really hesitate when I need to buy... I don't really have to think twice."[19] Housewives across *all* locations spend money without questioning the cost. For example, Jill opines that she "never know[s] what anything costs,"[20] and Kim receives laser treatments while admitting, "I don't know what I paid—I just give him my card."[21] It is both conspicuous consumption *and* a complete disregard for cost that indicate one's class status on-screen.

And this message is further strengthened via the Housewives' disregard for their own economic hardship(s). The Housewives continuously consume despite eviction notices, divorce, and declining business. After a breakup with her financial breadwinner, Kim continues to "shop and act like the bill's never gonna come."[22] Neither a collapsed economy nor crumbling personal finances can stop the Housewives from living out their material dreams. And while such portrayals are problematic for the ways in which programming emphasizes consumerism with no acknowledgement of the real forces (i.e., consumer debt) that influence—or are influenced by—consumerism, the message that women should spend *through* financial troubles complements Bravo's commercial goals of prioritizing advertiser needs above those of the audience.[23] But when one considers the economic disparities facing females in the United States, and the fact that females earn only 77 cents for every dollar earned by males,[24] *TRHW*'s suggestion that females engage in limitless spending encourages a materialistic lifestyle that many female viewers at home cannot (and/or should not attempt to) afford.

More than just this, while *TRHW*'s focus on consumerism reinforces the notion that females are shoppers first and foremost, it is also problematic as it focuses so much attention on merely *one* aspect of the women's lives. In this regard, the Housewives' propensity to shop receives so much attention because it operates in accordance with late consumer capitalism. As audiences watch the women celebrate successes and attempt to solve life's problems via consumption, viewers are encouraged to do the same. *TRHW* contains so much content centered on a consumer-driven lifestyle because it bodes well for those who provide the bread and butter for Bravo: advertisers. And here is where media's commercial logic takes hold. By repeatedly tying all of life's situations back to the act of consuming, *TRHW* capitalizes on the cultural moment in which females find themselves increasingly involved in a "mass luxury movement,"[25] and suggests that one's identity can be celebrated and embraced— or fixed and erased— through consumption. By underscoring every aspect of life with consumerism, audiences are unable to avoid the onslaught of messages convincing them to buy, and still buy more. Yet as scholars have argued,[26] this consumerism results in a false sense of empowerment that deflects discussion away from the larger social structures such as patriarchy and capitalism, and deflects our understanding of women as anything more than shoppers by trade.[27]

But more than just tangible goods, the capitalist class is also signified by elite treatment, access to celebrities, and professional services that cater to the stars. This is one of the benefits of being the bourgeoisie. Elite treatment (i.e., VIP treatment at Indie races and having Christian Dior send shoe samples directly to one's home) is framed as one of the many perks unavailable to average individuals. Multiple Housewives use the same jewelers as Madonna and Jessica Simpson, hire chefs who cook for Tyra Banks, and rent Merv Griffin's estate for a weekend getaway. They live in the same neighborhoods as Dick Cheney, go shopping with Natalie Cole, and play golf with Mark Wahlberg. These connections operate ideologically by conveying that the Housewives—while seemingly relatable on-screen—are *not* relatable to the working-class at all, thereby strengthening class separations between the

Housewives and viewers at home. In this way, feminist political economy suggests that *TRHW* does the ideological work of encouraging audiences to *envy* those in the capitalist class, while simultaneously accepting the fact that such a life is fundamentally out of reach for many female fans.

Additionally, membership in the capitalist class is also complicated by imposters. These are individuals who actively pursue admittance into the capitalist class and/or those who struggle to keep up once inside. By portraying these imposters as desperately trying to get in with the capitalist class, the capitalist class ideal is reified as that which many strive to achieve. On *TRHW*, two groups of imposters exist: those who have been ousted from the capitalist class and those who pretend to be much better off than they are.

The first group of imposters includes those who have experienced a fall from grace. These women were once extremely wealthy but through life-changing events were forced to leave the capitalist class behind. The fall from grace is often prompted by divorce, and many of these stories revolve around the imposters' lack of wealth and their struggle to maintain (or pretend to maintain) their previous quality of life. Tammy, Lauri, Sonja, Shereé, Adrianna, and Danielle were all left seemingly broke after divorce. On *TRHW*, many divorcees are shown desperately trying to regain entrance into the capitalist class. Despite females' gains in career advancement and education, *TRHW* continues to suggest that females must still be "saved" by men (at least financially), if they are to live a comfortable, happy life. For example, Danielle sets out to find a wealthy man to provide for her financially, so that she can return to the lifestyle to which she was accustomed. She even visits websites such as www.wealthymen.com to find him. Lauri and Tammy similarly discuss how much they miss the Orange County lifestyle and its limitless wealth, although Lauri is later granted re-admittance via her marriage to George in season three. Here, George is positioned as Lauri's Prince Charming who—along with his wealth—rescued her from the working-class life she was forced to endure. Damsel in distress, indeed. Applying feminist political economy, however, these portrayals are integral to understanding *TRHW* as a gendered text, as they demonstrate a point of convergence between patriarchy and capitalism. These on-screen moments perpetuate patriarchal ideologies that situate males as the breadwinners and protectors of the "lesser" sex, while simultaneously linking such patriarchal social relations to consumerism and class (both of which are guided by, and operate under capitalism).

The second category of imposters includes those who *are* doing well financially, but pretend to be much better off than they are. *TRHW* calls attention to how these Housewives are out of place among the capitalist class and exposes them for their masquerade. By repeatedly questioning the imposters' presence and focusing on what they do *not* have, *TRHW* makes clear that certain individuals should not be mistaken as members of the capitalist class. There are true members of the capitalist class and those who pretend. Illustrating this, Alex and her husband, Simon, are repeatedly framed as seeking membership into the upper class to which they do not belong. The couple attends events such as Opening Night at the MET in an effort to rub elbows with influential socialites; they rely on expensive jewelry, designer clothes, and a French au pair to communicate class status. Throughout the seasons, however, the couple's attempts are repeatedly exposed as merely a façade, as programming frames the other Housewives as the haves while Alex and Simon are the have-nots. On *Miami,* it is Cristy who is framed as the imposter, and the cast's "realization" of this occurs when she crashes Lea's fundraising gala without paying her dues. Wealthy from a previous marriage to a professional athlete, Cristy is characterized as cheap and socially inept for high society. On *D.C.*, Michaele and her husband are the subjects of derision as they attempt to keep up appearances despite a failing business and mounting debt. The couple is exposed for pretending to pick up the tab for a lavish birthday party, and later sneaking into the Congressional Black Caucus Dinner. In fact, audiences are primed in the very first episode to understand the couple as out of their league, when Lynda states that they are on a "second-tier level" and associating with them "just seems so unnatural."[28] *TRHW* takes social divisions based on class and economic wealth and uses them to justify the mocking and degrading of others. And while there are moments of contestation where Bravo's editing encourages audiences to view the casts' comments as elitist and rude, the prevailing message is that those in the capitalist class are not only different, but *better*, than those who are not. Outside of these specific portrayals, visual attempts at class separation also occur in *TRHW* opening shots, as footage zooms in on signs for exclusive neighborhoods such as Coto de Caza, and the opening of metal gates as if allowing viewers (i.e., the have-nots) admittance into a class previously off-limits.

Importantly, the presence of such imposters also illustrates that there is an internal hierarchy among the Housewives themselves. Simply being among the capitalist class is not good enough; the Housewives must have the best, newest, and most expensive of everything to *continuously* validate their membership. From a commercial standpoint, this internal hierarchy does the ideological work of encouraging even those audience members who are in the capitalist class that they, too, should spend. Achieving membership in the capitalist class is not good enough, as membership is constantly tested and must constantly be proven if one is to stay in good standing. Linking back to feminist political economy, such a message reifies the notion that females' worth (and contribution to society) is largely determined by their level of consumerism, and perpetuates the ideology that females (alongside their homes, wardrobes, cars, etc.) must always be reworked and improved.

In contrast to the capitalist class, *TRHW* also communicates ideologies of class through its treatment of the working class. When working-class individuals are included, they are often framed as less than and beneath the Housewives. As Housewives across locations denounce all that is cheap and indicative of the working class, this abhorrence applies to tangible goods and *people* as well. On-screen, working-class individuals are repeatedly associated with being homeless, drug addicts, mentally unstable, dirty, poorly behaved, morally lax, dangerous, and unhappy.

To illustrate this, when Lisa Vanderpump takes her son to visit a music institute in Hollywood, her voice-over describing the area as "very toxic" is coupled with visual close-ups of homeless individuals, young adults in grunge rock attire, and scantily clad women.[29] Visual footage emphasizes how different Lisa is from the "toxic" environment, in her designer pink jacket, white jeans, and heels; this scene is followed by footage of Lisa inside the school, inquiring if they have a "problem with drugs." Similar sentiments are illustrated when Lisa visits the Department of Motor Vehicles (DMV). Footage of diverse clientele (of various racial and classed groups) is spliced with Lisa stating, "So we showed up where the DMV was—it was in some God-forsaken place . . . I was kind of fearing for my life."[30] While these instances assign negative attributes to the working class, they also imply that the capitalist class, conversely, is *not* susceptible to the countless ills or vices of the working class.

In another example, Shereé becomes upset when her blind date invites her to go dancing in an area visually coded as the "Projects." As audiences watch Shereé in the back seat of a chauffeured car, there are close-ups of Shereé's hands clutching her purse and looking out the window anxiously. Shereé asks if the driver knows where he is going, as footage cuts from inside the car to what Shereé sees on the outside—liquor stores, a check-cashing business, and a "Wings R Us" restaurant with African Americans outside. This footage is coupled with the sound of police sirens and flashing lights, indicating that Shereé is no longer in her seemingly safe, upper-class community. As the car arrives at the strip mall where Shereé meets her date, dramatic music and police sirens continue in the background. Shereé steps out of the car, asking, "Is this a joke?"[31] Clearly out of her comfort zone, audiences are encouraged to interpret working-class neighborhoods as dangerous and indicative of crime.

In addition to being dangerous, the working class is also framed as mentally unstable, dirty, and lacking morals. For example, Jeana's daughter decides to leave the University of California-Berkley because she did not fit in—an outcast status spurred by the fact that she doesn't "live in a tree," "smoke trees," or eat food "from a trash can."[32] In a later episode, Jeana and Kara explore Berkley's campus while visual footage zooms in on people sitting in trees and vagrant individuals walking around.[33] As Jeana opines

that said individuals have some "screws loose," Kara contends, "I was intim-
idated and a little bit scared of the idea of the homeless people and maybe
them being drug addicts or drunks or violent." These comments are followed
by footage of Jeana and Kara pointing out the "different" individuals, while
Kara notes that it is "kind of like being at the zoo." Pointing at a homeless
person, Kara exclaims, "There's one, there's one!" Finding "tree people" and
homeless individuals is made into a game: a "Where's Waldo?" of sorts but
with the middle- to lower-classes. Thus it is not only the Housewives who are
mocked for *pretending* to be upper class, but also average individuals who
never were to begin with.

Similarly, when NeNe goes on a shopping spree with Lisa Hartwell, she
juxtaposes wealthy individuals against those who are not.[34] Stating that everyone on Rodeo Drive looks "very rich . . . clean . . . like they don't need a
bath," Nene's comments suggest that those who are *not* wealthy are inherent-
ly unkempt and unclean. Certain types of behavior, a lack of manners, and/or
lack of etiquette are also par for the course when it comes to the working
class. As every location contains references to appropriate and inappropriate
class behavior, membership in the capitalist class is a matter of how one
conducts him/herself. Intertwining gender and class, many of these behaviors
depend on stereotypical gender scripts. Being among the elite necessitates
that women be passive, have proper etiquette, and always be polite. They are
not to be too aggressive, too assertive, or too demanding lest they be labeled
for it. As LuAnn contends, a person's manners convey "a lot about where
they come from."[35] *TRHW* also ties a lack of morality to the working-class,
providing yet another neoliberal facet of reality TV.[36] This is evidenced
when Mary learns of her youngest daughter's newfound knowledge of "sex-
ting."[37] As her daughter opines, "You put me in public school, not me." It is
the association with working-class children that—according to *TRHW*—has
corrupted her.

Even within the Housewives' group, there are also times when working-
class individuals infiltrate their exclusive social circles, and programming
emphasizes how dangerous they can be. In *New Jersey,* Danielle's association with her ex-convict friend Danny brings a slew of drama and threats of
violence in season two. Danny's presence is marked by his paternalistic need
to protect Danielle, and by his connection to violent gangs such as the Hell's
Angels. In one episode, a miscommunication leaves Danielle, Danny, and his
entourage without seating at a charity event. Amidst the confusion, Danielle
purports that The Brownstone should think twice before making Danny and
his friends "feel unwelcome," which is followed by Danny causing a scene in
front of hundreds of guests. Danielle explains that nothing will be "dignified
if these boys cut loose," which is then spliced with dramatic music and
footage of the Housewives peacefully discussing how to rectify the situation.[38] The Housewives' seemingly logical reaction is juxtaposed against

Danny's, as viewers watch him angrily call the Housewives "punks" and proclaim that he is about to "get stupid" as he paces around the room.[39]

While these portrayals situate the working class as a menace to the capitalist class, perhaps the most prominent means by which the working-class factors into programming is when it is used to discredit another member of the cast. Here, a working-class background is used against the Housewives as ammunition in their many wars of words. In all but one location (*Beverly Hills*), the Housewives use class background as a source of ridicule and degradation. For example, an argument between Tamra and Gretchen prompts Jeana's reminder to "remember her [Tamra's] background," to which Gretchen laughs, "She's white trash!"[40] Michaele is mocked when the Housewives find out that she previously worked as a makeup artist at a department store; as Mary asserts, Michaele has "definitely changed her station in life."[41] Kim is ridiculed for being raised in a "trailer park,"[42] while Danielle taunts Teresa, claiming, "I saw the house you lived in, Teresa, before you moved into the mansion!"[43] Thus while many Housewives are upper-class in their current state, *TRHW*'s focus on background suggests that nobody can outgrow their roots—especially not if those roots are planted in the working class.

Thus with so much focus on the capitalist class ideal, *TRHW* also relies on the same neoliberalism that scholars argue is inherent to reality TV.[44] Neoliberalism is based on a preoccupation with individualism and freedom, and links improvement with personal choices and behaviors. It suggests that failure under the free market is one's personal fault rather than indicative of structural inequalities and challenges.[45] In accordance with such ideology, *TRHW* suggests that it is only through hard work and dedication that one can ascend into the capitalist class. Multiple Housewives suggest that the American Dream is possible for everyone, with enough sacrifice and hard work. Michaele states, "You work hard, you give a lot of love, and you end up at the White House,"[46] while Vicki frequently cites her own success as evidence that the American Dream is possible for all. Past odds are easily overcome, as illustrated when NeNe recounts her rags to riches story,[47] and when Shereé contends, "I was upper middle class growing up, but I left that behind for upper class."[48] Upward mobility is seemingly a matter of *choice*. In many ways, this neoliberal ideology is problematic for its reliance on individualism, and for the ways in which programming neglects to include social, economic, or political pressures that make possible (or *im*possible) the American Dream. *TRHW* fails to acknowledge how social and institutional structures make the American Dream attainable for only a select group of people (i.e., white, capitalist class, male), and pays no attention to how axes of identity complicate the process. Instead, the good life is presented as *proof* that the American Dream is attainable, while Bravo glosses over the ways in which social and economic hierarchies privilege some while disadvantaging others. By making invisible the larger structures that affect one's success under free-market capitalism, critical concerns regarding said structures remain unquestioned and intact.

But more than vague instructions on how to achieve the American Dream, *TRHW* also alludes to what comprises the American Dream: luxury. In *Beverly Hills*, for example, Taylor is shown climbing out of a bright yellow sports car in a blue dress and high heels. The camera slowly pans up her thin, tan legs as she steps out onto Rodeo Drive. Her voice-over explains that she grew up in a "normal, middle-class family," and is coupled with footage of her shopping at high-end retail stores. As she states, "I've always had a feeling inside of me since I was small, that there was something really big for me in my life."[49] Audiences are encouraged to understand Taylor's dream as shopping on Rodeo Drive. Similar sentiments are echoed by Alexis: "You know when you're a little girl you picture your life one way, but you never really think or know if you're going to get the lifestyle you want. I have a very fortunate lifestyle. The glitz and the glam and the $1500 shoes and I got it. I mean, I *got* it."[50] Complicating gender and class, these scenes suggest that the American Dream is inextricably tied to material goods, but also have profound implications for what big dreams females are encouraged (or suggested) to have. The females' on-screen aspirations do not speak to education, career, or civic service. Instead, marrying into money and enjoying the spoils of limitless wealth are placed at the top of the list.

Of course, this is not to say that challenges to *TRHW* classist behaviors does not exist. Rather, *TRHW* do contain moments that position these attitudes as shallow, materialistic, pretentious, and unrealistic. Through visual cues such as cast member reactions, narrative contestation, kitschy music, and formulaic emphasis on the contradictions between the Housewives' words and actions, Bravo occasionally critiques such behaviors while capitalizing off of them. Within the tenets of commercial culture, these representations persist because they still operate under—and in fulfillment of—capitalist rules, regulations and incentives despite momentary contestation.[51] In many ways, the Housewives are portrayed as out of touch with the world beyond their suburban safe havens, in part *because* of their class. As Kimberly states, "One of the interesting things about Coto is that you're living behind the Orange curtain, and that can be good, and that can be bad . . . it's easy to forget about the things the rest of the world has to worry about."[52] There are also objections to the Housewives' obsession with consumerism, often from family members who argue that the Housewives' preoccupation with materialism has changed their loved ones for the worse. And even as *TRHW* suggests that all of life's events warrant a shopping spree, consumerism is occasionally exposed for its inability to deliver on its promise of bliss. It is unable to take the place of real relationships and solve real problems. It is empty and transparent. True to Bravo form, it is this out-of-touch reality—

these moments of "reality"— that audiences are meant to find pleasure in, to envy and abhor at the exact same time.[53]

MONEY CAN'T BUY YOU CLASS: FANS' ONLINE RESPONSES

In examining fan discussions on Bravo's official message boards (http:// boards.bravotv.com), it must first be noted that many fans identify as working class. Because of this, when issues of class enter the discussion, many viewers align themselves with the working-class. Many fans position themselves as *counter* to depictions of the capitalist class. They argue that the working-class is more caring, moral, and kind. They assert that they are more relatable, relationship-oriented, and more in tune with reality than the Housewives themselves. Numerous fans contend that working class individuals are better off in life, despite the fact that the Housewives have it easier financially. Thus as countless fans juxtapose their experiences, attitudes, and values against *TRHW*'s image of class, there is an overwhelming attitude that the viewers are better off than they, despite the capitalist class's glitz and glam.

Because they identify as the working class, many fans take offense to the Housewives' disparaging attitude *toward* the working class. For example, in response to the *Beverly Hills* scene where Lisa equates Hollywood with violence and drugs, one viewer posts:[54]

> I like Lisa, but I was a little surprised [by] what she said about the Hollywood music scene. My hubby was a drummer that played the Hollywood clubs, and he didn't do drugs. Neither did the rest of his band. Quite a few of the musicians have jobs as graphic designers, accountants, etc., and do the music part time. I'm sure that some Hollywood music people do drugs, but not all. My guess is that there is more drug use in Beverly Hills than the streets of Hollywood.

In another *Beverly Hills* episode, Lisa's comments about the DMV are likewise unwelcome. As one fan writes, "Lisa at the DMV office, welcome to our world honey . . . some of those 'eclectic' folks at the DMV were probably the same folks cutting your lawn, cleaning your pool and cleaning your home . . . you sank a few notches in that episode for me." Jeana and Kara's game of find-the-bums prompted a similar pushback as one viewer wrote, "Hey Jeana, they aren't 'bummers,' they're people." However, while there *is* a clear distinction between "us" as working-class viewers and "them" as upper-class Housewives, such distinctions are not always proffered in a productive way. While political economic analysis interrogates how resistance is enacted by media consumers, it is argued here that working-class individuals take issue with the messages seen on-screen, although their comments fail to push the envelope in a progressive direction. Instead, fans point out the Housewives' offensive remarks and stop there.

When it comes to audiences' perceptions of the Housewives' class standing, there is also the pervasive belief that the Housewives are nouveau riche. As new money, the Housewives are criticized for their spending habits and inability to make economically sound decisions. Viewers contend that the Housewives do not know how to act in high-class society, and do not represent the true elite. This behavior is addressed across all message boards, as fans suggest that despite the Housewives' class status, they have no class at all. As one *Atlanta* fan writes, "NeNe, Kim, Shereé and DeShawn are spot-on representations of new money stupidty [sic]. Spend, spend, spend on anything and everything that might give the appearance of class and style."

Being new money, however, is also understood as behaving inappropriately. In fact, every message board contained the mantra, "money can't buy you class," which was directed at the Housewives. This sentiment is used in relation to the Housewives' tendency to gossip and create drama, and emerged in response to the Housewives' boasting about how much money they have, how much commodities cost, and their incessant proclamations about how much class they have. The mantra speaks to the Housewives' use of designer labels as markers of class, and their erroneous assumption that having a padded bank account guarantees high-class status. It is also in this regard that a number of online fans characterize this "bad," low-class/no-class behavior as "low rent." As a phrase rarely heard in *TRHW*, such comments suggest that there is a certain type of behavior that is characteristic of the working class— and that behavior is tacky and distasteful. Thus even as many fans identify as working class, class online means one of two things: the capitalist versus working-class, or a set of behaviors. In the former, many fans use their own experiences to assess where the Housewives fall within the social hierarchy. When it comes to behavior, fan comments perpetuate the notion that behaviors culturally associated with the capitalist class are "better than" those linked to the working class, despite the fact that most fans identify with the latter. In addition to this, the "money can't buy you class" mantra is also used to convey a sense of superiority over the Housewives. By invoking such rhetoric, fans are able to turn the tables, per se, and proffer judgment on how high class (or not) the Housewives really are. But even here, this phrase holds an extra layer of meaning as many fans use the phrase to make fun of the Housewives and the classed image(s) that they sell on-screen, thereby perpetuating the divisive ideologies concerning economic and social class in the United States.

Related to questions of class, online fans also speculate about the Housewives' validity as bona fide members of the capitalist class, specifically as it relates to financial resources. Drawing on the concept of imposters, many fans look to programming as well as secondary information for evidence that the Housewives are pretending to be upper class.[55] As John Fiske contends, this secondary information "extend[s] the fan's pleasures by extending the primary text,"[56] and takes the form of news articles, tabloids, mainstream interviews, and/or blog posts. In fact, there is at least one Housewife (often more) in every series whose financial wealth and class status comes under investigation by these online sleuths. In the majority of cases, fans utilize public information such as bankruptcy filings, foreclosure notices, tax records, divorce filings, and interviews to prove that the Housewives are simply putting on airs when it comes to their wealth.

Also related to portrayals of class are fans' critiques that the Housewives are all too consumed by material wealth. Many fans suggest that the House-wives have a perverted sense of what is— and is not— important in life. Viewers critique the Housewives' propensity to spend large amounts of money on frivolous items while more important matters are simultaneously ignored. On the *New Jersey* boards, Teresa is ridiculed for spending $120,000 on furniture when she could not pay her bills, and *Orange County* fans critique Lynne for getting plastic surgery when she could not pay her rent. *Atlanta* fans comment on Shereé buying expensive clothes while ignoring her son's need for braces, and criticize NeNe for buying her son $6,500 worth of suits instead of paying for college tutors. *New York City* fans critique Alex's shopping for high-couture fashion before finishing her home renovation, and *Miami* fans discuss how Adriana cannot afford her son's private school but can afford private stripping lessons.

In all of these instances, many fans argue that it is the Housewives' self-absorbed personalities that guide their focus on material goods. This focus, according to fans, is couched in the Housewives' obsession with image; consumerism is understood as a marker of one's status and key to the House-wives' goal(s) of "keeping up with the Joneses." As one *New Jersey* fan writes, "To them status is everything so they go out of there [sic] way to show people what they have, what they can get, and how easy they can have anything and everything." But a sizable portion of fans also address how such obsessions can have a negative effect on one's personal life. A number of fans argue that the Housewives' emphasis on wealth creates spoiled children, wrecks personal relationships, and persuades some women to settle for unhealthy relationships in exchange for the "lifestyle." As one *Atlanta* fan writes, "What kind of people are these women? If their lives consist of only D&G, Gucci, Prada, etc. . . then I actually feel bad for them because it is truly pathetic." Another *Orange County* fan argues, "It seems a rather empty existence, always trying to get more and bigger . . . more money, bigger house, bigger breasts, better car . . . where is our society going?" Thus while the series encourages conspicuous consumption, message board responses suggest that while some fans buy into the messages they see on screen, they also actively negotiate and criticize the shallowness of a life guided by material goods.

Related to this, an overwhelming number of fans argue that money cannot buy *happiness*, either. As one *Orange County* fan posts, "I have never seen 'happiness' in a Neiman Marcus catalog, jewlery [sic] store or on a car lot. Where do you shop?" Here, a prominent critique is that *TRHW*'s focus on consumerism leads to a life that is all but void of "stuff." As another *Orange County* viewer contends, "I've been rich, I've been poor. Having money is easier . . . But money doesn't make you happy. Purses don't hug back. Manolos [sic] don't send birthday cards or call out of the blue to say hello . . . They are isolating and insulating and creating their own hell." Fan comments suggest that the Housewives' vapid consumerism is exactly that—*vapid*. It leads to an empty life full of credit card debt and failed relationships, where nobody is happy in the long run. This over-the-top consumption is seen by some as little more than a transparent attempt to maintain status, but ultimately fails to deliver on its promise of fulfillment.

But the inherent emptiness of consumerism only complicates the fact that not all fans deplore the Housewives' spending habits. A number of fans admire, envy, and demonstrate a desire to participate in the same consumer culture chaos propagated by the show. In every message board examined, there was at least one inquiry (often more) about consumer goods and services. These viewers asked for information on brands and/or where they could obtain commodities seen on *TRHW,* such as jewelry and clothes to shoes and purses. Beyond the axiomatic, however, these inquiries demonstrate that some fans' critique of consumer culture existed alongside a desire to participate in it.[57] Applying feminist political economy, these comments suggest that the commercial logic behind this female-oriented program is working. As one *Beverly Hills* fan exclaimed, "This show really makes me want the stuff!"

And from a feminist political economic stance, it is here where the contradictions inherent in fans' online posts are brought to bear; while a number of fans critique the Housewives spending, some of those same fans simultaneously admire their lifestyle. In fact, many fans contend that should they ever find themselves in a similar situation (with similar resources) they would do the same. They would hire nannies, go on exotic vacations, and buy thousand-dollar shoes just because. They would spend just like the Housewives. In this way, fans' online critiques of consumerism are fleeting, as online contestation does not necessarily translate to contestation in real life. Some of the same fans who abhor the Housewives for their capitalist-class attitudes and behaviors are the same fans who would adopt the *TRHW* lifestyle, if given the chance.

Complicating matters further, a number of viewers blame TV programming—including *TRHW*—for failures in the United States' economy. In unpacking *TRHW* text, however, it is argued that fans' issues with the United States economy are reductionist and fail to incorporate the larger social, political, and economic structures that are inextricably linked and influence (and are influenced by) each other. In focusing so much on consumerism, the franchise fails to address equally important, mitigating factors affecting the economy. On the *New Jersey* boards, for example, fans express frustration that they (as taxpayers) will be left to foot the bill for Teresa's reckless spending after she filed bankruptcy, although there is no discussion of the corporate entities that—since 2007—have filed for bankruptcy and greatly impacted the national economy. As viewers contend, *TRHW*'s programmatic crux of conspicuous consumption is *part of the problem*, as it glorifies and perpetuates ideologies about wealth, consumer spending, and debt. As one *New Jersey* fan writes, "What kind of message does it [*TRHW*] send to young people who are building their lives when they see this family living so far beyond their means even after being 'caught' with seemingly no real repercussions so far?" In this case, some viewers argue that the Housewives' focus on material wealth is inconsiderate given individuals' financial hardships, and contend that the Housewives are out of touch with the nation's economic realities. According to one *New York City* fan, "The show does promote horrible values of conspicuous consumption . . . In these difficult economic times with corrupt values, their behavior is really almost contemptuous and out of touch." Another *Atlanta* fan states, "There are too many people in this world who are struggling between buying prescription medication or food. Not designer clothes or botox parties." These comments, while addressing important economic issues such as the recession, fall in line with reality TV's neoliberalism, as fans hold *individual consumers* responsible for the collapse of the U.S. economy. Rather than addressing how economic and political institutions play a vital role, fans instead suggest that it is because of individual behavior(s) that such problems have arisen, and it is only through correcting individual behavior can they be resolved.

Additionally, the on-screen message that one's "true" class can be transcended via conspicuous consumption and/or access to wealth is also addressed online. Viewer assessment of the Housewives' class status is partially mitigated by the lifestyles that they had prior to becoming wealthy. Much like programming, fans suggest that despite their new money, it is impossible for the Housewives to escape their earlier, working-class selves. On the *New Jersey* boards, for example, multiple viewers state that it is possible to "take the girl out of Patterson but not Patterson out of the girl." Similar sentiments are found across the *Atlanta* boards, where fans contend, "You can take the b**ch out of the ghetto, but you can't take the ghetto out of the b**ch." An *Orange County* fan opines, "you may be able to take the girl [Tamra] out from the wrong side of the tracks but you can't take those dirty tracks out from the girl!!" Thus when it comes to discussion of *TRHW*, there are two competing ideologies at play. First, harkening back to the House-wives' class status of yesteryear suggests that it is impossible to escape the class into which one is born. But most fans who address the Housewives' class do not link the seemingly impossible ascendency to the upper class to larger structural issues such as barriers to upward mobility and education. Instead, they link inability to improve one's class status (again) to individual female behavior. Yet using phrases such as "made good" when referring to the Housewives suggests that fans consider there to have been a step up in the Housewives' status, however superficial. While programming perpetu-ates ideologies of a class-based society grounded in social and economic hierarchies, the structural power relations that guide these hierarchies ulti-mately remain unquestioned by fans. In line with neoliberal ideology, many suggest that it is because of the *individual*—not the *system*—that women remain tied to their former classed selves.

Finally, as most fans suggest that it is the individual and not larger struc-tures that determine ascendency into the capitalist class, it is perhaps unsur-prising to find that when it comes to the American Dream, the majority of online comments *applaud* the Housewives for overcoming obstacles on their own. Here, the majority of comments fail to include consideration for the economic and/or political contexts that make possible (or hinder) one's abil-ity to achieve the American Dream in the first place. For example, both Vicki and Bethenny are applauded for building their careers and making names for themselves, as fans recount their difficult past(s) as evidence of their dedica-tion and perseverance. Multiple fans champion the Housewives for pulling themselves up by their proverbial bootstraps, yet there is no consideration for how education, access to resources, or class privilege factors in. Some fans even reveal their own ambitions for achieving the American Dream, inspired by what they see on-screen. Viewers comment on how the program has shown them that they, too, can live like the Housewives. The lavish lifestyle is read as ideal, and seen as attainable for "regular, working folk" at home. As one *Orange County* viewer writes, "I watch it [*TRHW*] because it puts me in that state of mind like it's possible for me to have all that as well . . . maybe . . . we'll see."

GETTING BACK TO OUR PATRIARCHAL ROOTS: CONCLUSIONS & IMPLICATIONS

To return to Sut Jhally and Justin Lewis's critical assertion, "It is not usually one episode or one series that influences the way we think; [but rather] it is the aggregate of messages that enter our minds."[58] While mainstream rheto-ric suggests that *TRHW* offers little more than "mindless" entertainment, this chapter illustrates that it is much more than that. Across the entire franchise,

TRHW contains ideological suggestions about how women should—and do—navigate the contested terrain of class in the 21st Century.

In this way, *TRHW* contains a barrage of textual moments that uphold and maintain the status quo as they relate to social and power relations in the United States. While embracing neoliberal ideologies that suggest the American Dream is attainable for everyone, *TRHW* simultaneously mocks those who have not achieved said Dream and/or those who *choose* not to. Across the range of episodes explored, *TRHW* continues to rely on economic and social relations that are hierarchical in form and unequal in treatment, while ignoring the structural institutions that privilege some while disadvantaging others. Programming overlooks, for example, how access to capital is required to obtain higher education, and how higher education is increasingly necessary to achieve the American Dream.[59] Programming glosses over how female empowerment via consumerism is bound to patriarchal logic that privileges the male gaze as validation for female worth, and neglects to call attention to how axes of identity influence the Housewives' lives as they play out on screen. Instead, viewers see one-dimensional images of capitalist women living the good life. Hence linking the aforementioned portrayals to media's commercial structure, it is argued that there is a strong undercurrent of consumerism that guides *all* of *TRHW* depictions on-screen. Whether one is attempting to improve class status by purchasing a Mercedes Benz or correcting bad behavior via new clothes, the franchise unabashedly suggests that all problems can be resolved through participation in consumer culture. Operating in accordance with capitalist goals, *TRHW*'s focus on consumerism services the network's commercial goals and is dually appealing to advertisers. In sum, it "drive[s] people to go out and buy things."[60]

Here, feminist political economy extrapolates the many ways in which Bravo sacrifices more well-rounded representations of class in exchange for programming that follows a tested formula for profit. Because it is much easier (and safer) to perpetuate classist tropes than it is to challenge them, it is this commercial logic that guides what female viewers do (and do not) see in this popular media text. And while such hegemonic ideologies are reified on-screen, it must be noted that these portrayals are not achieved *solely* through the Housewives' real behaviors—they are also achieved via Bravo's crafty editing techniques that play up stereotypes, drama, and conflict in an attempt to attract audiences and advertisers.[61]

Yet these images are not simply taken at face value by *TRHW* fans. Instead, they are complicated by fans' active negotiation, and participation with *TRHW* text. Paradoxically, as fans critique *TRHW* on-screen portrayals they perpetuate them, too. From a feminist political economic perspective, this online participation is problematic in a couple of ways.

First, fans responding to *TRHW* are overtly critical of programming. They evaluate and critique problematic messages, point out inconsistencies and contradictions, and are skeptical of the reality of *TRHW*. On one hand, such critiques proffer hope (and evidence) that viewers are far from passive dupes blindly accepting television's ideological messages. Despite *TRHW*'s regressive representations, fans are not wholly accepting the series' suggestions about class. Instead, they rework, reconstitute, and sometimes *resist* them in place of more realistic understandings of the world in which they live. On the other hand, even though some fans are seemingly less likely than the average viewer to believe *TRHW*'s claims, many still read much of the text in line with Bravo's intent. In so doing, these fans uphold the ideologies that reproduce less than egalitarian social and power relations. More than simple interpretation, while some fans *understand TRHW*'s portrayals as problematic, many of these same fans *reproduce* those same ideologies through their interaction(s) online.

Yet in an effort to avoid celebrating and/or romanticizing fans for their critical disposition, it must be acknowledged that such resistance does not equate to subversions of power. Simply because a fan contests the Housewives' messaging in an online setting does not guarantee intervention in real-life processes offline. In fact, the contradictory nature of many of the fans' online posts suggests that while resisting *TRHW*'s various ideological messages, fans are—at the same time—participating in the same systems of power and the same codes of conduct online and in their own lives. In the end, it is these negotiations that seemingly make the problematic images okay to female fans. Through feminist political economy, it is argued that online interactivity allows fans to feel empowered by critiquing the system, without necessitating that they embody subversive practices in their private lives. The systems of power remain intact.

In addition to this, the role of females in perpetuating patriarchal capitalism also extends beyond their discursive comments online. In this regard, females' *mere involvement with the text online validates its reproduction.* Females play a role in upholding the problematic portrayals— no matter how much they resist— simply by logging in and talking about *TRHW*. The more audiences talk about the program, the more buzz that is created for Bravo. And it does not matter if that buzz is good or bad— what matters is that it exists. Because online participation leads to more loyal and engaged viewing, females' online participation creates economic capital for media corporations from the cultural work that fans provide for *free* each and every time they log on.[62] *TRHW* fans are allotted the online space for interactivity in exchange for the free cognitive work they provide for Bravo. Although such labor is often considered "pleasurable work,"[63] it is from this work that Bravo tweaks *TRHW* storylines and narrative arcs just enough to respond to its audience,[64] while holding tight to the franchised formula that has proven itself financially fruitful. They tweak the formula, but never *change* it. Audience participation, therefore, is never transformative. The illusion of interactive empowerment and influence gives way to a more fine-tuned media text that continues to be guided by commercial logic, and fueled by the female fans themselves.[65]

REFERENCES

Andersen, Robin. "The Thrill is Gone: Advertising, Gender Representation, and the Loss of Desire." In *Sex & Money: Feminism and Political Economy in the Media*, edited by Eileen Meehan and Ellen Riordan, 223-239. Thousand Oaks: Sage Publications, 2002.

Andrejevic, Marc. *iSpy: Surveillance and power in the interactive era*. Kansas: University Press of Kansas, 2007.

Andrejevic, Marc. *Reality TV: The Work of Being Watched*. Oxford: Rowman & Littlefield Publishers, 2004.

Bagdikian, Ben. *The New Media Monopoly*. Boston: Beacon Press, 2004.

Baym, Nancy. *Tune In, Log On*. Thousand Oaks: Sage Publications, 2000.

Bury, Rhiannon. *Cyberspaces of Their Own: Female Fandoms Online*. New York: Peter Lang Publishing, 2005.

Chocano, Carina. "A Perverse, Televised, Postfeminist-feminine-status Olympics." *The New York Times Magazine*, November 2011.

Clifford, Stephanie. "We'll Make You a Star (if the Web Agrees)." *New York Times*. Accessed April 23, 2013, http://www.nytimes.com/2010/06/06/business/06bravo.html.

Cox, Nicole. "A Little Sex Appeal Goes a Long Way: Feminist Political Economy, Commodification, and TLC's 'What Not to Wear'." *Kaleidoscope*, 10 (2011): 19-36.

Cox, Nicole and Jennifer Proffitt, "The Housewives Guide to Better Living: Promoting Consumption on Bravo's 'The Real Housewives.'" *Communication, Culture & Critique* 5, no. 2 (2012): 295-312. doi: 10.1111/j.1753-9137.2012.01126.x.

Creeber, Glen. "Analysing Television: Issues and Methods in Textual Analysis," in *Televisions: An Introduction to Studying Television*, edited by Glen Creeber, 26-43. London: British Film Institute, 2005.

Dominus, Susan. "The Affluencer." *New York Times*. Accessed July 19, 2013, http://www.nytimes.com/2008/11/02/magazine/02zalaznickt.html?pagewanted=all&_r=.

Douglas, Susan. *Enlightened Sexism*. New York: Times Books, 2010.

Huffington, Christina. "Women and Equal Pay: Wage Gap Still Intact, Study Says." *The Huffington Post*. Accessed July 19, 2013, http://www.huffingtonpost.com/2013/04/09/women-and-equal-pay-wage- gap_n_3038806.html.

"I am woman, hear me shop." *BusinessWeek*. Accessed October 1, 2011, http://www.businessweek.com/bwdaily/dnflash/feb2005/nf20050214_9413_db_082.htm.

Jhally, Sut and Justin Lewis. *Enlightened Racism: The Cosby Show, Audiences, and the Myth of the American Dream*. Boulder: Westview Press, 1992.

Hill, Annette. *Reality TV: Audiences and Popular Factual Television*. London: Routledge, 2005.

Koff, Lori. "'Real Housewives of Beverly Hills' breaks ratings records finale night." *The Examiner*. Accessed April 23, 2013, http://www.examiner.com/the-real-housewives-in- national/real-housewives-of-beverly-hills-breaks-ratings-records-finale-night.

Krugman, Paul. "The Death of Horatio Alger." *The Nation*. Accessed April 23, 2013, http://www.thenation.com/article/death-horatio-alger.

Martin, Michele. "An unsuitable technology for women? Communication as circulation," in *Sex & Money: Feminism and Political Economy in the Media*, edited by Eileen Meehan and Ellen Riordan, 49-59. Thousand Oaks: Sage Publications, 2002.

Meehan, Eileen. *Why TV is Not Our Fault: Television Programming, Viewers, and Who's Really in Control*. Oxford: Rowman & Littlefield Publishers, 2005.

Mosco, Vincent. *The Political Economy of Communication*. Los Angeles: Sage Publications, 2009.

Murray, Susan and Laurie Ouellette. *Reality TV: Remaking Television Culture.* New York: New York University Press, 2009.

Nordyke, Kimberly. "Bravo's 'Real Housewives of Atlanta' Finale Sets Ratings Records." *The Hollywood Reporter.* Accessed April 23, 2013, http://www.hollywoodreporter.com/blogs/live-feed/real-housewives-atlanta-finale-set- 95226.

Ouellette, Laurie. "Take Responsibility for Yourself: *Judge Judy* and the Neoliberal Citizen." In *Reality TV: Remaking Television Culture,* edited by Susan Murray and Laurie Ouellette, 223-242. New York & London: New York University Press, 2009.

Ouellette, Laurie and James Hay. *Better Living Through Reality TV.* Malden, MA: Blackwell Publishing, 2008.

Riordan, Ellen. "Intersections and New Directions: On Feminism and Political Economy." In *Sex & Money: Feminism and Political Economy in the Media,* edited by Eileen Meehan and Ellen Riordan, 3-15. Thousand Oaks: Sage Publications, 2002.

Ross, Sharon. *Beyond the Box: Television and the Internet.* Malden, MA: Blackwell Publishing, 2008.

Seidman, Robert. "Bravo sets record with the finale of "The Real Housewives of Orange County" and the premiere of 'The Real Housewives of New York City.'" *TV by the Numbers.* Accessed April 23, 2013, http://tvbythenumbers.zap2it.com/2010/03/05/bravo- sets-record-ratings-with-finale-of-the-real-housewives-of-orange-county-and-premiere- of-real-housewives-of-new-york-city/44007/ .

Sgroi, Renee. "Joe Millionaire and Women's Positions: A Question of Class." In *The Gender and Media Reader*, edited by Mary Celeste Kearney, 344-354. New York: Routledge, 2012.

Storey, John. "Rockin' Hegemony: West Coast Rock and Amerika's War in Vietnam." In *Cultural Theory and Popular Culture*, edited by John Storey, 88-97. Harlow, England: Pearson, 2012.

The Real Housewives of Atlanta. *My Ego is Bigger Than Your Ego.* TV. Bravo. 2009

The Real Housewives of Atlanta. *Scrambled Egos.* TV. Bravo. 2009.

The Real Housewives of Atlanta. *Throwing Shade.* TV. Bravo. 2009.

The Real Housewives of Atlanta. *Unbeweavable.* TV. Bravo. 2009.

The Real Housewives of Atlanta, *Welcome One, Welcome ATL.* TV. Bravo. 2008.

The Real Housewives of Atlanta. *White Hot.* TV. Bravo. 2010.

The Real Housewives of Beverly Hills. *Charity Cases.* TV. Bravo. 2010.

The Real Housewives of Beverly Hills. *Chocolate Louboutins.* TV. Bravo. 2012.

The Real Housewives of Beverly Hills. *It's My Party and I'll Spend If I Want To.* TV. Bravo. 2010.

The Real Housewives of Beverly Hills. *Life, Liberty and the Pursuit of Wealthiness.* TV. Bravo. 2010.

The Real Housewives of Beverly Hills. *The Higher the Heel, the Closer to God.* TV. Bravo. 2012.

The Real Housewives of D.C. *Disloyal to the Party.* TV. Bravo. 2010.

The Real Housewives of D.C. *Foreign Relations.* TV. Bravo. 2010.

The Real Housewives of D.C. *Nation Building.* TV. Bravo. 2010.

The Real Housewives of D.C. *Welcome to the District.* TV. Bravo. 2010.

The Real Housewives of New Jersey. *Country Clubbed.* TV. Bravo. 2010.

The Real Housewives of New Jersey. *Into the Lion's Den.* TV. Bravo. 2010.

The Real Housewives of New York City. *Fashion Week.* TV. Bravo. 2008.

The Real Housewives of New York City. *On Their High Horses.* TV. Bravo. 2009.

The Real Housewives of Orange County. *Are They for Real?* TV. Bravo. 2008.

The Real Housewives of Orange County. *Be Nice to the New Girl.* TV. Bravo. 2007.

The Real Housewives of Orange County. *Friends, Enemies, and Husbands.* TV. Bravo. 2009.

The Real Housewives of Orange County. *It's All About Choices.* TV. Bravo. 2009.

The Real Housewives of Orange County. *The Housewives are Back!.* TV. Bravo. 2007.

The Real Housewives of Orange County. *Who's Your Daddy?* TV. Bravo. 2009.

White, Mimi. "Ideological analysis and television." In *Channels of Discourse, Reassembled: Television and Contemporary Criticism*, edited by Robert Allen, 161-204. Chapel Hill: The University of North Carolina Press, 1992.

Wyatt, Justin. "Weighing the transgressive star body of Shelley Duvall." In *Sex & Money: Feminism and Political Economy in the Media,* edited by Eileen Meehan and Ellen Riordan, 147-163. Thousand Oaks: Sage Publications, 2002.

NOTES

1. Robert Seidman, "Bravo sets record with the finale of "The Real Housewives of Orange County" and the premiere of 'The Real Housewives of New York City,'" *TV by the Numbers,* accessed April 23, 2013, http://tvbythenumbers.zap2it.com/2010/03/05/bravo-sets-record-rat-ings-with-finale-of-the-real-housewives-of-orange-county-and-premiere-of-real-housewives-of-new-york-city/44007/.

2. Lori Koff, "'Real Housewives of Beverly Hills' breaks ratings records finale night," *The Examiner,* accessed April 23, 2013, http://www.examiner.com/the-real-housewives-in-nation-al/real-housewives-of-beverly-hills-breaks-ratings-records-finale-night.

3. Kimberly Nordyke, "Bravo's 'Real Housewives of Atlanta' Finale Sets Ratings Records," *The Hollywood Reporter,* accessed April 23, 2013, http://www.hollywoodreporter.com/blogs/live-feed/real-housewives-atlanta-finale-set-95226.

4. Nicole Cox and Jennifer Proffitt, "The Housewives Guide to Better Living: Promoting Consumption on Bravo's 'The Real Housewives,'" *Communication, Culture & Critique* 5, no. 2 (2012): 295-312, doi: 10.1111/j.1753-9137.2012.01126.x.

5. Annette Hill, *Reality TV: Audiences and Popular Factual Television* (London: Rout-ledge, 2005).

6. Message board comments included in analysis come from Bravo's official message boards (http://boards.bravotv.com).

7. Ben Bagdikian, *The New Media Monopoly* (Boston: Beacon Press, 2004).

8. Vincent Mosco, *The Political Economy of Communication* (Los Angeles: Sage Publica-tions, 2009).

9. Justin Wyatt, "Weighing the transgressive star body of Shelley Duvall," in *Sex & Mon-ey: Feminism and Political Economy in the Media,* ed. Eileen Meehan and Ellen Riordan (Thousand Oaks: Sage Publications, 2002), 147-163.

10. Mosco, *The Political Economy of Communication.*

11. Riordan, "Intersections and New Directions."

12. Cox and Proffitt, "Housewives Guide," 297.

13. Michele Martin, "An unsuitable technology for women? Communication as circulation," in *Sex & Money: Feminism and Political Economy in the Media,* ed. Eileen Meehan and Ellen Riordan (Thousand Oaks: Sage Publications, 2002), 51.

14. The Real Housewives of Atlanta, *Welcome One, Welcome ATL,* TV, Bravo, 2008.

15. Renee Sgroi, "Joe Millionaire and Women's Positions: A Question of Class," in *The Gender and Media Reader*, ed. Mary Celeste Kearney (New York: Routledge, 2012), 344-354.

16. Cox and Proffitt, "Housewives Guide," 301.

17. The Real Housewives of Orange County, *Be Nice to the New Girl,* TV, Bravo, 2007.

18. The Real Housewives of Beverly Hills, *The Higher the Heel, the Closer to God*, TV, Bravo, 2012.

19. The Real Housewives of Beverly Hills, *Chocolate Louboutins,* TV, Bravo, 2012.

20. The Real Housewives of New York City, *Fashion Week,* TV, Bravo, 2008.

21. The Real Housewives of Atlanta, *Unbeweavable,* TV, Bravo, 2009.

22. The Real Housewives of Atlanta, *Scrambled Egos,* TV, Bravo, 2009.

23. Eileen Meehan, *Why TV is Not Our Fault: Television Programming, Viewers, and Who's Really in Control* (Oxford: Roman & Littlefield Publishers, 2005).

24. Christina Huffington, "Women and Equal Pay: Wage Gap Still Intact, Study Says," *The Huffington Post,* accessed July 19, 2013, http://www.huffingtonpost.com/2013/04/09/women-and-equal-pay-wage-gap_n_3038806.html.

25. "I am woman, hear me shop," *BusinessWeek,* accessed October 1, 2011, http://www.businessweek.com/bwdaily/dnflash/feb2005/nf20050214_9413_db_082.htm.

26. Robin Andersen, "The Thrill is Gone: Advertising, Gender Representation, and the Loss of Desire," in *Sex & Money: Feminism and Political Economy in the Media*, ed. Eileen Meehan and Ellen Riordan (Thousand Oaks: Sage Publications, 2002), 223-239.

27. Nicole Cox, "A Little Sex Appeal Goes a Long Way: Feminist Political Economy, Commodification, and TLC's 'What Not to Wear'," *Kaleidoscope*, 10 (2011): 19-36.

28. The Real Housewives of D.C., *Welcome to the District*, TV, Bravo, 2010.

29. The Real Housewives of Beverly Hills, *It's My Party and I'll Spend If I Want To*, TV, Bravo, 2010.

30. The Real Housewives of Beverly Hills, *Charity Cases*, TV, Bravo, 2010.

31. The Real Housewives of Atlanta, *White Hot*, TV, Bravo, 2010.

32. The Real Housewives of Orange County, *Are They for Real?* TV, Bravo, 2008.

33. The Real Housewives of Orange County, Who's Your Daddy? TV, Bravo, 2009.

34. The Real Housewives of Atlanta, *My Ego is Bigger Than Your Ego*, TV, Bravo, 2009.

35. The Real Housewives of New York City, *On Their High Horses*, TV, Bravo, 2009.

36. Laurie Ouellette, "Take Responsibility for Yourself: *Judge Judy* and the Neoliberal Citizen," in *Reality TV: Remaking Television Culture*, ed. Susan Murray and Laurie Ouellette, (New York & London: New York University Press, 2009), 223-242.

37. The Real Housewives of D.C., *Foreign Relations*, TV, Bravo, 2010.

38. The Real Housewives of New Jersey, *Into the Lion's Den*, TV, Bravo, 2010.

39. Ibid.

40. The Real Housewives of Orange County, *Friends, Enemies, and Husbands*, TV, Bravo, 2009.

41. The Real Housewives of D.C., *Disloyal to the Party*, TV, Bravo, 2010.

42. The Real Housewives of Atlanta, *Throwing Shade*, TV, Bravo, 2009.

43. The Real Housewives of New Jersey, *Country Clubbed*, TV, Bravo, 2010.

44. Ibid.

45. Laurie Ouellette and James Hay, *Better Living Through Reality TV* (Malden, MA: Blackwell Publishing, 2008).

46. The Real Housewives of D.C., *Nation Building*, TV, Bravo, 2010.

47. The Real Housewives of Atlanta, *Throwing Shade*.

48. The Real Housewives of Atlanta, *Welcome One, Welcome ATL*.

49. The Real Housewives of Beverly Hills, *Life, Liberty and the Pursuit of Wealthiness*, TV, Bravo, 2010.

50. The Real Housewives of Orange County, *It's All About Choices*, TV, Bravo, 2009.

51. John Storey, "Rockin' Hegemony: West Coast Rock and Amerika's War in Vietnam," in *Cultural Theory and Popular Culture*, ed. John Storey (Harlow, England: Pearson, 2012), 88-97.

52. The Real Housewives of Orange County, *The Housewives are Back!* TV, Bravo, 2007.

53. Carina Chocano, "A Perverse, Televised, Postfeminist-feminine-status Olympics," *The New York Times Magazine*, November 2011, 58-59.

54. It is because of the personal nature of many discussions that I have chosen to omit specific user names and message board forums from direct quotes. Message board examination demonstrated that although the boards are "public," they still represent an intimate space where fans discuss a variety of very personal matters. Thus in light of producing ethical research based on responses where there is some expectation of privacy, I have listed only the series board, but not the forum thread.

55. Bury, *Cyberspaces of Their Own*.

56. Ibid, 64.

57. Cox and Proffitt, "Housewives Guide."

58. Sut Jhally and Justin Lewis, *Enlightened Racism: The Cosby Show, Audiences, and the Myth of the American Dream* (Boulder: Westview Press, 1992), 35.

59. Paul Krugman, "The Death of Horatio Alger," *The Nation*, accessed April 23, 2013, http://www.thenation.com/article/death-horatio-alger.

60. Susan Dominus, "The Affluencer," *New York Times*, accessed July 19, 2013, http://www.nytimes.com/2008/11/02/magazine/02zalaznick-t.html?pagewanted=all&_r=0.

61. Susan Douglas, *Enlightened Sexism* (New York: Times Books, 2010).

62. Marc Andrejevic, *Reality TV: The Work of Being Watched* (Oxford: Rowman & Littlefield Publishers, 2004).

63. Sharon Ross, *Beyond the Box: Television and the Internet* (Malden, MA: Blackwell Publishing, 2008), 25.

64. Stephanie Clifford, "We'll Make You a Star (if the Web Agrees)," *New York Times*, accessed April 23, 2013, http://www.nytimes.com/2010/06/06/business/06bravo.html .

65. Andrejevic, *iSpy: Surveillance and Power.*

Chapter Six

Frugal Reality TV During the Great Recession: A Qualitative Content Analysis of TLC's *Extreme Couponing*

Rebecca M. Curnalia

In 2011, The Learning Channel (TLC) introduced *Extreme Couponing* as a documentary-style reality TV program centering on the "big haul" of practically free goods people were able to purchase using coupons. The show drew steady viewership, averaging 1.9 million viewers during the first season.[1] It was also anecdotally linked to increased couponing during the Great Recession. [2] At the height of the recession, couponing increased nearly 30 percent.[3] The structure of the show followed a clear and consistent narrative pattern: each segment of the 30-minute show followed one extreme couponer. Couponers gave tours of their stockpiles, discussed how and why they couponed, then went on an "extreme" shopping trip.

Though the show had steady viewership, it also sparked controversy. Couponers' stockpiles were compared to hoarding.[4] It was argued that extreme couponers were costly for companies, and that extreme couponers took advantage of the system.[5] There was also a rise in newspaper thefts as people, allegedly inspired by the show, tried to accumulate coupons. [6]

It is difficult, if not impossible, to know whether *Extreme Couponing* caused increases in newspaper thefts and increases in couponing, particularly during a down economy when many cash-strapped consumers were looking for ways to save money. But research can and should explore elements of the show that may instruct and inspire couponers, and explain how shows like this may affect American cultural values in the new, post-recession economy. Reality TV shows like *Extreme Couponing*, that feature odd lifestyles, offer viewers the opportunity to experience extreme couponing vicariously through reality TV. At the same time, the show provided shopping tips and therefore may have made this seem like a realistic solution to people's financial problems.

This chapter presents the findings of a directed content analysis of the first season of *Extreme Couponing*. Directed analysis is used to explore content when clear categories or themes are established in advance, but researchers want to explore the latent content within existing themes.[7] I report on the elements of the show that make extreme couponing seem practical, realistic, and involving to viewers, such as show content that creates a sense of identification through parasocial interaction and homophily with the "everyday people" featured on the show. I argue that shows like *Extreme Couponing* normalize "extreme" behaviors, and in fact frame couponing as a source of financial security in a down economy. The implication of this genre of frugal lifestyle TV is that people have to take personal responsibility to protect and provide for themselves and their families during times of financial crisis.

INTERPERSONAL CONNECTIONS WITH REALITY TV CHARACTERS

Identification is a concept from rhetoric that addresses how people create a sense of similarity and difference between themselves and others through communication.[8] Consubstantiation is the process of identifying one thing with another, whereas division is the way that people are different from each other. Burke argued that "repetition" and "reinforcement" create and sustain identification. Therefore, the repetition of elements in television shows, such as the direct-to-camera self-reflections, narrative descriptions of characters' behaviors and feelings, and personal revelations prevalent in reality TV shows, may create identification. Interestingly, this identification can be positive, such as watching a show because a person sees similarities between characters on TV and him or herself. But it may also be negative, such as watching shows because viewers see themselves as significantly different from those on TV.

Media can also identify one object, idea or concept with another. For example, rhetoricians have explored the use of identification in Food Network programming.[9] Food Network programming identifies food with "good life science" in that the programming identified food with "leisure, technology, and social distinction."[10] In this programming, food preparation, presentation, and ultimately tasting creates a sense in the audience of how they too can live the good life through consumption. Other researchers have raised concerns that "transformation TV," such as *What Not to Wear*, has a similar emphasis on consumption by making people feel insecure and teaching them how to commodify themselves through self-branding.[11] *Extreme Couponing* exists in this genre of lifestyle TV that centers on identification between consumerism and "living the good life," but the show adds the twist that one can live the good life, even with limited means, by using coupons.

In media effects literature, identification is defined somewhat differently. It is perceived similarity with characters seeing things from the TV character's perspective, and having a sense of vicarious experience through TV characters.[12] People who identify with reality TV characters have learning-related motives, increased perceptions of the realism of the show, and tend to be more involved in the show's content.[13]

Media effects theorists discuss other similar concepts, including parasocial interaction and homophily. Parasocial relationships are the perceived interpersonal relationships people develop with TV characters,[14] and homophily is the perceived similarity between viewers and characters on TV.[15] Typically, these are conceptualized as individual orientations toward media that lead to involvement in content,[16] but the types of media content that may inspire these perceptions of TV characters warrants exploration.

Horton and Wohl suggested that personae, or "real" people who are also TV personalities, are particularly influential due to the "illusion of intimacy."[17] Intimacy is the sense that viewers "know" TV characters. Horton and Wohl explained that there are several characteristics of TV content that increase parasocial interaction: a) Personae offer a comfortable relationship by being dependable and predictable. This is achieved through adherence to specific production elements that make content consistent. b) The personae create an "illusion of intimacy" by being informal and conversational. c) The personae will "blur" the lines between him or herself and the audience by interacting in natural and friendly ways with other people on the program and by interacting with the viewing audience through the camera. These scripting, editing, and production elements are very common aspects of reality TV, and they also may increase media effects.

Homophily is related to the formation of parasocial relationships.[18] Homophily includes perceptions of similarity in terms of thoughts, behaviors, status, class, economic situation, and culture.[19] Homophily, then, is similar to Burke's concept of consubstantiation, or positive identification, but distinct in that it focuses specifically on similarities in background between TV characters and viewers.

I argue that features of *Extreme Couponing*—that the people are not actors, they are shown in their homes with their families and friends, and that production and editing are used to create a coherent narrative for the audience[20]—are likely to increase identification, homophily, and the development of parasocial relationships. Indeed, research has suggested that feeling an interpersonal connection with TV characters is related to regular consumption of reality TV.[21] It remains unclear, though, *how* exactly this interpersonal connection—that is, identification, homophily, and parasocial relationships—is incited by reality TV content, particularly as this "similarity" may be created and sustained by characters that live extreme or obscure lifestyles.

NORMALIZING AND TEACHING *EXTREME* BEHAVIOR

In addition to the interpersonal aspects of reality TV use, these programs are also used by viewers for personal identity reasons and for information. [22] Normalization is a concept related to the ideology embedded in television content, which explains that TV constructs popular culture through the selective representation of reality. [23] TV, in essence, teaches people how to live by imparting values. Cultural studies theorists argue that culture is created, influenced, and reinforced by the content on television, which reinforces materialist and consumer culture in the United States. Television, therefore, is a source of identity for people: We learn whom we should be by watching the carefully scripted, produced, and edited messages on TV. These messages become the codes, or cultural rules, by which we live. [24]

Perceived realism gets at the perception of the accuracy of what is depicted in TV programming, and previous research has established that realism increases effects. [25] People report learning more from reality TV shows that seem authentic, or realistic. [26] Therefore, the realism of the depiction in reality TV shows coupled with the potential to identify with the characters in these shows, may "normalize" peculiar lifestyles, as is seen in *Extreme Couponing*. They are, in effect, creating a "new normal" for middle-class Americans in this post–Great Recession economy.

The very fact that these types of shows air on "The Learning Channel" suggests that they are intended to be both entertaining and instructional: They are teaching us how we could live by showing us how others live. Boyle and Magor made this same point about shows like *Dragon's Den*, which promote and teach people about entrepreneurship. [27] They pointed out that the BBC included content on their website for the show that taught people how to start their own businesses, thus framing the show as educational. TLC has done this with *Extreme Couponing*. In addition to clips of the show and information about featured couponers, TLC's website featured tips about how to "take charge of your everyday" [28] and "family finance ideas." [29]

Therefore, the second goal of this research is to explore the nature of frugal reality TV shows by looking at *Extreme Couponing* as one example of this type of programming, and to explore the ways that American values may have been reinforced and re-envisioned in TV content during the Great Recession. The consequences of these unique features of lifestyle reality TV are that the characters and production elements in the show may be imparting or updating cultural codes at a vulnerable time in American history.

METHOD

A directed content analysis of season 1 of *Extreme Couponing* was conducted. Season 1 was selected for analysis as it set the standards for later seasons, and it was also when some recurring extreme couponers were first introduced. This season also had the highest Neilsen ratings compared to subsequent seasons.[30] In April 2011, when the show premiered, it boasted 2.06 million viewers and a 1.3/3 rating for adults age 18 to 49.[31]

A stratified sample of the first season was used. Beginning with the first episode, odd numbered episodes were analyzed. Six episodes, featuring 13 extreme couponers, were analyzed using a directed analysis. Each show had two segments, and each segment followed a different extreme couponer. The units of analysis for this study were the individual segments of the show, so there were 12 segments analyzed. The couponers included J'amie and Tiffany in Episode 1; twins Tai and Tarin and male couponer Nathan in Episode 2; Desirae and Stephanie in Episode 5; Amber and Tammilee in Episode 7; Amber and Amanda in Episode 9; and Joni and Angelique in Episode 11.

Directed analysis was used to analyze the content of each segment. Directed analysis begins by qualitatively, but objectively, coding media content into themes or categories that are defined based on existing theory and research.[32] Though it is more pre-defined than typical grounded or thematic qualitative analysis, directed analysis allows the researcher to collapse and create categories while coding, and also includes identifying themes and trends in latent content after the initial coding. Initially, the coding scheme used here included identification, parasocial interaction/intimacy, homophily, and information. After coding the first episode, it was clear that the distinction between identification and homophily was not pronounced. Those categories were collapsed, and subsequently three types of identification/homophily emerged: Identification/homophily in terms of a) behavior, b) thoughts, and c) background. Also, after initial coding, it was clear that much of the narration for the show was actually instructional rather than informative (i.e., offered explicit instructions and advice about how to coupon), and that there was also explicit discussion of common American values, or cultural codes. Therefore, these two categories were also added to the coding scheme.

RESULTS AND DISCUSSION

Building interpersonal connections

Interpersonal connections between couponers and home viewers were examined through the lens of identification (overlap in perspectives; vicarious experience), parasocial interaction (informality and intimacy), and homophily (similarities in terms of background and behavior). In general, *Extreme Couponing* had several conventions that increased the potential for these types of involvement. The couponers featured in the show were diverse, often depicted with friends and families, had a familiar backstory, described their feelings to the viewers, and were supported by onlookers in the show.

Diversity of couponers

The couponers in the show came from diverse family, racial, and socioeconomic backgrounds, and from different geographic regions. The diversity of the portrayals in the show meant that most Americans could likely identify with at least one of the featured couponers in the first season.

Couponers featured in the show were often mothers, but also included men, married couples without children, and single women. "The couponing divas," twins Tai and Tarin, were single without children and Tammilee and Amanda were both married without children. On the other hand, some of the couponers had large families to provide for, such as Joni who had nine children and Tiffany who had seven. Couponers often described how their children reacted to, or helped with, couponing, and how couponing was a way they provided for their children.

There were both Caucasian and African American couponers, and couponers were from all over the United States, including Maryland, Missouri, Illinois, Arizona, Kentucky, Washington State, Florida, Georgia, Nevada, Ohio, and New York. In Episode 7, it was acknowledged that coupons, stores, and coupon policies vary based on region, and some areas are more difficult to coupon in compared to others. In keeping with this, different couponers featured on the show used different strategies to work within their regional grocery store's coupon policy. Therefore, in addition to increasing the potential geographic homophily by moving around the country, doing so was also an instructional strategy in that it demonstrated how couponing strategies varied by region.

Couponers were also from economically diverse backgrounds, representing upper- and middle-class families, and some couponers' education and professional backgrounds were highlighted during the show. For example, Tammilee had an MBA, Amber was a full-time nurse, and Angelique was a gymnastics coach. The first couponer featured on the show, J'amie, lived in an upper-middle class home, as did Stephanie, Amber, and Joni. On the other hand, more modest middle-class-homes were also represented, such as those of Nathan, Desirae, Tammilee, Amanda and Angelique. Therefore, in terms of socioeconomic status, couponing is depicted as something fundamentally middle-class.

It is not surprising that relatively affluent, educated middle class people were featured in *Extreme Couponing* given the data available on the people who are likely to use coupons. Research conducted in 2010 suggested that college-educated, metropolitan people with household incomes over $100,000 are more likely to redeem coupons.[33] Research has also suggested that self-perceived affluence, rather than merely income, predicts coupon use.[34] This may be why each couponer appeared to be a financially stable member of the middle class, but had a personal explanation for why they used coupons.

The "economic hardship" background story

Each of the couponers explained why he or she began couponing as part of the character development at the beginning of each segment. These disclosures were typically brief, close-up, direct-to-camera personal revelations in which couponers, sometimes with great emotion, explained the circumstances that led to their couponing. For all but three of the people on the show, the reason for couponing was a personal history of economic hardship.

Three of these economic hardships were the outcome of *job losses* during the Great Recession. J'amie's husband lost his job. She explained, "I cried for two straight days" and was "really scared that I couldn't shop the way I was used to shopping . . . I wouldn't be able to go out with my girlfriends again because I wouldn't be able to afford it." In Episode 7, Amber had a similar story. She started couponing when her husband's construction company folded, and she described how she went back to work when she was seven months pregnant. She called it a "scary time," and she only "made about $200 a month." Lastly, Tammilee lost her job in management and had to "rebalance the family budget." Like J'amie, she described "being scared" and wanting to "maintain the life that we're used to." In addition to rationalizing the extreme behavior depicted in this show, these backstories that focused on job losses resonated at a time that unemployment and underemployment were persistent issues among the middle-class.

Three economic hardship stories stemmed from *growing up in families that were frugal or not financially stable.* Tai and Tarin explained that they were raised in a large family with limited means. They told the story of couponing with their mom every Sunday evening because their family of five "had to stretch their dollar." Similarly, Angelique also explained that she "grew up really poor" and "started working at a really young age" so she "didn't like the thought of spending money." These stories are also striking, as moving out of poverty and into the middle-class is a quintessential American story, and something that each of these couponers had managed to accomplish. During the Great Recession, there was a sense among those in the middle-class that they might slip backward into poverty. Indeed, many people did.[35] As early as 1989, Barbara Ehrenriech pointed out that the middle-class had anxieties about losing their tenuous grip on wealth, particularly in terms of their children not earning a place in the professional middle class.[36] During the Great Recession, these fears became realities as "one of every 12 white-collar jobs in sales, administrative support, and nonmanagerial office work vanished in the first two years of the recession; [as did] one of every six blue-collar jobs in production, craft, repair, and machine operation"[37]

The four remaining economic hardship stories had to do with *life events* that led to financial instability. Desirae described her financial difficulties after having a child and "living paycheck to paycheck." Stephanie was injured and began couponing when she was unable to work. Joni started couponing when she was going through a divorce, which she described as a "very scary moment, because as a parent you're supposed to provide for your kids." Amanda explained that she coupons because her grandma "relies on me" and that her grandma was "on a limited income."

The background stories of the people featured on *Extreme Couponing* echo the difficult circumstances of the middle class during the Great Recession. NBC News reported that the middle class was hit the hardest during the recession, with household income dropping for 13 years and extended family members increasingly relying on each other for support.[38]

Even when the stories did not center on a specific financial hardship, the struggle to pay for necessities was also a theme. The stories that did not center on economic hardship were focused on people's uses of the savings from couponing. For example, Tiffany couponed to help put her seven kids through college. Nathan explained that couponing "brought his family financial stability" and "allowed him to donate $50,000" in goods to charity. In Episode 9, Amber explained that she was the sole financial support for her family, so she and her husband collected and clipped coupons to help support their teenage boys.

Couponing as a "sport" and hobby

In addition to being a source of financial help, couponing was also framed as a fun activity. In Episode 7, Amber described it as a way to "get time to myself" and said, "it's like a video game." Nathan described himself as a "marksman" but "instead of hunting deer, I'm hunting deodorant." Later, he explained, "I'm trying to target what I'm buying." Amanda described the feeling after getting nearly $2,000 worth of groceries for less than $20 as being similar to winning in the Olympics. Angelique, on the other hand, explained that "Everybody has their hobby; couponing is mine." So, extreme couponing was depicted as an enjoyable pastime that also helped pay the bills and support the family.

Depictions with friends and family

In addition to the potential for identification and homophily based on couponers' backgrounds, and linking couponing to other types of common hobbies, the participation of the couponers' family members in the show promoted parasocial relationships. Couponers were shown interacting with their families and spouses in their homes, with family members working together clipping coupons, and with family and friends shopping. Viewers became part of the close circle of friends and family, as they were introduced to the daily lives of the couponers and went along with them on their extreme shopping trips.

Couponers were typically shown with their kids. Joni discussed how her two oldest kids had moved out, and she likes to have food for them and their significant others because it "saves them a lot of money." Her daughter told viewers that she goes by once a week, and gets essentials like shampoo and toilet paper. In Episode 9, Amber explained that she has three teenage boys "who eat a lot." In the show, her husband and her sons went shopping with her. Stephanie also had teenage sons, and her son's friends were shown shopping her stockpile. She said "My house is popular in the neighborhood. It's the house that all the kids end up at because I've got so much food." Stephanie framed the "extreme" shopping trip as an opportunity to teach her son about saving money. She observed, "I think I taught him a bunch" and "hopefully I taught him a little bit about rolling with the punches" and "taught him a lot about just how much you can get." Tiffany also framed couponing as a "family affair," and was shown couponing and shopping with her kids. These interactions build identification and homophily between the couponers and viewers, by depicting them as parents who are involved with their children and their children's friends. This also increases the sense of parasocial interaction for viewers, as people watching the show get to "know" the couponers as parents, friends, and members of the community.

Extended family members and friends were also part of the couponing experience in the show. Amanda was shown shopping with her grandma, who had given her a list of needed items. She explained, "Grandma is the most important person in my life" and "I'd do anything for her because she's done anything she could for me." Similarly, Nathan shopped with his mom, who had taught him how to coupon. She "started couponing 30 years ago." He was teased by his mom that he was "being shy" about being good at math, which helps him with his couponing. Twins Tai and Tarin were shown clipping coupons together, sharing their stockpile, and shopping together on their birthday. In the show, they showed their mother's old coupon box and explained that their mom taught them how to save money. Lastly, Desirae shopped with her friend "to catch up and so she could help with the haul" and joked with her friend throughout the trip. The interesting thing about the people who shopped with extended family members and friends is that they seemed to have a good sense of humor, further creating the sense of intimacy and closeness that is central to parasocial interaction.

Viewers were able to see characters interact with their friends and family members, were shown friends and family being part of the process of couponing, and saw others benefiting from the "big haul" and stockpiles of extreme couponers. In many ways, viewers become part of couponers' inner circle of family and friends by meeting their kids, friends, spouses, and extended family in the show, and by watching couponers interact with their family and friends. This, in addition to the glimpse inside the homes and the personal disclosures of the couponers themselves, create intimacy with viewers.

Describing thoughts and feelings

In addition to the intimate glimpse at the personal struggles and family lives of the couponers, people in the show also described their feelings throughout the show. This emotional disclosure further enhances the sense of closeness, and also allows viewers to vicariously experience the anticipation, fear, relief, then pride that couponers felt after they completed "the big haul."

When J'amie's total reached $1,000, she says, "I might start to panic a bit; that amount is not in my wallet today." She explained that she felt "pressure" and described how her heart was racing and her stomach hurt due to anxiety. Angelique described "nervousness" and feeling "scared" and that she "was up all night worrying about this." During the checkout in Episode 7, Amanda also told the camera that she was "absolutely terrified" because the total was over $1500. Some shoppers, like Joni, described feeling tired and sore due to the long shopping trip. Amanda was shown snapping her fingers at her husband and becoming aggressive as her checkout became stressful. These descriptions and depictions of couponers' thoughts and feelings allowed the viewer to vicariously experience the anxiety and thrill of the successful shopping trip, and introduced game-like elements, particularly the feelings of stress, struggle, and winning.

Ultimately, the tension is relieved and the payoff is the thrill of getting a good deal. Amber explained, "Any time I can land a really great deal, it feels like I'm on crack" and that saving money "makes me hot." The twins, who shopped on their birthday, described the check-out as "a grand finale of this great birthday." And Tiffany described her joy after checkout: "being able to say that you saved over $1,000 on groceries in a trip is pretty crazy to me." In the end, Angelique said she felt "proud of myself" for completing the transaction. This thrill at checkout may be why people who had overwhelming stockpiles continued to coupon. Stephanie described herself as "obsessed" with coupons, and that she "think[s] about them sun up to sun down." Indeed, several of the couponers described their perception of couponing as an ongoing "lifestyle" or continued "obsession." For example, Tai and Tarin said it "is definitely a lifestyle; we eat it, sleep it, breath it, dream about it."

The onlookers

Further reinforcing the sense of suspense and excitement that the couponers were describing during checkout, there were also onlookers in the grocery store who watched the checkouts, commented on them, and clapped for the extreme couponers, much like a studio audience for a game show. Onlookers said that J'amie's checkout was "just awesome" and "pretty cool," and people cheered for her when they heard her total. Both Amber, from Episode 7, and Desirae were acknowledged with clapping when they checked out too. An onlooker who watched Tiffany's checkout declared, "that's unbelievable . . . I say 'go, girl, go!'" Nathan was shown donating his extreme couponing haul to spouses of American troops who thanked him profusely for his hard work and heartfelt donation.

The people who shopped with the extreme couponers also commented on how amazing their outcomes are. Stephanie's teenage son said "She may not think it's good enough" but he thought it was "really good." Amanda's grandmother was also impressed. She said, "That's what you call being smart and savin' money" and remarked that "it's great . . . You saved me a lot of money."

The presence of onlookers and supportive family and friends creates a sense of social acceptance for the "extreme" behavior depicted in the show, suggesting that extreme savings is admirable. This reinforces the perception in viewers that they too *should* be doing this. Couponing is depicted as a praiseworthy, socially acceptable way to live. This compliments the surprisingly pronounced instructional content in the show.

INSTRUCTIONAL ELEMENTS

Each of the shows included over one dozen tips, explanations, and definitions to help viewers understand couponing, types of coupons, and coupon policies, though some tips were repeated in later shows, such as explaining "peelie" coupons, catalinas, rainchecks, and the importance of comparing price per ounce. Most of these tips came from the narrator, who provided statistics, definitions, and explanations of what the couponers were doing. But the couponers themselves also offered instructions to home viewers by describing how they accumulated, organized, and used their coupons. Featured couponers reported spending between 6 and 50 hours collecting, organizing, and using their coupons each week.

The narrative style of the show reinforced the process of couponing to help viewers understand what is involved in each step. Each segment of the show began with a tour of the people's stockpiles, discussed their strategy for collecting and organizing coupons, then showed them planning their "extreme" shopping trip, and lastly viewers watched the actual shopping trip. The repetition of this process reinforced the keys to successful couponing: organizing, planning, and being aware while shopping.

Collecting and organizing

Generally, the couponers had to have a large stockpile of coupons. Each had their own way of accumulating coupons: J'amie got hers from other people, as did Amber in Episode 7. Tiffany explained that she got hers from stores, newspapers, and the Internet. Tammilee also pointed out that "there's coupons everywhere," even places like social networks. Amanda also explained, "Always look out for items that are on sale that have coupons stuck on them." Joni was the only couponer who reported using a clipping service. Nathan, on the other hand, reported clipping 20 or more coupons at a time, presumably from newspapers.

On the more extreme end, some of the couponers went dumpster diving for coupons, such as Desirae, Amber from Episode 7, and Amber from Episode 9.

Most of the shoppers also used Internet coupons. Stephanie explained that she had five computers to print coupons from, since Internet coupons are typically limited to two prints per computer. Stephanie also reported taking the newspapers from the driveways of foreclosed homes.

Given the quantity of coupons and the need to match those coupons to sales, extreme couponers often described the need for a well-organized coupon stockpile. Tai and Tarin used a hanging file system organized by date. Nathan, on the other hand, had a bin that was organized by date and type. Other couponers used bins and binders to organize their clipped coupons by type. Having organized coupons makes planning the shopping trip somewhat easier.

Planning

There were two types of planning emphasized in the show: planning the trip and knowing how much and when to stock up on products. Couponing was described and depicted as a process that required forethought and careful planning. Most of the couponers reported using blogs and websites to help them plan their shopping trips. In addition to having a detailed list, planning also involved organizing shopping lists in the order of aisles in the store, preordering certain items to save time and be considerate of other shoppers, and sorting shopping lists into multiple transactions to maximize savings and check out more quickly.

In addition to having a plan about what to buy and how much to buy, couponers were also encouraged to know when to buy certain products and gauge how much they may need. Stephanie explained that one should know how often things go on sale and how much one is likely to use so "you know how much to buy." Later, in Episode 9, Amber clarified that things go on sale every two to three months, so people should stock up enough to get to that next sale. In Episode 7, Amber explained that grocery deals have "seasons." Tai and Tarin also pointed out that people needed to "know exactly *when* to cash in on discounts." In several episodes, the narrator explained what is worth stocking up on anytime, like mustard and frozen foods, because those foods are good for long periods of time.

Being a conscious shopper

Once couponers were at the store, the attention to detail and careful decision making continued. Throughout the show there were three lessons about being a conscious shopper while in the store: compare items, be open to trying different products, and watch everything at checkout very closely.

Compare prices. Viewers were advised to always compare the price per ounce for items, because the smaller item is often the cheapest when using a coupon. For example, Tai and Tarin pointed out that when a coupon does not restrict sizes, people should shop in the travel-sized product aisle to get the deepest discounts. They noted, "Small sizes can offer some of the biggest savings." Nathan reiterated this when he explained, "The value size is not always a value. Pay attention."

Try new things. The couponers also warned viewers against brand loyalty and encouraged viewers to be willing to try new things. For example, Angelique said that to get big savings, "you have to be willing to try a new product." Similarly, Joni pointed out that "we've learned not to be product loyal anymore. If I can get a product for free, it's gonna be just as good."

Be alert at checkout. Lastly, viewers are advised to watch everything at checkout, and make sure items ring up correctly and that all of the coupons scan correctly. Tai and Tarin explained that people must "watch every detail at checkout," which was reiterated by several other couponers, including Angelique and Amanda, who were the two top savers in the program. Couponers explained that all of the effort put into organizing and planning can be wasted if products ring up incorrectly at checkout.

Extreme couponers as lifestyle "experts"

All of the details provided by the extreme couponers about each step in their couponing trip were arranged in a narrative that had the same repetitive plot points: accumulating and organizing coupons, planning trips, consciously and comparatively shopping, then attentively checking out. Tania Lewis described this approach to lifestyle television as "popular expertise" in that seemingly "ordinary" people dispense domestic advice in reality TV programming using identification, entertainment, and instruction.[39] The practical, "lay" nature of the advice, approachability of the couponers, vicarious thrill of the shopping trip, and social support by onlookers, friends, and family, all reinforce that these featured couponers are everyday lifestyle experts, dispensing useful tips to viewers and teaching them practical ways to save money and preserve their standard of living. Therefore, the remarkable organization and focused attention of the couponers were in many ways extreme, as the title of the show implies. On the other hand, the repetition of these behaviors by couponers who were otherwise similar to many middle-class people, and the identification of this as a hobby that offers financial security made it seem rather normal and, in many respects, admirable.

CULTURAL CODES: THE IMPORTANCE OF WEALTH

As expected and in keeping with the economic climate in America, wealth and financial security were central themes in *Extreme Couponing*. J'amie, the first couponer featured on the show, was shown putting on make-up, and she said, "My image is very important to me" and she speculated that it is "the way I look that says I have a lot of money." Her comments reflected a recurring theme in *Extreme Couponing*: Coupons are a form of currency and stockpiles are a source of security, so couponing pays dividends, much like having a job. It is, therefore, framed as well worth the time, meticulous attention to detail, and organization required.

Coupons are money

Throughout the show, couponers and the narrator described their coupons as "money" and discussed their cash value. As Desirae said, "coupons to me are money; you wouldn't believe how much money people throw away." J'amie had a similar view of coupons. When showing her coupons to the camera, she said, "This is money, right here . . . I don't need money, I need these!" Angelique also described coupons as "gold."

Coupons were also described as a way to save money so that people could purchase other things that were important to them. When touring Stephanie's nice, upper-middle-class home the narrator said "It hasn't always been a party," and went on to describe how she had back problems and her husband worked two jobs. When she was laid up she started researching couponing as a way to save money. She said her husband was able to quit his second job, she has a nice new Jeep and an impressive house and explained that "all of that I got because I coupon." Similarly, Tamilee used her coupon savings to take a vacation for her husband's 40th birthday.

The most important part of the show was the finale of each segment where the total retail value of the purchases and the final purchase price were shown on the screen, revealing couponers' percentages saved. This segment drove home the financial benefits of couponing. In the episodes analyzed here, extreme couponers' percentage savings ranged from 93 percent to 103 percent. Only one shopper actually made money by shopping: Angelique received $57 in gift cards for her coupon overages on an order worth over $2,000. In a more "typical" extreme shopping trip, Joni purchased $3,159 worth of groceries for $46. Amanda also saved 99 percent, paying under $20 for $1,959 worth of groceries. In all, the idea that coupons are "like money" was reinforced when the narrator reiterated the retail value of the goods and the amounts paid.

Security in the form of a stockpile

The stockpile of goods each couponer had accumulated was also described as a type of wealth and protection from financial downturns. When discussing his stockpile, Nathan said, "It's almost like an insurance policy; you don't get paid if you lose your job and your family still has to eat. So this is what a stockpile's for." Tai and Tarin described their stockpile as being similar to a savings account: "it's all money in the bank" and "we don't look at it as pasta sauce, we look at it and see $5."

Throughout the show, the narrator enumerated the goods in each person's stockpile and estimated the retail value of the contents. Retail values ranged from around $15,000 to over $75,000, suggesting that couponing can help people amass significant "savings." In episode 9, Amber, who had a stockpile worth over $40,000, said that she feeds her family of six on $50 a week and that, "for people who don't coupon, I'd definitely say you need to start and start immediately. Why not go out and get some of these great deals that are available for anybody?" Indeed, couponing was framed as a source of security for families that any parent *should* want to provide. As Amber said in episode 7, "I'm a mom, so I want to protect and provide" and "I'm just using the resources that we have and making the most of it."

Saving money is a "job"

Given that coupons were framed as money, and stockpiles were depicted as a form of insurance or an investment in the security of the family, it was a logical extension to also frame couponing as a type of job. Tammilee, who had lost her job in management, explained, "I do apply some of the tools I used in business" such as "organization with notes and knowing what I have in my stockpile." The narrator went on to explain, "Nowadays, Tamilee uses her MBA more to monitor the supermarket [rather] than the stock market." Further reinforcing this theme, when Tammilee was checking out, one onlooker said, "That's better than a part-time job!" Similarly, Desirea argued, "It's a job, but I like doing it. If I didn't have coupons we'd probably be living paycheck to paycheck. We wouldn't be where we are today." Similarly, in Episode 7, Amber explained that she quit her job because she "earned way more" by couponing, and Stephanie's husband quit his second job because they did not need the extra income after she began couponing.

It is interesting that, at a time that unemployment hovered around 9 percent[40] and underemployment was nearly 20 percent,[41] the people in the show and the producers framed couponing as a way of *earning money* and protecting one's family from unemployment. Several features of the show, including the value of the stockpiles and demonstrating the savings realized by shoppers on the show, suggested that couponing is a job that pays well compared to other alternatives like part-time employment. Ouellette and Hay argued that reality TV is a new kind of "social work"[42] and also a new form of charity[43] for people who would have received health-related and financial help from the state before the era of federal welfare reform. Indeed, though the actual shopping trips depicted in this show were extreme, the message to Middle America was clear: You can maintain your standard of living even with unemployment and depressed wages, but it's your job to make it happen.

IMPLICATIONS

In the new economy, in which middle-class wages were depressed, wealth diminished, and long-term unemployment was persistent, frugal reality TV shows like *Extreme Couponing* place responsibility back on the middle-class for protecting and maintaining their standard of living. The show depicts couponing as a middle-class activity that many others have successfully used to overcome financial hardship. The show then provides specific strategies that anyone can use to save money while grocery shopping that are not "extreme." The supportive comments of family members and onlookers further reinforce couponing as a worthwhile and socially acceptable activity.

The findings here support the conclusion that consumerism as a cultural value was reinforced in the show, *Extreme Couponing*, though consumers were warned to be conscious and flexible. The backgrounds and personal stories of the couponers reflected traditional middle-class values, such as wanting to be secure, maintaining their standards of living, giving to others, and having nice things. These consumer values were adjusted to accommodate the reality of the "new economy" by focusing on money-saving tips. The message implied in these episodes overall was that Americans can still live the good life by being frugal. In fact, saving money by using coupons was depicted as an alternative to having a job, as a way to provide security for one's family during times of economic hardship, and a way to maintain the consumer lifestyle that is the cornerstone of American material culture. This message was delivered by diverse, middle-class people across the United States whose back stories and daily lives promote identification and homophily, and through production elements and editing throughout the show that invite viewers to have parasocial relationships with the couponers.

Thinking about other popular shows during the Great Recession, such as *Storage Wars, American Pickers, Pawn Stars, Shark Tank, Auction Hunters*, and *Hardcore Pawn*, there was a clear trend in reality TV to introduce the middle-class to new ways of living the American dream. In shows like *Extreme Couponing*, lifestyles that may have seemed peculiar, desperate, or even low-class, were depicted as acceptable, even admirable.

Frugality was reinforced by the onlookers who cheered on the extreme couponers as they checked out, the narrator explaining the simple strategies to save money while grocery shopping, and the couponers themselves revealing how much money they had saved and the other things—like college educations, new cars, and homes—they were able to pay for because of couponing.

Unfortunately, the show ignored the fact that couponing can be expensive. If people do not have money to spend on groceries, regardless of how much money could be saved using coupons, they simply do not have the means to accumulate coupons, pay the balance due, and maintain a stockpile. Purchasing multiple weekly newspapers, paying clipping services, and purchasing or building storage for stockpiles are an ongoing expense for people who live this lifestyle. The narrator in *Extreme Couponing* mentioned that one couponer spent up to $2,000 per year just to accumulate coupons, but that was the only expense other than time mentioned in the shows analyzed here.

By glossing over the very real costs of couponing in general, and extreme couponing in particular, the show offers an unrealistic and unattainable panacea to the economic hardships plaguing Americans. Indeed, these everyday lifestyle experts may have further undermined empathy for the working poor and impoverished, as the tone of the show suggested that couponing is something that anyone can do if they are willing to put in the effort. This subtle message may further reinforce the post-welfare era American belief that hard work and persistence can help people dig themselves out during an economic collapse. Indeed, as the Great Recession continued, public support for government "safety net" programs steadily declined.[44] Further, as employment prospects improved, people became less supportive of welfare programs.[45] Joni, who donated most of her extreme shopping trip spoils to charity, pointed out at the end of her segment, "There is no reason people should go hungry today. We walked out with over $3,100 worth of stuff for $45. If we can do it, anyone can do it." The subtext of the advice about saving money to maintain one's lifestyle is that people need only plan, organize, and be conscious consumers to survive the worst economic downturn since the Great Depression.

REFERENCES

Barker, Chris. *Cultural Studies* (3rd ed.). Thousand Oaks: Sage, 2008.

Bonner, Jessie L. "'Extreme Couponing' Inspires Cult of Grocery Store Savers" *Huffington Post*, accessed on February 5, 2013, http://www.huffingtonpost.com/2011/07/07/extreme-couponing-grocery-stores_n_892069.html.

Boyle, Raymond and Maggie Magor, "A Nation of Entrepreneurs? Television, Social Change, and the Rise of the Entrepreneur," *International Journal of Media and Cultural Politics* 4 (2008): 125-144.

Burke, Kenneth. *A Rhetoric of Motives.* Berkley: UC Press, 1969.

Busselle, Rick W. "Television Exposure, Perceived Realism, and Exemplar Accessibility in the Social Judgment Process," *Media Psychology* 3 (2001), 43-67.

Davidson, Merle M., "Extreme Couponing Goes too Far," *Editor & Publisher* 144 (2011): 58.

Dougherty, Sheila. "Flat-out Greed Outweighs Savvy Frugality in TLC's *'Extreme Couponing,'*" *Advertising Age* 82 (2011): 13.

Godlewski, Lisa R. and Elizabeth M. Perse, "Audience Activity and Reality Television: Identification, Online Activity, and Satisfaction," *Communication Quarterly* 58 (2010): 148-169.

Ehrenreich, Barbara. *Fear of Falling: The Inner Life of the Middle Class.* New York: Pantheon, 1989.

Eyal, Keren and Alan M. Rubin, "Viewer Aggression and Homophily, Identification, and Parasocial Relationships with Television Characters," *Journal Of Broadcasting & Electronic Media* 47 (2003): 77-98.

"Extreme Couponing Fades Away—For Good?" accessed on February 5, 2013, http://couponsinthenews.com/2012/12/06/extreme-couponing-fades-away-for-good/

Gorman, Bill. "TLC premiers second season of *Extreme Couponing*," TV By the Numbers, accessed February 5, 2013, http://tvbythenumbers.zap2it.com/2011/09/01/tlc-premieres-second-season-of-extreme-couponing/102251/

Hall, Alice. "Perceptions of the Authenticity of Reality Programs and Their Relationships to Audience Involvement, Enjoyment, and Perceived Learning," *Journal of Broadcasting & Electronic Media* 53 (2009): 515-531.

Hearn, Alison. "Insecure: Narratives and Economies of the Branded Self in Transformation Television," *Continuum: Journal of Media & Cultural Studies* 22 (2008): 495.

Hsieh, Hsiu-Fang and Sarah E. Shannon, "Three Approaches to Qualitative Content Analysis," *Qualitative Health Research* 15 (2005): 1277-1288.

Horton, Donald and R. Richard Wohl. "Mass-Communication and Para-Social Interaction: Observations on Intimacy and Distance," *Psychiatry* 12 (1956): 215-229.

Hutchinson, Kevin L., "The Effects of Newscaster Gender and Vocal Quality on Perceptions of Homophily and Interpersonal Attraction," *Journal of Broadcasting* 26 (1982): 457-467.

Jervis, Rick. "Crazy for Coupons, Man Stockpiles Goods," *USA Today* (August 18, 2011): 03a.

Klein, Ezra. "Wonkbook: The Real Unemployment Rate is 11 Percent," *Washington Post*, accessed April 30, 2013, http://www.washingtonpost.com/blogs/wonkblog/post/wonkbook-the-real-unemployment-rate-is-11-percent/2011/12/12/gIQAuctPpO_blog.html.

The Learning Channel. "Take Charge of Your Everyday," accessed on February 5, 2013, http://tlc.howstuffworks.com/home/takecharge.htm.

———. "Family Finance," accessed on February 5, 2013, http://tlc.howstuffworks.com/family/family-finance.htm

Lewis,Tania, *Smart Living: Lifestyle Media and Popular Expertise*. New York: Peter Lang Publishing, 2008.

Margalit, Yotam. "Explaining Social Policy Preferences: Evidence from the Great Recession," *American Political Science Review* 107 (2013): 80-103.

McCroskey, James C., Virginia P. Richmond, and John A. Daly, "The Development of a Measure of Perceived Homophily in Interpersonal Communication," *Human Communication Research* 1 (1975): 323-332.

Meister, Mark. "Cultural Feeding, Good Life Science, and the TV Food Network," *Mass Communication & Society* 4 (2001): 165-182.

Mittal, Banwari. "An Integrated Framework for Relating Diverse Consumer Characteristics to Supermarket Coupon Redemption," *Journal of Marketing Research* 31 (1994): 533-544.

Nabi, Robin L., Erica N. Biely, Sara J. Morgan, and Carmen R. Stitt, "Reality-Based Television Programming and the Psychology of Its Appeal," *Media Psychology* 5 (2003): 303-330.

O'Donnell, Victoria. *Television Criticism*. Los Angeles: Sage, 2007.

Ouellette, Laurise and James Hay, *Better Living Through Reality TV*. Malden: Blackwell Publishing, 2008.

Peck, Don. "Can the Middle Class Be Saved?" *The Atlantic*, accessed May 1, 2013, http://www.theatlantic.com/magazine/archive/2011/09/can-the-middle-class-be-saved/308600/.

Pew Research Center for the People & The Press, "Partisan Polarization Surges in Bush, Obama Years: Trends in American Values: 1987-2012," accessed May 9, 2013 http://www.people-press.org/2012/06/04/section-4-values-about-government-and-the-social-safety-net/.

Schoen, John W. "Great Recession Still Slamming the Middle Class," NBC News, accessed April 28, 2013, http://www.nbcnews.com/business/economywatch/great-recession-still-slamming-middle-class-994834.

Seidman, Robert. "Wednesday Cable Ratings: 'Extreme Couponing,' 'Storage Wars' Lead Night + 'Real World,' 'Justified,' 'Mythbusters' & More," accessed on February 8, 2013, http://tvbythenumbers.zap2it.com/2011/04/07/wednesday-cable-ratings-extreme-couponing-storage-wars-lead-night-real-world-justified-mythbusters-more/88695/.

Turner, John R. "Interpersonal and Psychological Predictors of Parasocial Interaction with Different Television Performers," *Communication Quarterly* 41 (1993): 443-453.

United States Department of Labor Bureau of Labor Statistics, "Labor Force Statistics from the Current Population Survey," accessed April 30, 2013 http://data.bls.gov/timeseries/LNS14000000

Webley, Kayla. "Extreme Couponing," *Time* 178 (2011): 36.

"Well-off and Well-coiffed Adults use Coupons More, New Research Shows," *Business Wire*, accessed April 28, 2013, http://www.businesswire.com/portal/site/home/permalink/?ndmViewId=news_view&newsId=20100525006709&newsLang=en.

NOTES

1. Bill Gorman, "TLC premiers second season of *Extreme Couponing*," TV By the Numbers, accessed February 5, 2013, http://tvbythenumbers.zap2it.com/2011/09/01/tlc-premieres-second-season-of-extreme-couponing/102251/.

2. Jessie. L. Bonner, "'Extreme Couponing' Inspires Cult of Grocery Store Savers," *Huffington Post*, accessed on February 5, 2013, http://www.huffingtonpost.com/2011/07/07/extreme-couponing-grocery-stores_n_892069.html.

3. Kayla Webley, "Extreme Couponing," *Time*, 178 (2011), 36.

4. Sheila Dougherty. "Flat-out Greed Outweighs Savvy Frugality in TLC's '*Extreme Couponing*,'" *Advertising Age* 82 (2011), 13.

5. Merle Davidson, M., "Extreme Couponing Goes too Far," *Editor & Publisher* 144 (2011), 58.

6. Rick Jervis, "Crazy for Coupons, Man Stockpiles Goods," *USA Today*, August 18, 2011, 03a.

7. Hsiu-Fang Hsieh and Sarah E. Shannon, "Three Approaches to Qualitative Content Analysis," *Qualitative Health Research* 15 (2005), 1281.

8. Kenneth Burke. *A Rhetoric of Motives* (Berkley, CA: UC Press, 1969), 21-26.

9. Mark Meister, "Cultural Feeding, Good Life Science, and the TV Food Network," *Mass Communication & Society*, 4 (2001), 165-182.

10. Ibid, 173.

11. Alison Hearn. "Insecure: Narratives and Economies of the Branded Self in Transformation Television," *Continuum: Journal of Media & Cultural Studies* 22 (2008), 495.

12. Lisa R. Godlewski and Elizabeth M. Perse, "Audience Activity and Reality Television: Identification, Online Activity, and Satisfaction," *Communication Quarterly*, 58 (2010), 151.

13. Ibid, 159.

14. Donald Horton and R. Richard Wohl. "Mass-Communication and Para-Social Interaction: Observations on Intimacy and Distance," *Psychiatry* 12 (1956), 215.

15. Hutchinson, K. L., "The Effects of Newscaster Gender and Vocal Quality on Perceptions of Homophily and Interpersonal Attraction," *Journal of Broadcasting* 26 (1982), 457-467.

16. Keren Eyal and Alan M. Rubin, "Viewer Aggression and Homophily, Identification, and Parasocial Relationships with Television Characters," *Journal of Broadcasting & Electronic Media* 47 (2003), 77.

17. Donald Horton and R. Richard Wohl, "Mass-Communication and Para-Social Interaction," 216.

18. John R. Turner, "Interpersonal and Psychological Predictors of Parasocial Interaction with Different Television Performers," *Communication Quarterly* 41 (1993), 447.

19. James C. McCroskey, Virginia P. Richmond, and John A. Daly, "The Development of a Measure of Perceived Homophily in Interpersonal Communication," *Human Communication Research* 1 (1975), 323-332.

20. Robin L. Nabi, Erica N. Biely, Sara J. Morgan, and Carmen R. Stitt, "Reality-Based Television Programming and the Psychology of Its Appeal." *Media Psychology* 5 (2003), 304.

21. Ibid, 321.

22. Ibid, 321.

23. Chris Barker, *Cultural Studies* (3rd ed.), (Thousand Oaks, CA: Sage, 2008), 9.

24. Victoria O'Donnell, *Television Criticism*, (Los Angeles, CA: Sage, 2007), 158.

25. Busselle, R. W. "Television Exposure, Perceived Realism, and Exemplar Accessibility in the Social Judgment Process," *Media Psychology* 3 (2001), 43-67.

26. Alice Hall, "Perceptions of the Authenticity of Reality Programs and Their Relationships to Audience Involvement, Enjoyment, and Perceived Learning," *Journal of Broadcasting & Electronic Media* 53 (2009), 527.

27. Raymond Boyle and Maggie Magor, "A Nation of Entrepreneurs? Television, Social Change, and the Rise of the Entrepreneur," *International Journal of Media and Cultural Politics* 4 (2008), 138.

28. The Learning Channel, "Take Charge of Your Everyday," accessed on February 5, 2013, http://tlc.howstuffworks.com/home/takecharge.htm.

29. The Learning Channel, "Family Finance," accessed on February 5, 2013, http://tlc.howstuffworks.com/family/family-finance.htm.

30. "Extreme Couponing Fades Away—For Good?" accessed on February 5, 2013, http://couponsinthenews.com/2012/12/06/extreme-couponing-fades-away-for-good/.

31. Robert Seidman, "Wednesday Cable Ratings: 'Extreme Couponing,' 'Storage Wars' Lead Night + 'Real World,' 'Justified,' 'Mythbusters' & More," accessed on February 8, 2013http://tvbythenumbers.zap2it.com/2011/04/07/wednesday-cable-ratings-extreme-couponing-storage-wars-lead-night-real-world-justified-mythbusters-more/88695/.

32. Hsiu-Fang Hsieh and Sarah E. Shannon, "Three Approaches to Qualitative Content Analysis," 1281.

33. "Well-off and Well-coiffed Adults use Coupons More, New Research Shows," *Business Wire*, accessed April 28, 2013, http://www.businesswire.com/portal/site/home/permalink/?ndmViewId=news_view&newsId=20100525006709&newsLang=en.

34. Banwari Mittal, "An Integrated Framework for Relating Diverse Consumer Characteristics to Supermarket Coupon Redemption," *Journal of Marketing Research* 31 (1994), 541.

35. Don Peck, "Can the Middle Class Be Saved?" *The Atlantic*, accessed May 1, 2013, http://www.theatlantic.com/magazine/archive/2011/09/can-the-middle-class-be-saved/308600/.

36. Barbara Ehrenreich, *Fear of Falling: The Inner Life of the Middle Class* (New York, NY: Pantheon, 1989), 262-263.

37. Don Peck, "Can the Middle Class Be Saved?" 1.

38. John W. Schoen, "Great Recession Still Slamming the Middle Class," NBC News, accessed April 28, 2013, http://www.nbcnews.com/business/economywatch/great-recession-still-slamming-middle-class-994834.

39. Tania Lewis, *Smart Living: Lifestyle Media and Popular Expertise* (New York, NY: Peter Lang Publishing, 2008), 4-6.

40. United States Department of Labor Bureau of Labor Statistics, "Labor Force Statistics from the Current Population Survey," accessed April 30, 2013 http://data.bls.gov/timeseries/LNS14000000.

41. Ezra Klein, "Wonkbook: The Real Unemployment Rate is 11 Percent," *Washington Post*, accessed April 30, 2013, http://www.washingtonpost.com/blogs/wonkblog/post/wonkbook-the-real-unemployment-rate-is-11-percent/2011/12/12/gIQAuctPpO_blog.html.

42. Laurise Ouellette and James Hay, *Better Living Through Reality TV* (Malden, MA: Blackwell Publishing, 2008), 64-66.

43. Ibid, 38-39.

44. Pew Research Center for the People & The Press, "Partisan Polarization Surges in Bush, Obama Years: Trends in American Values: 1987-2012," accessed May 9, 2013 http://www.people-press.org/2012/06/04/section-4-values-about-government-and-the-social-safety-net/.

45. Yotam Margalit, "Explaining Social Policy Preferences: Evidence from the Great Recession," *American Political Science Review* 107 (2013), 80.

Chapter Seven

Bigger, Fatter, Gypsier[1]: Gender Spectacles and Cultural Frontlines in *My Big Fat American Gypsy Wedding*

Gordon Alley-Young

My Big Fat American Gypsy Wedding's (*MBFAGW's*) use of gypsy, a slur to some, implies a singular culture. Gypsy or gipsie is Middle English for Egyptian though ethnic Roma originate from the Indian subcontinent.[2] Irish Travellers, (gypsies, tinkers, or travellers), are nomads with roots in fifth century Ireland[3] who, DNA suggests, are a unique ethnicity.[4] Understanding these groups' cultural, linguistic and social histories will facilitate analyzing their popular representation in *MBFAGW*.

ROMA AND TRAVELLERS: A SHARED HISTORY OF MARGINALIZATION

The Roma arrived in the Middle East around 1000AD from the Indian sub-continent for unknown reasons.[5] Roma migrated across Europe and around the world. Fourteenth-and fifteenth-century Romanian and Spanish documents mention *gypsies'* metalwork and names their homeland as Little Egypt: location unknown.[6] Early Roma claimed they were exiled nobility.[7]

From the 1400s European nations exiled and/or restricted Roma dress, language and culture.[8] In 1600s Portugal, Roma were used to replace or to be sexual companions for colonists in Africa.[9] Meanwhile in Britain, Oliver Cromwell's land seizures and Catholicism ban[10] and later the Irish famine[11] lead Travellers to emigrate. McVeigh argues that the Travellers were a distinct nomadic group before the famine and thus ethnically distinct from Irish famine exiles.[12]

Englishman Jacob Bryant studied the Roma language in 1776, noting Indo-Iranian similarities and Greek/Slavic loan words.[13] In 1777, German Johann Rudiger saw Roma as Hindi, while others correctly noted Punjabi.[14] The Travellers' language, Shelta, uses modified Gaelic and English words and grammar.[15] Both languages are not shared with outsiders, and this creates suspicion and hostility.

Fischel estimates there were 1.5 million Roma in pre-WWII Europe,[16] and they helped the Jews during WWII (e.g., Bulgaria). The Nazis banned *gypsy* intermarriages, ordered their sterilization[17] and sent them to separate camps in places like Auschwitz.[18] The Roma Holocaust is estimated at 200,000-500,000 or more.[19] Such mistreatment and bias have likely contributed to the Travellers' and Roma's insular cultural orientations.

Both groups currently face rejection. In 2004, Ireland stated that Travellers were not an ethnicity, effectively limiting legal recognition of racism against them. Yet, legal recognition does not eliminate racism as the Roma's example illustrates.[20] In 2009, France paid Roma to leave the country.[21] England evicted 86 Traveller families in 2011 from their land;[22] others had already been moved to build Olympic facilities.[23] In the United States, Maryland's 2008 ban on fortune telling was challenged as anti-Roma.[24]

The cultures do share characteristics. Both emphasize self-employment, wealth displays and borrowing money inside the community.[25] Both often emphasize a clean house that excludes pets.[26] Both are often Christian,[27] though Catholic Travellers are conspicuous in the Protestant US South.[28] Despite similarities, reductive labels like *gypsy* overlook both groups' historical and cultural differences.[29] Most people only know *gypsies* through popular culture.[30] An early fortune teller depiction appears in Dutch painter Bosch's *The Haywain Triptych* (1510).[31] Early European representations of Roma show dark skin, long hair, earrings and "outlandish attire."[32] Early Traveller depictions show an exotic other that Burke argues is closer to mainstream Irish identities than is acknowledged.[33]

Modern media depict Travellers as romantic nomads and serial criminals like the TV series *The Riches*.[34] Similarly, Nat Geo TV depicted Roma as mafia-like in the reality series *American Gypsies*, drawing threats of civil action.[35] Most of the United States' estimated one million Roma avoid publicity, fearing the bias they historically faced in Europe.[36] The US's estimated 12,000 Travellers receive media attention out of proportion to their modest population.[37]

MBFAGW AS A POPULAR CULTURAL TEXT FOR ANALYSIS AND CRITIQUE

MBFAGW's women are objectified as frontiers/lands and this affects how they are treated in society. Roma and Travellers face more poverty and domestic violence with less education[38]; their children are often bullied.[39] Media stereotypes are used to justify this violence.[40] Smith argues that technology brings us into closed cultures, like the Roma, while creating misrepresentations that influence for generations.[41] *MBFAGW*'s first season drew 1.6 million viewers per episode and inspired two specials and a second season.[42] While the series is new it relies upon the same, stereotypical "outlandish attire"[43] and exotic other imagery found in Europe's earliest popular representations of Roma and Travellers.[44]

This study uses Objectification Theory to argue "women are treated *as bodies*," here bodies of land or frontiers "that exist for the use and pleasure of others."[45] Women in *MBFAGW* are thus constructed, protected, claimed, inhabited or visited like frontiers/lands. Post-colonial and Feminist theories provide insight into women's conflation with land. Archetype Theory helps to unpack *MBFAGW*'s frontier/land constructions that rely upon "primordial or archaic images" that speak to our culture's collective unconscious and inform our ideas of virtue (e.g., mothers), villain (e.g., shadow/whore) and our gender roles (e.g., anima/animus).[46]

PROTOCOLS FOR ANALYZING POPULAR CULTURE

Fiske studies are popular on three levels. The first is the primary text, in this case, the first season of *MBFAGW*.[47] Secondary analysis examines publicity (e.g., commercials) and criticism of the series' prominent and obscured themes. An article charging the British series with racism that discourages viewing is clearly criticism.[48] Yet audiences will watch when asked not to. An article mocking two stars of the British series while urging audiences to tune in is arguably promotion wrapped in criticism.[49] The third level of analysis examines audience responses (e.g., satire, fantasy, debate, creation) on online message boards.

The textual levels are connected and mutually influential. For example, viewers go online to support/refute/qualify criticisms and publicity. Series producers then respond to this audience discussion in how they construct future episodes of the series. The textual levels thus are a cycle or as some have described popular culture, a "circuit."[50]

This study reports capta, socially constructed knowledge,[51] to address three questions: (1) How does *MBFAGW* construct women's bodies as cultural frontiers/lands? (2) What are the socio-cultural implications of

MBFAGW's constructions of women? (3) How can existing analyses of real-ity TV help us to interpret this series? This is a study of *MBFAGW's* first season (eight 42-44 minute episodes), notable criticism and publicity texts and online postings. Analysis of the series finds four representational catego-ries of woman as cultural frontiers or lands. These representations are woman as (1) Virgin Territory, (2) Motherland, (3) No-Man's-Land and (4) Tourist Attraction. The subsequent discussion defines the categories using textual evidence that is read through a lens of critical scholarship and theory.

FINDINGS AND ANALYSIS OF REPRESENTATIONAL CATEGORIES

Representation One: Woman as Virgin Territory

Virgin territory has not been touched, explored or developed and takes time to access. *MBFAGW's* brides are valued like a frontier is for being un-touched. De Beauvoir argues, "A virgin body has the freshness of secret springs, the morning sheen of an unopened flower, the orient luster of a pearl on which the sun has never shone."[52] Landscape makes this territory treach-erous, "Virgin lands have always fascinated explorers; mountain-climbers are killed each year because they wish to violate an untouched peak."[53]

The virgin territories of *MBFAGW* sit atop symbolic mountains of bridal skirt built of (rhine)stone and fabric that keep their grooms at a distance. The dress becomes an impermeable feature of the landscape (body) that restricts its contamination. Episode one's Shyanne wears 14,000 stones. Her groom must contort himself over this mountain to get a brief, chaste kiss at the altar. The bride's mother warns her to do no more than kiss on her wedding night. The groom must let nature take its course if he is to conquer this territory.

Post-colonial theorists argue that the native woman's body is a frontier conquest to the Western man. Fanon argues that French men abolished the veil in Algeria to possess the women, if only visually.[54] Cultural outsiders express this same territoriality about Roma/Traveller woman. In response to charges of *MBFAGW's* racism on www.romanichal.net "Luther" (June 8, 2012) writes, "Where can I buy one of those Romanichal chicks for my club?"[55] The comment degrades the women but also shows his desire to possess them visually in his strip club. On Internet Movie Database (IMDb) "Sacknballs" (June 20, 2012) writes, "They may not be whores, but they are wearing whore's uniforms."[56] This comment reflects both society's harsh judgment of and attempts to regulate public displays of female sexuality.

MBFAGW's brides are the maiden archetype, the female protagonist of fairy tales like *Sleeping Beauty* and *Rapunzel* where the hero knight, who conquers lands for his monarch, now seeks a virgin body of land of his own. The groom, like the knight, must cut through swathes of brush (crinoline) or scale her mountain peak (rhinestone skirt) to claim his prize. A land claim requires that the knight must leave his mark on the land. Shyanne's dress is 75 pounds. and she tapes her hips with gauze to minimize scarring. This mark is a blemish on the virgin territory and stakes the claim of its owner. In the British series, brides tape disposable diapers to their hips. Literally the bride is back in diapers, and like a new baby, she is symbolically reborn and clean.

Even a glimpse of virgin territory is thrilling. As Shyanne reaches the church in her carriage her grandmother exclaims, "Here it comes. It's coming, look!" Shyanne becomes an undiscovered heavenly body, an untouched ice floe that floats into sight. Once occupied, man transforms this land. De Beauvoir writes, "Grotto, temple, sanctuary, secret garden—man, like the child, is fascinated by enclosed and shadowy places [. . .] which wait to be given a soul: what he alone is to take and to penetrate seems to be in truth created by him."[57] Gliatto evokes the secret garden when reviewing *MBFAGW* for *People Magazine* by describing the dresses as "the only romantic bloom allowed" to women.[58] The power of virgin territory is an illusion. Man alone will inhabit and give her a soul. Without him she is fallow land or no-man's-land.

MBFAGW constructs passive women and conquering men. Brides are immobilized land waiting for men to claim them. In episode eight, bride Nettie struggles with her dress stating, "It's just so hard to move. I need help at all times." Nettie's dress foreshadows the social immobility she will experience in a patriarchal world. Those who would not immobilize themselves are audience members to others' immobilization. On www.romanichal.net "Coco" (June 13, 2012) writes, "I have been watching the show, and although I find it entertaining [. . .] I know its [sic] not good for the people its [sic] portraying."[59] On the same site "Petra" (June 8, 2012) writes, "Though I'm far from stupid I fell for it" and "Shelby" (July 3, 2012) offers, "Sorry for my part in condoning the disrespect to all of you by watching it at all."[60] Viewers' comments, like those of some media critics,[61 62 63] either reject the US/UK series or atone for watching it, yet they do participate in the women's domination by watching and (inadvertently) promoting it via their comments. Viewers and critics, by participating in another's cultural domination, called hegemony,[64] reflect their own cultural domination by the media.

Virgin territory is always in viewers' minds as they constantly map the virginity of the bride's bodies in language. In an analysis of 175 online postings made on Amazon[65] and IMDb,[66] words describing women's sex or sexuality appeared 102 times. Words describing women not having sex or not acting sexually include virgin(ity) (11 mentions); self-respect(ing) (5 mentions); modesty (3 mentions); good, moral (2 mentions); boundaries, chaste, good, ladylike, new, old maid, pure, self-esteem, self-preservation, self-righteous, waiting (1 mention). Excluding "new," (an object) and the pejorative "old maid," these words are positively connoted and/or describe positive actions/states. Words describing women having sex or acting sexually include whore(ish) (15 mentions); sex—includes variations (8 mentions); object, double standard(s), slut(s/iest) (3 mentions); bra, dirty, filthy, grinding, nipple(s), skimp(y), smutty, stripper(esque) (2 mentions); ass, booty, bootie, butt, cock tease, Johns, mate, navel, paraded around, penetration, promiscuous, prostitute, satisfying, sin, skank, skeeves, STD, target practice, unbuttoned, used (1 mention). These are words negatively connoted, used in a negative context and/or used to keep the discussion focused on women's sexual excess.

Virgin territory brides possess fantasy power that stems from the patriarchal power that immobilizes and objectifies. Large dresses are mistaken for real social power. The power of the fantasy is undeniable as we see in episode two when father Pat Baby and his 14-year-old daughter Priscilla switch gender archetypes. Seeing her coming-out dress, Priscilla slips into her male archetype (animus) stating, "It's so pretty I want to kiss it." The altar is where a *gypsy* girl receives her first kiss. Meanwhile, her father evokes his feminine archetype (anima) stating, "It makes me wish I was a cross-dresser." Pat Baby comments that he wants to temporarily inhabit women's fantasy power space but only temporarily. Priscilla's comment projects her as the groom who takes control by kissing "it," the virgin land. The power of the male is clear in this fantasy. Priscilla does not need the pretext of cross-dressing to choose the animus.

Constructing women as virgin territory is the work of series producers, critics and audiences. We cannot deny the role of the series' subjects who participate in the constructions. The ideologies underlying these media constructions predate our nation, though have since become pervasive in the Roma, Traveller and US culture. In the subsequent representations, virgin territory is transformed into different, though still problematic, landscapes.

Representation Two: Woman as Motherland

From *MBFAGW's* perspective, Roma/Traveller men compensate for a nomadic life by creating a physical/psychological homeland out of their wives. The Roma/Traveller wife assumes partial responsibility for defending this land from others. Though her children might leave her temporarily, the motherland is never truly devoid of life to care for. Culturally, Mother Nature has long symbolized women's life-giving and nurturing capacities, but *MBFAGW* constructs motherland as the only socially accepted option for a virgin territory after marriage.

Motherland imagery is not new. Mayo personified India as a downtrodden mother.[67] Gandhi reinterpreted Mayo's book, derided as racist, personifying Mother India as woman's role in India's independence battle. Gandhi's Mother India wears homespun cloth, as do her children, is a guardian of tradition and stands for chastity, purity, self-sacrifice and suffering.[68]

We see the virtues of Mother India throughout *MBFAGW*'s first season episodes as the women give of themselves, exuding purity and domesticity. The motherland feeds her people through tradition (family recipes), self-sacrifice (women are shown dieting on vegetables and vinegar) and resource-fulness (stretching a food source). In episode four, Laura teaches Amber how to feed many with little; Laura revels in being productive and multiplying her resources. Ritualized cleaning represents the purity of Mother India and on another hand, the woman's body blurs into domestic surfaces as she becomes them through her ritual. She transmits cultural virtues enforcing chastity (e.g., Mellie is chaperoned on a date) and honor. For instance, a commercial "sneak peek," meant to attract viewers to a post-season-one special, focuses solely on Nettie and Mellie preparing to fight others to defend their family's honor.

Similar to Mother India, Mother Ireland representations date from the 9th century poem "The Hag of Beare."[69] Kearns notes, "She has been invaded and betrayed [. . .] the diaspora is a result of her suffering. Mother Ireland has been abandoned and fallen victim to famine."[70] Similarly, *MBFAGW* constructs Roma/Traveller women as a safe haven from US society to which man can to return and from which he can never be exiled. In episode six, Heath and Alyssa buy a trailer home as Heath must travel to find work. Alyssa is motherland, a piece of home that he will always have with him wherever he is. Similarly Nettie (episode 4) is the archetypal mother image taking in any family member needing her care, including her divorced sister Mellie. Heart imagery is evident in several dresses, notably in a coming, out dress for Priscilla, in episode two. Though only fourteen and neither a wife nor a mother, foregrounding the heart constructs Priscilla as a potential future motherland. The motherland construction transforms women into a place where a young man's symbolic heart yearns to return (i.e., the heartland) while it also constructs him as an exile in a foreign land.

People grow and thrive from the motherland's resources and energy, which it is expected that she will give freely. The dresses she wears as a bride foretell her motherland destiny. The dresses highlight her fruitfulness and reproductive vigor in her ample bosom and hips that demonstrate her capac-ity for suffering under the weight of many children by bearing 75-pound dresses. Dresses exaggerate the fullness of hips to the extreme. They become not the hips of single women but hips big enough to bear a people's approval. The bodice is more prominent through the addition of jewels symbolic of the wealth of the motherland's people and the resources available to nurture her future generations. In episode five, cultural outsider Tamara holds a jewelry party to show the wealth that her infant Jackson will benefit from as a future marriage prospect. She sits in a jeweled gown as community members come by to survey her as much as they survey the jewelry. A motherland's resources must be affirmed as plentiful.

Like the Mother Nature archetype, the motherland is a landscape that has survived difficult seasons. In episode seven, we meet Annie who has been rhetorically frozen out of the community for breaking the rules and having a child before marriage with her cousin. At her wedding Annie, already a mother, appears in a winter snowflake dress, her body, a landscape for seasons and a territory symbolically enduring with struggle, a nod perhaps to her own Spartan living conditions. Annie, like the motherland, is shaped by the seasons and by her society.

Post-colonial theorist Mohanram argues that woman is central to the embodiments of nations because of the role her body plays in reproducing the nation but paradoxically in this discourse, she is denied agency.[71] Katrak similarly critiques how Gandhi's Mother India's imagery is restricted to the domestic sphere as her emancipation becomes secondary to nation building.[72] *MBFAGW* constructs Roma/Traveller women as choosing to become motherland, existing solely for the benefit of men and children. In reality, the series minimizes the fact that motherland is the sole socially acceptable role that the woman is allowed to play—unlike Mother Ireland whose children are exiled by famine, the motherland is never separated from her children. In episode eight, Laurel remarks, "Romney women never escape our kids." The word "escape" disrupts the series' altruistic construction of women as all-giving motherland and hints at Laurel and other women's desire to leave the motherland for an individual identity and singular personhood—desires that the series either overlooks or deems selfish.

Audience members posting on IMDb[73] question the health of the children's upbringing, express wishes to see the young women in college and question the legality of the lifestyle and parenting practices. As much as this study also asks critical questions about how women are constructed and portrayed, it is not the place of those cultural outsiders to save the women. This is disempowering to the women as this makes the decisions for them just as Mayo argues for Britain to rescue Mother India.[74] Western society at the time of Mother India and Mother Ireland placed the same restrictions on women as Woolf argues that her writing career was plagued by an archetype called the Angel of the House "who was so constituted that she never had a mind or a wish of her own."[75] The motherland exists because of this Angel and, whatever we might call her, she is not the exclusive property of Roma/Traveller culture; she is alive and living in the United States.

The Motherland construction creates misunderstanding of the power that women have to shape the culture. Constructing Roma/Traveller women as a nationalistic saints is perhaps meant to overcome existing stereotypes of poor personal hygiene and lacking morals but in so doing it develops new misconceptions. The construction is an altruistic one that precludes individual subjectivity and passes the onus on for future generations of women to follow suit. *MBFAGW* personifies motherland in its representation of Nettie as altruistically sustaining family life and cultural values in contrast to no-man's-land, a land that is undomesticated at best and self-annihilating at worst as exemplified in episode four's "Wild Gypsy Mellie."

Representation Three: Woman as No-Man's-Land

No-man's-land was the name for the land between two opposing soldiers' trenches in WWI. Persico notes the 14th-century origins of the word stating, "The term was believed to have been used originally to define a contested territory or a dumping ground for refuse between provinces and fiefdoms."[76] If Motherland is the preferred archetype constructed for Roma/Traveller wives, then no-man's-land is the shadow that lies below the surface. On one hand, she is tempting to men, because in a culture where women are defined by their connection to men she is not under any man's control, but she threatens to castrate the men who wander in her midst.

As a divorced woman, Mellie is "used" in the eyes of her community. In episode one, groom Michael only accepts his bride Shyanne because she is "clean" stating, "I want something new, I don't want something used." *Gorger* (*non-gypsy*) men are kept away from the Motherland or virgin territory, but the borders are relaxed around Mellie as a *gorger* man attempts to court her. In both the *gorger* and *gypsy* cultures she is framed as a dumping ground for each culture's refuse. In episode five, a car speeds by a group of *gypsy* women, of which Mellie is a part, and ambush them yelling, "Dirty little sluts!" The verbal refuse lands on Mellie who is shown responding as opposed to other women in the group who are defined by marriage or virginity.

The fact that Mellie is constructed as a dumping ground for the *gorger's* refuse (sexual anxiety as verbal abuse) signals her precarious position as a desirable and unattached exotic other. In *gypsy* culture she is constructed as the location of her ex-husband's refuse (anger as domestic violence) and sister Nettie's refuse (chastity anxiety as lectures and physical violence). Women within her culture deposit their refuse on her as a failed motherland in their expressed anxieties about life without men. Mellie's *gorger* man is symbolically killed (dumped) at the end of episode four in the no-man's-land that is constructed between the two cultures.

Mellie's social circle fears that she will threaten their status as Motherland. Mellie lies at their frontiers and if unchecked, she threatens to overtake their territories. She must be controlled and restricted for the fear that she will encroach and take over. Nettie punishes and banishes Mellie from the group and makes her wait in the car while the women receive manicures. Nettie is always carefully watching and restricting Mellie's movements. The fear of encroachment is most intense when outsiders are near her (e.g., in the grocery store, in the casino). Nettie may never reclaim Mellie into Mother-land but she is not willing to have her annexed by the other side. Nettie states, "I'm trying to show her and teach her, but it's like she doesn't want to be taught." Episode four narrator Ellen K. seems to share in Nettie's domesti-cating mission asking, "With Mellie intent on enjoying herself, will she be able to behave?" In a picture promoting season one, Mellie is dressed in a plain, pure white wedding gown, deemed a *gorger*-style dress in the series. Her bouquet is slumped, hand is on hip, head is cocked and her eyes are rolled up. The message is clear. Mellie is neither Motherland nor *gorger*-wife.

No-man's-land is constructed and maintained largely by and through the efforts of women like Nettie and Mellie. Audience members and critics argue that Roma and Traveller men directly control women but in no-man's-land men are passive or symbolic. When Mellie flirts with men in the casino and while shopping, they look at her with restrained anticipation. Their reactions prefigure how viewing audiences are meant to regard promos in which Mel-lie hangs out of the window of a truck speeding down the highway. In episode six, as Mellie fist-fights with a bridesmaid in front of a courthouse where her nephew is married, men watch from a distance and record her. They do not quite know how to react to her; she is a treacherous land.

Patriarchy exists symbolically within Nettie and Mellie's psyche. They are presented as having internalized the cultural codes of objectification; they self-objectify by regarding "themselves as objects to be looked at and evalu-ated."[77] Nettie is constructed as having accepted her and Mellie's status as cultural territories, and she assumes responsibility for Mellie. When Mellie's nephew Heath chaperones her date with her *gorger* boyfriend, he states that it is he who will not allow her to date; but in reality he is an envoy of Mellie who has asked him to attend and negotiate rules of engagement. Mellie takes over from Nettie when she rejects her *gorger* boyfriend and reaffirms support of *gypsy* society at the conclusion of episode four; this ending shows that Mellie has internalized the importance of Motherland.

Post-colonial theory would consider lands caught between the dominant Western culture and the marginalized Eastern culture as hybrid spaces with each side vying to define the space. Similarly, the people inhabiting these spaces are cultural hybrids as there exists an uneasy status quo between the two sides. On the one hand, there is no truly native state to which this land can return and racism prevents the West from fully accepting the post-coloni-al territory as home. It is a battle for control that is couched in terms of land, but it is fought for bodies and minds.

Standpoint theory would argue that, caught between two patriarchal cul-tures, Mellie is in the perfect space to "critique patriarchal practice and ideology."[78] Yet Mellie does not reflect on patriarchy and ideology but in-stead reflects an internalized patriarchy.

We cautiously survey Nellie's surface for indentations like her overuse of alcohol and risk-taking behavior, and we do not attempt to ask what these indentations might hide. A critic echoes, "It appears that no effort is going to be made to address the disturbing questions you may have after watching [. . .]. Do these child marriages last? Is domestic violence a problem in this culture?"[79] Series producers do not intend to for us to remain in this space because it raises more questions than the narrative structure is willing or able to answer. Staying too long might alienate viewers from the tourist attraction—a space that is designed for and is most pleasurable to them.

Representation Four: Woman as Tourist Attraction

Woman as tourist attraction gives the cultural outsider or tourist a cultural experience with a *real gypsy*. There is nothing real or authentic about this attraction. The tourist attraction is the archetype of the passive, exotic native woman epitomized in countless post-colonial critiques with which Westerners seek to find and have experiences. To this end, producers pose and place the attraction where she will have the greatest impact. While other lands are off-limits, claimed, or dangerous this is a well-trodden land that invites outside visitors.

Levell describes Victorians at Indian cultural exhibits saying, "The touristic act of travelling across time and space, consuming other places, peoples and their culture through exhibitionary spectacles, served to widen the horizon of the Victorian's imagination and simultaneously shifted the boundaries of the actual and the imaginary."[80] Like these Victorian exhibits, in episode two Priscilla is encouraged to walk Boston's streets as an exhibitionary spectacle that blurs fantasy with reality. We are meant to believe she wears her culture even though her dress was designed by someone outside of her culture. TV allows the audiences to witness her juxtaposed with US urban culture without leaving the comfort of their own cultural spaces.

Baudrillard wrote about simulacra, as objects or images that stand in for a real object or image that either no longer exists or never existed in the first place.[81] Early representations of the "outlandish attire" are taken to be real when they may have been simulacra performances (e.g., early fortune tellers who performed to satisfy Western expectations). Even if there is a precedent for this imagery, it is by no means natural or authentic. The British series speaks directly to the Disney movies that young *gypsy* virgin brides covet for their bridal style and these films that copy popular representations of princesses are themselves performed social conventions. *MBFAGW* obscures these influences, leading us to believe that we are in an authentic space.

MBFAGW is a play on *My Big Fat Greek Wedding* during which a woman from a Greek-identified family marries a man from a WASP (White, Anglo Saxon, Protestant) family. Here, size (large dresses, bodies), bright colors and big personalities denote ethnicity. Using this logic, anything that is perceptually more intense than the mainstream society is ethnic *gypsy* or *Greek*. Baudrillard argues that Disneyland is an imaginary fantasy that in part exists to convince us that California and America are real.[82] In a similar way, pedestrians in episode two experience Priscilla as a cultural tourist attraction, a place to take a vacation (where sights, sounds and colors are more intense) from real life (their lives are real; Priscilla is a fantasy). Likewise, featured dressmaker Sondra Celli's website is split into two separate sites—"classic couture" and "bling"—that might as well be reality and fantasy.[83]

In series promotional photos, *gypsy* women walk Boston in multi-colored neon track suits or elaborate dresses, and pedestrians (tourists) snap pictures with cell phones as one might with a New York City street performer posing for pictures with tourists while dressed as the Statue of Liberty. One could argue that the joke is one perpetuated by the Roma/Travellers by flaunting excess that feeds into cultural outsiders' expectations to fund expensive weddings via a reality show performance. Yet while the glowing tourist attraction appears to symbolize freedom in its visual excess, like Lady Liberty's torch, she is immobilized, an object for others to experience. People pose not with her as a person but against her like a theme park backdrop that she provides. Level argues that Western tourists have sought to collect such sensory experiences of exhibitionary spectacles from the Victorian age onward.[84]

Critic Lowry notes a pseudo-social scientific perspective with the TLC network framing the show as a "subcultural oddity."[85] Critic Genzlinger counters, "This isn't a sociological study; there's nothing respectful about the way the people here are portrayed."[86] Similarly on IMDb,[87] viewers collaborated on a list of 28 things (many offensive) learned from the series compiled in the trope of a tourist guidebook or pseudo-anthropological field notes. The list of *things learned* are eye opening for what they reveal about Western cultural perspectives.

On www.romanichal.net [88] "Jennifer" (May 21, 2012) writes, "I have watched this show, and have tried to find information about this lifestyle, I'm curious about this lifestyle." "Mario," (May 22, 2012) as moderator writes, "We are a race not a lifestyle." "Holly" (May 23, 2012) writes, "I've always had this romantic notion of "gypsies" and travellers and the lifestyles they lead." "Darlene" (May 28, 2012) writes, "I do not know any gypsies but would soooo love to." The women's comments resemble those of tourists investigating an exotic, all-inclusive resort. "Mario" (July 19, 2012) concludes, "This little blog can't compete with a lying international media phenom." " Mario's " blog competes with a TV review of *MBFAGW* in *People Magazine* (3.6 million weekly US readers [89]) that describes the show as, "gentle, winning and sympathetic."[90] "Laurie" (May 23, 2012) speaks to the influence of international media as she asks, "Is there a producer you [Mario] can get in touch with to pitch a show to him about the way Gypsys really live? The Real Housewives of Gypsys?" "Laurie" says she would watch a real show. "Laurie" presents herself as a good judge of real. If we apply Baudrillard's theory of simulacra[91] to "Laurie's" comments, she is real (America) and *MBFAGW's* women are fantasy (Disneyland).

"Laurie" illustrates the problems with tourist attractions. Their authenticity is assessed by tourists who are the least qualified to determine realness. Tourist attractions face heavy pressure to deliver culture that the tourist cannot find at home. Tourist attractions benefit in the short term. For instance, online comments claim that series producers allegedly provide financial compensation for the dresses, parties and alcohol in addition to the increased attention gained by *MBFAGW's* stars. The long term consequence is best described by "JD" (June 22, 2012) who writes, "Perception is the NEW reality and whenever the truth is twisted for ANY reason, the long-term problem is that it becomes very VERY difficult to untwist the misconceptions borne of a warped unchallenged presentation."

MBFAGW AS REALITY TELEVISION CULTURE

Kavka's three-generation framework for interpreting reality television is useful here for the insights it provides into *MBFAGW*. *MBFAGW* reflects the characteristics of Kavka's third generation of reality television that she argues is "a key genre for [. . .] clarifying the process through which contemporary celebrity is produced, maintained and consumed."[92] This generation of reality TV is premised on reviving the celebrity of faded stars and projecting average people as everyday celebrities. It is no consequence that *MBFAGW* does not significantly address its subjects' poverty, marginalization, teenage pregnancy, domestic violence and alcohol use because problem solving is not the concern of this reality generation. The focus is less on intervening in individual lives, Kavka argues, and more "on using the material of personal lives to intervene in the economies of celebrity culture."[93]

The series emphasis on *real* and *authentic* culture is central to third-generation reality programs. Kavka argues that third-generation reality programs foreground authenticity (e.g., a *real-life gypsy*) while not always displaying the construction (e.g., stylists, production assistants) that underlie these *authentic* performances.[94] With everyday celebrity shows like *MBFAGW,* the focus quickly becomes anti-talent that Kavka defines as "ignorance, malapropisms, turning one's bottom to the camera and slapping it."[95] A subgenre of anti-talent is monstrous femininity[96] that we see in Mellie who, while publically intoxicated, falls down and inadvertently exposes her breast. She also fist-fights at her nephew's wedding. When anti-talent and monstrous femininity are the stuff of celebrity, each new episode must top what has come before.

Constructing individual reality performers as personifications of regions, nations and cultural frontiers is not exclusive to *MBFAGW*. *Jersey Shore/ Geordie Shore*, *The Real Housewives of Atlanta/Beverly Hills/Miami/New Jersey/New York/Orange County/Vancouver*, and *Yukon Men* are just three examples of this phenomenon from third-generation reality TV. One media critic conflates both *MBFAGW* and *American Gypsies* with "shows with 'Housewives' or 'Jersey' in the title."[97] The problem is not that these shows focus on regions, nations or cultures, but that they construct complex social-historical contexts through the singular characteristics of individual perform-ers.

DIRECTIONS FOR FUTURE INQUIRY

The representations analyzed in this study reinforce patriarchal ideologies to the detriment of marginalized groups like the Roma, Travellers and women who are minorities within these co-cultures. Given the intense scrutiny given to the media production, framing and construction of Roma and Traveller life, one is left to wonder what indigenous storytelling would look like creat-ed within, by and for Roma and Travellers. Mobile and personal communica-tion technology makes this possible. If this self-narration was studied, per-haps we might see some of the same representations that are critiqued here as Roma and Travellers exist within a larger US cultural context. It would be naïve to expect that by studying a self-narration project one would uncover some authentic, native or real Roma or Traveller, but analysis might yield insight into the cultural discourses/repertoires that inform identity construc-tions for Roma and Travellers.

One wedding story that was not referenced in this analysis that deserves further study was Annie's lesbian wedding to Linda, a *gorger* woman. Their story breaks from many of the conventions featured in the series analyzed here. While the series focuses on ornamentation and objectification, Anna pawns her family jewelry to pay for her modest wedding at which neither she nor Linda wear a heavily constructed dress. Anna's family members have reservations, and yet they show up. The couple is unfettered by many of the traditions that constrain the other women, and they even play with gender constructions in a tongue and cheek fashion. Juxtaposing gay and lesbian Roma and Traveller wedding narratives to hetero-normative wedding narra-tives is worthwhile for these and a host of other reasons.

Finally, from a cultural standpoint, this study does consider Roma and Traveller ethnic identity construction in a small way by commenting on real and authentic versus fantasy and imaginary constructions of the culture. Ad-ditionally interesting are attempts to identify featured Roma and Travellers with Europe (e.g., England) as a strategy of whiteness.[98] The problem with this is that it downplays both groups' migratory histories and the Roma's roots in the Indian subcontinent. This also applies to Irish Travellers as Ignatiev argues that the Irish were not historically considered White under the WASP definition of whiteness.[99] On one hand, perhaps the series is respecting the participants' self-identifications (e.g., women are shown describing themselves as "English gypsies"); on the other hand, it is arguably an attempt on the part of the series producers to *mainstream* the performers and thus make them more relatable to the dominant (white) cultural group with which many viewers will identify. Either way, this seems an important area for further analysis, as it seems when studying *MBFAGW* that we have only just seen below the first of many levels of televisual crinoline.

REFERENCES

AAM: Alliance for Audited Media. "Research and Data: Top 25 U.S. Consumer Magazines for December 2012." AAM: Alliance for Audited Media. December 31, 2012. http://www.auditedmedia.com/news/research-and-data/top-us-consumer-magazines-for0december-2012.aspx (accessed May 7, 2013).

Allen, Peter. "Gypsies Paid to Leave France Face Tough New Measures to Prevent Their Return." Mail Online. October 1, 2010. http://www.dailymail.co.uk/news/article-1316906/Gypsies-paid-leave-France-face-tough-new-measures-prevent-return.html (accessed December 1, 2012).

Alley-Young, Gordon. "Big Fat Gypsy Weddings." In *The Multimedia Encyclopedia of Women in Today's World* (Electronic Version), by Carol K. Oyster and Jane E. Sloan Mary Zeiss Strange. Sage, 2011.

Amazon. "Customer Reviews: Virgin Gypsy Brides." Amazon. 2012-2013. http://www.amazon.com/Virgin-Gypsy-Brides/product-reviews/B008K3XJI4/ref=cm_cr_dp_qt_see_all_top?ie=UTF8&showViewpoints=1 (accessed July 31, 2013).

Baudrillard, Jean. *Simulations*. New York: Semiotext(e), 1983.

Bullock, Alan, and Stephen Trombley (Editors). *The New Fontana Dictionary of Modern Thought* (3rd edition). New York: Harper Collins, 1999.

Burke, Mary S. *Tinkers: Synge and the cultural history of the Irish Traveller*. New York: Oxford University Press, 2009.

Café, Rebecca. "Dale Farm: Who are the UK's Travellers." BBC News. September 23, 2011. http://www.bbc.co.uk/news/uk-15020118 (accessed December 1, 2012).

Darby, Seyward. "Big Fat Disgrace: TLC's 'My Big Fat Gypsy Wedding' is Wildly Misleading." *The New Republic*. May 31, 2011. http://www.newrepublic.com/article/books-and-arts/89173/my-big-fat-gypsy-wedding-tlc-traveller-roma (accessed December 1, 2012).

DeBeauvoir, Simone. *The Second Sex*. New York: Random House, 1989.

Donovan, Josephine. *Feminist Theory: The Intellectual Traditions of American Feminism*. New York: Continuum Publishing Company, 1993.

Drucker, Johanna. "Humanities Approaches to Graphical Display." *Digital Humanities Quarterly*, 5, 1, 2011: http://www.digitalhumanities.org/dhq/vol/5/1/000091/000091.html#.

du Gay, Paul, Stuart Hall, Linda Janes, Hugh MacKay, and Keith Negus. *Doing Cultural Studies: The Story of the Sony Walkman*. London: Sage, 1997.

Fanon, Franz. *A Dying Colonialism*. New York: Grove Press, 1967.

FFT: Friends, Families and Travellers. "Bullying Facts and Figures." FFT: Friends, Families and Travellers. 2006. http://www.gypsy-traveller.org/your-family/young-people/bullying/facts/ (accessed December 1, 2012).

Fischel, Jack R. *Historical Dictionary of the Holocaust* (2nd ed.). Lanham, MD: Scarecrow Press, 2010.

Fiske, John. *Reading the Popular*. Boston: Unwin Hyman, 1989.

———. *Television Culture*. London : Routledge, 1987.

Fraser, Angus. *The Gypsies: The Peoples of Europe*. Malden, MA: Blackwell Publishers, 1995.

Fredrickson, Barbara L., and Tomi-Ann Roberts. "Objectification Theory: Towards Understanding Women's Lived Experiences and Mental Health Risks." *Psychology of Women Quarterly* 21 (1997): 173-206.

Genzlinger, Neil. "A Turbulent Romney Family Working as Psychic Healers." *New York Times*, July 17, 2012: C4.

———. "If Carmen Had Made it To the Altar." *New York Times*, April 28, 2012: C1.

Gliatto, Tom. "My Big Fat American Gypsy Wedding." *People*, May 7, 2012: 48.

Hancock, Ian F. *Ame Sam e Rromane Džene/We Are the Romani People*. Hertford, UK: University of Hertfordshire Press, 2005.

———. "Romanies and the Holocaust: A Reevaluation and Overview." In *The Historiography of the Holocaust*, by Dan Stone, 383-396. New York: Palgrave-MacMillan, 2004.

Hough, Jennifer. "DNA Study: Travellers a Distinct Ethnicity." *Irish Examiner*. May 31, 2011. http://www.irishexaminer.com/ireland/dna-study-travellers-a-distinct-ethnicity-156324.html (accessed January 18, 2013).

Iaccino, James F. *Psychological Reflections on Cinematic Terror: Jungian Archetypes in Horror Films*. Westport, CT: Praeger, 1994.

Ignatiev, Noel. *When the Irish Became White*. New York: Routledge, 1996.

Internet Movie Database. "Board: 'My Big Fat American Gypsy Wedding' (2012)." Internet Movie Database. 2012. http://www.imdb.com/title/tt2245937/board/?ref_=tt_bd_sm (accessed May 10, 2013).

Kabachnik, Peter. "The Culture of Crime: Examining Representations of Irish Travellers in Traveller and The Riches." *Roma Studies*, 2009: 49-63.

Katrack, Ketu H. "Indian Nationalism, Gandhian 'Satyagraha,' and Representations of Female Sexualities." In *Nationalisms and Sexualities*, by Andrew Parket, Mary Russo, Doris Sommer and Patricia Yaeger, 395-406. London: Routledge, 1992.

Kavka, Misha. *Reality TV*. Edinburgh, UK: Edinburgh University Press, 2012.

Kearns, Caledonia. *Motherland: Writings by Irish-American Women About Mothers and Daughters*. New York: HarperCollins.

Kenrick, Donald. *The Roma World: A Historical Dictionary of the Gypsies*. Hertfordshire, UK: University of Hertfordshire Press, 2004.

LaCalle, Charles A. "Racism and the Roma: Gypsies Suffer from Discriminarion in Europe and America." *The Harvard Crimson*. November 10, 2009. http://www.thecrimson.com/article/2009/11/10/gypsies-gypsy-europe-against/ (accessed December 12, 2012).

Levell, Nicky. "Reproducing India: International Exhibitions and Victorian Tourism." In *Souvenirs: The Material Culture of Tourism*, by Michael Hitchcock and Ken Teague, 36-51. Burlington, VT: Ashgate Publishing, 2000.

Littlejohn, Georgina. "Cheers! My Big Fat Gypsy Wedding star Josie McFadyen Celebrates Her Birthday With a Semi-Clad Night on the Town." Mail Online. June 12, 2012. http://www.dailymail.co.uk/tvshowbiz/article-2159064/My-Big-Fat-Gypsy-Wedding-star-Josie-McFadyen-celebrates-birthday-semi-clad-night-town.html (accessed December 1, 2012).

Lowry, Brian. "My Big Fat American Gypsy Wedding." *Daily Variety*, April 27, 2012: 11.

Mairson, Alan. "National Geographic's 'American Gypsies' Leads to a Potential Class Action Lawsuit by the Romani Community." *Society Matters: How the National Geographic Society Could Create a New Blueprint for Journalism*. July 26, 2012. http://societymatters.org/2012/07/26/national-geographics-american-gypsies-leads-to-a-potential-class-action-lawsuit-by-the-romani-community/ (accessed May 17, 2013).

Marechal, AJ. "TLC Wedded to 'Gypsy.'" *Daily Variety*, June 15, 2012: 36.

Mayo, Katherine. "Mother India." *Project Gutenberg Australia*. 1927. http://gutenberg.net.au/ebooks03/0300811h.html (accessed May 24, 2013).

McVeigh, Robbie. "'Ethnicity denial' and racism: The case of the government of Ireland." *Translocations: The Irish Migration, Race and Social Transformation Review*, 2 (1), 2007: 90-133.

Mohanram, Radhika. *Black Body: Women, Colonialism, and Space.* Mineapolis: University of Minnesota Press, 1999.

My Big Fat Gypsy Mockery. 2011-2012. http://www.romanichal.net/ (accessed May 2, 2013).

Nakayama, Thomas K., and Robert, L. Krizek. "Whiteness: A Strategic Rhetoric." *Quarterly Journal of Speech* 81 (1995): 291-309.

News, BBC. "Irish Travellers: 'A House is Like a Prison'." BBC News. July 22, 2009. http://news.bbc.co.uk/2/hi/europe/8140429.stm (accessed December 1, 2012).

O'Riain, Sean O. *Solidarity With Travellers: A Story of Settled People Making a Stand for Travellers.* Dublin: Roadside Books, 2000.

Persico, Joseph E. *Eleventh Month, Eleventh Day, Eleventh Hour: Armistice Day 1918 World War I and Its Violent Climax.* New York: Random House, 2005.

Smith, Jerilyn. *The Marginalization of Shadow Minorities (Roma) and Its Impact on Opportunities.* PhD diss., Purdue University, 2008.

South East Wales Women's Aid Consortium. "Domestic Abuse and Equality: Gypsy and Traveller Women." Equality and Human Rights Commission. October 1, 2010. http://www.equalityhumanrights.com/uploaded_files/Wales/domestic_abuse_and_gypsy_travellers.pdf (accessed December 12, 2012).

The Scottish Gypsies of Scotland. "The Early History." *The Scotish Gypsies of Scotland.* 2004. http://www.scottishgypsies.co.uk/early.html (accessed October 2012, 21).

Thomas, Barbara A. "Case Study: Dislocation of Roma and Irish Travellers for the 2012 London Olympic Games." *UW Bothell Policy Journal*, Spring 2008: 1-3.

Webley, Kayla. "Hounded in Europe, Roma in the US Keep a Low Profile." *Time.* October 13, 2010. http://www.time.com/time/nation/article/0,8599,2025316,00.html (accessed December 1, 2012).

Woolf, Virginia. "Professions for Women." In *Virginia Woolf on Women and Writing*, by Virginia Woolf, 57-63. London: The Women's Press, 1979.

NOTES

1. Channel 4 (UK) catchphrase cited in Darby, "Big Fat Disgrace."
2. Hancock, *Ame Sam e*, 9.
3. O'Riain, *Solidarity With Travellers*, 8.
4. Hough, "DNA Study."
5. The Scottish Gypsies of Scotland, "The Early History."
6. Fraser, *The Gypsies*, 53.
7. Fraser, *The Gypsies*, 100.
8. The Scottish Gypsies of Scotland, "The Early History."
9. Fraser, *The Gypsies*, 169.
10. News, BBC. "Irish Travellers."
11. Kabachnik, "The Culture of Crime," 52.
12. McVeigh, "Ethnicity Denial," 109.
13. Fraser, *The Gypsies*, 100.
14. Ibid.
15. Binchy cited in McVeigh, "Ethnicity Denial," 113.
16. Fischel, *Historical Dictionary*, 105.
17. McVeigh, "Ethnicity Denial," 102.
18. Fischel, *Historical Dictionary*, 107.
19. Hancock, "Romanies and the Holocaust," 392.
20. McVeigh, "Ethnicity Denial," 98.
21. Allen, "Gypsies Paid to Leave."
22. Alley-Young, "Big Fat Gypsy Weddings."
23. Thomas, "A Case Study," 1-2.
24. LaCalle, "Racism and the Roma."
25. Café, "Dale Farm."
26. Ibid.

27. Ibid.
28. McVeigh, "Ethnicity Denial," 114.
29. Café, "Dale Farm."
30. Kabachnik, "The Culture of Crime," 50.
31. Fraser, *The Gypsies*, 122.
32. Ibid.
33. Burke, *Tinkers*, 112.
34. Kabachnik, "The Culture of Crime," 50.
35. Mairson, "National Geographic's."
36. Webley, "Hounded in Europe."
37. Kenrick 2004 as cited in Kabachnik, "The Culture of Crime," 51.
38. FFT: Friends, Families and Travellers, "Bullying Facts and Figures."
39. South East Wales Women's Aid Consortium, "Domestic Abuse and Equality."
40. McVeigh, "Ethnicity Denial," 121.
41. Smith, *The Marginalization of Shadow Minorities*, 77.
42. Marechal, "TLC Wedded," 36.
43. Fraser, *The Gypsies*, 122.
44. Burke, *Tinkers*, 112.
45. Fredrickson and Roberts, "Objectification Theory," 175.
46. Iaccino, "Psychological Reflections," 4.
47. Fiske, *Reading the Popular; Television Culture.*
48. Darby, "Big Fat Disgrace."
49. Littlejohn, "Cheers!"
50. du Gay et al, *Doing Cultural Studies*, 4.
51. Drucker, "Humanities Approaches."
52. DeBeauvoir, *The Second Sex*, 154.
53. Ibid.
54. Fanon, *A Dying Colonialism*, 154.
55. "My Big Fat Gypsy Mockery."
56. Internet Movie Database, "These women sure act pretty whorish."
57. DeBeauvoir, *The Second Sex*, 154.
58. Gliatto, "My Big Fat," 48.
59. "My Big Fat Gypsy Mockery."
60. Ibid.
61. Genzlinger, "If Carmen," C1.
62. Littlejohn, "Cheers!"
63. Lowry, "My Big Fat," 11.
64. Bullock and Trombley, "The New Fontana," 387-388.
65. Amazon, "Customer Reviews."
66. Internet Movie Database, "Message Boards."
67. Mayo, *Mother India*, Chapter VIII.
68. Katrack, "Indian Nationalism," 397-398.
69. Kearns, *Motherland*, xiv.
70. Ibid, xii.
71. Mohanram, *Black Body*, 59.
72. Katrack, "Indian Nationalism," 400.
73. Internet Movie Database, "Message Boards."
74. Mayo, *Mother India*, Chapter VIII.
75. Woolf, "Professions for Women," 59.
76. Persico, *Eleventh Month*, 68.
77. Fredrickson and Roberts, "Objectification Theory," 177.
78. Donovan, *Feminist Theory*, 89.
79. Genzlinger, "If Carmen," C1.
80. Levell, "Reproducing India," 48.
81. Beaudrillard, *Simulations*, 2.
82. Ibid, 24.

83. Celli, "Enter Classic Couture, Enter Bling Site."
84. Levell, "Reproducing India," 37-38.
85. Lowry, "My Big Fat," 11.
86. Genzlinger, "If Carmen," C1.
87. Internet Movie Database, "Things we've learned from this show."
88. "My Big Fat Gypsy Mockery."
89. AAM: Alliance for Audited Media, "Research and Data."
90. Gliatto, "My Big Fat," 48.
91. Baudrillard, *Simulations*, 24.
92. Ibid, 145.
93. Ibid, 146.
94. Ibid., 150.
95. Ibid, 159.
96. Ibid, 163.
97. Genzlinger, "A Turbulent," C4.
98. Nakayama and Krizek, "Whiteness," 300-301.
99. Ignatiev, *When the Irish*, 2-3.

Chapter Eight

Odd or Ordinary: Social Comparisons Between Real and Reality TV Families

Pamela L. Morris and Charissa K. Niedzwiecki

INTRODUCTION

A large portion of television programming today is devoted to so-called reality television. Reality shows dominate ratings, especially among the viewers whom the majority of networks consider most valuable, those 18 to 49.[1] As of 2010, an estimated 600 reality series have aired on American television, accounting in that year for approximately 40 percent of prime-time programming.[2] Networks continue to roll out new reality TV series every season. In particular, the documentary-style subgenre of reality television (variously called the docusoap, docudrama, or cinéma vérité style), which follows the everyday life of a person or group, is a popular format. A number of these shows depict families who are at the same time both ordinary and unusual. In some ways, they resonate with viewers who remark, "That's just like me." However, part of the appeal of reality television is that it also takes the viewer a step away from the real world. In this sense, reality television families are also chosen by producers for their deviance from societal norms. In the words of one of our study participants, reality TV families "are, socially speaking, on the outside of the spectrum for a traditional definition of what a family is." Indeed, this non-normality is part of the shows' popularity, as stated by another study participant: "I think that's what makes the reality show interesting to people. You don't want to watch just normal people; you want to watch abnormal people."

When we think of families on TV, classic family shows like *Leave it to Beaver* and *Ozzie and Harriet* automatically come to mind. There is a mother, father, and children—traditionally two. However, families have changed dramatically since these shows, and now it is not uncommon to see many different configurations of families portrayed on television, including singles, divorcees, gays and lesbians, and extended families. According to Stephanie Coontz in *The Way We Never Were,* such shows were actually only a myth and were not representative of actual families in that time period which suffered from some of the same socioeconomic problems (violence, child abuse, poverty) we have today.[3] Even in the past, a few families shown on television did not fit into the stereotypical norms of what is considered to be family. *The Brady Bunch,* for example, challenged the traditional family unit by featuring a divorcee and a widower couple that brought together their two families of three children each. Today, shows like *Modern Family* portray not only the traditional family but also a step-family and gay family, and *The New Normal* portrays a surrogate who is having a baby for a gay couple.

Reality television in particular has challenged family stereotypes. The unconventional Osbourne family, which featured a veteran heavy metal rocker dad, Ozzie, wife and manager of the household, Sharon, and two out-of-control teenagers, Jack and Kelly, debuted on MTV in 2002. The show was MTV's all-time, highest rated, regular series with more than 6 million viewers.[4] The show challenged existing family stereotypes by showing chaos and airing foulmouthed language ("shut the fuck up and go to bed.") on reality TV instead of traditional parents like *Leave It To Beaver*'s June and Ward Cleaver who maintained control over their children.

Reality TV continues to push the boundaries of what is considered to be a traditional family with shows like *Sister Wives,* which introduced polygamy in mainstream media. *Sister Wives,* produced by Figure 8 Films, premiered on TLC in 2010. The series features Kody Brown, his four wives, and their combined 17 children. In the episode, "Meet Kody and the Wives," the viewers are introduced to Kody and his three wives (Meri #1, Janelle #2, and Christine #3) and later Robin (#4). The family is portrayed to be similar to any large family with the exception that there is only one husband and multiple wives. Some of the older children are featured in the opening series showing how they help their large family with tasks such as cooking, raking the yard, and helping with the younger children.

The series, one of two we looked at for this study, claims to "shatter stereotypes, revealing a side of polygamy that has never been seen before."[5] All of the wives entered marriage of their own free will. One wife, Christine, explains how she wanted to fit into a polygamous family as the third wife to avoid jealousy with the first two wives.[6] Each wife is shown in her section of a home built specifically for polygamists with Kody and their children. Meri (wife #1) has one child and is working on her degree in social work. Janelle (wife #2), who has six children and works full-time outside of the home, says she would rather work than stay at home and clean. Christine (wife #3), is a stay-at-home mother who is expecting her sixth child, Truly, and enjoys home schooling her five biological children as well as Janelle's six, who she also considers her "own children."[7] All of the children featured in the introduction have positive comments about their large family and find their family no different from other families except they are polygamists.

Other TLC reality TV shows are not as politically or religiously controversial as *Sister Wives* but feature families that are unusual in terms of how many children they have, such as *Jon and Kate Plus 8* and *19 Kids and Counting,* or who have some physical distinction as in *Little People, Big World.* All three shows feature a traditional married couple though, which makes them more socially acceptable than the Browns of *Sister Wives.* The fascination with these families is their large family size (versus today's average family of about two children) or their adjustment to physical challenges in the real world.

TLC's coverage of the Duggar family began with the documentary *14 Children and Pregnant Again* in 2004, showcasing their large, conservative family. Four more documentaries followed, and in 2008, the Duggars landed their own television series. It was called *17 Kids and Counting*, which became *18 Kids and Counting,* and is now *19 Kids and Counting.* Since their television debut, the Duggar family has been in front of the camera for nearly a decade. As a result of this longevity, the audience size is tremendous and there are several web sites and blogs devoted to the Duggars; these are updated by *TLC*, the Duggar family, and loyal fans. Filmed at the family's home in Arkansas, *19 Kids and Counting* shows the Duggars taking part in various everyday activities. The characters in this documentary-style reality television show, Jim Bob and Michelle Duggar and their 10 boys and nine girls, do things differently as a result of their size and religion. They are over quadruple the size of the average American family and practice a strong Independent Baptist religion. Their children wear ultra-conservative clothing, such as long dresses and modest bathing suits for the girls, have names all beginning with the letter "J," and mentor each other.

The Duggar's show was chosen to be studied because of the family's unique size and religious practices. With 11 seasons, the show has grown in popularity and viewers are discovering more about the family's uniqueness. The Duggars are a real family, but what makes them special is how uncommon their lifestyle is, a lifestyle that has been scrutinized and admired throughout their many years on television. As a result, viewers have vastly different perspectives on the family and their interactions.

In one of her numerous papers on reality TV, Alice Hall wrote: "The potential importance of reality programs is not based solely on their popularity. The shows also claim researchers' attention because of their potential to offer unique insights about the way audiences make sense of media texts."[8] Inspired by this statement, we formed research questions that asked whether watching reality television families stimulates viewers to make comparisons between themselves, those they know, and the families on the screen, as suggested by social comparison theory, and if so, on what topics comparisons are made. We also wondered whether exposure to reality TV families, with all of their eccentricities, leads viewers to develop positive or negative attitudes about the structure and activities of real-world families. For example, such nonnormative or eccentric families may make us view our own family foibles as less unusual or view a family's behavior as deviant. For as Hall later wrote, "Although most contemporary reality programs are not intended to teach, they have the potential to inform audiences about a variety of topics, including about the way people behave and interact with each other,"[9] and "one of the things viewers feel they may be able to pick up from the shows is a better understanding of human nature and behavior."[10]

BACKGROUND

Reality TV

Researchers have studied a number of aspects of reality television, including the categories and themes of shows, reasons why audiences watch reality TV, and perceptions of realism and authenticity. Although scholars have debated the role of voyeurism as a motivation for watching reality TV, we agree with researchers Nabi and colleagues, who found that reality TV audiences "watch—and they think others watch—not to see sexual behavior per se but because they like to watch interpersonal interactions and because they are curious about other people's lives."[11] Our focus groups agreed that these programs are watched partly out of mere curiosity. One participant stated: "Society is just nosey, and it's almost like we're bored with our own lives, so we sit down, we watch someone else's, and it's interesting. And this is so different that people do get a better world view or whatever. This part of us wants to know what other people are doing. It's the nosiness of us all." A few researchers have begun to examine the effects of increased reality television viewing, a topic particularly relevant given its ubiquitousness on nightly TV schedules.

Researchers have also started to recognize that the potential power of reality TV goes beyond its ability to entertain us. In her book on reality TV, Annette Hill observed that "the power of reality programming is that it can provide both entertainment and information at the same time."[12] On a scholarly level, Alice Hall has suggested that, stemming from earlier work about factual television's ability to influence audience members, the more realistic a reality TV program, the more likely it is that viewers *learn* from the program[13]; "factuality heightens the sense that a program is relevant to the world and that it will therefore be associated with perceived learning."[14] Translated to reality TV, Hall hypothesized that viewers learn from reality television shows perceived as real or authentic, more than would be the case for scripted shows. In fact, "perceived learning is likely to reflect the degree to which a specific text contributes to an audience member's social construction of reality."[15] Hill made similar statements in her book, stating that "when audiences watch reality TV they are not only watching programmes or entertainment, they are also engaged in critical viewing of the attitudes and behavior of ordinary people in the programmes, and the ideas and practices of the producers of the programmes."[16]

Social Comparison Theory

Rose and Wood wrote that in contrast to news programs "the majority of reality fare depicts common people engaging in uncommon (wilderness survival, international travel) and common (dating, home redecorating) tasks, giving viewers the chance to compare and contrast their own lives with those of the show's 'protagonist'."[17] This alludes to social comparison theory, first defined and studied by Festinger through his work with small groups at the Research Center for Group Dynamics at MIT.[18] The theory posits that we determine our own social and personal worth on the basis of how we measure up against others in similar domains (i.e., attractiveness, intelligence, success). We develop our attitudes through comparison to other people and their opinions (both favorable and unfavorable). Typically, we seek to compare ourselves with someone against whom we believe we should have reasonable similarity, a comparison of affiliation. For example, students would compare themselves with other classmates to determine how well they did on an exam. Alternatively, we also compare to those who are different, where the comparison is called a contrast. Social comparison is a ubiquitous social phenomenon; it provides "useful information about where one stands in one's social world, feeling better about oneself, and learning how to adapt to challenging situations."[19]

Comparison can be made in both directions—upward social comparison and downward social comparison.[20] Upward social comparison occurs when we compare ourselves with people who we deem to be socially better than we are in some ways. On the other hand, downward social comparison leads us to compare ourselves to those less fortunate. People who are low in self-esteem were found to be more likely to make downward comparisons because of a greater need for self-enhancement.[21] A 2012 Today.com survey also found that people who watch reality TV have a lower self-esteem than those who don't.[22] This relates to the concept of "schadenfreude"—taking pleasure in the misfortune of others, which establishes superiority to others such as hoarders, or people getting drunk and arrested on reality TV.[23] However, there is a tendency to stop comparing oneself with others who are divergent, especially if others are perceived as different from oneself in relevant dimensions such as morals and values. Smith and associates also found emotions, such as contempt and scorn, aimed at people who violate a basic social norm such as the traditional heterosexual marriage.[24] This is evident in *Sister Wives,* where polygamy goes against the prevailing social norm of monogamy in marriage. Although social comparison theory has been applied to several different contexts such as small group processes, health and justice, and television's influence on girls' body image, there have not been studies done using social comparison theory for people in reality TV shows. Television, however, is an obvious place to look for social comparisons. In fact, in her book, Hill included an observation made by Richard Hoggart, a cultural historian of the 1960s: "Television is a major source of 'people watching' for comparison and possible awareness of how different and similar we are to other people, and how different or similar our own culture is to other cultures."[25]

In the social sciences, social comparison is considered a central feature of human social life; comparisons with others play an important role in evaluating and constructing social reality. Social comparison theory is about "our quest to know ourselves, about the search for self-relevant information and how people gain self-knowledge and discover reality about themselves."[26] In a review of current social comparison research, Buunk and Gibbons wrote that "what these studies reveal once again, is that Festinger underestimated the importance and especially the ubiquity of social comparisons. They occur frequently and, in many cases, automatically—oftentimes without full awareness."[27] The authors continue: "It would appear that social comparison is now thought to be any process in which individuals relate their own characteristics to those of others. It is even assumed now that impression formation (or person perception) necessarily involves some social comparison."[28]

Given the availability of reality TV and its characteristic depiction of real people in unscripted situations, one would assume a vast opportunity for social comparison. What social comparisons are made and the effects of these comparisons provide a fruitful avenue of study. Because it is seen as real, participants may position themselves with respect to characters on reality TV. Such comparisons have gone unstudied, but not unnoted, by reality television scholars. For example, in her book, Hill cited Professor Shaun Moores who wrote: "Broadcasting provides viewers and listeners with a constant 'stream' of symbolic materials from which to fashion their senses of self . . . this flow of images and sounds is creatively appropriated by social subjects as they seek to put together personal identities and lifestyles."[29] Hill further cited John Ellis who wrote: "Audiences of reality programming are involved in exactly the type of debates about cultural and social values that critics note are missing from the programmes themselves: on the radio, in the press, in everyday conversation, people argue the toss over 'are these people typical?' and 'are these really our values?'"[30]

METHOD

The data for this study were collected using focus group interviews. A total of eight faculty and staff and 28 students were recruited from a state university in the U.S. Midwest to participate in six focus groups (with six participants each). These took place in February and March, 2013. At the beginning of each focus group, participants were shown either an episode of *Sister Wives* ("Meet Kody and the Wives") or two episodes of the Duggar family series, *17 and Counting* ("O Come All Ye Duggars") and *18 and Counting* ("Duggars' New Additions"). Following a short break, the focus groups assembled for a semi-structured interview led by one member of our research team. The other members of our team took notes during the interviews, which were also video- and audio-taped and later transcribed. During the interview, participants discussed reality television in general to warm up, and then were guided to discuss the families they saw.

Following the completion of all transcription, our research team of three individually read the transcripts and then met to establish a list of themes. These themes described the ways participants made comparisons between the reality TV families and real-world families and situations they knew. We established themes by employing thematic analysis. Once themes were established, we then assigned two coders to each transcript, with each coder working on four of the six transcripts. Coders met after coding one transcript to compare coding and adjust as needed. The following table lists the themes coded and the average number of instances coded across all transcripts.

RESULTS

Participants in our focus groups reported having watched a wide variety of reality television programs. From *Keeping Up with the Kardashians* and *Jersey Shore* to *Cake Boss*, and *Say Yes to the Dress* to *Breaking Amish*, everyone reported having seen at least a few reality television shows. Participants described reality television in general as scripted, staged, and dramatized, entertaining, outrageous, and obnoxious, and degrading, embarrassing and trashy. However, after viewing episodes of *Sister Wives* and *18/19 and Counting,* shows focused on the life of families, albeit unusual ones, focus group participants used very different words to describe them. These included culturally stimulating, informative, enlightening, a new perspective, insightful, educational, genuine and eye opening. Participants indicated that these two reality shows had something to teach; one participant stated that "they are teaching people to be culturally aware and culturally sensitive to people who are different from them." Another participant thought these families "could view it as almost like their job to show people that it's okay to

Table 8.1.   Social comparison themes coded from transcripts

Theme	Average Count
Religion/Conservatism	81
Perfection/Lack of Conflict	50
Marriage/Parents' Relationship	48
Gender roles and Stereotypes	40
Family Unity/Teamwork	40
Parent-Child Relationship	28
Money/Environmental Impact	25
Communication	24
Child-Child (Sibling) Relationship	22
RTV Family Perspective (put myself in their place)	13

think the way they do, and that you don't have to follow necessarily what the world says."

While almost all participants felt that the level of happiness of the families depicted (and resulting lack of conflict) was unrealistic, they also commented that in many other ways the shows were realistic. Participants discussed and were surveyed about the six dimensions of media realism proposed by Hall (2003): plausibility, typicality, factuality, narrative consistency, perceptual persuasiveness, and emotional involvement. Although participants watched only a limited number of the show episodes, and this is too small a sample size from which to draw statistical conclusions, we report in Table 8.2 the mean values for these six dimensions of realism across all focus groups (1= Strongly Disagree to 5=Strongly Agree).

With very little prompting, participants began to compare the families in these shows to their own experiences and to their own families. Further probing by the researchers about the families on the shows generated many types of comparisons (Table 8.1). In this chapter we will discuss the following types of social comparison found in our focus groups: demographic, family relationships (e.g. parent-child, sibling, and marriage), religion/conservatism and perspective taking.

Demographic Comparisons

Both shows depict families with many children, and a simple comparison made by participants was that of basic demographics. We observed that participants made this type of comparison early in the focus group interviews, as if to put themselves in the frame of mind of a large family in

Table 8.2.   Mean values for dimensions of media realism

Dimension	Mean
Plausibility: The potential to occur in the real world.	3.23
Typicality: Something that could happen to me or to people like me.	1.89
Factuality: Accurately represents a specific, real world event or person.	3.26
Emotional Involvement: ability to evoke an emotional response. Viewers are involved with or relate to media characters.	3.66
Narrative Consistency: Consistent, coherent story, without holes or unexplained events.	3.60
Perceptual Persuasiveness: How real the images look.	3.97

anticipation of making further connections between RTV families and real-life families. Because few participants themselves came from large families, participants often instead looked for affiliation by sharing experiences based on large families they knew in their schools or communities. For example, one participant stated: "It reminds me of one of my friends from home. She has nine other brothers and sisters, so they have a pretty large family and I feel like sometimes it's chaotic just like this . . . I was thinking of her family when I was watching it sometimes, to, like, see if anything was similar." Another participant shared: "There's a family that went to my school, and when I was in high school . . . they had seven kids and they just all were like one year right after the other. Of course, it's not as many as 19, but they did seem to get along really well, and I'm pretty sure they were a fairly conservative family." A few participants likened the Browns or Duggars to experiences with close extended family, including this participant: "It's more like when we were younger and all of the cousins would be together. We would all stay in the same three-bedroom house for a week with, like, 40 people, and so we did the whole, no TV, kids were always outside all day just by themselves kinda playing or whatever." Even where specific families were not called out for comparison, participants associated the RTV families with general knowledge about contemporary families. For example, one participant stated about *Sister Wives*: "Because blended families have become so natural lately, that didn't seem unusual to me."

Family Relationships

By far the most common type of comparison made was regarding relationships within families. We further divided this theme into the following: overall family (teamwork and roles), parent-child relationship, child-child (sibling) relationship, and parent-parent (marriage) relationship.

Participants noted repeatedly that both of the RTV families were strongly bonded, worked together as a team, and delegated the work of a large family into specific roles—mainly using upward comparison. For example, one participant noted that the Duggars are a positive role model for families in the real world: "They all work really hard to work together and everything, and I think that cohesiveness as a group is something that a lot of families should strive for, if they can." Of *Sister Wives*, a participant said: "I liked how they shared tasks and worked out a system that people were happy with what they were contributing. I think that's a great idea." Another, generalizing what was seen on *Sister Wives* to real families, said: "The whole concept of the community raising your child and stuff is something that I think Americans don't value enough."

More specifically, participants compared how these RTV families worked together in ways either similar to or different from their own. One comment about the Duggars was: "The entire family is like one unit, like everybody got along and it seemed like everybody helped together on projects and stuff like that, that was really cool. Growing up with my siblings, it was almost like, me and my sibling, we never really worked together as like a team, so to speak, so I thought that was really cool." Not all participants saw the extremely strong family unit as a positive characteristic. Thus, there was some downward comparison. These participants felt that these large families resulted in a lack of individuality, something they valued in their own, smaller families. For example, a participant summed up the Duggar family this way: "everyone seemed very similar in this family . . . I just don't feel like you get a personality; it's kind of like an overarching 'This is the family personality'." Another participant thought that unlike the Browns and Duggars, real families *can* function without eliminating the individuality of each member, and thus provided a contrast comparison: "(I) come from a very strong family, strong Catholic family, with very family-oriented values. . . . we have a ton of cousins, but we're all individuals. Like, we're crazy, but we all love each other, but we're all like our own person, nobody's just like the other . . . I think the lack of individuality [in the show] kinda creeps me out."

Most of our participants were college-age students (19-21), and they tended to focus on the roles of the children in these large reality TV families. Some found positive models in the relationships between the children and parents, although it often offered a contrast to their own families, such as for this participant: "I mean, you saw that girl in a polka-dot top and a long skirt hauling wood and stuff. I was never helping my dad with building projects." Overwhelmingly, participants lamented the lack of individual time between the parents and children in these large families, where in both shows, older siblings are shown to act in the place of parents. Typical of these downward comparisons is this participant's statement: "I'm very close with both of my parents, and I would find it very hard not to have a one-on-one connection. I'm sure they do in a way, but it'd be very hard, considering all the kids. And they have other siblings to look up to, but it's not the same as a parent." Another participant, reflecting on whether she would like to be part of either of these reality TV families, said: "I think sometimes people grow up thinking 'It'd be fun to have a big family,' because there just seems to be a lot of cool stories. But specifically this one, I think it's too big . . . because it's just *too* big, there's not enough time with the parents."

Most of the discussion about sibling relationships in the RTV families fell into two categories. The first was that the siblings got along too well to be realistic, in comparison to their own experience:

> They only show positive things on the show. Like, you never see any of the kids really getting in trouble, or you never see any of the siblings…like the older siblings complaining about always having to take care of the younger siblings. There's never much, like, sibling rivalry that *I* would consider normal, or fighting, bickering, things like that. So I feel like they try to make it seem like they're all a lot happier than maybe they really are.

The second was that older siblings became pseudo-parents for the younger ones, and participants felt this was a concern. For example, one participant used her experience (affiliation) to frame her comments:

> I have two siblings and I'm still considered like a mini-mom because I was the oldest and my parents, as soon as they could, were leaving me home with them and having me babysit, and I just can't even imagine having such a hierarchy of different ages to worry about. It would feel like there were probably four moms and three dads or something, and you would kinda just go to the older siblings almost before you'd go to the parents.

Not only was the role difficult for the caregiving siblings, but also for the younger ones who may fail to benefit from the "wisdom of elders." In a downward comparison, one particularly insightful participant stated:

> I think of all of the perspective that they (my parents) bring when I ask them for advice, or like when I go to grandparents [for advice]. So though the pseudo-parents can *physically* take care of these younger children, I wonder if there's a lack of really high-quality communication because they don't have enough life experience to speak to some matters.

Participants also discussed the marriages in the RTV families. Participants found the Duggar parents' marriage to be conservative and traditional, but also too happy and conflict-free to be realistic. Stereotypes were also noted by participants: "Not just gender, but the husband takes care of the boys and does all the hard work; the wife is kinda submissive to the husband. So it's not only gender, but it's also, like, marital roles." Gender and marital stereotypes were also observed in the Brown household: "The wives are in the kitchen. I mean, did you see him once helping out in the kitchen? No. He was out in the living room playing with kids, you know, being the fun dad, and the moms are the ones taking care of making the food. He's the one with the big chain power saw." In addition to Kody's stereotypical male gender role, viewers of *Sister Wives* noted he was also relatively uninvolved with the raising of his children, and were critical of him: "I got every feeling that he could go out of the picture and the family would function just fine . . . his role is to bee-bop in there and, plant the seed, and bee-bop out."

The *Sister Wives* marriages are more novel than that of the Duggars and resulted in more diverse comments from participants. On one hand, participants found that the marriages "worked." For example, "The way he (Kody Brown) integrates all three of them and the way they interact with him and such really, truly is a marriage—three different marriages—which, you know, is traditional in my mind." Another positive observation (an upward comparison) about the Browns was that "I'm looking at it from the standpoint that both parents are present, which is something that maybe is not the norm today, you know, to have the dad and the mom." Despite this apparent normality of the individual Brown marriages, other participants were more skeptical of the Brown's television appearance. One remarked: "You're three wives sitting with one dude? You know, there's got to be someone that'll go, 'Well is it like a party?' Because what do we think of in polygamy? We think pedophile...we think patriarchal . . . you know, there's got to be a freak flag in there somewhere, right?"

Religion and Conservatism

An obvious basis for comparison in the RTV families in our study was the religious and conservative values prominent in these shows. Participants felt that the Duggars enact conservative Christian roles: "The girls are in the house in the kitchen or taking care of the kids while the boys are playing. So it's just like . . . a stereotypical conservative family." Although participants acknowledged being brought up with "Midwestern Christian values," they felt that the Duggars were unusual (a comparison of contrast). One participant said: "I feel like I'm a religious person, but I still think that they take it too far." Some participants made comparisons to real-world families that were like the Duggars but still found dissimilarities. One participant said:

> These very kind of conservative Christian families that home-school their kids . . . that tend to want to make all of their kids the same and have everything just perfect in this way. Those families tend to be a lot like this. They're all kind of . . . Family A is just like Family B is just like Family C and they're

all just like this . . . I mean, I've known families like that, and you just want to shake the kids like "Come outside! Play! Run down the street and, you know, kick the dog. Like, do something!"

Participants who viewed *Sister Wives* also thought that faith and religion were very strong themes in the show, themes that contrasted with their own experience. One participant said: "Their family is so strong, like the foundation of their family is their faith, and that's so not how my family operates." Another said "There were moments where I felt like the show was really just trying a little too hard to promote their faith."

A sub-theme was that participants felt that both families isolated themselves, particularly through the practice of homeschooling and, in the case of the Browns, later sending their children to a school where everyone was of their same faith (and practiced polygamy). Participants noted that neither family interacted with many people different from themselves. Such isolation, they felt, had negative repercussions (downward comparison). For example, one participant wondered, about the Duggar family: "Psychologically . . . what does that do from a communication perspective? How are you taught to communicate with people that have different views than you?" Similarly, a viewer of *Sister Wives* said that "97 percent of the world is not like that . . . how are they going to be able to adapt when they've been so censored and sheltered by Kody and the moms? You know, you live in an area where all your neighbors are polygamists, you go to a polygamist school."

Overall, when talking about this theme, participants were largely unable to make clear comparisons of affiliation—the reality TV families were just too out of the ordinary. For example, a participant who viewed *Sister Wives* said: "They're not traditional, so it's interesting to me to keep my mind open on watching a polygamist family and . . . to try very hard *while* I'm watching the show not to judge." Another said: "It seems very odd to us here because . . . people do this, I don't know where, but it doesn't happen here."

Perspective taking

An interesting form of comparison that took place among our focus group participants was perspective taking—that is, imagining oneself as a member of the reality TV family and evaluating that imagined experience. This may have occurred if participants were seeking comparisons of affiliation but could not identify a real-world experience with which to make a comparison. For example, after viewing *Sister Wives*, one participant remarked: "I don't have children because I don't want the responsibility, but if I had another family that would help me raise that child, I might do it, you know." Another viewer of *Sister Wives* was comfortable putting herself into the Brown's neighborhood, if not the family: "I like all three of those women. I wouldn't be comfortable in the family, but I sure would like them as my neighbors, all three women. I *like* those women. They work well together . . . and wouldn't you like to be with neighbors like that, you know? So, to surround myself with people in that true character, yeah, I'd be their friends." Our student participants often put themselves into the shoes of the children in the RTV families. In particular, one participant returned to the theme of the siblings as pseudo-parents, picturing herself and her reaction to being one of the Duggar children: "If I were them and I had to take care of all these kids growing up and was always holding a little child...it would almost make me not want to have some of my own, just because I've been doing it for so many years that would I want to have children of my own and just keep doing it year after year after year?" Others pictured themselves with regard to being in an isolated, conservative family:

> I don't think they have many outside influences, like we talked about, with nobody else being on the show. So that's like all they know. They don't know how to be any different or . . . like what would happen if they did do something different; they're almost, like, afraid of it, like Oh my gosh, what's going to happen to me if do this and I'm told not to?

Like the participant who felt comfortable as the Brown's neighbor, a viewer of the Duggars didn't want to be one of the many children, but a more peripheral figure such as Anna, who married the oldest Duggar son: "I would find it highly interesting to marry into a family like that, of 18, 19 kids. I think that would be like a culture shock in itself. So I think that kind of relationship. . . . I would—like, that would be the character that I would become emotionally attached to, to see what happens, because it's like an outside force."

Odd or Ordinary?

Overall, participants found both similarities (affiliation) and differences (contrast) between the RTV families and themselves. The differences, said our participants, are one reason people do watch reality television, for the novelty: "I *wouldn't* be drawn in if I felt like I understood their experiences." At the same time, participants are aware that part of what these shows do is begin to normalize reality TV family units: "While we have this dichotomy right now, the more and more opportunities we're given to normalize what has been traditionally seen as abnormal activity, that dichotomy is probably breaking down more quickly than we anticipate."

What was probably most surprising to us, however, was the large number of comments about the normality of these reality TV families—the upward comparisons and the attempt to find comparisons of affiliation. For example:

"Even if we see these people engaged in these activities and they are, in our perspectives, overly scripted or conflict has been added in, introducing these characters in this situation forces you to see this as a normal activity." Similarly, in another focus group, a participant said: "I found it interesting due to the fact that it allowed me to have these insights into an experience that I'm not aware of that allowed me to see it as a normal experience." Perhaps the best and most simply put statement about the "ordinary-ness" of RTV families was this: "There's no cookie-cutter family, even though we like to think that there is. The biggest thing that I noticed about them is they seem like a family." Participants were aware, however, that while abnormal and odd families do attract viewers, too much would also be detrimental to viewership. In particular, TLC, the network hosting both of our shows, knows how far it can push the agenda of introducing non-normative families. One of our participants remarked:

> Obviously TLC is putting this on for a reason, but this family wouldn't bring in the cameras if it was extremely dysfunctional . . . TLC isn't putting this show on to show the negative effects of polygamy. So some of it has to be staged because they have to be a normal working family to be on TLC's network . . . otherwise, then everyone in the media would just have an uproar about polygamy and evidence A would be this show.

LIMITATIONS/FUTURE DIRECTIONS

The limitations of our study included minimal exposure to episodes of the shows used (about 45 minutes), giving participants only a short period of time to develop perceptions of or comparisons with the reality TV families. Additional episodes could have changed their perceptions of the families; for example, in *Sister Wives* the addition of wife #4, Robin, occurs later in the show and may have resulted in a change in perception of the Browns. Additionally, both shows chosen were from the same network, TLC; other networks might have portrayed families in a different way and with a different mix of entertainment and education. Both shows also were similar in that they portrayed white, conservative, deeply religious families. Using families that offered a different type of nonnormality would be likely to affect the topics, types, and frequency of comparison by focus groups. Future studies should examine whether social comparisons with reality TV families happen with other, more diverse, reality shows.

Another limitation of our study was the use of focus groups. By their nature, focus group samples provide a limited selection of participants; our groups were primarily white, middle-class students with Midwestern values about families. Their responses may not be generalized to other audience groups. Future research should consider using more diverse audience members (including more parents) to see whether they interpret and respond to the reality TV families in a similar way.

Finally, our use of social comparison theory could be a limitation. As noted, the theory, over time, has been expanded to cover a wide variety of human behavior. Festinger himself noted that such expansion might result in a lack of scientific rigor.[31] While this makes the theory flexible enough to apply to a mediated situation such as reality TV, it may also be vague enough to lack rigorous guidance about results.

Future directions may include using additional episodes—or an entire season—of the reality TV shows and more diverse audiences, as well as looking for social comparison among viewers of other reality TV shows that depict families, such as those on other networks. An interesting related study could examine the relationship between social comparison theory and actual changes in opinions or attitudes about real families resulting from the viewing of reality TV. We also thought that in a larger study, the linking of quantitative data regarding Hall's dimensions of realism with a quantification of the type/number of comparisons viewers make would provide an interesting future analysis. Finally, applying a different theory, such as attribution theory, could add another perspective to a similar study by looking at the internal and external attributions of a family member's behavior.

DISCUSSION/CONCLUSIONS

The reality TV shows were "ordinary" enough to allow viewers to relate to them and compare them to their own families, such as having fun when the Duggars made their own slip 'n' slide or working out in the yard with the entire family as in *Sister Wives*. But, at the same time, the families were "odd" enough to allow viewers to regard them as different from their own families. For the Duggars, the large size (19 kids) of the family made them different from most families and for *Sister Wives*, the three moms and one dad went against societal norms of one mom and dad. This created downward comparisons by participants because these oddities violated their personal expectations for families. However, as these lifestyles were portrayed over a long period of time, viewer acceptance of the families' oddities may have helped change attitudes or created more acceptance of these types of families. This is why it is important to look at depictions of reality TV because they have the power to change viewers' attitudes towards people who are odd or different from them. One participant noted that greater acceptance and tolerance of homosexual lifestyles resulted from mainstream media exposure (unlike other earlier lifestyles that predated mass exposure to television); and perhaps media exposure to other non-normative family lifestyles (such as the Brown's) would have similar results. This participant concluded about *Sister Wives*: "I don't know so much that it's educational, but I believe it has opportunities to be transformational."

Whether or not watching these types of reality TV programs actually changes perceptions or just provides us with oddities for our entertainment, is yet to be fully explored. We took a step toward answering this question by listening to audience's social comparisons of affiliation and contrast, both upward and downward, regarding the shows *Sister Wives* and *19 and Counting*, and concluded that there is a potential for some types of reality TV to provide education as well as entertainment. Ultimately, however, we—and our participants—remained skeptical about the agenda of reality TV's creators. A participant summed it up by asking us: "Do you think TLC is trying to break stereotypes by putting on a program like that, or further stereotypes, or just entertain people and make money, maybe it comes down to that?"

REFERENCES

Barnhart, Aaron. "How Reality TV Took Over Prime Time." *Kansas City Star* (Kansas City, MO), December 6, 2010. http://www.kansascity.com/2010/12/04/2497484/how-reality-tv-took-over-prime.html

Buunk, Abraham and Frederick X. Gibbons. "Social Comparison: The End of a Theory and the Emergence of a Field." *Organizational Behavior and Human Decision Processes* 102, no. 1 (2007): 16.

Carter, Bill. "Tired of Reality TV, But Still Tuning in." *New York Times* (New York, NY), September 13, 2010. http://www.nytimes.com/2010/09/13/business/media/13reality.html?_r=0s

Coontz, Stephanie. *The Way We Never Were: American Families And The Nostalgia Trap.* New York, NY: Basic Books, 1992.

Festinger, Leo. "A Theory of Social Comparison Processes." *Human Relations* 7 (1954): 117-140.

Kompare, Derek. "Extraordinarily Ordinary: The Osbornes as 'An American Family'." In *Reality TV: Remaking Television Culture*, edited by Susan Murray and Laurie Ouellette, 100-122. New York, NY: New York University Press, 2008.

Gibbons, T. *Sister Wives*. "Meet Kody and the Wives," Season 1, Episode 1. DVD. Figure 8 Films. Silver Springs, MD: The Learning Channel, 2010.

Hall, Alice. "The Impact of Reality Programs' Perceived Factuality on Viewers' Senses of Suspense and Learning." Paper presented at the Annual Meeting of the International Communication Association, New York, NY, May 2005.

Hall, Alice. "Viewers' Perceptions of Reality Programs." *Communication Quarterly* 54 no. 2 (2006): 193.

Hall, Alice. "Perceptions of the Authenticity of Reality Programs and Their Relationships to Audience Involvement, Enjoyment, and Perceived Learning." *Journal of Broadcasting & Electronic Media* 53 no. 4 (2009): 519.

Hazlett, Courtney. "Reality Check for Reality TV Fans: You're More Neurotic," *Today.Com*, November 29, 2012. http://www.today.com/entertainment/reality-check-reality-tv-fans-youre-more-neurotic-1C7320186

Hill, Annette. *Reality TV: Audiences and Popular Factual Television.* New York, NY: Routledge, 2005.

Nabi, Robin L., Erica N Biely, Sara J. Morgan, and Carmen R. Stitt. "Reality-based Television Programming and the Psychology of its Appeal." *Media Psychology* 5 (2003): 324.

Rose, Randall L. and Stacy L. Wood. "Paradox and the Consumption of Authenticity Through Reality Television." *Journal of Consumer Research* 32 no. 2 (September 2005): 284.

Sister Wives, Season 1. DVD. produced by Figure 8 Films. Silver Springs, MD: The Learning Channel, 2010.

Smith, Richard, Terence Turner, Ron Garonzik, Colin Leach, Vanessa Urch-Druskat, and Christine Weston. "Envy and Schadenfreude." *Personaliy & Social Psychology Bulletin* 22 (1996): 158-168.

Suls, Jerry and Ladd Wheeler, eds., *Handbook of Social Comparison: Theory and Research* (*The Springer Series in Social Clinical Psychology*), New York: Springer Publishers, 2000.

Wills, Thomas A. "Downward Comparison: Principles in Social Psychology." *Psychology Bulletin* 90 (1981): 245-271.

NOTES

1. Bill Carter. "Tired of Reality TV, But Still Tuning in," *New York Times* (New York, NY), September 13, 2010, http://www.nytimes.com/2010/09/13/business/media/13reality.html?_r=0s

2. Aaron Barnhart. "How Reality TV Took Over Prime Time," *Kansas City Star* (Kansas City, MO), December 6, 2010, http://www.kansascity.com/2010/12/04/2497484/how-reality-tv-took-over-prime.html

3. Stephanie Coontz, *The Way We Never Were: American Families And The Nostalgia Trap* (New York, NY: Basic Books, 1992).

4. Derek Kompare, "Extraordinarily Ordinary: The Osbornes as "An American Family"." In *Reality TV: Remaking Television Culture,* ed. Susan Murray and Laurie Ouellette (New York, NY: New York University Press, 2008), 100-122.

5. *Sister Wives,* Season1, produced by Figure 8 Films (Silver Springs, MD: The Learning Channel, 2010), DVD.

6. *Sister Wives,* "Meet Kody and the Wives," Season 1, Episode 1, directed by T. Gibbons, produced by Figure 8 Films (Silver Springs, MD: The Learning Channel, 2010), DVD.

7. Ibid.

8. Alice Hall, "Viewers' Perceptions of Reality Programs," *Communication Quarterly* 54, no. 2 (2006): 193.

9. Alice Hall, "Perceptions of the Authenticity of Reality Programs and Their Relationships to Audience Involvement, Enjoyment, and Perceived Learning," *Journal of Broadcasting & Electronic Media* 53, no. 4 (2009): 519.

10. Ibid, 528.

11. Robin L. Nabi, Erica N. Biely, Sara J. Morgan, and Carmen R. Stitt, "Reality-based Television Programming and the Psychology of its Appeal," *Media Psychology* 5 (2003): 324.

12. Annette Hill. *Reality TV: Audiences and Popular Factual Television* (New York, NY: Routledge, 2005), 106.

13. Hall, "Perceptions of the Authenticity of Reality Programs."

14. Alice Hall, "The Impact of Reality Programs' Perceived Factuality on Viewers' Senses of Suspense and Learning" (paper presented at the Annual Meeting of the International Communication Association, New York, NY, May 2005): 6.

15. Ibid, 6.

16. Hill, *Reality TV*, 9.

17. Randall L. Rose and Stacy L. Wood, "Paradox and the Consumption of Authenticity Through Reality Television," *Journal of Consumer Research* 32, no. 2 (September 2005): 284.

18. Leo Festinger, "A Theory of Social Comparison Processes," *Human Relations* 7 (1954): 117-140.

19. Abraham Buunk and Frederick X. Gibbons, "Social Comparison: The End of a Theory and the Emergence of a Field," *Organizational Behavior and Human Decision Processes* 102, no. 1 (2007): 16.

20. Thomas A. Wills, "Downward Comparison: Principles in Social Psychology," *Psychology Bulletin* 90 (1981): 245-271.

21. Ibid.

22. Courtney Hazlett, "Reality Check for Reality TV Fans: You're More Neurotic," *Today.Com,* November 29, 2012, http://www.today.com/entertainment/reality-check-reality-tv-fans-youre-more-neurotic-1C7320186

23. Richard Smith, Terence Turner, Ron Garonzik, Colin Leach, Vanessa Urch-Druskat, and Christine Weston, "Envy and Schadenfreude," *Personaliy & Social Psychology Bulletin* 22 (1996): 158-168.

24. Ibid.

25. Hill, *Reality TV*, 98.

26. Mettee and Smith, 1977, as cited in Buunk and Gibbons, "Social Comparison," 3.

27. Buunk and Gibbons, "Social Comparison," 12.

28. Ibid, 16.

29. Hill, *Reality TV*, 90.

30. Ibid, 9.

31. Jerry Suls and Ladd Wheeler, eds., *Handbook of Social Comparison: Theory and Research (The Springer Series in Social Clinical Psychology)*, (New York: Springer Publishers, 2000).

Chapter Nine

The Lolita Spectacle & the Aberrant Mother: Exploring the Production and Performance of Manufactured Femininity in *Toddlers & Tiaras*

Leandra H. Hernandez

Lolita, the sexualized girl-child who first appeared in Nabokov's 1958 novel *Lolita* and later in many films based on the novel, is now a cultural icon that has recently dominated Western popular culture.[1] Lolita, represented by sexualized images of prepubescent girls that are often referred to as "nymphets" or "nymphettes,"[2] dominates the American imaginary and is exemplified in TLC's *Toddlers & Tiaras*. In this series, prepubescent, sexualized girls (ranging from six-month-old infants to tweens) compete in beauty pageants with highly regimented hair, makeup, costumes, and on-stage performances. The pageant queens frequently resist participation in the pageants and are forced to endure hours upon hours of training to perfect their smiles, stage walks, and their talent acts to ensure that they will be the most beautiful, feminine girl at the beauty pageant.

Taken together, what type of ideal femininity does *Toddlers & Tiaras* create? How does one "do" femininity in *Toddlers &* Tiaras? How is femininity produced and performed in the television series? These are the questions that inspire and guide this analysis. This essay argues that the femininity performed and portrayed in *Toddlers & Tiaras* is not normal or natural, it is bought and consumed via multiple avenues, and it is an identity performance that the young beauty pageant contestants must constantly practice, perfect, maintain, and regulate. Although some might perceive beauty pageants to be a traditional performance of femininity, *Toddlers & Tiaras* constructs a new definition of femininity that resonates with contemporary ideologies about the celebration of the body, extreme attention to personal appearance, and personal transformation.[3] These ideologies partially "comprise a commercially driven postfeminism" which both creates and legitimates reality television shows such as *Toddlers & Tiaras*.[4] Moreover, this postfeminist identity performance is one that is almost always forced upon the young girls by their mothers who, in the process, relive their pageantry days of the past and seek national fame and recognition for their daughters' successful performances.

Situated within postfeminist conceptualizations of femininity, the first part of this essay will explore the literature surrounding the commodification of girlhood, as well as how young girls are encouraged to perform postfeminist notions of femininity in accordance with girls' expected life scripts. Then, an analysis will be conducted of *Toddlers & Tiaras* that exemplifies the sexual commodification of girls, the gender and feminine performativity associated with their participation in beauty pageants, and the demonization of motherhood in the series as the young girls' mothers are the principal drivers behind their daughters' commodified femininities and participation in the pageants.

THE EMERGENCE OF POSTFEMINISM

Postfeminism is a concept and movement that is rife with contradictions. It emerged in the late 20th century as a break from feminism, and the term has been appropriated in numerous contexts for a variety of reasons.[5] Postfeminism has been used to signal death and termination of feminism, as well as the generational shift where young feminists use the term to establish their identities as being separate from second-wave feminism.[6]

The definition and conceptualization of postfeminism that will be used as the theoretical framework for this essay is drawn from Tasker and Negra's[7] work on postfeminism. According to feminist scholars, postfeminism constantly insists upon the argument that feminism is redundant and bleak, and it characterizes feminism and feminists in negative and unattractive ways.[8] Diane Negra writes:

> By caricaturing, distorting, and (often willfully) misunderstanding the political and social goals of feminism, postfeminism trades on a notion of feminism as rigid, serious, anti-sex and romance, difficult, and extremist. In contrast, postfeminism offers the pleasure and comfort of (re)claiming an identity uncomplicated by gender politics, postmodernism, or institutional critique.[9]

Postfeminism presents itself to women as a more attractive alternative to feminism. It commodifies feminism and encourages women to engage in high levels of consumption to make them look and feel younger and more beautiful. Yvonne Tasker and Diane Negra note that postfeminism perpetuates women as "pinups," cornerstones of commercialized beauty culture. Postfeminism has "offered new rationales for guilt-free consumerism, substantially reenergizing beauty culture and presiding over an aggressive mainstreaming of elaborate and expensive beauty treatments to the middle class."[10] Advertisements, television shows, magazines, and news articles abound that stress the importance of bodily maintenance, regulation, and surveillance. Ranging from increased usage of hair, nail, and skin services to pubic hair waxing, Botox, and liposuction, it is evident that postfeminism encourages hyperconsumption and extreme regulation, management, and surveillance of one's own (female) body. Taken together, this signals a reinvestment in capitalist patriarchy, which is particularly evident in *Toddlers & Tiaras*. In this series, the girls and their families partake in numerous expensive beauty treatments, including tanning, manicures and pedicures, wigs, fake teeth, and the purchasing of beauty pageant costumes that cost, at the low end, at least a few hundred dollars to, at the high end, at least a few thousand dollars.

Furthermore, another key concept associated with postfeminism is the illusion of choice.[11] Genz and Brabon note that postfeminism, in addition to commoditizing feminism's fight for equal rights, takes the collective, unifying aspect of feminism and instead transforms it to deemphasize the political and emphasize individual choice, empowerment and lifestyle.[12] Michelle M. Lazar extends this point when she notes that postfeminism is co-optative and achieves co-optation by harnessing feminism to discourses that neutralize its radical potential.[13] As a result, it both "takes the 'bite' out of feminism [and] characteristically leaves traditional femininity remarkably intact."[14] Postfeminism reverses feminism's well-known motto "the personal is political" and perverts it to emphasize its individualistic agenda.[15] Postfeminism presents the illusion of solving the "choice" dilemma that women face on a daily basis. Diane Negra argues that never has the popular culture landscape been as dominated by fantasies and fears about the life choices that women make as it is today. She questions the contradictions associated with postfeminism's illusion of choice:

> [W]hy, at a moment of widespread and intense hype about the spectrum of female options, choices, and pleasures available, do so few women actually seem to find cause for celebration? Why does this period feel so punishing and anxious for many?[16]

Therefore, in summation, postfeminism emphasizes that feminism is no longer necessary: it is dead and no longer timely because women have achieved all of their second-wave feminist goals. Moreover, it is obsessed with beauty, youth, and bodily maintenance and regulation. Women can become fulfilled, empowered, and more feminine *only* if they engage in postfeminism's advocated hyperconsumption. However, this raises the question of how postfeminism conceptualizes femininity. What is considered feminine in postfeminism? How does one *do* (youthful) femininity in accordance with current postfeminist discourse?

POSTFEMINIST CONCEPTUALIZATIONS OF FEMININITY

Sarah Projansky notes that the current proliferation of discourses on girlhood coincides with the proliferation of postfeminist discourses.[17] Postfeminist discourses productively engender new forms of femininities.[18] Within these discourses, femininity is often based upon a woman's sexuality, as opposed to traditional definitions such as empathy, nurturance, and passivity, among others. Numerous femininities have emerged within postfeminist discourse; however, the two that are of particular focus for this paper include the mean girls discourse (which is an extension of the girl power discourse) and the Lolita/pageantry discourse. Taken together, these postfeminist femininities can shed light upon how femininity is produced and performed in *Toddlers & Tiaras.*

Mean girls: Girls are not sugar and spice and everything nice

The mean girls discourse focuses on new pathologies of girl power. In this discourse, mean girls are aggressive, potentially violent bullies.[19] Girls' relational aggression focuses less on physically harming other girls and more on damaging girls' relationships and social status.[20] Whereas the vulnerable girl initially occupied the public view, the mean girl has replaced her in public consciousness.[21] Certain feminist scholars and criminologists note that the constructions of violent girls in the media are fueled by aforementioned notions of gender equality and the notion that "girls can do it, too."[22] This is also partially a backlash to feminist research reaffirming traditional notions of femininity, including the ideas that women are more caring, nurturing, and relationship-focused than men.[23] Jessica Ringrose argues that the recent shift from the universalized vulnerable girl to the universalized mean girl is "universalizing, essentializing, [and] gender-differentiat[ing]," and thus creates a new template and a new framework for normal girlhood that moves along the girlhood continuum from nice, vulnerable girl to mean, aggressive girl.[24] Drawing upon scholars Austin and Walkerdine, Jessica Ringrose notes that "femininity is re-pathologized, any expression of aggression from girls is 'wrong', and violence is re-constituted as 'other' to the feminine."[25]

Jessica Ringrose and Valerie Walkerdine discuss in length the middle-class mean girls' discourse and argue that meanness is now a dominant motif for Western girlhood. They argue that it does "not disturb the traditional boundaries of appropriate femininity, but rather entrenches them."[26] Thus, meanness lies within the boundaries of normative, repressive femininity. Girls and women trespass into the aggressive, mean realm, which is supposed to be inhabited only by boys and men. Ringrose and Walkerdine refer to this as "girls' incapacity for rational fraternity."[27] When there is not a fit and girls and women cannot rationally enjoy these new subjectivities in positive ways, the age-old story of femininity reappears, stressing that girls and women are still plagued by lack and risk slipping into ways of cruelty and violence.[28] The relational aggression that girls perform by intentionally withdrawing relationships as a means of hurting or controlling another child, excluding children from play groups, and spreading rumors about another child falls under the "guise of a pathological feminine behavior, a disease even, that must be treated to prevent peer rejection, depression, loneliness and much worse."[29] Jessica Ringrose summarizes the issues associated with relational aggression:

> From what began as a feminist-inspired challenge to male-biased science on aggression, we find a developmental literature on girls' relational aggression that constitutes a near total objectification of the girl for whom gender-differentiated behavior is invented through scales that pathologize subjects via their approximation to relational aggression. This pathologization occurs in the way direct aggression is held as a neutral, normative masculine standard of aggression against which the feminine is constructed as indirect, repressed, and aberrant. This feminine and masculine binary opposition reconstitutes the gender-dichotomized symbolic terrain where the feminine originates as lack—as universally different, inferior and 'other' to the masculine.[30]

Thus, images of the mean girl in contemporary society are caught up in Girl Power discourses. Postfeminists and anti-feminists argue that girls' success and power that they experience from school success and in masculine worlds of work and pleasure inevitably lead to manipulation, aggression, and meanness. Girls' pathological nature sabotages them, and feminism is to blame because this meanness and aggression is a failure of feminist goals and *claims* of girls' success.

Pageantry: the Lolita effect

The second type of postfeminist femininity that will be discussed is the notion of pageantry. Children's beauty pageants began in the late 1950s when America's Junior Miss Pageant was created as a high school scholarship program in Mobile, Alabama. Now, numerous pageants have emerged nationwide for girls of all ages, and one example of a reality television show that chronicles the experiences of young pageant contestants is TLC's *Toddlers & Tiaras*. Children's beauty pageants comprise a billion-dollar industry, gaining support both from corporate sponsors and the families of the contestants, who pay excessive sums to enroll their children in the pageants and also to buy the entire kit and caboodle, including dresses, performance costumes, makeup, wigs, extensions, fake nails, fake teeth, and tans. Furthermore, pageants have produced numerous support industries, including photographers, publishers, grooming consultants, and costume designers, among others. Participating in beauty pageants is a highly classed activity, considering that those who are not affluent or middle-class are often discouraged by the high price tags associated with pageantry.[31]

Many scholars have explored the issues associated with child pageantry. Jenny Kitzinger and Henry Giroux note that childhood innocence has now become a cultural panic, causing politicians to present themselves as protectors of childhood innocence by attempting to implement policies defending childhood innocence.[32] However, Giroux argues that now, childhood innocence has emerged as a means to advance a "conservative political agenda based on so-called family values, in which middle-class white children are viewed as more valued and deserving of the material resources and cultural goods of the larger society than are poor and nonwhite children."[33] This resounds Diane Negra's work, in which she argues that postfeminist ideologies work to propagate conservative, capitalistic values by emphasizing the woman's retreat to the home and also the extensive levels of consumption she must enjoy to make herself more beautiful at the expense of poor, lower-class minorities.[34]

Child beauty pageants, according to Henry Giroux, are exemplary sites for examining how the discourse of innocence mystifies appropriating children's bodies in a culture and society that sexually commodifies them.[35] He argues:

> Not only do child beauty pageants function as a pedagogical site where children learn about pleasure, desire and the roles they might assume in an adult society, they also rationalize and uphold commercial and ideological values within the larger society that play an important role in marketing children as objects of pleasure, desire, and sexuality . . . As sites of representation, identity formation, consumption and regulation, the dominant and assigned meaning attached to these events have to be understood in terms of how they align with other cultural sites engaged in offering mostly young girls regressive notions of desire, femininity, sexuality, beauty, and self-esteem.[36]

This sexually commodified girlhood that Giroux discusses has been termed "Lolita." The "Lolita Effect" has been defined by M. Gigi Durham as "the distorted and delusional set of myths about girls' sexuality that circulates widely in our culture and throughout the world, that works to limit, undermine, and restrict girls' sexual progress."[37] The sexy little girl is a familiar figure in today's cultural landscape: the curvy, make-up—stained nymphet, the scantily clad music video child dancer, and the sexy teeny-bopper film and television show stars across the world.[38] M. Gigi Durham argues that the Lolita girl occupies a contradictory space in society: she is simultaneously a symbol of female empowerment and the embodiment of the "chauvinistic beauty myth. She invokes the specter of pedophilia while kindling the prospect of potent female sexuality."[39]

Lolita discourses characterize the Lolita as a girl who is empowered via sexuality and consumption. This characterization engages a postfeminist conceptualization of the sexy, desirable girl and young woman.[40] Within this consumer discourse, girls are powerful citizens with powerful buying power who utilize their shopping for girlie products as an expression of empowered choice.[41] Jackson and colleagues note that "a key shift around the sexy production of femininity is from a construction as object (of the male gaze) to one as subject, confident and agentic enough to express herself as sexually knowing and desiring."[42] This is evident in music videos, advertisements, and reality television shows such as *Toddlers & Tiaras* where girls wear tight, body-revealing clothing and engage in sexual posing, self-touching, gyrating dances, and other sexualized acts. This child sexualization discourse positions the Lolita as being influenced by and emulative of these sexualizing modes.[43]

Taken together, postfeminist conceptualizations of femininity include the strong, empowered, successful girl; the aggressive, violent girl; and the beautified, sexy Lolita. Various analyses have been conducted on postfeminist performances of femininity in reality TV shows, including femininity, plastic surgery and self-improvement in *The Swan*;[44] the domestication of cosmetic surgery on *Extreme Makeover* and *Nip/Tuck*;[45] and connections of beauty pageant femininity and cosmetic surgery in various reality television shows.[46] However, to date, an analysis has not been conducted of the performance and production of (postfeminist) femininity in child beauty pageants. An analysis of *Toddlers & Tiaras* is necessary because American popular cultures presents and perpetuates representations of normative gender performances. Anoop Nayak and Mary Jane Kehili posit that cultural studies analyses of popular culture texts "may have a great deal to say about the changing world in which we live and the types of gender identities that are being envisioned."[47] Furthermore, the presentation of the girl subjects in *Toddlers & Tiaras* speaks both to "the changing role of media in the normalization of performances of femininity, as well as to the affiliation of many young women with post-feminist politics in the United States."[48]

Toddlers & Tiaras has the potential to result in two possible outcomes (of many): it could shape young girls' and parents' perceptions of how a true, beautiful, feminine child should act and the consumption activities in which she should engage to attain this postfeminist femininity, or it could result in an encoding of these representations as an aberrant type of girlhood, a repulsive femininity that makes viewers' skin crawl and results in harsh judgment of both the young pageant queens *and* their aggressive mothers who exploit their daughters for fame and recognition under the rhetoric of "their choice." A critical cultural analysis of *Toddlers & Tiaras* can help us understand more fully how the show sexually commodifies the girls who participate in the beauty pageants, the construction of the worthwhile girl subject *only* because of her consumption abilities and the power her outer beauty can buy, and the role of pageant mothers in this bodily commodification.

THE PRODUCTION AND PERFORMANCE OF FEMININITY IN *TODDLERS & TIARAS*

This essay analyzes three key moments (out of many) in *Toddlers & Tiaras* from seasons 3 and 4. Seasons 3 and 4 were chosen because the author had access to all episodes of these two seasons. This analysis indicates that the femininities performed represent the main postfeminist conceptions of femininity, specifically the mean girls and the pageantry Lolita femininities, and that the girls' mothers are the main driving forces behind their participation in the pageants.

MEAN GIRLS: "SHE REALLY IS GONNA BE SOMEBODY"

One of the femininities performed in *Toddlers & Tiaras* is the mean girls femininity. It is evident in numerous episodes that young girls become very irritated with each other and become extremely hypercompetitive, not wanting to lose their grand supreme title. The grand supreme title in *Toddlers & Tiaras* is not only a highly coveted honor, but it is also accompanied with thousand-dollar cash prizes and some sort of material prize, including a Disney canopy bed, life-sized trophies and a life-sized Barbie Jeep or car, among other prizes. Thus, some of the young pageant contestants become hypercompetitive to ensure they win; as a result, they become very aggressive when they interact with other contestants.

For example, in Season 3, Episode 18, the viewer chronicles the pageantry experiences of Makenzie, Danielle, and twins Scarlett and Isabella. Four-year-old Makenzie is one of the most popular pageant contestants in the American child pageant circuit. Despite her young age, she is a national winner and thus is well known and respected at all American pageants. Eight-year old Danielle Kirby, an up-and-coming rookie, was prepping to go onstage to perform her "beauty walk" after Makenzie. When Danielle saw Makenzie, she instantly became aggressive and sassy, rudely sneering at her mother and even dismissing other contestants. As soon as Makenzie finished her beauty walk, Danielle gets into a fight with her mother. The scene cuts to an interview with Danielle's mother, Tedi, who tells the camera, "She can get a *little* diva attitude on pageant day. She can sometimes get a little agitated." The scene cuts back to Danielle and Tedi struggling, with Danielle saying, "She keeps taking my spotlight. And she's like (mimics Makenzie's walk). She's taking my spotlight, yes she is. She's probably going to be on TV! I *hope* they cut that out." Tedi tells Danielle, "It's okay. She's a baby." Tedi then tells the camera that Danielle gets annoyed when she sees other girls taking the spotlight because she wants the attention and spotlight to *only* be on her, and that this leads Danielle to get annoyed with other girls. Danielle then shoos off another contestant in the waiting room, saying, "Go! I'm done with you." Tedi concludes by noting that Danielle would never hurt the other contestants, and then the scene cuts to Danielle slapping her little brother and shaking her fist at her mom. Danielle then sees another girl with an outfit similar to hers and says, "That just doesn't go with my flow." Tedi says, "You look at all the children, and some kids have it and some kids don't. I *know* she has it."

This scene explicates very clearly what Jessica Ringrose and Marnina Gonick term the mean girls discourse.[49] Danielle is very sassy, egotistical, and competitive, and she constantly mocks and badmouths other contestants. This aggression plays out in actual encounters with other girls, when she tells them to leave her sight because she's "done with them." Moreover, Danielle's hypercompetitiveness is fueled by her desire to win the cash prizes, the life-sized trophies, and the success that accompanies winning a supreme title. She vies for the monetary prizes and recognition that reward her successful performance of postfeminist femininity. She mentions to the camera, "If I don't win, I'll start punching some judges." However, when she loses, she begins to weep profusely on stage, expressing her sadness about not winning and about not being rewarded for what she thought was an ideal, well-practiced feminine performance. She constantly cries to her mother that she was so sad she lost, despite all of the practicing she did to perfect her (postfeminist feminine) performances. Also, Tedi implies that a major component of her daughter's success *is* the diva attitude she possesses. This mean girl, diva sass is precisely, according to Tedi, what is going to put her daughter a step ahead of the rest of the contestants.

To a certain extent, Danielle's mean girl-ness is accepted and even encouraged. Furthermore, in addition to Danielle's mother, other parents encourage their daughters to be hypercompetitive in order to win large cash sums and other prizes. Part of the discourse of hypercompetitiveness in *Toddlers & Tiaras* is a never-ending cycle in which the daughters absolutely *have* to win because their parents have spent thousands of dollars on their pageantry precisely so that they can win. It becomes evident throughout the series that many mothers force this imposed identity performance upon their daughters as they live out old pageant dreams and wishes vicariously through their daughters' bodies. This is exemplified in Danielle's mother, who constantly tells her daughter, "I did *not* spend this much money on you for you not to win. Now get out there and win!" Another example of this is in the 12th episode of season 4 where the viewer is introduced to four-year-old Victoria. Tammi, Victoria's mom, tells the camera, "The funnest thing about seeing her win is that *I* made her look like that. And *I* won. It's addicting!" Lastly, in the 12th episode of season 4, baby Brystol's mom tells the camera:

> We're not losers by any means. When it comes to pageants, losing is not an option. The family is very competitive. So am I. whenever she wins a crown, I win a crown. If I have to take out a second mortgage on my house to do what it takes, then I would do it. Am I crazy? No. I do what it takes to win.

Thus, the mothers of the prepubescent Lolitas not only compromise their children for fame, but they also instill hypercompetitive values and traits in their daughters as a means of "adding fuel to the fire" so that the daughters will become competitive and win. Furthermore, the pageant mothers frame their daughters' pageant participation under the rhetoric of choice, stating that the daughters can quit pageantry whenever they choose to do so, although that is rarely ever the case. Thus, performing the mean girls discourse is accepted, even encouraged, for pageant girls in *Toddlers & Tiaras* because it is seen as a way for them to enact their (false) power and attain the grand supreme titles, cash prizes, and the fame that accompanies winning success.

THE SEXUALIZED PAGEANTRY LOLITA: SHIRLEY TEMPLE AND DOLLY PARTON

Although the mean girls' discourse might not be as explicit in every *Toddlers & Tiaras* episode, the sexualized pageantry Lolita femininity is not only performed in every episode, but also encouraged and emphasized. Although numerous clips could have been chosen for this analysis, the two that I chose to include are the Shirley Temple and Dolly Parton performances. These clips are particularly interesting because of the ways the girls heavily practice the routines; the ways their mothers and fathers spend thousands of dollars on costumes, props, and routine/beauty pageant coaches; and the ways that all of these performances together show what it means to be a "lady"—or, rather, a very feminine girl—in a postfeminist world.

Shirley Temple

The first example of the sexualized Lolita is Mia, a four-year-old girl who performs as Shirley Temple during the 11th episode of season 3. She is performing at a celebrity-themed pageant show, and the rules for the dance skits require that the skits be based upon a conceptualization of 1920s and 1930s Hollywood. Mia performs as a less traditional Shirley Temple, taking stage in a black and white plaid cropped top with a tie, a black and white petticoat glitter tutu skirt, white knee-high socks, and black Mary Jane patent leather flats. Her blonde hair has volume-adding curly extensions added to it, and her makeup is done as if she were a 1950s pin-up girl. As the performance begins, Mia looks like a little doll as she walks on stage with a large white and pink lollipop. The large white and pink lollipop symbolizes innocent girlhood, yet it could also symbolize adolescent sexuality and sexual prowess, as the large lollipop is frequently perceived as a sexualized candy or object. In a finalizing, shattering blow, Mia's symbolized innocent girlhood is eradicated when she throws her lollipop to the ground and begins gyrating furiously to a hip-hop beat. Mia's dance skit, which lasts 35 seconds, is solely comprised of what *Toddlers & Tiaras* has now termed the "Shirley Temple Chest Bump." Her dance includes her facing the crowd with her arms up, alternating her chest thrusts and her hip thrusts, and ending her routine with her chest bump moves, showing the crowd how well she can shake her rear end.

The production and performance of femininity in Mia's routine was dependent upon the scripts and props that she needed to perform successfully, as well as the high amounts of consumption that furnished her costumes, props, body maintenance, and her entry into the pageant. Mia's costume and performance simultaneously and paradoxically symbolize and embody both innocent girlhood and the sexualized Lolita. Her costume and lollipop prop initially provide a false sense of innocent girlhood, which vanishes once the sexy young dancer comes to life.

Dolly Parton

The second example of the sexualized Lolita is Maddy from the 11th episode of season 4, whose skit is entitled "Doing Dolly Parton." Four-year-old Maddy begins her clip by saying, "I want to show the judges how beautiful I am." Maddy's Dolly Parton outfit is special to her because it is the same Dolly Parton outfit her mother used when she was a beauty pageant participant. The Dolly Parton outfit includes a platinum blonde curly wig and a purple satin jewel-bedazzled dress. The clincher, though, is the fake boobs and fake buttocks that accompany the costume. In order for Maddy to be a realistic representation of Dolly Parton, she needs the enhanced breasts and buttocks. The clip shows Maddy's mom attaching her fake breasts and her fake buttocks, what her mom calls "the fake extra enhancers." Maddy's mom notes that the enhancers are important because everyone "all of a sudden realizes that she's *really* Dolly because she has the enhancements."

This example of Maddy's performance as Dolly Parton is a two-part exemplar of both the sexualized Lolita and the artificiality and unnaturalness of postfeminism's conceptualization of femininity. First, Maddy is a product of sexually commodified girlhood. Performing as Dolly Parton sexualizes her, especially with the addition of her fake breasts and buttocks. Furthermore, her sexualized commodification is compounded when her mother and grandmother note that money is not an issue concerning Maddy's pageantry because they always know that she will win and that they will "get the money back." Yet again, similar to Danielle's hopeful win and Mia's Shirley Temple performance, Maddy's perfect performance of femininity is expected to be rewarded monetarily. In this scene, Maddy's body becomes a commodity that can be exploited for monetary gain and a better pageant reputation. Maddy's grandma tells viewers that pageantry "runs in their blood," implying that being a feminine, sexual beauty queen is natural for them and that they have at least two generations of experience in utilizing girls' bodies for monetary gain and pageant fame. However, there is nothing natural about Maddy's femininity in this scene. The traditionally dominant ideology of femininity argues that it is natural and inherent, but Maddy's performance disputes this notion. Her femininity is not natural and inherent; rather, it is artificially implemented in order to feign the naturalness needed to make her representation appear realistic. Her femininity in this scene needs to be restaged with fake breasts and buttocks and constantly regimented via repeated practice sessions and extensive bodily maintenance in order for her performance to appear as a representation of both *real* femininity and *real* Dolly Parton. There is no escaping the idea of consumer capitalism, production, and consumption associated with postfeminist ideals of girlhood and femininity, especially in pageantry, considering that Maddy's grandmother has spent over $400,000 in costumes, pageant enrollment fees, travel, performance coaches, nails, tans, and other bodily regimens necessary to make Maddy the perfect, feminine beauty queen. Postfeminism's illusion of solving the choice dilemma for women runs rampant in these scenes as the parents and grandparents consistently argue that participating in pageants is the girls' choice, not theirs, and that they would without a doubt pull their girls out of pageants at the girls' requests. However, this argument is not persuasive, considering that the girls are sexualized commodities who earn their parents and grandparents fame, reputation, and monetary prizes when they succeed. Most of the girls do not have a choice regarding participating in pageants, and this is evident in the loud screams, crying fits, and rageful thrashings that occur when girls no longer want to participate and resist the constant practice sessions. Thus, Maddy and her fellow sexualized Lolitas are both rewarded for and by their successful performances of femininity.

DISCUSSION: PEDAGOGICAL PRACTICES PLAYED OUT ON YOUNG FEMALE BODIES

TLC's *Toddlers & Tiaras* is a postfeminist reality television show that sexually commodifies prepubescent girls. It chronicles the extreme bodily maintenance and regulation that prepubescent girls are subjected to as their mothers force them to participate in these pageants. All of this body maintenance, practice, and performance is done in hopes that one lucky (and highly overdone) girl can win the ultimate grand supreme title, along with a large cash prize and other materialistic gifts. Here, girls are treated as commodities that are put on display and modeled for others' consumption purposes so that they can win cash prizes and fame. Catherine Driscoll discusses the position of girls in patriarchy and capitalism and notes that daughters "are a kind of money—an evaluation of property and wealth and an extension of reproductive and familial labor into the world."[50] Although she is explicitly discussing girls as traded family commodities via dowries and marriage systems, the point still stands that girls in capitalism are represented by notions of consumption and commodification. In *Toddlers & Tiaras*, this point is furthered even more when the prepubescent girls' consumption and commodification is sexualized. Driscoll further notes that "the significance of late modern girls to consumption is not that they consume (everybody does), or that their sexuality is in fact bound up in commodification, but that they are perceived to derive an inordinate amount of pleasure from commodification and commodity fetishism."[51] Christine Griffin furthers this point when she notes that girls and girls' bodies are represented as both consuming objects and objects of consumption, especially for male heterosexual desire and consumption.[52] Jessica Ringrose and Valeria Walkerdine elaborate upon the notion of girls as both subject *and* object:

> If we think about what is and has been demanded of women, who have always had to be desirable, presentable, consumable, we can think about what is happening under neo-liberalism as an intensification of feminine as site (both subject and object) of commodification and consumption. The new importance of the feminine is intimately linked to the rise of the psychological subject, a rational subject of choice, flexibility, who has to have the necessary skills to succeed in the constant necessity to change oneself.[53]

Additionally, in preparation for the pageants, the young girls' parents subject them to extreme forms of bodily modification, such as spray tanning; tanning booths; manicures and fake nails; pedicures; eyebrow waxing and threading; fake teeth; hair coloring; excessive use of facial and hair products; and consumption of candy and "go-go" juice, a mix of sodas and energy drinks to keep them awake, bubbly, and hyper. This extreme body maintenance and regulation is prioritized by the parents of the young pageant participants, as they try to make their daughters the most beautiful (read feminine) participants at the pageant. Furthermore, it is accepted, even encouraged, for the girls to perform traits of the mean girls discourse as a means to attain rewards for flawless performances of postfeminist femininity. Taken together, conceptualizations of femininity as natural are disputed: femininity is artificial, imposed, regimented, and practiced, and this is very evident in the beauty pageant spectacle.

The spectacle, first introduced by Guy Debord, refers to the various images used by the media to represent the world.[54] These images and messages are transmitted simultaneously and globally, and M. Gigi Durham notes that spectacles urge consumers to purchase products and that they are a useful way to think about girls' sexuality in a social context.[55] The child beauty pageant, in particular, is a spectacle that not only puts girls on display for consumption, but simultaneously encourages girls and women to perform the femininities they see in the show and engage in consumption processes to attain that femininity. They also encourage men to consume the young bodies on display. Henry Giroux notes that child beauty pageants tell us what we have become as a society by thinking critically about how ready "we are to sell our kids on the beauty block."[56] This is reminiscent of the mothers who force their daughters to compete in pageants to "make their daughters famous," although it quickly becomes evident that the mothers are the ones vying for the fame and attention.

Furthermore, in addition to sexually commodifying the prepubescent Lolitas, *Toddlers & Tiaras* also uses the Lolita bodies as sites of pedagogy[57] to teach women what "true femininity" and "true womanhood" are: artificial, regimented, practiced, and characterized by high amounts of consumption. It is not a coincidence that the show airs on TLC, also known as The Learning Channel, and its slogan is "Life Unscripted!" *Toddlers & Tiaras* shows girls and women what scripts they have at their disposal to attain the perfectly feminine postfeminist performance, and it also sets women down their postfeminist life-cycle path. Diane Negra discusses life-cycles as the different postfeminist phases women are supposed to go through in their lifetime. Adult phases include getting married; having children; retreating from work to the home/domestic space to engage in motherly and domestic duties; and then engaging in hyperconsumption to make one's body more beautiful, including consuming creams, Botox, plastic surgery, and other extreme forms of bodily modification.[58] The femininity presented in *Toddlers & Tiaras* teaches girls how to be feminine (in a postfeminist sense) and sets girls on their postfeminist life-cycle path: if, at such a young age, the prepubescent girls are already engaging in performative, feminine identities, then transitioning to the next postfeminist life-cycle is a logical progression. This not only perpetuates postfeminism, but it also depoliticizes girls, in addition to sexually commodifying them. Instead of embracing a childhood that includes sports, dolls, and education, the prepubescent Lolitas engage in and perform a childhood that sexually commodifies them and puts them on display for the male gaze so that others can consume them.

Perhaps what emerges as most fascinating through an analysis of *Toddlers & Tiaras* is the role of the pageant mothers in this perpetuation of the commodification of their daughters' bodies. Although this analysis initially intended to focus on the young beauty queens at the forefront of the pageant spectacle, the role of the mothers in facilitating this constant commodification cannot go unaddressed. For the young girls, successful femininity is articulated through constant performance of the ultimate embodiment of postfeminism: the illusion of choice, high levels of consumption and regimentation, and putting one's self on display to be judged. In this series, it may seem that the young girls have high hopes and aspirations to become the next Miss America; however, as the series unfolds, it becomes apparent that these aspirations are generally forced upon the pageant queens by their mothers and family members. Just as successful childhood femininity is articulated by extreme attention to one's body and extreme attention to the physical so that one can win prizes and fame, "successful maternal femininity" is articulated in this television series by endorsing and borderline forcing daughters to participate in pageantry, even at the expense of their pocketbooks and daughters' forceful resistance.

CONCLUDING THOUGHTS

TLC's *Toddlers & Tiaras* is a reality television series that endorses and showcases postfeminist notions of femininity. Prepubescent mean girls and Lolitas in the series endure hours upon hours of practice to perfect their performances of femininity, and they undergo multiple bodily modifications in order to be the most beautiful, feminine girl at the pageant. This is done in the hope of winning cash prizes, life-sized trophies, and all the fame that money can buy. Mothers frequently encourage their daughters to perform traits associated with the mean girls discourse because they have spent thousands of dollars for their daughters to win, and their daughters need to "do whatever it takes to win," even if it means being rude, sassy, and mean to other pageant contestants. Furthermore, the prepubescent Lolitas are sexually commodified during their routines as they perform choreographed routines dressed as Dolly Parton, Shirley Temple, *Pretty Woman's* Julia Roberts, Lady Gaga, and others, and it becomes evident that the femininity produced and performed in *Toddlers & Tiaras* is unnatural, artificial, regulated, modified, and imposed upon the girls. Mothers in the series argue that the girls' participation is to give them high self-esteem and so that they can have fun, but it becomes apparent that many of the mothers live their old pageant dreams and wishes vicariously through their daughters' bodies. These are new representations in the American consciousness that present aberrant, non-normative modes of motherhood as it relates to daughters in beauty pageants.

Henry Giroux argues that "concerned educators, parents, and activists must begin to challenge and counter such representations, ideologies, and social practices as part of a cultural politics that makes issues of pedagogy and power central to its project."[59] My hope is that, with this analysis, I have uncovered how *Toddlers & Tiaras* uses girls' bodies as sites of pedagogy to teach other girls and women what it means to perform postfeminist notions of femininity. We must take seriously how beauty pageants and other cultural sites position girls in terms of how they are to think of themselves through images and performances in order to fully understand how girls' bodies are utilized as sites for the production and performance of knowledge, the knowledge that is supposed to teach other girls and women how to be feminine—a true woman—in a postfeminist world. Henry Giroux and M. Gigi Durham urge parents, educators, and activists to pressure schools to study popular culture as a "serious object of analysis," and also to work with children to help them become more media literate.[60] Only then can we hope that girls will critically consume images of the sexualized Lolita in *Toddlers & Tiaras* and other television shows and advertisements so that they can demystify the images and "learn the knowledge and skills that enable them to be cultural producers capable of creating public spheres informed by representations that honor and critically engage their traditions and experiences."[61]

REFERENCES

Albright, Julie. "Lolita online: Sex and under-aged smoking on the Internet." *Journal of Critical Psychology*. (2005).

Banet-Weiser, Sarah, and Laura Portwood-Stacer. "'I just want to be me again!': Beauty pageants, reality television and post-feminism." *Feminist Theory*, 7. (2006): 255-272.

Debord, Guy. "Commodity as spectacle." In *Keyworks in Cultural Studies II*, edited byM. Gigi Durham & Douglas Kellner, 117-121. Malden: Blackwell, 2006.

Driscoll, Catherine. *Girls: Feminine adolescence in popular culture and cultural theory*. New York: Columbia University Press, 2002.

Durham, M. Gigi. *The Lolita Effect: The Media Sexualization of Young Girls and What We Can Do About It*. Woodstock: The Overlook Press, 2008.

Genz, Stephanie, and Benjamin Brabon. *Postfeminism: Cultural Texts and Theories*. Edinburgh: Edinburgh University Press Ltd., 2009.

Gill, Rosalind, and Jane Arthurs. "Editors' introduction: New femininities?" *Feminist Media Studies, 6*. (2006): 443-451.

Gillis, Stacy, and Rebecca Munford. "Harvesting our strengths: Third wave feminism and women's studies." *Journal of International Women's Studies*, 4. (2003): 1-6.

Giroux, Henry. "Nymphet fantasies: Child beauty pageants and the politics of innocence." *Social Text*, 57. (1998): 31-53.

Giroux, Henry. *Stealing innocence: Corporate Culture's War on Children.* New York: Palgrave, 2000.

Giroux, Henry. "Child beauty pageants: A scene from the "Other America." Truthout, 2009. http://archive.truthout.org/051109A.

Gonick, Marnina. *Between Femininities: Ambivalence, Identity and the Education of Girls.* Albany: SUNY Press, 2004.

Gonick, Marnina. "Between "girl power" and "reviving Ophelia": Constituting the neoliberal girl subject." *NWSA Journal*, 18. (2006): 1-23.

Griffin, Christine. (2004). "Good girls, bad girls: Anglocentrism and diversity in the constitution of contemporary girlhood." In *All about the Girl: Culture, Power, and Identity*, edited by Anita Harris, pp. 29-43. New York: Routledge, 2004.

Hawkesworth, Mary. "The semiotics of premature burial: Feminism in a post-feminist age." *Signs: Journal of Women in Culture and Society*, 29. (2004): 961-985.

Jackson, Sue, Tiina Vares, and Rosalind Gill. "'The whole playboy mansion image': Girls' fashioning and fashioned selves within a postfeminist culture." *Feminism & Psychology*, 23. (2013): 143-162.

Kitzinger, Jenny. "Defending innocence: Ideologies of childhood." *Feminist Review*, 28. (1988): 77-87.

Lazar, Michelle. "Entitled to consume: Postfeminist femininity and a culture of post-critique." *Discourse & Communication, 3.* (2009): 371-400.

Marwick, Alice. "There's a beautiful girl under all of this: Performing hegemonic femininity in reality television." *Critical Studies in Media Communication*, 27. (2010): 251-266.

Merskin, Debra. "Reviving Lolita? A media literacy examination of sexual portrayals of girls in fashion advertising." In *Contemporary Readings in Social Problems,* edited by Anna Leon-Guerrero & Kristine Zentgraf, 97-103. Thousand Oaks: Pine Forge Press, 2004.

Nayak, Anoop, and Mary Jane Kehily. *Gender, Youth, and Culture: Young Masculinities and Femininities.* Houndmills: Palgrave, 2008.

Negra, Diane. *What a Girl Wants? Fantasizing the Reclamation of Self in Postfeminism.* New York: Routledge, 2009.

Nelson, Sarah. *Incest: Fact and myth.* Edinburgh: Stramullion Press, 1987.

Projansky, Sarah. "Mass magazine cover girls: Some reflections on postfeminist girls and postfeminism's daughters." In *Interrogating postfeminism: Gender and the politics of popular culture*, edited by Yvonne Tasker & Diane Negra, 40-72.

Ringrose, Jessica. "A new universal mean girl: Examining the discursive construction and regulation of a new feminine pathology." *Feminism & Psychology*, 16. (2006): 405-424.

Ringrose, Jessica. "Successful girls? Complicating post-feminist, neo-liberal discourses of educational achievement and gender equality." *Gender and Education*, 19. (2007): 471-489.

Ringrose, Jessica, and Valerie Walkerdine. "Regulating the abject: The TV makeover as site of neo- liberal reinvention toward bourgeois femininity." *Feminist Media Studies*, 8. (2008): 227-246.

Ringrose, Jessica, & Valerie Walkerdine. "What does it mean to be a girl in the twenty-first century? Exploring some contemporary dilemmas of femininity and girlhood in the West." In *Girl Culture: An Encyclopedia,* edited by Claudia Mitchell & Jacqueline Reid-Walsh, 6-16. Westport: Greenwood Press, 2008.

Rush, Florence. *The Best Kept Secret: Sexual Abuse of Children.* New York: McGraw-Hill, 1980.

Tait, Sue. "Television and the domestication of cosmetic surgery." *Feminist Media Studies*, 7. (2007): 119-135.

Tasker, Yvonne, and Diane Negra. *Interrogating Postfeminism: Gender and the Politics of Popular Culture.* Durham: Duke University Press, 2007.

Walkerdine, Valerie. *Daddy's Little Girl.* Cambridge: Harvard University Press, 1997.

Worrall, Anne. "Twisted sisters, laddettes, and the new penology: The social construction of 'violent girls.'" In *Girls' violence: Myths and Realities*, edited by Christine Alder & Anne Worrall, 41-60. New York: SUNY, 2004.

NOTES

1. Julie Albright, "Lolita online: Sex and under-aged smoking on the Internet," *Journal of Critical Psychology* (2005). Debra Merskin, "Reviving Lolita? A media literacy examination of sexual portrayals of girls in fashion advertising," in *Contemporary Readings in Social Problems*, edited by Anna Leon-Guerrero & Kristine Zentgraf. (Thousand Oaks: Pine Forge Press, 2004), pp. 97-103. Valerie Walkerdine, *Daddy's Little Girl*, (Cambridge: Harvard University Press, 1997).

2. Albright, "Lolita online." Jenny Kitzinger, "Defending innocence: Ideologies of childhood," *Feminist Review*, 28 (1988): 77-87. Merskin, "Reviving Lolita?" Sarah Nelson, *Incest: Fact and Myth*, (Edinburgh: Stramullion Press, 1987). Florence Rush, *The Best Kept Secret: Sexual Abuse of Children*, (New York: McGraw-Hill, 1980).

3. Sarah Banet-Weiser and Laura Portwood-Stacer, "'I just want to be me again!': Beauty pageants, reality television and post-feminism," *Feminist Theory*, 7 (2006): 255-272. Diane Negra, *What a Girl Wants? Fantasizing the Reclamation of Self in Postfeminism*, (New York: Routledge, 2009).

4. Banet-Weiser & Portwood-Stacer, "I just want to be me again!" p. 257. Negra, *What a Girl Wants?* Sarah Projansky, "Mass magazine cover girls: Some reflections on postfeminist girls and postfeminism's daughters," edited by Yvonne Tasker & Diane Negra.

5. Stephanie Genz and Benjamin Brabon, *Postfeminism: Cultural Texts and Theories*, (Edinburgh: Edinburgh University Press Ltd., 2009). Negra, *What a Girl Wants?*

6. Genz & Brabon, *Postfeminism*. Stacy Gillis and Rebecca Munford, "Harvesting our strengths: Third wave feminism and women's studies." *Journal of International Women's Studies*, 4 (2003): 1-6. Mary Hawkesworth, "The semiotics of premature burial: Feminism in a post-feminist age," *Signs: Journal of Women in Culture and Society*, 29 (2004): 961-985.

7. Yvonne Tasker and Diane Negra, *Interrogating Postfeminism: Gender and the Politics of Popular Culture.* (Durham: Duke University Press, 2007).

8. Ibid.

9. Negra, *What a Girl Wants?*, p. 2.

10. Tasker & Negra, *Interrogating Postfeminism,* p. 3.

11. Negra, *What a Girl Wants?*

12. Genz & Brabon, *Postfeminism.*

13. Michelle Lazar, "Entitled to consume: Postfeminist femininity and a culture of post-critique," *Discourse & Communication*, 3 (2009): 371-400.

14. Ibid, p. 373.

15. Genz & Brabon, *Postfeminism.* Negra, *What a Girl Wants?*

16. Negra, *What a Girl Wants?*, p. 5.

17. Projansky, "Mass magazine cover girls."

18. Lazar, "Entitled to consume." Rosalind Gill and Jane Arthurs, "Editors' introduction: New femininities?" *Feminist Media Studies*, 6 (2006): 443-451.

19. Jessica Ringrose, "A new universal mean girl: Examining the discursive construction and regulation of a new feminine pathology," *Feminism & Psychology*, 16 (2006): 405-424.

20. Ibid.

21. Marnina Gonick, *Between femininities: Ambivalence, Identity and the Education of Girls.* (Albany: SUNY Press, 2004). Ringrose, "A new universal mean girl."

22. Anne Worrall, Twisted sisters, laddettes, and the new penology: The social construction of 'violent girls,'" in *Girls ' violence: Myths and Realities*, edited by Christine Alder & Anne Worrall. (New York: SUNY, 2004), pp. 41-60. Ringrose, "A new universal mean girl."

23. Ringrose, "A new universal mean girl."

24. Ibid, p. 407.

25. Walkerdine, *Daddy's Little Girl.* Ringrose, "A new universal mean girl," p. 407.

26. Jessica Ringrose & Valerie Walkerdine, "What does it mean to be a girl in the twenty-first century? Exploring some contemporary dilemmas of femininity and girlhood in the West," in *Girl Culture: An Encyclopedia,* edited by Claudia Mitchell & Jacqueline Reid-Walsh. (Westport: Greenwood Press, 2008), pp. 6-16.

27. Ibid, p. 10.

28. Ringrose & Walkerdine, "What does it mean to be a girl in the twenty-first century?" Ringrose, "A new universal mean girl."

29. Ringrose, "A new universal mean girl," p. 411.

30. Ibid, p. 411.

31. Henry Giroux, *Stealing Innocence: Corporate Culture's War on Children*, (New York: Palgrave, 2000).

32. Kitzinger, "Defending innocence." Giroux, *Stealing innocence.*

33. Giroux, *Stealing Innocence,* p. 42.

34. Negra, *What a Girl Wants?*

35. Giroux, "Child beauty pageants: A scene from the 'Other America.'"

36. Ibid.

37. M. Gigi Durham, *The Lolita Effect: The Media Sexualization of Young Girls and What We Can Do About It*, (Woodstock: The Overlook Press, 2008), p. 12.

38. Ibid.

39. Ibid, p. 24.

40. Sue Jackson, Tiina Vares, and Rosalind Gill, "'The whole playboy mansion image': Girls' fashioning and fashioned selves within a postfeminist culture," *Feminism & Psychology*, 23 (2013), 143-162.

41. Ibid.

42. Jackson, Vares, & Gill, "The whole playboy mansion image." Gill & Arthurs, "Editors' introduction."

43. Jackson, Vares, & Gill, "The whole playboy mansion image."

44. Alice Marwick, "There's a beautiful girl under all of this: Performing hegemonic femininity in reality television," *Critical Studies in Media Communication*, 27 (2010): 251-266.

45. Sue Tait, "Television and the domestication of cosmetic surgery," *Feminist Media Studies*, 7 (2007): 119-135.

46. Banet-Weiser & Portwood-Stacer, "'I just want to be me again!'"

47. Anoop Nayak, and Mary Jane Kehily, *Gender, Youth, and Culture: Young Masculinities and Femininities*, (Houndmills: Palgrave, 2008), p. 34.

48. Banet-Weiser & Portwood-Stacer, "'I just want to be me again!'" p. 255.

49. Marnina Gonick, "Between "girl power" and "reviving Ophelia": Constituting the neo-liberal girl subject," *NWSA Journal*, 18 (2006): 1-23. Jessica Ringrose, "Successful girls? Complicating post-feminist, neo-liberal discourses of educational achievement and gender equality," *Gender and Education*, 19 (2007): 471-489.

50. Catherine Driscoll, *Girls: Feminine Adolescence in Popular Culture and Cultural Theory*, (New York: Columbia University Press, 2002), 59.

51. Ibid, p. 110.

52. Christine Griffin, "Good girls, bad girls: Anglocentrism and diversity in the constitution of contemporary girlhood" in *All About the Girl: Culture, Power, and Identity*, edited by Anita Harris. (New York: Routledge, 2004), pp. 29-43.

53. Jessica Ringrose and Valerie Walkerdine, "Regulating the abject: The TV makeover as site of neo- liberal reinvention toward bourgeois femininity," *Feminist Media Studies*, 8 (2008): 227-246, pp. 230-231.

54. Guy Debord, "Commodity as spectacle" in *Keyworks in Cultural Studies II*, edited by M. Gigi Durham and Douglas Kellner. (Malden: Blackwell, 2006), pp.117-121.

55. M. Gigi Durham, *The Lolita Effect.*

56. Henry Giroux, "Child beauty pageants."

57. Henry Giroux, "Nymphet fantasies: Child beauty pageants and the politics of innocence," *Social Text*, 57 (1998): 31-53.

58. Negra, *What a Girl Wants?*

59. Henry Giroux, "Nymphet fantasies," p. 48.

60. Giroux, "Nymphet fantasies." Durham, *The Lolita effect.*

61. Giroux, "Nymphet Fantasies," p. 47.

Chapter Ten

Manifest Masculinity: Frontier, Fraternity, and Family in Discovery Channel's *Gold Rush*

William C. Trapani and Laura L. Winn

Go West, young man, and grow up with the country. –Popular mid-1800s call to Westward expansion. [1]

There isn't one man in America, if he's got anything inside him, who wouldn't want to be here with us. –Jack Hoffman, [2] *Gold Rush* Season One Episode One.

A decade ago, James McDaniel wrote convincingly of the ways in which the American attachment to conquering empty terrain had been triumphantly ported to the virtual age as the new landscape of American national power. Or, as he put it, "what could be more recurrent in the American experience than the wish for new, uncharted territory?" [3] Central to his account was the way the original Westward expansion depended on sublimating the libidinal energy of the tall tale and its characters (such as Davy Crockett) into the usable social discourse of American exceptionalism and its companion call to embody the frontier spirit. Although not essential to McDaniel's account, there is, throughout, the presumption that the frontier had been depleted and hence that a new, albeit digital, space had to emerge in order to function as the surplus space for the voracious American territorial appetite. As such, "combination" became the master trope of the Internet's dawn with new frontiers to conquer with restrained and scientifically oriented heroes guiding us into a lighter, safer and more enlightened age.

Even as recently as his essay was written, however, McDaniel could not have predicted the veritable explosion of reality television programs that portray hyper-masculinized men returning to (literal) frontiers once more to find fame and fortune (*American Loggers, Ax Men, Bering Sea Gold, Coal, Deadliest Catch, Ice Road Truckers, Saw Dogs,* e.g.). In this essay, we explore the force of such shows by examining the identification structures at play in the Discovery Channel hit show *Gold Rush.* Attending both to the specificity of its idiosyncratic particularities as well as assessing its generic traits as they are informed by and play a significant role in the constitution of hyper-male programming, we consider the cultural and rhetorical force of the show through a quite different register of sublimation. Centered on the trope of "division," today's rugged frontier functions—following the logic of such shows—not merely as a terrain onto which an already constituted body projects its virility.

Instead, in these contemporary accounts a "troubled" subject rediscovers itself, first and foremost, by leaving the trappings of society and domesticated family life. In the process, he renews himself, the nation, and the "brotherhood" of man through the rigors of work and self-denial. Read from this angle, shows that could have illustrated the surprisingly humble (and humbling) path of narcissism instead veer back toward a perverse delusion of an apolitical space in which national troubles are conveniently removed. Put differently, we argue that *Gold Rush*—and by extension many of the programs that follow its generic form—is problematic not merely because it figures political and personal entanglements as "bothersome," but because it does not represent those concerns at all. Here, we follow the insights of Homi Bhabha who has suggested that

> "masculinism" as a position of social authority is not simply about the power invested in the recognizable "persons" of men. It is about the subsumption or sublation of social antagonism; it is about the repression of social divisions; it is about the power to authorize an "impersonal" holistic or universal discourse on the representation of the social that naturalizes cultural difference and turns it into a "second"-nature argument. [4]

Or, put finally, it is because the male is freed not just by sole ownership of a territory, but because through the sheer force of his will he ushers forth a perfectly sanitized space free from political strife that we find the show(s) both hysterical (in the psychoanalytic sense) and dangerous (in the political sense).

We advance these arguments by first considering twin discourses of collapse: the collapse of the national ideals and mission and the putative assailing of the American male. Throughout our aim is not to determine the truth-value of either of these claims, nor is it to trace the political interest served by advancing them; rather our interest is limited to the narrow effort to demonstrate the psychic dislocation (supposedly) affecting men in America today. [5] Second, we read the 19th Century advance to the "frontier" against the proliferation of hyper-masculine reality programs today. Identifying narrative characteristics no doubt appealing to those over-animated by the "decline of man" thesis, we suggest that the slate of macho television programs, and *Gold Rush* in particular, offers a rehabilitative discourse for the hysterical male. Finally, we conclude by attending to the reconfiguration of social space necessary for that rehabilitation. There we suggest that fantasy provided by masculine television is "escapist" not merely in the sense that it succeeds by eliminating the presence of others from its imagery, but because that disconnection and mastery over social space becomes its principal, arguably its singular, goal. In simpler terms, discovering gold is ancillary to the cause itself; it is, at best, an enabling alibi that gives legitimacy to the central purpose of the show: to effect a reconnection to the symbolic order in which men are once again in charge even if it is because all others have been evacuated from the scene.

THE (NEW) "MASCULINITY CRISIS": THE (MASCULINITY) CRISIS OF THE "NEW"

Would it not take undue space, it would take little effort to demonstrate that a specter of national anxiety dominates descriptions of the current cultural, economic, and political age. Indeed, lamentations over economic disruptions, the polarization of the public and its political apparatus, hostility to identity politics and its demands for recognition, a general crisis over the family and its breakdown, and a rhetoric bemoaning a loss of American control over geopolitics following the Cold War's end have all come to characterize a certain restlessness—a nation unmoored. It was, of course, not supposed to be this way. Americans, long weaned on Cold War narratives of national triumphalism, were no doubt surprised that spending the Soviet Union onto the "ash heap of history," as Ronald Reagan had once directed, had not inaugurated the long-promised pacific era.

But if the New World Order's "bad surprise" was that there was to be no immediate end to politics, perhaps nothing has been figured as more troubling to national unity than the oft-circulated predictions that ethnic and religious Balkanization abroad might be mirrored at home by divisive multicultural demands. Time and time again, the heroic narrative of a nation united was recast as a house divided by the internecine squabbles over political clout, social standing and economic advantage. As Paolo Virno frames it in his *A Grammar of the Multitude*, the lines between the political and the social have collapsed and we have all been exposed to the dread of "not feeling at home" of being "exposed omnilaterally to the world"—of all becoming, in short, a dislocated multitude for which all is not, to put it mildly, "peaches, cream and honey."[6]

If things have been bad for the country, they are, we are told, even worse for its men. For years (if not for decades), popular and political discourse has been suffused with cries of the decline of male power. While the 1980s and 1990s each saw their various "crises" of masculinity—often attributed to systemic efforts to promote feminism, political correctness or multiculturalism, today's masculinity issues appear less tied to *being* controlled than in *losing* control (of authority, of oneself, e.g.). Indeed, the recent economic meltdown that began in 2007 set off the newest and perhaps deepest yet anxiety over the role of men in the social order. One noteworthy essay, written just six months before the first episode of *Gold Rush* aired, asks provocatively whether we have seen "The End of Men" In that article, Hanna Rosin details the dramatic ascent of women in salary, job status and social prestige relative to their male counterparts. It was her account of male resignation and anger in the face of these changes, and her vivid description of a male support group for "dead-beat dads" that caught the eye of many. According to Rosin, a male social worker leading the group began by relaying his own childhood spent watching traditional nuclear families on television which he characterizes as a "check [that] bounced a long time ago." She recalls he opened one session by saying:

> "Let's see," he continues, reading from a worksheet. What are the four kinds of paternal authority? Moral, emotional, social, and physical. "But you ain't none of those in that house. All you are is a paycheck, and now you ain't even that. And if you try to exercise your authority, she'll call 911. How does that make you feel? You're supposed to be the authority, and she says, 'Get out of the house, bitch.' She's calling you 'bitch'!" El-Scari has their attention, so he gets a little more philosophical. "Who's doing what?" he asks them. "What is our role? Everyone's telling us we're supposed to be the head of a nuclear family, so you feel like you got robbed. It's toxic, and poisonous, and it's setting us up for failure." He writes on the board: $85,000. "This is her salary." Then: $12,000. "This is your salary. Who's the damn man? Who's the man now?" A murmur rises. "That's right. She's the man." [7]

Surveying the cultural landscape, and in particular television's portrayal of men, clinical psychoanalyst and professor, psychiatry Dr. Gurmeet S. Kanwalof argues that men are experiencing a type of psychic malaise and that "the perception and image of heterosexual men in this country has never been as negative, de-idealized, and potentially harmful as it is now. And lots of men are feeling it." [8] Another commentator puts it even more succinctly, arguing that "America is now a very anti-masculine place." [9]

Given all of this, it is hardly surprising that in *Gold Rush* the acquisition of the gold functions first and foremost as a vehicle for the acquisition of a masculine self. As Todd Hoffman, arguably the show's central character, puts it in the first episode of the series, "I'm no miner, I'm just your average guy sitting here tired of making no money. So, like my forefathers, they balls'd (sic) up and they went out into the frontier." Given the perceived loss of autonomy throughout terrains of work and home in which they used to have unquestioned supremacy, it is hardly surprising that as the men complete the long journey from Oregon to Alaska Hoffman looks about the landscape and says almost reverently "This feels awesome . . . it feels like I'm coming home."[10]

MALE HYSTERIA

The so-called crisis of masculinity, however real (or not) it might be in its actual economic, cultural and social dislocations and transformations, exhibits classic traits of hysteria. In the following section, we advance just that claim but suggest that while it is certainly possible to diagnose the aimless, scattered and emotional male of contemporary culture as if it were a perfect analog to the figure of the panicky female that must be slapped back into sense, it is far more profitable to understand today's man as hysterical because he is no longer able to invest effectively in the structures of power on which his own identity and power depends. Eric Garland puts the problem this way:

> Every male in America grows up with these older images of masculinity— soldier, cowboy, farmer, family man—and fewer men than ever are able to connect their real lives to those archetypes. Something in recent years has changed for men. . . . Our images draw a picture of man against the elements, man in his natural state using his wits, man as a strong-willed individual in a world of uncivilized chaos. The reality of living in America is being funneled into one sclerotic, outdated institution after another.[11]

For our purpose it is less relevant whether these transformations *should* cause men to act hysterically than that the pervasive discourse suggests men should be expected to act hysterically.

Clinical and cultural accounts of hysteria are notoriously—and tortuously—convoluted, troubled with interested political and social control ambitions. It is a history so murky that, as Elain Showalter notes, one commentator has analogized it to being "so amorphous...[that it] is like trying to write a history of dirt."[12] Indeed, its continuously wrinkled narrative has been so distended from its own genealogical account that it caused Lacan to lament: "How convincing the process of remembering was with the first hysterics!"[13]

Any discussion of hysteria, however, cannot but begin with Freud's discussion of the hysteric in *Group Psychology and the Analysis of the Ego*. There he notes,

Supposing, for instance, that one of the girls in a boarding school has had a letter from someone with whom she is secretly in love which arouses her jealousy, and that she reacts to it with a fit of hysterics; then some of her friends who know about it will catch the fit, as we say, by mental infection. The mechanism is that of identification based on the possibility or desire of putting oneself in the same situation. The other girls would like to have a secret love affair too, and under the influence of a sense of guilt they also accept the suffering involved in it. It would be wrong to suppose that they take on the symptom out of sympathy. On the contrary, the sympathy only arises out of identification, and this is proved by the fact that infection or imitation of this kind takes place in circumstances where even less pre-existing sympathy is to be assumed than usually exists between friends in a girls' school. [14]

Freud's account places identification beyond our control. Indeed, through a spectatorial process in which the recognition of consubstantiality demands the viewer of hysteria herself become hysterical, a type of contagion inhabits the subject, forcing her outside of her normal behavior. Here, Freud's anxiety is that the circulatory nature of the disease places the patients outside the analyst's grasp because they are constantly at the whims of whatever might catch their eye. Or as Killingsworth and Palmer reframe his concern, the body of the hysteric is "eloquent" but "the mind cannot interpret its meaning [because] the psychoanalyst who listens to the voice of the ego gets nowhere and must instead listen to the body." [15]

As the nature of a clinical diagnosis of hysteria and its difficult cure are beyond our interest here, we turn to Judith Butler's work in *The Psychic Life of Power* to better understand the identificatory relay of hysteria. Borrowing from psychoanalysis, in that work Butler argues that the interpellative hail to "become" someone else carries within it a guilt structure one seeks to be acquitted from. In clarifying and supplementing Althusser's too basic account of interpellation, Butler demonstrates that the response to a hail is figured in advance by the general condition of his or her desire to be something "other;" desire which, at least initially, places them at some vulnerability to the law. Given this, she implies, we ought not to think of identification as an end-state in which the subject is finally realized, but rather as a necessary stage in which the newly enshrined subject must prove their innocence and worth. As Butler notes, " If the mastery of a set of skills is to be construed as an act of acquitting oneself, then this master of savoir-faire defends one against an accusation; quite literally it is accused declaration of innocence . . . [which requires] a display or proof of guiltlessness in the face of the demand for confession implied by an insistent accusation." [16]

It is here that we discover the latent guilt that circulates about reality TV's macho moment. It is not the oft-commented viewer's guilty pleasure that is being satisfied, but rather the character's pleasure at no longer feeling guilty for failing in their "normal life" (as a father, husband, provider e.g.). As

Michael Kimmel noted in his groundbreaking work *Manhood in America*, for a man to be successful he must become so in front of other men. He argues,

> If manhood could be proved, it had to be proved in the eyes of other men. From the early nineteenth century until the present day, most of men's relentless efforts to prove their manhood contain this core element of homosociality. From fathers and boyhood friends to our teachers, co-workers, and bosses, it is the evaluative eyes of other men that are always upon us, watching, judging. [17]

Read this way, the hysteria on display in *Gold Rush* (and in similar shows), is a type of confession, but not of the subject confessing his crimes to an authority, but rather of the authority confessing his incompleteness back to the barred subject. To understand this we must understand that within the Lacanian formulation the hysteric is that subject which does not ask "What is the value or love I should have for the big Other?" but instead, incessantly worries over whether the Other loves him. The hysteric, then, is precisely that subject that seeks a master in the big Other, but importantly a master whose authority is beyond question such that its love validates the existence and worth of the subject and in the process closes over the fundamental lack that propelled that subject to find a master in the first place.

It is precisely the impossibility of loving the symbolic order that produces the hysteric; that is, the terror visited upon the authority and the law denies any opportunity to identify with its structure and as a consequence the subject becomes hysterical, now viciously turning on the master in the very place where it is thought to reign. In this way, hysteria is indeed an eloquent sign. It is a sign that the symbolic order is thought to be ill — for the law can no longer be understood as a site of authority. [18]

It is, we are suggesting, not at all coincidental that the boom in hyper-masculine television is occurring at the same moment as a corresponding lamentation at masculinity's loss. Such shows offer a rhetoric of rehabilitation not only for the characters on the screen but for the viewers who, following the contagion-like nature of hysteria Freud articulated, are equally over-determined by their loss of a trustworthy symbolic order.

Those looking to understand reality television by scanning its entry at the popular pseudo-encyclopedia *How Stuff Works.com* however, might be forgiven for assuming that some alien mastermind had successfully orchestrated the most effective and comprehensive coup of all time. Indeed, in its few short pages, the piece offers both a level-headed genealogy of the slow-moving evolution of radio and then television network producers' long-standing search for alternative (and less costly) story formats and a sort of wide-eyed wonder at the breadth and speed by which "reality" has conquered America's living rooms. Indeed, the overall impression is that while the country was looking the other way for the merest moment, someone surreptitiously swapped the well-worn and comforting slate of shows for something exotic, strange and a little disturbing. The description begins with the following opening passage, inviting readers to imagine that

> you're home on the couch in front of your new plasma screen with a few hours to kill. You start channel-surfing and come across a show with people slurping a concoction of maggots and hissing beetles for a chance to win 50 grand. On channel after channel you see shows with truckers driving across treacherously icy roads in Alaska, two people telling folks what not to wear, and crab fisherman braving a mother of a storm. Now you're asking yourself, when did Elaine, Jerry, George and Kramer get replaced by Lauren, Heidi, Audrina and Brody? Who in the world are New York and Tila Tequila, and why do they have their own shows? Just when did reality TV get to be so popular? And, finally, how do people come up with this stuff—and how real are these shows anyway? Reality TV has morphed from radio game show and amateur talent competition to hidden camera stunt show to dating show to documentary-style series. The genre now encompasses unscripted dramas, makeover sagas, celebrity exposés, lifestyle-change shows, dating shows, talent extravaganzas and just about any kind of competition you can think of (and a few that you probably can't). [19]

As effective as the folksy conceit of a viewer caught off-guard by the sudden occupation of their television set might be at conveying the massive shift in the television landscape, staging the piece in this fashion has the unfortunate consequence of covering over a central truth about today's television: everyone sees (through) it. Indeed, reality television is hardly subtle. Its casting, themes, challenges, weekly dramas and outcomes are neither unexpected nor particularly intricate in design. This ubiquity and transparency does not—of course—make its rhetorical force as a rehabilitation technology any less important. Rather, it presses us to inquire into the types of enjoyments viewers receive in choosing particular shows over others.

To that point, the public has made its choice quite clear: *Gold Rush* is a ratings monster. It is the Discovery Channel's top-rated show, and for a remarkable 13-week period during its second season in 2012 it was the most watched show in all of television by the coveted 18-49 year old male demographic. [20] But while its powerful ratings are surely one testament to its symbolic sway over millions of Americans, when even that venerable grey lady the *New York Times* suggests that they, too, prefer watching the spate of macho shows because they are infinitely more fascinating than "the leave-nothing-but-your-footprints, green kind of eco-travelers [who] are too mellow and conscientious to be interesting to watch" you know a type of sea-change in cultural viewing habits has occurred. As they put it

> the burly, bearded, swearing men who blow methyl hydrate into their own transmissions and welcome storms as breaks from boredom and a chance to

"go four-wheeling with a big rig" (as they put it) are much better television. But how does the excitement we find in the adventures of these guys and the miners they serve—as well as the commercial fisherman on the Discovery Channel—comport with the efforts, expressed on other channels, to keep the seas and tundras pristine? That ideological conflict is another adventure on television.[21]

Certainly, there are no end of commentators reflecting on our collective fascination with males exhibiting a return to traditional—even primal—forms of masculinity. A staff writer for the *Washington Post*, for example, greeted the season premieres of *Storage Wars* and *Gold Rush* with an opening two paragraphs that would quite comfortably sit among the prose and insights offered by many contemporary cultural and critical studies journals, arguing that,

> If you broaden the definition of American exceptionalism to include rooting through the contents of abandoned storage units or spending your last few dollars to trot off to the Alaskan wilderness to backhoe for gold, then America is looking mighty exceptional indeed. At least on television. A&E's *Storage Wars* . . . and Discovery's *Gold Rush: Alaska* . . . are really just further ruminations on the perceived crises of national masculinity and consumer confidence.[22]

No doubt the utopian fetishization of sudden and spectacular accumulation of wealth drives much of the reality television genre, and it is certainly a key component of *Gold Rush*. Again, it is hardly coincidental that a show about unemployed men hitting the road to strike it rich in an alluring industry such as gold mining would do so well in the midst of America's greatest economic meltdown in 70 years. To be sure, the producers miss no opportunity to remind viewers of (what was) the escalating price of gold and how even a modest haul could change these miners' fortunes. The show description, for example, is steeped in this type of "get-rich-quick" sensibility:

> *Gold Rush: Alaska* follows six men who risk everything in the face of an economic meltdown—their families, their dignity, and in some cases, their lives—to strike it rich mining for gold in the wilds of Alaska. Inspired by his father Jack Hoffman, Todd Hoffman of Sandy, Oregon, leads a group of greenhorn miners to forge a new frontier and save their families from dire straits. . . . With the price of gold on the rise, [Todd] came up with a plan to mine for the mineral in southeast Alaska, where there's an estimated $250 billion worth of gold. The mine at Porcupine Creek is located in the heart of one of the last great wildernesses, where weather conditions can change in an instant. The claim is surrounded by the largest bald eagle population on earth, and a nearby river is the site of a year-round salmon run. Grizzly bears and moose sightings happen daily, and the team must be prepared for some seriously close encounters. Armed with the hope and ferocity to rekindle the

original American Dream, *Gold Rush: Alaska* shines a spotlight on this group of enthusiasts. In essence, these are the new "'49ers," going back to the roots this country was founded on: hard labor, blood, sweat and tears. The men put it all on the line in the biggest gamble of their lives, and the hunt is on to strike it rich—or go bust. [23]

There, in the Discovery Channel's promotional discourse we find the culmination of this hysterical identificatory chain: it is that men are willing to take "the biggest gamble of their lives" that makes us watch. It is their complete and absolute re-dedication to the symbolic order that provides the only possible "relief" from the otherwise complete failure of the symbolic order. Gavin Mueller underscores this point, arguing that our viewing enjoyment comes not from their success, but from their work, suggesting that we are fascinated by shows that depict

> the decline of American industrial labor. In shows like *Coal* and *Gold Rush*, squads of aging, grizzled white men risk death to extract whatever minerals remain in the corners of America's dwindling wilderness, while equally grizzled petty bourgeois bosses nervously bark orders at them while sweating about their investment. The meager pleasures of these shows come from watching rusty boys playing with rusty toys, the ghosts of organized labor (for these workers are anything but organized) grasping to the only thing they have left: nostalgic masculinity. [24]

It is crucial to emphasize the point that the audience's affective purchase does not turn on any demonstrable proof that the gamble will pay off—that the order is indeed worth our investment. At the height of *Gold Rush*'s dominance the crews had yet to turn a profit for almost two full seasons. Indeed, throughout its run, ratings have been high whether the miners were losing or making money. [25] On a recent junket to New York to meet with journalists and promote the show, Todd Hoffman spoke at length about the relative non-relevance of financial gain to the overall value of the mining experience. As he put it,

> Here's the reality of helping people: It hurts to help. If it doesn't hurt to help, you're probably not really helping. It hurts to give something up and create a job sometimes. It hurts to open up an opportunity, have someone take the opportunity, then burn you with it. When you stick your neck out there, there are people who want to cut it off. There are tons of people who hate success. There's tons of armchair warriors. Like I say, if you're a hero to your family, those guys can kiss our ass. Sometimes you find that there's two types of people. People who go out and make shit happen and there's people who go "Wow, what just happened?" We're kind of those guys who will either screw it up so bad that no one will touch it, or we'll get some success out of it. So we just kind of go after it. When you have that type of spirit in you, you can make some catastrophic errors. I care a lot about my faith and my family. But the

show's coming out and I'm hoping that I'm going to get edited to perceive my real feelings: How much I care about my guys, how much I care about my country, how much I care about my faith. Am I being a good dad? Am I being a good husband? That's kind of taking the place of when you're young and you're like, "I want to make a million dollars." Once you have kids, you don't give a crap about that stuff. Now this being famous celebrity B.S. is just a tool to accomplish those three goals that I told you about. It's just an avenue. It's not "Oh boy, I'm famous. I can't wait to sign autographs." I'm the average everyday guy. So is this guy. We don't give a shit. Having said that, it's just a tool to represent our faith and provide for our family. It's a tool to look out there to average guys and say, "Guys, I'm just like you. I don't have a perfect marriage. I've lost a lot of money. Brother don't give up," and offer some hope.[26]

We leave it to the reader to determine whether they find Hoffman's seemingly earnest commitment to traditional family values endearing or retrograde (or both). In our view, and borrowing the work and language of Avital Ronnell, we would instead categorize Hoffman's "devil-may-care" attitude an exemplary case of what Ronnell has called the pathology of the "loser son."

So as not to be seen as trafficking in mere ivory tower intellectualism and the disparagement of particular types of labor, we want to be clear that labeling his sensibility that of a "loser" is to underscore that it demonstrates a refusal to accept any tempering of the "paternal residue" regardless of consequence so that, as Ronnell puts it, "When all is said and done, [the son] gets off on defeat, whether this be construed as defeating their neighboring others or along the lines of various forms of self-defeat and a mock-up suicidal finale." Her point—and by extension ours—is that what from one angle looks like a dedicated father and husband caring for his family at all costs becomes, from another angle, a zealotry-fueled insistence on paternal authority despite the consequences. In this sense, the loser son seeks validation and valorization because he "tried" when in fact what is taking place is an

> insistent reversion to the paternal, even where it has been disqualified yet continues to run out the clock, [which] still models the essential pull of authority. As a starting point that does not look back or look down, the paternal still has a hold on power, the way it is shaped, the way it is justified and used.[27]

What is clear from both the television show and from his interview is that Hoffman's commitment to his masculinity entails leaving his family and putting their finances at risk by selling everything possible to raise funds for his mining operation, evincing a "father knows best" paternal impulse that, while infectious (in the Freudian sense described earlier) is also resolutely committed to its authority and assertion of primacy. It is to the scene of that exercise of control, the "new" frontier, that we now turn.

FRONTIER FANTASIES: EMBRACING THE RETURN OF THE DISTRESSED

If the 18th-century forging of the American nation required valorizing an interstitial space between the old and new worlds to create a sense of "home," it did so by plying the middle ground between extravagant European decadence and the civilization of the West.[28] Although it was an assemblage rather than any single technology that helped articulate the grand design of America's perfect "placement," it is difficult to overstate the role that travel and travel writing had in forging the national image. Indeed, no other genre of literature enjoyed greater popularity or prominence than travel narratives.[29] From the nation's earliest days, a discourse of mobility, sutured with political treatises on the "natural rights of man," the aesthetic sublime of the American wilderness, and discourses on the supremacy of European races, served as a mechanism of distinguishing and exalting the American national character.[30]

If the brutal sanitation of the West has made contemporary travel there something of a perversion—it is a land made accessible precisely because the "wildness" that such travel often seeks has been vanquished—it is perhaps no less important in its nation rebuilding effect than those travel narratives that helped found the nation's heroic origin. Indeed, the West is often characterized as the place where one can experience the last vestiges of real America. To a significant degree it is the sublime space of "the West"—its great vastness, imagined freedom of mobility, and the monumental fortitude it is thought to take to thrive in that environment—that has afforded the landscape its seemingly limitless power for renewal. If, as Kord and Krimmer suggest, "Westerns are America's most enduring mythical genre," it is because the plasticity of that genre and the terrain in which it is set "permits the straightforward exportation of Western themes into the real world of U.S. politics."[31] The West, in short, is where Americans have always imagined big things can become possible. In this vein, fascination with the awesome scope of a gold-mining project is analogous to interest in the construction of other Western sublime marvels such as the Hoover Dam and Mt. Rushmore. As Richard Guy Wilson has argued, the consumption of such grand endeavors draws spectators precisely because it is visible proof of the heroic accomplishments of which we imagine ourselves capable.[32]

Although he was not principally concerned with "size" itself, much of Thomas Farrell's life was dedicated to understanding the magnitude of discourse. Following Aristotle's insight that magnitude is one avenue of "inventional logic," Farrell's own work spoke volumes (another metaphor of magnitude) about the force necessary to ground discourse with mattering.[33] As we understand it, to consider magnitude in this manner helps underscore the point that discourses *impress*; they fashion a call to attention and, subsequently, they offer a sense of value and scale by which we weigh our future options. Here, too, however, things are not always so clear. Indeed, size may not matter at all. In the Western world at least, gigantism has long been associated with the strange and grotesque. It can overwhelm, and prove difficult to take in. Indeed, such forces can prove "uncanny or *unheimlich* . . . neither homey nor protective."[34] Historian Michel-Rolph Trouillot has echoed these points in language that recalls the sublime force of something beyond comprehension; something that is both awesome and awful in its magnitude. As he puts it,

> The bigger the material mass the more easily it entraps us: mass graves and pyramids bring history closer while they make us feel small. A castle, a fort, a battlefield, a church, all these things bigger than we that we infuse with the reality of past lives, seem to speak of an immensity of which we know little except that we are part of it. Too solid to be unmarked, too conspicuous to be candid, they embody the ambiguities of history. They give us the power to touch it, but not to hold it firmly in our hands—hence the mystery of their battered walls. We suspect that their concreteness hides secrets so deep that no revelation may fully dissipate their silences."[35]

Just as frontier narratives emphasized the dangerous but God-given duty to conquer territory, producers revel in showing the grueling labor and physical strain required to brave the elements. Just as the original gold rush and land grabs of the mid-nineteenth century promised upward mobility and a fast pass to social status, today's reality television lures its characters (and audiences) with seductive and sumptuous imagined lifestyles well beyond their present reach. And, just as frontier narratives often pitted men against treacherous forces (Indians, nature, women, domesticity), the lead characters on the shows are hyper-masculinized. Routinely depicted as the titular head of a traditional household of a wife and children they leave behind in order to support, the men are also chronically restless, poor managers of money, unable or unwilling to take a "normal" job (even if it would pay more and more regularly than their adventurous choice). Indeed, it is this call to something "other," something outside the bounds of conventional family dynamics that is most often tied directly to their irrepressible masculinity. In an episode most noteworthy for other contestations over masculinity and male responsibility, for example, the camera focuses on miner Greg Remsburg using a bulldozer across a wide expanse of soil cleared of all vegetation. In a tone that suggests he's speaking out loud to himself, he opines, "Some people think the American Dream is a two-story house with a white picket fence, two new cars out in the driveway, and, uh, I'd give that up any day of the week. This is the American Dream, this is what it is."[36]

Exactly what that dream requires to make it work is put to the test when, in one episode in the middle of season two, a squabble breaks out between

Todd Hoffman and his mechanic and fabricator James Harness. With dwindling days left before temperatures drop below mining capabilities, a repair is needed on the machine that uses water pressure to separate gold from the recovered dirt, but Harness's girlfriend has unexpectedly arrived, marking the first time that a wife or significant other has been seen on any of the mining sites since the show began. While the rest of the crew can do little but wait till the part is repaired, Harness (who is the only one capable of fixing the part) plays with his girlfriend around the site, at one point panning for gold with her in a nearby stream. Incredulous, Hoffman says out loud to himself "What the heck? Look at James—he's like teaching his girlfriend how to pan right now. What the heck? He's supposed to be welding on that thing," later adding "This ain't a love story, it's a frikkin gold mine."[37]

Making matters worse, before he even looks into the repair, Harness and his girlfriend get in a truck and drive to the local town for what the narrator describes as "a couple of days of R and R" and for what Harness, speaking to an in-truck puts thusly: "It's my job to make sure they keep running. I accepted it so I'll follow it through. It doesn't mean I can't have fun in the meantime."[38]

Somewhat predictably, when he does return several days later, a heated exchange ensues between Hoffman and Harness with each expressing disappointment in the other (their "hurt" actually). For his part, Hoffman is concerned that Harness does not seem to be committed to the work effort and that he doesn't know if Harness is "there" with them. Harness, taking offense at being chastised, responds that he's always been there to support Todd and that he's not going to have anyone say anything negative about his girlfriend. The following dialogue ensues:

> Harness: If you wanna talk about Catherine, she's been very patient, ok? So you guys can get that shit out of your mind right now.
>
> Hoffman: Ok, ok, well I've never said anything negative about Catherine—she's a great lady.
>
> Harness: So just keep her out of it. This is between you and me and this machine right here that I don't want to come between us.
>
> Hoffman: Dude, neither do I. Dude, I'm your fan. I'm a James Harness fan.[39]

The set piece concludes with the two agreeing to focus on work, and while Harness is working in the background Hoffman opines to the camera, "Me and this guy together, you know I dream up crap and he can frikkin make it. I'm like a fat Batman and he's like a broken down Robin. So, I don't want that team to ever end."[40] As the exchange makes clear, this is a realm of men and their machines; nothing less and (especially) nothing more is acceptable.

From the vantage point of the man on a mission to forge himself on the frontier, Harness's violations are almost too obvious to mention, but what is particularly striking is that from Hoffman's perspective all of his failures are *spatial*: he has allowed his girlfriend to enter the work site and to distract him from his needed labor, he is in all the wrong places of the worksite doing all the wrong things, he leaves and goes into town[41] and perhaps, most damning of all, he is not "here" where Hoffman is. Harness has punctured the illusion of control Hoffman imagines he has over his crew, but his fundamental sin is that he has punctured the frontier space by allowing the world to return to the frontier; to the mission.

How might we best understand the entailments of this set of spatial violations? Rather than rehearse tired categorizations of public/private divides or work through the argument that lamentations over the "lost" public sphere are misguided because there never was such a thing, we would rather make the point that it is not the actuality or possibility of such clear divisions between public and private, work and recreation, or—in this case, friends and girlfriends, that should concern us so much as it is the effort to purify and maintain those distinctions themselves.

For Rosalyn Deuetsche, the lamentation over lost public space—or equally the celebratory talk over its refilling—functions less as a narrative that will spur democratic dialogue, but rather as the "cover story" for an agoraphobic. For just as democracy is a form of society that is "destroyed" the moment that it is positivized, a democratic public space cannot be a lost object that we want but do not have; rather public space may be "the space that we as social beings are in but do not particularly want." She continues,

> The story of the lost public makes its narrator appear to be someone who is comfortable in, even devoted to, public space—someone who . . . is ill at ease when exiled from the public square. But while the story gives the impression that its speaker is unafraid of public space, it transforms public space into a safe zone. The lost public sphere is the place where private individuals gather, and, from the point of view of reason, seek to know the social world objectively. There, as citizens, they "find" the object—"society"—that transcends particularities and differences. There, society becomes possible. Founded like all impartial totalities on the loss of others, the lost public sphere closes the borders of the very space that to be democratic must remain incomplete.[42]

In discussing the political entailments of "public" art in urban centers, Deutsche is, of course, speaking about a setting a world away from the one we consider here. But her insightful point that it is the very subjects that clamor for the clear division between life spheres because they claim to relish the public are, in fact, an agoraphobics who fear the terror of the collapse of such distinctions is powerfully instructive to its own purposes. Translated for *Gold Rush* and for the countless other shows that mirror its macho reclamation of

America and the American male, we might instead suggest that the constant discourse of frontier work as a sacrifice done in the name of the family is in fact a cover story, an alibi, for a subject that wants nothing at all to do with them—who feels completely out of place in contemporary society and only at "home" when as far away from the actuality of *that* space as possible. The real terror of *Gold Rush*, from that perspective, is not whether miners might or might not discover gold, but what repressed masculinist fantasies are being served by the effort and what the return of their supposed repression will bring on us all.

REFERENCES

Bhabha, Homi K. "A Good Judge of Character: Men, Metaphors, and the Common Culture." In *Race-ing Justice, En-gendering Power: Essays on Anita Hill, Clarence Thomas, and the Construction of Social Reality*, edited by Toni Morrison, 232-250. New York, Pantheon Books, 1992.

Danielewski, Mark Z. *House of Leaves*. New York: Pantheon Books, 2000.

Deutsche, Rosalyn. *Evictions: Art and Spatial Politics*. Cambridge, MA: MIT Press, 1998.

Farrell, Thomas. "Sizing Things Up: Colloquial Reflection as Practical Wisdom." *Argumentation* 12 (1998): 1-14.

Freud, Sigmund. *Psychology and the Analysis of the Ego* (1921), Standard Edition, 18: 107.

Fuss, Diana. *Identification Papers*. London: Routledge, 1995.

Garland, Eric. "The Crisis of American Masculinity," *Eric Garland.com*, last date modified December 20, 2012, http://www.ericgarland.co/2012/12/20/the-crisis-of-american-masculinity/

Gold Rush. "No Guts, No Glory." Amazon.com video, 43:33, December 3, 2010, http://www.amazon.com/No-Guts-Glory/dp/B004FKRYWS.

Kanwalof, Gurmeet S. "The Masculinity Crisis, Male Malaise, and the Challenge of Becoming a Good Man," *Psychology Today*, last modified June 18, 2011, http://www.psychologytoday.com/blog/psychoanalysis-30/201106/the-masculinity-crisis-male-malaise-and-the-challenge-becoming-good-ma

Killingsworth, M. Jimmi and Jacqueline Palmer. "The Discourse of 'Environmentalist Hysteria'. *The Quarterly Journal of Speech* 81 (February, 1995): 1-19.

Lacan, Jacques, *The Four Fundamentals of Psychoanalysis*. Alan Sheridan (Trans.). Jacques-Alain Miller (Eds.). New York: W.W. Norton & Company, 1981 [1973].

McDaniel, James P. "Figures for the New Frontiers, From Davy Crockett to Cyberspace Gurus,"*Quarterly Journal of Speech* 88, no. 4 (2002): 91-111

Metz, Winifred Fordham, "How Reality TV Works," *How Stuff Works*. Last date modified December 7, 2007, http://electronics.howstuffworks.com/reality-tv.htm.

Rosin, Hannah. "The End of Men," *Atlantic Monthly*. Last modified June 8, 2010, http://www.theatlantic.com/magazine/archive/2010/07/the-end-of-men/308135/.

Showalter, Elaine. *Hystories: Hysterical Epidemics and the Modern Media*. New York: Columbia University Press, 1997, 15.

Trouillot, Michel-Rolph. *Silencing the Past: Power and the Production of History*. Boston: Beacon Hill, 1995.

Virno, Paolo. *A Grammar of the Multitude: For An Analysis of Contemporary Forms of Life*. Translated by Isabella Bertoletti et al. Cambridge, MA: MIT Press, 2004.

Wilson, Richard Guy. "American Modernism in the West." In Thomas Carter (ed.) *Images of an American Land: Vernacular Architecture in the Western United States*, 291-319.Albuquerque: University of New Mexico Press, 1997.

NOTES

1. Although this well-known call has long been attributed to Horace Greeley, more contemporary accounts attribute it to John Soule. As we have neither the knowledge, nor the interest, in settling the question we leave it unattributed.

2. Gold Rush Alaska, "No Guts, No Glory,"*Amazon.com* video, 43:33, December 3, 2010, http://www.amazon.com/No-Guts-Glory/dp/B004FKRYWS.

3. James P. McDaniel, "Figures for the New Frontiers, From Davy Crockett to Cyberspace Gurus," *Quarterly Journal of Speech* 88, no. 4 (2002): 92.

4. Homi K. Bhabha, "A Good Judge of Character: Men, Metaphors, and the Common Culture," in *Race-ing Justice, En-gendering Power: Essays on Anita Hill, Clarence Thomas, and the Construction of Social Reality*, ed. Toni Morrison, (New York, Pantheon Books, 1992), 242.

5. "Today" should be understood somewhat elastically. No doubt many would argue this "assault" has been underway since the late 1960s if not earlier.

6. Paolo Virno. *A Grammar of the Multitude: For An Analysis of Contemporary Forms of Life*, trans. Isabella Bertoletti et al, (Cambridge, MA: MIT Press, 2004), 26.

7. Hannah Rosin, "The End of Men," *Atlantic Monthly*, last modified June 8, 2010, http://www.theatlantic.com/magazine/archive/2010/07/the-end-of-men/308135/.

8. Gurmeet S. Kanwalof, "The Masculinity Crisis, Male Malaise, and the Challenge of Becoming a Good Man," *Psychology Today*, last modified June 18, 2011, http://www.psychologytoday.com/blog/psychoanalysis-30/201106/the-masculinity-crisis-male-malaise-and-the-challenge-becoming-good-ma

9. Eric Garland, "The Crisis of American Masculinity," *Eric Garland*, last date modified December 20, 2012, http://www.ericgarland.co/2012/12/20/the-crisis-of-american-masculinity/

10. *Gold Rush: Alaska*, "No Guts, No Glory."

11. Eric Garland, "The Crisis of American Masculinity."

12. Elaine Showalter. *Hystories: Hysterical Epidemics and the Modern Media*. New York: Columbia University Press, 1997, 15.

13. Jacques Lacan. *The Four Fundamentals of Psychoanalysis*. Alan Sheridan (Trans.). Jacques-Alain Miller (Eds.). New York: W.W. Norton & Company, 1981 [1973], 49-50.

14. Sigmund Freud, *Group Psychology and the Analysis of the Ego* (1921), Standard Edition, 18: 107.

15. M. Jimmi Killingsworth and Jacqueline Palmer. "The Discourse of 'Environmentalist Hysteria.'" *The Quarterly Journal of Speech* 81 (February, 1995): 5.

16. Butler, 118.

17. Michael Kimmel. *Manhood in America: A Cultural History*. New York: The Free Press, 1996, 26.

18. We borrow the use of the term "eloquent" in relation to this phenomenon from Fuss.

19. Winifred Fordham Metz, "How Reality TV Works," *How Stuff Works*, last modified December 7, 2007, http://electronics.howstuffworks.com/reality-tv.htm.

20. Amanda Kondolojy, "'Gold Rush #1 Among Men on All Television, Not Just Cable," *TV By The Numbers*, last modified February 27, 2012, http://tvbythenumbers.zap2it.com/2012/02/27/gold-rush-1-among-men-on-all-television-not-just-cable/122202

21. Virginia Heffernan, "Honk? No, Pray if You Hear a Loud Crack, *New York Times*, last date modified June 22, 2007, http://www.washingtonpost.com/wp-dyn/content/article/2010/11/30/AR2010113006133.html

22. Hank Stuever, "TV Reviews: 'Storage Wars' and 'Gold Rush: Alaska,' Tales from the Recessionary Frontier," last modified December 1, 2010, http://www.washingtonpost.com/wpdyn/content/article/2010/11/30/AR2010113006133.html

23. "About the Show: Gold Rush Alaska," Discovery Channel, http://dsc.discovery.com/tv-shows/gold-rush/about-this-show/gold-rush-alaska-about-show.htm.

24. Gavin Mueller, "Reality T.V. and the Flexible Future," *Jacobinmag*, http://jacobinmag.com/2012/10/reality-t-v-and-flexible-future/

25. Even more pointedly, ratings for the third season, one in which the Hoffman crew hit the "motherlode" and grossed over $1 million in gold recovery, were marginally lower than season

two (in which they did little better than break even) although they were still better than season one in which they lost money.

26. Brandon Wenerd, "6 Things you Need to Know about Gold Mining and Reality TV, By Todd and Jack Hoffman of 'Gold Rush'," *BroBible*, last date modified November 9, 2012. http://www.brobible.com/entertainment/article/todd-hoffman-gold-rush-interview

27. Avital Ronnell, *Loser Sons: Politics and Authority*. (Champagne-Urbana: University of Illinois Press, 2012) 33.

28. On the need for an indigenous American literature (in the broad sense) as a means of forestalling an endless cycle of revolutions, see Susan Scheckel, *The Insistence of the Indian: Race and Nationalism in Nineteenth-Century American Culture*. (Princeton: UP, 1998) 9.

29. Jeffrey Alan Melton,"Touring Decay: Nineteenth-Century American Travel Writers in Europe." *Papers on Language and Literature* 35 (Spring, 1999): 206-222.

30. Thomas F. Gossett, "The Indian in the Nineteenth-Century." *Race: The History of an Idea in America*. (New York: Schocken Books, 1963) 228-252.

31. Susan Kord and Elisabeth Krimmer, *Contemporary Hollywood Masculinities: Gender, Genre and Politics*. (New York: Palgrave MacMillan, 2011) 61-62.

32. Richard Guy Wilson. "American Modernism in the West." In Thomas Carter (ed.) *Images of an American Land: Vernacular Architecture in the Western United States*, 291-319. (Albuquerque: University of New Mexico Press, 1997).

33. Thomas Farrell, "Sizing Things Up: Colloquial Reflection as Practical Wisdom." *Argumentation* 12 (1998): 1-14.

34. Mark Z. Danielewski, *House of Leaves*. (New York: Pantheon Books, 2000), 28.

35. Michel-Rolph Trouilot. *Silencing the Past: Power and the Production of History*. (Boston: Beacon Hill, 1995), 29-30.

36. *Gold Rush: Alaska*, "Lovestruck," Amazon.com video, 44:00, December 2, 2011, http://www.amazon.com/Lovestruck/dp/B0Bor6HDOAWI.

37. *Gold Rush: Alaska*, "Lovestruck."

38. *Gold Rush: Alaska*, "Lovestruck."

39. *Gold Rush: Alaska*, "Lovestruck."

40. *Gold Rush: Alaska*, "Lovestruck."

41. In a sidebar, Hoffman even notes that he "guesses" that Harkness is in town, but that he's not going to go there to find out. Underscoring the "spatial" puncturing argument we advance in the text, the "town" is understood to be toxic—the very idea that Hoffman would leave to retrieve or fire Harkness (even though he is gone for days) is, literally, unimaginable to Hoffman.

42. Rosalyn Deutsche, *Evictions: Art and Spatial Politics*. (Cambridge, MA: MIT Press, 1998), 326.

Chapter Eleven

Celebrity Rehab with Dr. Drew: A Wicked Brew of Fame, Addiction, and Cultural Narcissism

Christopher Mapp

Dr. Drew Pinsky is no stranger to the perils of addiction and fame. For more than 15 years, the man some call the "celebrity doctor" has worked with the rich and notorious as director of the Las Encinas Hospital treatment center in California. In this time, the host of the long-running radio show "Loveline" says he's seen a troubling trend emerge: an addiction to fame itself. Celebrities are becoming more dysfunctional, more demanding of entitlement, more "toxic"[1] in their behavior. Worse still, he fears audiences who are obsessed with watching these non-stop melodramas are following the celebrities down the rabbit hole of self-destruction. Pinsky calls it the "mirror effect" and he worries that non-celebrities interpret this dysfunctional lifestyle as "a game anyone can play" by adopting "the same unregulated, often troubling behavior that dominates reality TV and the Internet."[2]

So why would otherwise well-adjusted people preoccupy themselves with celebrities on a downward trajectory of misery and shame? That's easy, Pinsky explains. Our society, like the self-absorbed celebrities we love/ loathe, is becoming increasingly narcissistic, too. In a 2009 interview with *USA Today*'s Sharon Jayson, Pinsky said: "I speculate that that's what drives us toward this phenomenon of elevating people to almost godlike status. It's not so much that it's the glamour we like focusing on—rather it's the dysfunction. We're taking someone who needs to be a god and making them a god. Then we spend all our energy tearing them down."[3]

Perhaps no show on television embodies this dysfunctional trend more than Pinsky's own "Celebrity Rehab with Dr. Drew." The show's formula is simple enough. Celebrities struggling with addiction, whether to drugs, alcohol, sex, and so on, agree to spend 21 days at the Pasadena Recovery Center with a film crew present to record their "recovery process" 24 hours a day. There are rock stars (Steven Adler, former drummer of Guns 'N Roses), porn stars (Mary Carey), cultural icons (Rodney King), aging actors (Gary Busey). Nothing is off limits. The results at times can be gruesome, poignant, comical, even enlightening. Initially, the show was a ratings success. The formula, no matter how distasteful to some critics, seemed to work for VH-1, the network that aired it for six seasons (2008-2012).

Although Pinsky discontinued the series in 2013 because he grew tired of defending his methods and the outcomes, he has always defended the integrity of his show, arguing that it was never exploitative, but instead informative. "We unveil all the traumas and reveal what's going on with these people. We pull the curtain back and show you who these human beings are and where there is real suffering. It's a bait and switch. We're using the celebrity draw and trying it on people to show the reality. The celebrities have all been very pleased to be part of it because they want be an inspiration to other people," Pinsky said.[4]

Perhaps not all of the celebrities. Over the course of the first five seasons (the sixth and final season consisted of televised treatment for non-celebrities), five of the show's 50 participants died either from suicide or natural or drug-induced causes. The final celebrity death was former country singer Mindy McCready, who committed suicide on Feb. 17, 2013. Other celebrities who died after appearing on the show were Rodney King, Alice in Chains bassist Mike Starr, Taxi star Jeff Conaway and Real World's Joey Kovar. Despite the fact that 10 percent of the participants met an untimely death following their televised stints, Bob Forrest, a counselor with host Pinsky, defended the show. "These are late-stage addicts who've decimated their careers and lives," Forrest said. "But everybody's looking for somebody to blame, so it's Dr. Drew."[5]

Pinsky, a board-certified internist who also has worked for years as a professor of psychiatry, certainly has his supporters, too. He was described in an article in *The Atlantic* this way: "As a healer, Dr. Drew is fascinating. On the surface, his approach is scientific and slightly Dawkins-oid . . . but go below and you'll feel the cunning of the rural exorcist."[6] In a *Rolling Stone* piece from 2008, the year the show first aired and before the first celebrity died after appearing on the show, Pinsky was painted in magnanimous terms: "A cynic might be tempted to see Celebrity Rehab as little more than Pinsky's attempt to capitalize on what could be called a cultural addiction to celebrity addiction—Britney's shaved head! David Hasselhoff's hamburger meltdown!—all while enhancing his own celebrity. But the Doctor is an optimist at heart, an earnest believer that even the crassest mediums (talk radio, reality TV) can be subversively manipulated for altruistic means."[7]

No one has ever publicly accused Pinsky of directly causing these stars' demise, although some critics, like columnist Drew Grant ("Why it's time to shut down Celebrity Rehab, Salon.com, March 9, 2011) and members of the band Alice in Chains, whose bassist appeared on the show and then later died of an overdose, argue that it both takes advantage of celebrities at their weakest points and also trivializes self-diagnosed addictions, which leads to the type of celebrity narcissism Pinsky has himself railed against.[8] But complicating matters, unfortunate events have happened for which Pinsky said he was unfairly blamed, such as Rodney King's deadly heart attack. Following his exit from the show, Pinsky cited a heavy heart of his own for leaving the series behind. "It's very stressful and very intense for me," Pinsky told the *Today Show.* "To have people questioning my motives and taking aim at me because people get sick and die because they have a life-threatening disease, and I take the blame? Rodney King has a heart attack and I take the blame for that?"[9]

But the question has been raised by media critics and health care professionals about whether or not appearing on "Celebrity Rehab" contributed to these individuals' problems, or worse, hastened their eventual downfall.

"The show takes advantage of and uses people in deep distress because of their addiction as a way to draw viewers," said Ronald Hunsicker, president and CEO of the National Association of Addiction Treatment Providers (NAATP). "I can't think of another illness for which we would dramatize the struggles of individuals in such a graphic fashion."[10]

Some suggest these stylized struggles are just what the doctor ordered for ratings success. Dr. John Mariani, Director of the Substance Treatment and Research Service at Columbia University, told the *New York Times* in 2009 that Pinsky has a conflict of interest with his patients. "The problem here is that Dr. Drew benefits from their participation, which must have some powerful effects on his way of relating to them. He also has a vested interest in the outcome of their treatment being interesting to viewers, which is also not in their best interest. Treatment with conflicts of interest isn't treatment," Mariana said.[11]

Others have wondered publicly if Pinsky is not so much cynical and exploitative as hopelessly naïve, a doctor with a good heart who has spent too much time in the cozy, toxin-filled womb of Hollywood to know whether he's been played (and in doing so, unwittingly furthering the public's morbid fascination with celebrity self-destruction). As the writer David Amsden wrote in *Rolling Stone*: "He exudes so much irony-free sympathy that at times you can't help but wonder if he is delusional—someone who has spent so long on Hollywood's periphery that he no longer sees the difference between the desperate anonymous patients paying for his services at Las Encinas and the egomaniacs who were paid to be 'patients' on Celebrity Rehab."[12]

Pinsky counters by pointing out his show has never tried to glamorize addiction, which is anything but. Instead, death is sometimes a realistic by-product of a process that often goes awry. In other words, it comes with the territory.

"We are portraying the treatment of a fatal illness," Pinsky told *Entertainment Weekly* in a 2011 interview following the death of "Grease" and "Taxi" star Jeff Conway, arguably the show's most famous participant. Conway died from pneumonia that overwhelmed his drug-ravaged body just two months after the overdose of Alice in Chains bassist Mike Starr. "If you treat fatal diseases in a public program, people we treat are going to die."[13]

Others in the addiction industry were not convinced. Dr. Jeffrey Foote, cofounder of NYC's substance-abuse facility Center for Motivation and Change, laid a scathing attack at the feet of Pinksy himself, stopping short of pinning the deaths on the TV M.D. "How could this be working," Foote asked, "a doctor benefiting fame-wise and financially from patients' misery?"[14] Some, like scholar Peter Lawler, writing in the journal *Society*, are more pointed: "The celebrity physician to the celebrities, Dr. Drew Pinsky, is obviously laughing all the way to the bank."[15]

There is no doubt the doctor is making good money for his medical expertise. Pinsky, who also appears on the shows *Dr. Drew* on HLN and *Dr. Drew's Lifechangers* on the CW, was named in a $3 billion settlement case against drug-maker GlaxoSmithKline, which according to the government complaint, paid Pinsky $275,000 in 1999 to speak favorably about the anti-depresseant Wellbutrin SR in settings in which the educational intent was unclear.[16]

Writing in *Rolling Stone* magazine in 2011, Rob Sheffield asked if there was any depth Pinksy would not plumb. "The new season of Celebrity Rehab makes you marvel at how much he gets away with. In recent months, two former cast members have died, Jeff Conaway from *Taxi* and Mike Starr of Alice in Chains. You'd think that might cast a major shadow over the whole idea of televised detox, right? Yet Drew merely mentions them in passing: 'Sadly, this year we lost two of our own. But it only strengthens my resolve to fight this deadly disease.'" Sheffield continues: "It boggles the mind. If two *Dancing With the Stars* vets died in the line of duty—crushed in a fox-trot mishap, or trampled by an enraged *pasodoble*—it's hard to imagine that wouldn't be a big deal. But for Dr. Drew, it just proves the world needs more of him."[17]

Although Dr. David Sack, CEO of Promises, a rehab center popular with celebrities, questioned whether Pinsky was a "responsible physician" for treating his patients in an inferior television environment, Pinsky claims the cameras are precisely what these celebrities needed to seek help in the first place. "Here is a group of people who were unmotivated, and they come to be on TV and get paid. In spite of the distorted motivation, they come to treatment," Pinsky said.[18]

This startling assertion begs the question: do the celebrities come for treatment of their addictions, or do they come to feed their addiction to fame? Are they motivated by a true desire to get clean? Or is it simply a cynical ploy to stoke their egos and fuel their rampant narcissism? Whatever the case, Pinksy maintains that the important thing is getting them in the door of the rehab facility, where they can get treatment they otherwise might not seek. If it is narcissism leading the way, all the better, especially when you consider its pitiful psychological roots.

In their scientific study "The Mirror Effect," which examines the prevalence of narcissism among celebrities, Pinsky and his co-author S. Mark Young differentiate between narcissism and egomania. They posit that most narcissists are suffering serious psychological trauma stemming from past experiences, much of which can contribute to chemical dependency and other addictive tendencies.[19]

In "The Mirror Effect," Pinsky and Young write the following: "In common parlance, narcissism is often used as a synonym for egomania or excessive self-regard. In psychological terms, however, egotism and narcissism can be very different things. Egotists are preoccupied with themselves to an extreme degree. . . . Narcissism, on the other hand, springs from not self-involvement, but a disconnection with oneself. . . . Narcissistic individuals fixate on the reactions of others in order to shore up their own sense of self."[20]

This is consistent with research by Dr. Gad Saad, who writes in *Psychology Today* that celebrities often suffer from being stuck in a positive feedback loop, in which they never experience the kind of criticism that leads to self-correcting behavior. Absent this kind of constructive feedback, celebrities come to mistakenly believe they can do no wrong, and they can never be wrong. "Failure to receive any such feedback ensures celebrities will maintain their grandiosity," Saad writes.[21] One can only imagine how devastating it must be for the celebrities on *Celebrity Rehab* to get straightforward feedback from the group sessions or in one-on-one counseling with Dr. Drew and his assistants, namely the straight-shooting Bob Forrest, a former addict himself. Blogger Helen O'Reilly, writing for OurSalon.com, argues that for rehab to work successfully, it must happen covertly. "The basic text of the grandaddy of all twelve-step recovery programs, Alcoholics Anonymous, spells it right out: 'almost no one likes the self-searching, the leveling of pride' that the process demands. That leveling of pride starts with anonymity. Tell me; are there two more diametrically opposed concepts than 'anonymity' and 'celebrity?' And yet we react with surprise when we read that Mindy McCready is the fifth celebrity addict/alcoholic to have died in the last two years after appearing on Dr. Drew's show."[22]

Pinsky maintains that narcissism is typically mistaken for overabundant self-love, but actually it is a matter of self-loathing born out of emotional injury suffered in childhood. "It's a deep sense of emptiness and a deep disconnect between primary emotional experiences and second order representations of those experiences, such that feelings don't have much meaning and other people's feelings don't have much meaning. They have trouble with intimacy; they have trouble empathizing with other people, and the only way they feel good about themselves is sort of filling themselves up with the positive affects of other people," Dr. Drew told Gayle King in an interview on Oprah Radio.[23] For those celebrities suffering a lighter form of narcissism, Saad argues that some might even be able to muster enough self-insight to try to compensate for the sense of existential guilt they feel for being famous for little or no reason. Many do this by taking up pet causes or political crusades.[24]

Dr. Drew says his findings, based on survey research conducted in 2006 of 200 celebrities who took the Narcissistic Personality Inventory—show that "stars"—in this case, actors, musicians, reality show participants, and so on—are more narcissistic than the rest of the population.[25] But he points out that fame does not warp stars. Instead, they are drawn to the limelight like moths to a flame. These stars' rampant narcissism does not flow from celebrity, "but [it is] a primary motivating force that drives people to become celebrities."[26]

The most narcissistic type of celebrities, according to Dr. Drew's study, are female reality show contestants. But having a talent or a craft to devote oneself to, like music, for instance, helped buffer the narcissistic impulse. "People on reality shows, they're on TV because, 'Hey, it's just me! I just need to be on TV!'"[27]

Of course, anyone who has seen an episode of VH-1's *Behind the Music* knows that once celebrities achieve that exalted status, things often take a dark turn. Lawler writes, "Celebrities, generally speaking, are fairly irresponsible or selfish—out for themselves. They have less reason than we do not to be. They have rare opportunities to do whatever they want whenever they want. And not having been raised (as aristocrats once were) for their privileged lives, they usually aren't good at handling that freedom."[28]

Pinsky would call Anna Nicole Smith, who died of an overdose but never appeared on *Celebrity Rehab*, the "poster child" for this sort of malignant narcissism that leads to eventual self-destruction. But because most narcissists are acting out of emotional despair rather than self-interested malice, Dr. Drew suggests people should not put stars on a pedestal, but instead offer them empathy.[29] Unfortunately, he says far too often audiences relish the human train wrecks unfolding each season on screen.

In the same 2009 *USA* interview in which Pinsky defended giving the celebrities a platform to expose their own personal trauma and turmoil for the benefit and "inspiration" of the viewers, he chastised audiences who take solace in the reality stars' pain. Said Pinsky: "We should be concerned. It's anathema to what's healthy for humans—interpersonal experiences and being of service—as opposed to preoccupying oneself with extreme, chaotic, dysfunctional behavior and modeling those behaviors and wishing to be part of that and never experiencing a stable family life and not being able to trust other people or themselves. For those who say 'It's just fun,' why are you motivated to look at those people? Why gravitate to watching their troubles and their pathology? That's not OK. You feel better about your life with their misery. That's not what I call an admirable impulse."[30]

Pinsky thinks society has taken a turn for the worse over the last 100 years, before which medical experts debated whether narcissism even truly existed. Now, he says, psychiatric hospitals are overflowing with patients suffering from a constellation of narcissistic disorders.[31] The narcissistic interplay between celebrities and the society that worships and simultaneously destroys them is based in envy, an unhealthy outcropping of narcissism. But envy and jealousy are separate emotions, according to Pinsky. "I believe envy is what's being acted out here . . . Jealousy is, 'I want what you have.' That was back in what now seems like the more sanguine days of Lifestyles of the Rich and Famous, which seemed gross then, but now seems quite tame. And we've moved from jealousy to envy, which is, 'I want what they have and I must knock them down to my size.'"[32]

At the same time, Pinsky is asking us to understand the narcissistic impulses born from deep psychological trauma suffered by celebrities and empathize while capping our own narcissistic impulses. In an interview with conservative radio host Laura Ingraham, Pinsky said the following about the dangers of our society acting out its narcissistic impulses: "Healthy narcissism can give you a sense of confidence, a sense of ambition. But when it goes bad, it makes people prone to envy, and it gives them insufficient sense of empathy. So people lose the sense that other people have feelings of their own. And so it's easy to exploit. It's easy to think you're special. It's easy to act out in ways. We don't care."[33]

Of course, in terms of media, shows like Pinsky's are not the only ones offering the public garish glimpses into the excesses of celebrity. At least one British study examined the prevalence of alcohol-related stories in newspaper articles.[34] Of 186 articles examined involving alcohol-related themes, 45 of them featured celebrity drinking. Clearly, the public is enthralled by the chemical exploits of the rich and famous. And there are other addiction-themed reality shows, namely A&E's *Intervention*, a gritty series about regular people coming to grips with their dependencies, typically once their families and friends have staged an intervention. Although many of the show's subjects successfully get sober, the show has been criticized by some scholars for misrepresenting what addicts can realistically expect to encounter at treatment facilities and for perpetuating stereotypes and misconceptions about addiction.[35]

But that show is about regular people. It is doubtful many in its audience actively engage in the kind of envy Pinsky describes. On Celebrity Rehab, however, where the participants are screened, hired and paid for their time on the show, audiences are less forgiving. Seemingly, the public just can't seem to get enough when it comes to famous people behaving badly, if for no other reason than what Pinsky says amounts to "feeling better about ourselves." And Pinsky, often the titular head of the kinds of shows dishing this dirt, has kept them coming at a steady drip.

For Dr. Drew, the drug and booze rehab series spawned a side series on VH-1, the short-lived *Sober House*. It followed the celebrities as they tried to stay clean outside the strict confines of the Pasadena, California, facility in which *Celebrity Rehab* was filmed. Once this show played out, Pinsky followed it up with *Sex Rehab*, prompting a *Washington Post* editorial to shout "enough already." From that editorial, regarding what it considered the most pitiful moment of the first episode: "Most sadly, former swimsuit model Amber Smith, a *Celebrity Rehab* alum, arrives and tearfully tells Dr. Drew that now that she's conquered pain pills, the real issue (really) is sex. If that's what she wants us all to think, fine, but we wait in vain for the doctor to call her out on the actual disorder from which she seems to suffer—a problem he's actually written a book about already. Amber is addicted to her own narcissism, and to fame. He's too kind, that Dr. Drew."[36]

Too kind? Or too clever? There is no doubt Pinsky has guided countless addicts down the road to recovery. To this day, Pinsky still works tirelessly with addicts at the recovery center he's helmed for the last 20 years, just not on television anymore. And Pinsky, at least ostensibly, is reasonable about the limits of his shows' reach. As he told *Rolling Stone*, "Look, I'm not saying people are going to watch it and have some kind of epiphany . . . I see it more like turning the battleship just a little bit in a better direction. Fine, go out and make fun of Britney Spears if that's your impulse. But if I can get you to temper that with some understanding of the struggles going on with a person like that, then maybe (a) you can be a better person, (b) you go get help if you need it and (c) knock this bullshit off a little bit."

But it is also safe to say his forays into televised therapy have also contributed to the culture of celebrity worship of which he seems both disdainful and mystified. In an interview on the eve of the launching of his first episode of *Dr. Drew on HLN*, a news-oriented talk show, Pinsky was asked if he thinks our fascination with celebrities will ever wane.

"Not in the near term, I don't think. I don't see it lightening up in the near term," Pinsky said.[37]

Michael Hirschorn, executive VP of production at VH-1, openly stated that Celebrity Rehab sought both to capture and to capitalize on the audience's fervor for media fame. "The show is trying to take this moment of celebrity insanity—both the behavior of celebrities and our obsession with them—and try to explain why it's happening," Hirschorn said. "It's part of the 'celebreality' continuum, but it lives a little outside it. Obviously these are people who thrive on attention, but at the same time, the show is so raw that anyone will see it was far from a joy ride."[38]

Oddly enough, Pinsky—the celebrity doctor to the celebrities whose own celebrity has been enhanced thanks to his patients' personal pitfalls—says he's concerned that we as a society are "so focused on this stuff."[39]

"I don't know what it's gonna take to get people off of it, I really don't. So I don't know how to answer that cause that's sort of like trying to predict history, and I would want to do that with great caution," Pinsky said.[40]

If "history" is any guide, chances are it will wind up as a show somewhere with Dr. Drew's name on it.

REFERENCES

Alcoholism and Drug Abuse Weekly. February 4, 2008.

Amsden, David "Cleaning up with Dr. Drew," *Rolling Stone*, January, 24, 2008.

Armstrong, Jennifer. "Dr. Drew Pinsky's Bad Medicine?" *Entertainment Weekly*, June 17, 2011.

Dodd, Johnny. "They're so vain," *People*. April, 6, 2009. 57.

"Dr. Drew Hangs his shingle at HLN," www.multichannel.com. March 28, 2011.

Gaad, Sad. "I'm not a Doctor, but . . ." *Psychology Today*, November/December, 2009.

Grant, Drew. "Why it's Time to Shut Down Celebrity Rehab," *Salon.com*, March 9, 2011.

Halperin, Shirley. "Another Celebrity Rehab Death," *Hollywood Reporter*, March 1, 2013.

Herper, Matthew. "Feds Say Dr. Drew Was Paid By Glaxo To Talk Up Antidepressant," Forbes.com, last modified July 2, 2012.

Ingraham, Laura. "Why Do Celebs Behave Badly?" O'Reilly Factor (FOX News), March 19, 2009.

Jayson, Sharon. "Celebrity narcissism: A bad reflection for kids," *USA Today*, March, 17, 2009.

Kosovski, Jason and Smith, Douglas. "Everybody Hurts: Addiction, Drama, and the Family in the Reality Show *Intervention*," *Substance Use & Misuse*, 2011, 46:852–858. Taylor and Francis.

Lawler, Peter. "Celebrity Studies Today," *Society*. 47(2010): 420. Doi:10.1007/s12115-010-9353-z

Majeski, Ashley. "Dr. Drew Checks out of Celebrity Rehab," *Today*, May 2, 2013. Accessed August 20, 2013. http://www.today.com/entertainment/dr-drew-checks-out-celebrity-rehab-6C9751586

Nicholls, James. "UK News Reporting of Alcohol: An Analysis of Television and Newspaper Coverage." *Drugs: Education, Prevention and Policy*, June 2011; 18(3): 200–206.

Norris, Chris. "Hitting Bottom," *The New York Times*, December 30, 2009. Accessed August 20, 2013. http://www.nytimes.com/2010/01/03/magazine/03Pinsky-t.html?pagewanted=all&_r=0

Oprah.com/oprahradio/Dr-Drew

O'Reilly, Helen. "Attention Dr. Drew: It's Anonymity, not Celebrity that Makes for Successful Recovery," OurSalon.com, February 20, 2013. Accessed August 21, 2013, http://oursalon.ning.com/profiles/blogs/attention-dr-drew-it-s-anonymity-not-celebrity-that-makes-for

Parker, James. "Retching with the Stars," *The Atlantic*, November, 2009.

Pinsky, Drew and Young, S. Mark. *"The Mirror Effect: How Celebrity Narcissism Is Seducing America,"* (New York: Harper, 2009), 288.

Review of "The Mirror Effect: How Celebrity Narcissism Is Seducing America," in PW Review Annex, March 6, 2009.

Sheffield, Rob. "Why the Sleaze Doesn't Stick to Dr. Drew," *Rolling Stone*, August 4, 2011.

The Washington Post, "Sex Rehab's Dr. Drew just can't break his helper habit," October 31, 2009.

NOTES

1. Review of "The Mirror Effect: How Celebrity Narcissism Is Seducing America," in *PW Review Annex*, March 6, 2009.

2. Ibid.

3. Sharon Jayson, "Celebrity narcissism: A bad reflection for kids," *USA Today*, March, 17, 2009.

4. Ibid.

5. Shirley Halperin, "Another Celebrity Rehab Death," *Hollywood Reporter*, March 1, 2013.

6. James Parker, "Retching with the Stars," *The Atlantic*, November, 2009.

7. David Amsden, "Cleaning up with Dr. Drew," *Rolling Stone*, January, 24, 2008.

8. Drew Grant, "Why it's Time to Shut Down Celebrity Rehab," Salon.com, March 9, 2011.

9. Ashley Majeski, "Dr. Drew Checks out of Celebrity Rehab," *Today*, May 2, 2013. Accessed August 20, 2013. http://www.today.com/entertainment/dr-drew-checks-out-celebrity-rehab-6C9751586

10. *Alcoholism and Drug Abuse Weekly*. February 4, 2008.

11. Chris Norris, "Hitting Bottom," *New York Times*, December 30, 2009. Accessed August 20, 2013. http://www.nytimes.com/2010/01/03/magazine/03Pinsky-t.html?pagewanted=all&_r=0

12. Amsden, "Cleaning up with Dr. Drew."

13. Jennifer Armstrong, "Dr. Drew Pinsky's Bad Medicine?" *Entertainment Weekly*, June 17, 2011.

14. Ibid.

15. Peter Lawler, "Celebrity Studies Today," *Society*. 47(2010): 420. Doi:10.1007/s12115-010-9353-z

16. Matthew Herper, "Feds Say Dr. Drew Was Paid By Glaxo To Talk Up Antidepressant," Forbes.com, last modified July, 2 2012.

17. Rob Sheffield, "Why the Sleaze Doesn't Stick to Dr. Drew," *Rolling Stone*, August 4, 2011.

18. Armstrong, "Dr. Drew Pinsky's Bad Medicine?"

19. Drew Pinsky and S. Mark Young, *"The Mirror Effect: How Celebrity Narcissism Is Seducing America,"* (New York: Harper, 2009), 288.

20. Ibid.

21. Sad Gaad, "I'm not a Doctor, but . . ." *Psychology Today*, November/December, 2009.

22. O'Reilly, Helen, "Attention Dr. Drew: It's Anonymity, not Celebrity that Makes for Successful Recovery," OurSalon.com, February 20, 2013. Accessed August 21, 2013, http://oursalon.ning.com/profiles/blogs/attention-dr-drew-it-s-anonymity-not-celebrity-that-makes-for.

23. Oprah.com/oprahradio/Dr-Drew.

24. Gaad, "I'm not a Doctor, but . . . " 61.

25. Johnny Dodd, "They're so vain," *People*. April, 6, 2009. 57.

26. *PW Review Annex*; "The Mirror Effect . . ." 5.

27. Oprah.com/oprahradio/Dr-Drew.

28. Lawler, "Celebrity Studies Today," 420.

29. Dodd, "They're so vain," 57.

30. Jayson, "Celebrity narcissism . . . "

31. "Dr. Drew Hangs his shingle at HLN," www.multichannel.com. March 28, 2011.

32. Ibid.

33. Laura Ingraham, "Why Do Celebs Behave Badly?" *O'Reilly Factor* (FOX News), March 19, 2009.

34. James Nicholls, "UK News Reporting of Alcohol: An Analysis of Television and Newspaper Coverage." *Drugs: Education, Prevention and Policy*, June 2011; 18(3): 200–206.

35. Jason Kosovski and Douglas Smith, "Everybody Hurts: Addiction, Drama, and the Family in the Reality Show *Intervention*," *Substance Use & Misuse*, 2011, 46:852–858. Taylor and Francis.

36. *The Washington Post*, "Sex Rehab's Dr. Drew just can't break his helper habit," October 31, 2009.

37. "Dr. Drew Hangs his shingle . . . " 8.

38. Amsden, "Cleaning up with . . . "

39. Dr. Drew Hangs his shingle . . . " 8.

40. Ibid.

Chapter Twelve

"Born" Survivors and Their Trickster Cousins: Masculine Primitive Ideals and Manly (Re)Creation on Reality Television

Matthew P. Ferrari

I. INGESTING WILDNESS: POSITING A "MAN VS." SUBGENRE

In recent years, reality television has become an important site for projecting a cultural vision of masculinity defined by idealizations of man's struggle against nature. We might call it the "Man vs." subgenre, one that privileges the articulation of a socio-historical gender ideal known as the "masculine primitive,"[1] operating under the broader umbrellas of "travel and adventure" and "animals and nature" reality television. This grouping of shows relies most centrally on the spectacle of male bodies mobilized in outdoor spaces dealing with themes of survival, isolation, and forms of "primitive" contact, labor, or performance; of challenging the boundaries and habits of those bodies in extreme, exotic, and threatening places and situations; of escaping the modern socially disciplined body to one more "natural" or untamed by contriving survival scenarios which subject it to challenging environmental elements, plants and animals, climate extremes, sometimes "native" peoples and sometimes one another. I am referring to programs like *Survivorman*, *Man vs. Wild*, *Dual Survival*, *Going Tribal*, *Tribal Life*, *Last One Standing*, *Man vs. Monster*, *Yukon Men*, *Extreme Survival Alaska*, *Man Woman Wild*, *Wildboyz*, and *Mountain Men*, a few of the more obvious examples spanning the last 5-10 years. I argue that this generic grouping, and the performances herein, exhibit characteristics similar to the historical "masculine primitive" ideal that emerged in mid-19th-century America amidst rapid industrialization and urbanization, and is fundamentally rooted in a deep reverence for wild nature as the sacred space of masculine regeneration in the modern age.

As a brief introduction, consider the depiction of masculine primitive ideals in *Mountain Men* (History Channel). The cast of social actors is established in terms of a pious belief in ancient, outmoded ways of life associated with wild "nature" and living apart from (in time and space) civilization. As Eustice Conway explains, "These mountains are my life. This land is my life. I live it, live with it, breathe it. I live like people have lived for hundreds of thousands of years."[2] Or Marty Meierotto, who says, "I'm a man who has to be in nature because that's the only place I feel like I'm whole."[3] Rich Lews exclaims, "I'm not a people person. I'm not gonna conform to society."[4] *Mountain Men*'s opening voice-over establishes its cast in terms of isolation and confrontation with wild nature, but also as a threatened group faced with rarefied daily obstacles: "America's mountains are a natural barrier. Here, man's ambition collides with the ultimate power of nature. Some men seek to live here, beyond the bounds of civilization. They fight to survive, battling ruthless predators. And relying on ancient skills, to feed, clothe, and sustain their families. The last of their kind, they are . . . Mountain Men."[5] Finally, the titles alone for the show's "webisodes" suggest an array of masculine primitive values: "A Dying Breed," "Hard Living," "Facing Danger," "Skills to Pass On," "Loving the Wild," "Self-Reliance," "Alone in the Wild," "Country vs. City," "Man vs. Bear."[6] And yet, within the "Man vs." subgenre—or perhaps just standing alongside it in mimetic play—there are, as I will discuss, significant contradictions and disruptions of the ideal articulated through forms of de-mythologizing parody.

This essay explores the discursive boundaries and limitations of masculine primitive ideals by examining both their "pieties and parodies" across several key shows.[7] In doing so, I posit this socio-historical ideal—and its related terms—as a fruitful, if under-theorized basis for generically organizing and interpreting a particular vein of reality television production and its ideological implications for contemporary gender formation. This chapter will define "masculine primitive" ideals, and then present an analysis of their earnest, reverent expression in *Man vs. Wild* (with *Survivorman* an important inter-text), *Dual Survival*, and *Man Woman Wild*. These examples are then set against parodies of the "travel and adventure" and "animals and nature" subgenres. *Wildboyz* and other pertinent examples are posited as "tricksters" exposing the authoritative ideological construction of primitive masculinities as exemplary forms. Lastly, several explanations for the apparent surge in production of "Man vs." themed programs are considered.

II. "MASCULINE PRIMITIVE" IDEALS

One of the challenges of interrogating the varied iterations of the masculine primitive ideal lies in its semiotic flexibility and adaptability to social change, which is also crucial to understanding its historical persistence. Much like the closely related category of "nature" (or the "natural"), the "primitive" (and its many associated primitivisms) can play any number of roles, but the "primitive" and "natural" are fundamentally aligned in their rhetorical function of disguising ideological interests.[8] That is, much like framing or labeling something as a part of "nature"—or as merely "natural"—often serves to falsely render it timeless (i.e. ahistorical) and thus inevitable, the notion of a "primitive" or "natural" masculinity brings with it a host of related suppositions. That these two terms are so often placed in quotations serves to emphasize their role as flexible cultural constructs, along with the troubling specter of political effects left in their wake.

The links between "nature" and the "primitive" as fundamentally intertwined cultural discourses is not always immediately apparent. Kate Soper, in explaining how "nature" has functioned throughout history as the key "concept through which social conventions and cultural norms are continuously legitimated and contested," explains the association thusly: "Western configurations of nature—notably its association with the 'primitive', the 'bestial', the 'corporeal', and the 'feminine',—reflect a history of ideas about membership of the human community and ideals of human nature and thus function as a register or narrative of human self-projections."[9] It may go without saying, but the "primitive" has historically served very different social and ideological functions for men than it has for women. While it is not within the scope of this essay to outline these differences in detail, suffice it to say that cultural configurations of the "primitive" have, by and large, served primarily to empower men of Euro-Western descent while diminishing the status of women, non-Western populations, and people of color.[10] In short, for white men, the masculine primitive is more often cast as an ennobling ideal, while for most, if not all other populations, the construct functions through a powerful symbolic "othering" complicit in a long history of racial and sexual prejudice.[11]

According to R.W. Connell, "masculinities come into existence at particular places and times, and are always subject to change."[12] The masculine primitive, then, requires further grounding and qualification here. According to Rotundo, who first placed the two terms together, the masculine primitive emerged primarily for white, middle-class men in mid-19th-century America as one of three ideal types of manhood.[13] Citing evidence from written correspondences, literature, speeches (e.g. Theodore Roosevelt, it is a good thing to "make the wolf rise in a man's heart"), and a variety of other primary historical materials, Rotundo explains that "suddenly, natural passions and impulses had become a valued part of man's character."[14] This ideal arose during the convergence of certain historical circumstances—namely, the dissemination of Darwinian thought (and a concomitant "Social Darwinism" which sought to re-locate understandings of social dynamics in biological terms), widespread rural to urban migrations, a changing sexual division of labor, the introduction of intercollegiate sports, new scientific understandings of the human body and its norms, and last but not least, the emergence of anthropology—a "science of humanity" circulating new ideas about human origins and cultural diversity based in the study of colonized non-Western populations.[15] This ideal was rooted in a belief that "men—more than women—were primitives in many important ways," and while the forces of civilization might weaken or conceal this, all men "shared in the same primordial instincts for survival."[16] Viewing man as the "master animal" within the natural order, this gendered primitivism emphasized the importance of cultivating a "natural" physical strength and vigor, and the ability to access instincts for survival in the modern world.[17]

Although this ideal has adopted various guises over time, its underlying structures are relatively stable, arguably rooted in a patriarchal masculine impulse toward consolidating definitions of ideal manhood when perceived to be threatened or attenuated. Leo Braudy maintains that "much of human ritual and social organization" is obsessed with defending clear distinctions between masculinity and femininity, which may suggest "a deep-rooted human (or masculine) fear that they are arbitrary enough to be constantly in danger of erosion or forfeit."[18] So one way to shore up masculinity is to base it in something ostensibly "natural," biological, ancient, timeless; that is, buried in the deep recesses of a primitive pre-history, which, despite having no literal access to it, is strategically supported by popular naturalistic mythologies and a facile public acceptance of certain components of evolutionary theory.

The popular belief in a partial, "lost," latent, or "inner" masculinity is crucial to understanding any cultural expressions of a masculine primitive ideal. The role of the "primitive" in masculine gender formation, as suggested above, is in aiding the construction of a naturalistic myth of a "real," "true," "deep" or essential masculinity—one innately there to be accessed or re-created—rooted in imaginary origins. Johannes Fabian explains that the "primitive" is the key concept of temporalizing discourses, often functioning to naturalize subjects by removing them from historical time.[19] For Lovejoy and Boas, the use of the "primitive" in cultural discourses involves a "backward looking habit of mind" aimed at "recovering what has been lost."[20] Or, as Stanley Diamond explains, "primitivism is the puzzled search for what is diminished by civilization,"[21] and that "civilized man cannot know what he has gained until he learns what he has lost."[22] Whether it is discussions of "true" masculinity, the "natural man," "the wildman," the "deep masculine," or the "man-the-hunter" thesis, these are all various configurations of primitive masculinity involved in the political project of assigning actual or idealized male behavior to innate, biological, or so-called "natural" origins, and thus rendering it more immune to political critique. And where a "feminine primitive" in cultural discourses has more often configured women negatively as "victims of their biological nature as childbearers," the masculine primitive enacts myths of men as "free to express their biology, often in elaborate rituals of competition."[23] Braudy explains that, historically, notions of "true" masculinity are "tinged with, even steeped in, nostalgia for a lost masculinity," and that this "powerful form of masculinity is perpetually nostalgic in its judgment and standards."[24] Thus, the "masculine primitive" is merely one name for a cultural discourse observed by social historians to function as a gender norm or ideal, but it is also socially enacted or performed, and thus an (albeit indirect) agent in our modern gender formations.

While the nineteenth-century social conditions factoring into the emergence of the masculine primitive have changed greatly, most have not simply disappeared. Instead, many have intensified, transformed, or become more familiar through a repetition of these cultural tropes in literature, film, and television. Even though social Darwinism is not exactly in favor, it still carries great resonance in popular culture. A "survival of the fittest" mentality has considerable purchase as common sense wisdom. Connell explains that a belief in "real men," "natural man," and the "deep masculine" are a "strategic part of the modern gender ideology."[25] Along these lines, Kimmel argues that the present-day search for the "deep" masculine is "historically anachronistic, echoing late nineteenth-century masculinist complaints against the forces of feminization."[26] Thus, even though this particular masculine primitive ideal emerged most prominently over a century ago—one positing men as naturally aggressive and competitive, as "natural" warriors and hunters because of an evolutionary imperative to adapt and survive, where this exemplary form of masculinity is one that can (when called upon) willfully summon the primordial instinct from which man's physical strength and vitality flows, and where "true" and "deep" masculinity is possibly imperiled by the feminizing forces of civilization—it is still with us today in modified forms.

And yet I will argue further on that, through the repetition of certain expressive tropes of primitive masculinity, this ideal is increasingly familiar and untethered from its earnest nineteenth-century origins, and is thus more available to parody and other forms of critique. But first I wish to demonstrate how the "Man vs." subgenre of reality television is currently one of the most conspicuous cultural sites for earnest (and reverent) expressions of this form of masculinity, which we might understand as a privileged cultural site for the "willful summoning of past styles of cultural behavior as a way of dealing with the present."[27] And finally, while a significant portion of the gender imaginary expressed in contemporary popular cultural production is now much more expansive and diverse, the "Man vs." subgenre is part and parcel with historical patterns in which forward-looking ideals and values are interwoven with the impulse, as Braudy puts it, "to repeat compulsively an array of archaic gestures from the past."[28]

III. "BORN" SURVIVORS

For Bear Grylls, the ex-British Special Forces survival expert and host of *Man vs. Wild* (or *Born Survivor: Bear Grylls* in the UK, 2006-2011), his show's dramatic staging of an ostensibly one man vs. nature survival narrative provoked its own separate man vs. society narrative when it was revealed that certain survival sequences were staged, and the show's "born" survivor even slept in hotels at night, and not on location as suggested. Apparently viewers took the show's title(s) and stated premise too literally, expecting an authentic picture of one man's battle to survive in true wilderness isolation over a continuous period of days. The term "wild" signifies location, geography, but more importantly for reality television producers, it signifies danger and the opportunity to sell dramatic risk taking. Perhaps the most common role of the "wild"—and "nature" in general—utilized throughout the history of Western cultural narratives lies in its qualities to test humans, wherein "nature" enables conflict in the form of a bodily threat or challenge.[29] Quite often, these "tests" function as a means to demonstrate an exemplary masculinity through physical prowess (stamina, endurance, toughness, aggression), but also knowledge and technical expertise. The masculine primitive ideal in programs like *Man vs. Wild*, *Survivorman*, *Dual Survival*, and *Man Woman Wild* is expressed in the physical performance of survival prowess. But, a successful performance is contingent on the authenticity of the test—a real threat to survival through true wilderness isolation. And, as the public controversy surrounding *Man vs. Wild* appears to suggest, the sufficiency of wildness as a test of manhood lies in the conditions of one's isolation within it.

Each episode of *Man vs. Wild* begins with Grylls parachuting into some exotic location with only a few items to help him "survive" (usually a knife and canteen, but with some variation depending on the specific location and survival scenario). Dropping in from the sky is just one of the show's gimmicks for enhancing the impression of wilderness isolation, a formal device making it easier for the viewer to sympathize with Grylls's test. A related device is to only depict Grylls alone. We never see him receiving any kind of support or aid from the camera crew. Additionally, the sense of duration is manipulated such that this (self-proclaimed) modern "Robinson Crusoe"[30] appears to be out in the elements continuously for full days and nights.

Working in the codes of realism, these formal devices establish and intensify the sense of Grylls's isolation and wilderness hardships.

Grylls's survival performances emphasize his (supposed) embodiment of a masculine primitive ideal. Many of the "tests" wild nature offers Grylls, as we will see, would merely be outdoor "recreation" were it not for exigencies of the show's "survival" format. Given the dramatic conceit of dropping into the wild with a few essentials, Grylls is reliably compelled to demonstrate pre-modern methods of survival. In one episode, before descending a rock face, he exclaims, "I'm going to try to attempt this without any ropes or any other modern rock climbing aid."[31] Grylls often cites the influence of indigenous populations from each episode's specific region, taking on some of their symbolic status (as "closer to nature," and thus a strategic symbolic Othering by association). In one episode, Grylls explains, "This area was once home to many native Americans. I'm using some of their survival techniques to turn this driftwood into a raft."[32] After citing some gruesome statistics on white-water rafting deaths on the river over the last thirty years, Grylls undertakes the challenge without modern aids, and as is typical, highlights the physical toll on his body. He says, "My knees are taking a real pounding here."[33] In addition to depicting Grylls's physical durability, this "true" survivor is also successful in the hunt—shown tracking, killing, cleaning, cooking, and eating small game—and is more than willing to consume a host of wild plants and insects (like grubs, an excellent source of protein), highlighting the often sensational grotesqueries requisite of pre-modern survival methods. Through these performances, Grylls becomes a symbolic intermediary between civilization and the wild. He is, after all, a "born" survivor—it is in his (biological) "nature." So when it was revealed that, during the show's filming, he was actually sleeping in hotels at night, controversy ensued.

One of the show's producers divulged that some scenes were artificially staged or enhanced when, for example, a smoke machine was used to exaggerate the extent of poisonous gas from a volcano Grylls traversed.[34] Another example is the "wild" bronco Grylls attempted to lasso in one episode, the horse later revealed to be on hire from a local trainer.[35] Producers responded to the criticisms by re-editing some episodes and issuing a statement claiming all future episodes would be "100% transparent," but that for reasons of health and safety, some aspects of the show could not always be "natural to the environment."[36] *Born Survivor*'s original UK broadcaster, Channel 4, said in a statement that the show "is not an observational documentary series, but a "how to" guide to basic survival techniques in extreme environments. The programme explicitly does not claim that presenter Bear Grylls's experience is one of unaided solo survival."[37] The controversy resulted in a new disclaimer opening each episode: "The crew receives support when they are in potentially life-threatening situations," and "occasionally situations are presented to Bear so he can demonstrate survival techniques."[38] Among fans of survival television, *Survivorman*'s Les Stroud was touted as the more authentic survivalist through reference to the insufficient wildness of *Man vs. Wild*'s studio wilderness.

Programs like *Man vs. Wild* and *Survivorman* re-enact two powerful, interrelated myths regarding the supposed origins of proper manliness—first, an American myth of geographic mobility in which the re-creation of men, or masculine regeneration, is made possible through isolation in the wild.[39] In this way, these programs invoke the "frontier fable," with the pioneer (e.g. Les Stroud as Daniel Boone) elevated as the embodiment of the masculine primitive ethos. In this scenario, man going "into" the wild is perhaps as much about his leaving key relational "others" behind who are perceived to erode or blur the rigid binary on which the modern gender order relies for its stability—namely "civilization," the domestic sphere, and the feminine/feminizing associations therein. Second is the belief that "real" men have certain kinds of technical competencies, especially those that require the body's natural physical strength and vigor and do not rely on short-cuts or aids afforded by "modern" technologies. That a problem appears to arise for the viewer (or journalist) when core values of the masculine primitive are revealed to be artificially "presented" or staged by producers, and not fully lived, is indicative of the ideal's agency in the popular imaginary.

As might be expected, the fan discourse of reality television's survival shows takes up the project of evaluating how well each show lives up to a masculine primitive ethos, and for that matter, goes some way in defining its social parameters. The notion of Grylls's or Stroud's degree of isolation in the wild directly implicates the level and quality of fan engagement. On a forum like Survivalistboards.com, where presumably participants have made their own forays into survivalism and thus draw directly on that knowledge and experience, discussions of survival television focus on debates about authenticity and the particulars of survival scenarios. One participant echoes an earnest masculine primitive ideal, with women's inclusion merely a secondary or bracketed possibility, saying, "A 'real' survival show would pit a man (or woman) against the elements with nothing but the clothes on his/her back with no tools. That would impress me. Build shelter, hunt/trap/fish, make fire, heal thyself, etc. with nothing but your hands and whatever nature provides."[40] Les "Survivorman" Stroud is often lauded by fans as a more authentic survivor than Grylls. Stroud agrees with this assessment, stating, "They're right. What I do, I do for real. To really show survival, I had to go out and do it alone."[41]

By having a public debate on whether Bear Grylls or Les Stroud is the truer survivalist, fans have a chance to assert their own masculine (or feminine) values—whether "primitive," "marketplace," or otherwise. This dynamic is not exclusive to survival shows, but rather is a general part of what Justin Lewis calls "the popular epistemology of TV viewing."[42] The *Man vs.*

Wild controversy, though extending a set of value judgments from a specific cultural context, is rooted in the more general condition all reality television currently finds itself in—that of a "postdocumentary culture"[43] where "traditional codes of documentary realism intermingle with genres based in celebrity and artifice."[44] Some dimension of our viewing pleasure clearly resides in the game of judging a program's relationship to "real" life, regardless of the mode or format. "Just as with fiction," Lewis argues, "the notion of the authentic or real is an evaluative and interpretive tool in making sense of factual entertainment."[45] We know television is always part real and unreal, authentic and artificial, but how we make use of the relationship between television and reality is based in specific cultural contexts.

Where men are predominately the "born" or "natural" survivors in these shows, modifying the format to include traditional "others," or contrasting survival abilities, is revealing in how these shows configure a mythic quest for manhood and its ideological implications. After the initial success of *Man vs. Wild* (i.e. *Born Survivor*) and *Survivorman*, several variations on the theme emerged. For example, *Dual Survival* (Discovery) uses a similar format, but adds a man vs. man conflict involving two protagonists with often radically opposed survivalist philosophies. Dave, a former Army sniper, explains his philosophy in agonistic, defensive terms, with nature cast as the adversary, believing that "The elements are your enemy, and only the strong will survive,"[46] while his counterpart Cody, a "primitive living skills expert," articulates his survival philosophy in terms of ecological integration, awareness, or harmony. Cody says, "I pay attention to mother nature, because she's the boss. So I'm trying to think with her, not against her."[47] *Dual Survival* is designed to encourage viewers' identification with (or rejection of) distinct (re)iterations of a masculine primitive ideal and its different styles of embodiment. Cody's nature-spirituality and adoption of archaic lifestyle practices, like insisting on being barefoot even when placed in an arctic climate, leads Dave (a self-proclaimed "common sense kinda guy") to denounce Cody's methods as "bush hippy logic and mother nature stuff that I don't get."[48] Cody's explanation of his chosen methods reflect a nostalgia for primitive life-ways. As he says, "I do it to feel more connected to the planet. I do it because hundreds of thousands of people before me could and did."[49] When Dave is out hunting (small game), Cody is gathering (plants and snails). *Dual Survival* stages—much like the contest between Grylls and Stroud materialized in public discourse—a drama of contrasting and competing survival prowess and their particular effectiveness. While they work together fairly well, and both are depicted as inhabiting and fulfilling the ideal, their contrasting styles of primitive masculinity create channels for judgment not available in the solo format, extending the possibilities for viewer engagement and identification. Cody's "bush hippy logic," nature-spirituality, and insistence on foraging (over hunting) often serves to position

Dave by contrast as the more realistic, manly survivor. On the other hand, Cody's insights and wisdom often leave Dave appearing shallow and out of tune with nature. Ultimately they both succeed in their "test" in nature—they are both sufficiently "wild men." As we will see, however, other variations on the "Man vs." subgenre negotiate the performance of survival prowess and sufficient wildness somewhat differently, through more stark contrasts between the (white) manly ideals and their (symbolic) "others."

Man Woman Wild (Discovery) articulates how including women as "others" within a symbolically masculine primitive domain (e.g. wilderness) can serve to exempt men from needing to attain sufficient wildness (through success in isolation) required for the successful performance of a masculine primitive ideal. On the surface of it, these variations on the "Man vs." theme originate in the market logic of expanding audience appeal. From a producer's perspective, *Man Woman Wild* finally offers women viewers a character to more easily identify with, or gain access to, the masculine primitive domain. But ideologically, this scenario affords the opportunity for masculine re-creation through a dynamic Kimmel explains as "the successful symbolic reclamation of manhood possible only via the failure of traditional others, the exclusion of the other from that same mythic quest."[50]

The opening voice-over in *Man Woman Wild* establishes a bipolar distinction between men and women with regard to wilderness survival. Ruth, the show's female protagonist, opens with the question: "What happens when you drop a husband and wife into some of the most remote places on the planet? Fortunately, my husband Myke (Mykel Hawk) is a survival expert. He survived in some of the most dangerous places in the world. Myke's going to teach me how to stay alive in the wild."[51] At the outset, it appears Ruth is to be included in the "quest," that she might be allowed to cultivate and then demonstrate sufficient survival prowess, even possibly attaining through a symbolic conferral of the (masculine) primitive ideal her own re-creation. But the opening montage reminds us that Ruth is not a "born" survivor like Myke, further establishing her as the "other," with much to surmount in her quest. Some of the telling images include the following: Ruth recoils in horror from a snake, where Myke shows fearlessness; in disgust, she refuses to eat some creature while he does so decisively; Ruth awkwardly wields a shotgun and then struggles to manage its "kick" when fired. These opening images establish Myke as the one in possession of key features of the masculine primitive ideal—as one "naturally" strong, decisive, fearless, and skilled. While the viewer might hope for Ruth to achieve this ideal, well into the second season, Myke is still clearly ensconced as masculine primitive representative, as intermediary between primitive and civilized, with Ruth depicted as still unable (or unwilling) to adapt as effectively as Myke. Where Myke's role is to be the decisive and imperturbable body, rarely showing fear, weakness, or uncertainty ("the first thing we need to do is assess our situation by getting to a good vantage point, and then let's make a plan"),[52] Ruth's role is evidently to bring the hardships of wilderness survival to more vivid life for the viewer through effusive complaining, squeamishness, and general discomfort ("So, I climb up that rattlesnakey, crevicey, hideous rock?").[53] Ultimately, Myke is depicted to be more "at home" in the wild, and Ruth, even after numerous adventures, performs a form of gendered wilderness incompetence—making for great drama, of course—but therefore not in possession of the innate or "natural" wildness available to Myke.

In one episode, Ruth is sick from dehydration (having been unwilling to drink her own urine as Myke did), so Myke calls in first-aid support from the crew (located miles away) earlier than planned, though he is still apparently capable of continuing on, and expresses some disappointment for not enduring to reach their planned destination. Ruth's "failure," and in general, her inability to perform survival prowess on a par with Myke, exempts him from the same masculine primitive ideals (i.e. the prowess and skills) expected of Grylls, Stroud, or Cody and Dave of *Dual Survival* in gender isolation. Indeed, Myke's greatest challenge is apparently the encroachment of "culture" (i.e. the feminine and domestic sphere) upon his place in/as wild "nature." This comment from each episode's introduction indicates that his survival prowess is limited once the symbolic space of the "wild" is breached to include an unknown variable from the domestic sphere: "My military skills will go a long way, but there's no field manual for surviving with a spouse."[54] Ruth's mere presence and the symbolic fixity of her role as "other," even over the course of two seasons, casts Myke in terms of naturalistic myths of primitive masculinity rooted in biological difference. Furthermore, the social actors' relatively fixed symbolic status renders Ruth only capable of miming (but never fully inhabiting in her own right) Myke's masculine primitive survival prowess, a device that engenders a form of inadvertent parody. According to Taussig, "Parody is where mimicry exposes construction."[55] We might conclude of *Man Woman Wild*, then, that Ruth's hopelessly subordinate status in the duo (at least in terms of certain masculine primitive ideals)—her default role of parodying Myke's successful performance of primitive masculinity through an incompetent if entertaining mimesis—facilitates the commercial enactment and commodification of an outmoded style of masculinity that reifies harsh wilderness as the privileged domain of men and is fundamentally articulated through the cultural terms of gender essentialism. However, when viewed within the wider mediascape of masculine primitive performances on reality television, and when considering the extent to which these ideals are parodied and transgressed by (and for) its supposed subjects (i.e. heterosexual white men), the terms of their flexible construction and instability as a symbolic commodity becomes more transparent.

IV. TRICKSTER COUSINS

The masculine primitive ideal is at its core an equation of manhood with a certain kind of embodied (physical and technical) prowess. As we saw with reality television's so-called "born" survivors, this ideal is performed in terms of a decisive, brave, and durable body, but also one possessing certain kinds of knowledge, mental toughness, and technical skills. Ruth (*Man Woman Wild*) was predictably the only survivor not fully living up to (i.e. not permitted to) the ideal expected within the "Man vs." subgenre. In most respects, the masculine primitive ideal is part and parcel with exemplary masculinity, falling within "official" masculinity, which Horrocks explains as "resolutely heterosexual and butch."[56] However, I turn now to parodies of the genre and its ideal that, while still relying on a spectacle of masculinity in the wild, effectively talk back to it. Where Ruth's role was, I argue, to provide an unambiguous "other" whose counterposed failure served to symbolically affirm Myke's (and the male viewer's) embodiment of the ideal, and even mitigate its standards, what happens when men are "others" to their (own) ideal within the same (more or less) generic and thematic format?

Wildboyz (MTV), a *Jackass* spinoff featuring Steve-O and Chris Pontious, arguably accomplishes this, operating as a general parody of the wildlife-adventure genre. That is, borrowing Denith's definition of genre, *Wildboyz* works (to a great extent, at least) through the "imitation and transformation" of another "cultural production or practice."[57] Relatedly, I treat *Wildboyz* here in terms of parody's "critical intertextuality," or what Gray understands as a form that "reveals the hidden tricks and assumptions of its target genre(s)."[58] Establishing the meaning of the "Man vs." subgenre can only be accomplished by looking at the discursive continuities and differences across its different programs, which is the basis of genre theory. As Berry explains, a genre's meanings "exist only intertextually, in relation to conventions, forms, and motifs found in related texts."[59]

Wildboyz is aware of the typical earnestness and seriousness that suffuses the genre they mimic—of the genre's general reverence for other cultural traditions (e.g. Grylls invoking Native American tradition) and the natural environment (e.g. Cody's earnest reverence for nature). The show's scenes involve the formal interplay between a classic, omniscient voice-over narration (by a British actor, no less) providing factual information ("The long neck women of Mehong Sun wrap heavy brass coils about their necks, a tradition once believed to prevent them from marrying into other tribes."),[60] and the gross body, juvenile shtick of Chris and Steve-O ("Holy crap, we're in the middle of nowhere Thailand now! Oh yeah these women look great with long necks!").[61] The narration provides relevant cultural context and factual wildlife information (along with the local experts who serve as tour guides), referencing the generic form, but also pronouncing the incompetence and childish antics of the hosts. Chris and Steve-O only demonstrate enough knowledge of local culture and wildlife to deliver their usual puerile quip ("This animal here is Central America's Jaguarundi, and these are our jaguar undies.").[62] And ultimately, their mocking of a wild man style or ideal of masculinity ("Nobody's more of a 'wilderman' than old Steve-O.") is usually accomplished by exhibiting anything but the decisive, brave, and imperturbable body in possession of manly knowledge, mental toughness, and technical competence.

Historically, maturity in men is often established (rhetorically, at least) through the physical enactment of technical competence.[63] Unlike typical wildlife television guides who facilitate the genre's infotainment (e.g. *The Crocodile Hunter*'s Steve Irwin), where the successful negotiation and mastery of exotic, often dangerous wildlife by white men becomes the genre's symbolic currency, in *Wildboyz* it exists as a structured absence. Exotic wildlife, the untamed wilderness, the symbolic space where boys can be tested and possibly prove manhood, here becomes the playground or stage upon which white (adult) male bodies refuse to obey and enact this old ideal. By and large, they demonstrate no nature spirituality, no reverence for its grandeur, no special knowledge to negotiate its mysteries, nor the proper style of bravery and requisite physical powers through which to successfully implement that knowledge. Instead, they invoke these ideals by imitating the wildlife-adventure infotainment format, acting within its symbolic spaces and settings, only to fail in the performative motifs vital to their affirmation. Yet there is some symbolic blurring, and *Wildboyz*'s formal intimacy with the genre's ideals is not only disruptive or transgressive of the exemplary masculinities enacted as masculine primitive ideals—it is also complicit in some crucial ways.

Like proper "wildmen," Chris and Steve-O do masochistically seek out physical punishment, taking the pain, and certainly present a spectacle of toughness and durability (extending their corporeal daring from *Jackass* (MTV)) just like the genre's earnest "born" survivors. But for the *Boyz*, this arguably serves not to demonstrate some (imagined) nobility of violence and its concomitant pain, nor to invoke its power to confer manly status. They take pain not in order to master or sublimate it in a demonstration of mental toughness and self-discipline, but instead to turn it on its head through histrionic reaction—to transgress this criterion of heroic masculinity. Thus they render their bodies as variations of the grotesque and absurd, as "other" to the classical, obedient, disciplined body.[64] Still, as Cynthia Chris rightly points out, the *Boyz*'s often painful contact with "the wild" still functions primarily as a "disposable backdrop for the exhibition of white, masculine physical prowess and cultural mobility" (as it generally does for Grylls, Stroud, and the rest).[65] The "disposability" of nature, related to infotainment's obvious bias towards entertainment, is indicative of a much larger social problem involving the denial of environmental devastation and the human place (and complicity) within imperiled ecosystems, resulting in televisual media's general strategic avoidance due to the discomfort it might provoke in the viewer/ consumer. But, *Wildboyz* should not be taken as simply another gendered cultural artifact behaving according to the genre's wider history of reverent quests for masculine (re)creation/regeneration through wildlife "tests" and encounters—as another recuperation of archaic masculine forms and styles— if only because its ironic playfulness goes so far in unmasking internal contradictions found in masculine primitive ideals.

Consciously or not, Chris and Steve-O's goofy failure to achieve and revere certain masculine primitive ideals, especially within the specific generic form and symbolic settings of those ideals' cultural (re)iteration, exposes their construction. Their role within the genre is that of "The Trickster." Through their incompetence, they mock manly competence. They are brave if only to expose the equally real masculine potential for basic cowardice and childlike perturbability. And they are generally irreverent toward nature and its mysteries because the ideal tells them they ought not to be. Although, they do end each episode with this telling disclaimer, "Nobody's wilder than the *Wildboyz*. But the truth is we love animals and would never hurt one."[66] This reminds viewers that the indignities they inflict upon animals and themselves is only their version of a parodic critique serving to comment on humanity's troubled historical relations with wild nature. The figure of the trickster, Wicks explains, "Reminds us of our need to temper seriousness with sarcasm and irony;" but perhaps more importantly, to help "ensure that the leadership doesn't get too deeply entrenched in the seriousness of its positions."[67] Furthermore, the trickster archetype, according to Kipnis, can serve to diffuse differences and confrontations through its "ritualized form of irreverence."[68] I see the impious *Wildboyz*, then, as the trickster cousins of Bear, Les, Myke, Dave, and Cody, and reality television's other would-be avatars of reverent masculine primitive performances. Although such parodies of masculine primitive ideals may not be as abundant as their earnest, more reverent counterparts, the use of parody to disrupt and expose this particular style of official masculinity is evident elsewhere.

What Kimmel calls "the search for the deep masculine," the sense that "we have lost our ability to claim our manhood in a world without fathers, without frontiers, without manly creative work,"[69] represents a core part of the "Man vs." subgenre, if not its organizing principle. But there is plenty of evidence from the popular (Euro-Western) media imaginary beyond *Wildboyz* to suggest that this search is—in most respects at least—a fool's errand. During its nineteenth-century formation, the masculine primitive ideal was responding to the moment's shockwaves of industrial modernity—large rural to urban migrations, new scientific revelations about human origins and cultural development, and other key historical factors. In short, it was a new ideal. In the twenty-first century, earnest or romantic invocations of primal masculinity are increasingly easy to dismiss (or parody) as outmoded, unproductive, or unnecessary. And yet pieces of the ideal persist, even thrive in our ever-expanding wilderness of cable television. Kimmel argues that this contemporary search to shore up the boundaries of masculinity through the various concepts ("true" "natural" "deep" "wild" "primal") constellating around masculine primitive ideals, indeed echo the "late-nineteenth-century masculinist complaints against the forces of feminization."[70] But, he explains, "It is also developmentally atavistic, a search for lost boyhood, effort to turn back the clock to the moment before work and family responsibilities yanked men away from their buddies."[71] "Man vs." reality television, both its parodies and pieties, certainly reflects this search. Besides Chris and Steve-O's "bromance," by its fourth season *Man vs. Wild* invited Will Ferrell to join Grylls for a special episode, *Men vs. Wild*, set in Norway[72] (Ferrell was there, in part at least, to promote his film *Land of the Lost*, thematically related in its configuration of men demonstrating (in)competencies within a fictionalized primordial setting). Producers surely sensed Grylls's serious survival lessons needed some levity. The "coupling" played perfectly into Ferrell's now standard performance of a buffoon alpha male. The iconic man-child feigned rugged fearlessness despite being wholly ill-equipped for the conditions, a dynamic which bolstered Grylls's prowess while also parodying the entire masculine primitive survival project through Ferrell's comical incompetence.

Such parodies are visible elsewhere, like the many *Old Spice* commercials playing on masculine primitive ideals, such as the male animal (Centaur: "Double Impact, it's two great things: a moisturizer and body wash. I should know, I'm two great things: a man . . ." Woman: "And a provider."),[73] or the inner wildman "other" (literally removing an "outer" domesticated layer to reveal a wildman "rocker" within—"Somewhere in there, there's a man in there"),[74] inoculating against the potential emasculation of brand identification with bath products. The recent "Mountain Man" commercial for *Dr. Pepper 10*, "The Manliest Low-Calorie Soda in the History of Mankind," employs a similar parody of masculine primitive ideals, overtly expressing the notion of emasculation in advanced technological society. As *Dr. Pepper*'s official description for the soda claims, "Before we had tablet computers, computers, power steering, and vegans—men had non-ironic beards, hawk friends, and the ability to live off the land with nothing more than a *Dr. Pepper Ten*."[75] A mock disclaimer for the soda also parodies contemporary social prescriptions of sensitivity to wild nature when used for commercial purposes, but also reiterates (the silliness of) manliness as the demonstration of competence within its (nature's) own standards: "Disclaimer: No animals were harmed in the making of this commercial. They were only impressed. Really, really impressed."[76]

Some may also recall the episode of *The Office* (NBC) during which the suburban Michael Scott attempts being a "Survivorman."[77] Michael sub-scribes initially to the serious, existential masculine primitive view—the con-frontation with "wild nature" being a sacred rite promising manly (re)creation—saying, "Dwight will be driving me deep into the Pennsylvania wilderness where he will then leave me to either die or survive. This is a very personal, private experience in the wild that I wish to share with me, myself, and I. When I return, I hope to be a completely changed human being."[78] After his inevitable failure, he takes a comically dismissive view of the whole enterprise, saying, "I don't need the woods, I have a nice wood desk. I don't need fresh air, because I have the freshest air around—AC."[79] These send-ups of masculine primitive ideals suggest the discursive limitations of such binaries to begin with, and they are also indicative of the now well-established understanding of their status as performative tropes, as fantasies, in spite of their earnest cultural origins and ongoing appeal.

V. EXPLAINING PARODIES AND PIETIES FOR THE MASCULINE PRIMITIVE

Parodies and pieties for masculine primitive ideals on reality television re-mind us that the "primitive" has now become, as Torgovnik puts it, a "gener-al marketable thing," "a grab bag primitive;"[80] or, in other words, a free-floating signifier. She explains, "What's primitive, what's modern, what's savage, what's civilized, increasingly becomes hard to tell. . . . While the primitive has always been a construct or fantasy of the West, it used to be much more convinced of its veracity—convinced of the illusion of otherness it (primitivism) created."[81] Studlar understands this cultural dynamic as a form of "nostalgic primitivism"[82] while MacCannell argues that the primi-tive "does not really appear in these enactments of it," but instead, "the 'primitivistic' performance contains the image of the primitive as a dead form."[83] Donna Haraway similarly echoes this sentiment, arguing that the growth and intensification of our (in)human intimacies and interfaces with scientific and electronic technologies (to the extent of becoming prosthetics) render the central binaries of our classical Western episteme altogether blur-ry. "It is irrational," Haraway claims, "to invoke concepts like primitive and civilized. . . . The dichotomies between mind and body, animal and human, organism and machine, public and private, nature and culture, men and wom-en, primitive and civilized are all in question ideologically."[84] Yet perhaps this growing alienation and a global state of environmental panic are generat-ing renewed attempts at rehabilitating our sensitivity to the natural world, to relearning states of (im)mediacy that necessitate (discursive if not literal) distance from the so-called artificial and the synthetic, and renewed contact with the natural world.

While parodies of the masculine primitive highlight its own construction, and also the "irrationality" of taking it too seriously, its earnest expression persists—even grows—within the context of reality television. Les Stroud said of the survival shows now so common on cable, "The reality is, with everything going on in the world, the genre's exploding."[85] Extending Stroud's vague explanation, Strauss claims that "a decade of cataclysmic events—9/11, the global economic meltdown and disasters ranging from Hurricane Katrina to the Gulf of Mexico oil spill—appears to be energizing interest in the peace of mind that comes with survival skills."[86] Media historian Jan-Christopher Horak draws a similar conclusion. Tracing the history of visual wildlife media over the last eighty years, from classic documentaries to current proliferations within reality television's "animals and nature" subgenre, Horak argues that there is a correlation between the genre's overall growth in popularity and an increasingly irrefutable state of global environmental peril.[87] In its early 20th-century inception, the classic wildlife and travelogue documentaries accommodated previously unmet consumer desires to experience remote wildlife and exotic cultures, whereas today, Horak argues, much of the televisual wildlife presented can be seen as a form of "virtual rescue from the uncomfortable reality of the natural world."[88] That is, "animals and nature" reality television may be less about satisfying a curiosity for the exotic and more about enabling the viewer's sense of progress in developing a personal relationship with "nature" while simultaneously serving to insulate them from its ongoing devastation by humanity. Conveying serious concern for the present state of environmental devastation, especially through the documentary presentation of urgent scientific evidence, is apparently too much reality for corporate media's risk-averse production mentality and so remains largely repressed. Thus reality television's commitment to "infotainment" results in the continual blurring of fiction and reality in which wildlife (and the human cultures so often problematically associated with it) is consumed merely as image, backdrop, dramatic device, or prop, and not conveyed as part of a larger, imperiled ecosystem.

Still, the proliferation of "Man vs." programming cannot simply be explained away as a response to "cataclysmic events," or understood merely as a marketplace response to human alienation from the natural world—as an exploitation of consumer desires to develop personal relationships with "nature" from the uncomplicated distance of superficial infotainment. It is more complicated than this, and certainly must include the now more than century-old masculinist discourses in which, as Kimmel puts it, manhood is retrieved "by a confrontation with nature."[89] The "Man vs." genre, insomuch as one can be fruitfully demarcated, exists largely as the renewal and reiteration of much older "fantasies of masculine retreat and re-creation"[90] articulated through masculine primitive ideals. A political economic view could also be linked to the foregoing argument: the need for cheap programming to fill the growing number of cable channels and time-slots resorts to the time-tested desires of men wanting to affirm their manhood through the approval of other men (and women), especially in a moment of economic decline which makes it all the harder to acquire the markers of a successful marketplace masculinity. After all, demonstrations of successful masculinity are perhaps most centrally, according to Kimmel, "A defense against the perceived threat of humiliation in the eyes of other men."[91] When one is unable to achieve (one's own sense of) a successful marketplace masculinity (i.e. accumulation of wealth, status, and power), the masculine primitive contains within it the ideological (or mythical) antidote: the marketplace (as enervating, feminizing, domesticating, and over-civilizing) only weakens the "natural" man, subdues his "primal" potential, and attenuates his inner wildness and survival instincts which, in the final analysis, is all he really needs. An obvious irony, then, is that the lengthy history of masculine primitive ideals—a proffering of strategies for gaining manly affirmation through resistance to an overly "civilized" or market-defined identity—is also a history of those ideals' creative incorporation into that very same marketplace. Coinciding with the emergence of the nineteenth-century masculine primitive ideal was its reflection in myth and literature. As Kimmel explains, "If middle-class men were unable to venture to the west, or even a local pond, the tonic virtues of the wilderness could be brought to their homes; they could escape through fantasy."[92] And while the tricksters' parodies of "born" survivors may indicate the "softening" of exemplary, or hegemonic masculinities over the past few decades, this does not mean the "harder" masculinities are gone. The successful commodification of masculine primitive ideals seen in the "Man vs." genre also reaffirms and perpetuates such socio-historical standards of masculinity.

REFERENCES

"Bear Grylls 'Faked Toxic Volcano Fumes With a Smoke Machine' in New Born Survivor Fake Row." *Daily Mail Online*. Last modified August 12, 2007. http://www.dailymail.co.uk/news/article-474866/Bear-Grylls-faked-toxic-volcanic-fumes-smoke-machine-new-Born-Survivor-fake-row.html

Berry-Flint, Sarah. "Genre." In *A Companion to Film Theory*, edited by Robert Stam and Toby Miller, 25-44. Blackwell, 1999.

Braudy, Leo. *From Chivalry to Terrorism: War and the Changing Nature of Masculinity*. Random House Digital, Inc., 2010.

Buchbinder, David. *Studying Men and Masculinities*. Routledge, 2012.

Canterbury, Dave and Cody Lundin. "Shipwrecked." *Dual Survival*, season 1, episode 1. United States: Discovery Communications, June 11, 2010.

Chris, Cynthia. *Watching Wildlife*. University of Minnesota Press, 2006.

Connell, Robert William, and Raewyn Connell. *Masculinities*. University of California Press, 2005.

Corbett, Julia B. *Communicating Nature: How We Create and Understand Environmental Messages*. Island Press, 2006.

Corner, John. "Performing the Real: Documentary Diversions." *Television and New Media* 3, no. 3 (August 2002): 255-270. Quoted in Justin Lewis, "The Meaning of Real Life," In *Reality TV: Remaking television culture*, edited by Susan Murray and Laurie Ouellette. New York: NYU Press, 2004, 288.

Dentith, Simon. *Parody*. London: Routledge, 2000.

Diamond, Stanley. *In Search of The Primitive: A Critique of Civilization*. New Brunswick, NJ: Transaction Books, 1963.

Fabian, Johannes. *Time and The Other: How Anthropology Makes Its Object*. Columbia University Press, 2002.

Ferrari, Matthew. "Primal Giggles: Thoughts on Reality TV's Recent Pieties and Parodies of The 'Masculine Primitive.'" *Flow*, 10, no. 7. September 3, 2009. http://flowtv.org/

Gray, Jonathan. *Watching with The Simpsons: Television, Parody, and Intertextuality*. Taylor & Francis, 2006.

Grylls, Bear. *Man Vs. Wild: Season 1*. Chatsworth, CA: Distributed by Image Entertainment, 2007. DVD.

Grylls, Bear. *Man Vs. Wild: Season 3*. Chatsworth, CA: Distributed by Image Entertainment, 2009. DVD.

Haraway, Donna. "Simians, Cyborgs, and Women: The Reinvention of Women." *London and New York: Routledge*, 1991.

Hansen, Anders. *Environment, Media and Communication*. London: Routledge, 2010.

Hawke, Myke, and Ruth England. "Amazon." *Man Woman Wild*, season 1 episode 1. Discovery Channel, Aired July 16, 2010.

Horak, Jan-Christopher. "Wildlife documentaries: From classical forms to reality TV." *Film History: An International Journal* 18, no. 4 (2006): 459-475.

Horrocks, Roger. *Male Myths and Icons: Masculinity in Popular Culture*. New York: St. Martins Press, 1995.

Kelly, Tom and Sam Greenhill. "How Bear Grylls The Born Survivor Roughed it—In Hotels." *Daily Mail Online*, July 23, 2007. http://www.dailymail.co.uk/news/article-470155/How-Bear-Grylls-Born-Survivor-roughed--hotels.html

Kimmel, Michael S. *Manhood in America*. New York: Free Press, 1996.

Kimmel, Michael S. "'Born to run': Nineteenth-century fantasies of masculine retreat and re-creation (or the historical rust on Iron John)." *The Politics of Manhood: Profeminist Men Respond to the Mythopoetic Men's Movement (and the Mythopoetic Leaders Answer)*, ed. Michael S. Kimel (Philadelphia: Temple University Press, 1995), 115-50.

Kipnis, Aaron. *Knights Without Armor: A Practical Guide for Men in Quest of Masculine Soul*. Los Angeles, CA: Jeremy P. Tarcher. 1991.

Kurasawa, Fuyuki. "A Requiem for The Primitive." *History of the Human Sciences* 15, no. 3 (2002): 1-24.

Lewis, Justin. "The Meaning of Real Life." In *Reality TV: Remaking Television Culture*, edited by Susan Murray and Laurie Ouellette, 288-302. New York: NYU Press, 2004.

Lovejoy, Arthur O., and George Boas. *Primitivism and Related Ideas in Antiquity: Contributions to The History of Primitivism*. New York: Octagon Books, 1965.

MacCannell, Dean. *Empty Meeting Grounds: The Tourist Papers*. London: Routledge, 1992.

Martindale, Stone. "Discovery 'Man vs. Wild' Not so Rough After All?" *Monsters and Critics*. July 24, 2007. http://www.monstersandcritics.com/smallscreen/news/article_1334235.php/Discovery_Man_vs._Wild_not_so_rough_after_all

Moss, Mark. *The Media and the Models of Masculinity*. Lanham, MD: Lexington Books, 2011.

"Mountain Men: Web Exclusives." *History.com*. Accessed July 3, 2013. http://www.history.com/shows/mountain-men/videos

Rotundo, Anthony. "Learning About Manhood: Gender Ideals and the Middle-Class Family in 19th-Century America." *Manliness and Morality: Middle-Class Masculinity in Britain & America* 1940 (1800): 35-55.

Sabo, Don. "Pigskin, Patriarchy and Pain." In *Men's lives*, ed. Michael S. Kimmel and Michael A. Messner. (Macmillan Publishing Co, Inc, 1992), 99-101.

Slotkin, Richard. *Regeneration Through Violence: The Mythology of the American Frontier, 1600-1860*. Middletown, Conn: Wesleyan University Press. 1973.

Soper, Kate. *What Is Nature?: Culture, Politics and the Non-Human*. Oxford: Blackwell, 1995.

Steve-O, Chris Pontius, and Manny Puig. *Wildboyz:* Complete Seasons 3 & 4. United States: MTV Networks, 2006.

Strauss, Gary. "Survival Shows are Now the Fittingest on Television." *USA Today*. August 27, 2010. http://usatoday30.usatoday.com/life/television/news/2010-08-27survivaltv27_ST_N.htm

Stroud, Les. Interview on "Fox and Friends." *Fox News*. February 9, 2011. http://www.youtube.com/watch?v=bsp1pUut9h4

Studlar, Gaylyn. "Wider Horizons: Douglas Fairbanks and Nostalgic Primitivism." In *Back in the Saddle Again: New Essays on the Western,* edited by Edward Buscombe and Roberta E. Pearson, 63-76. London: BFI Publishing, 1998.

"Survival Show Faces 'Fake' Claim." *BBC News*. last modified July 23, 2007. http://news.bbc.co.uk/2/hi/entertainment/6911748.stm

Taussig, Michael T. *Mimesis and Alterity: A Particular History of the Senses*. New York: Routledge, 1993.

Torgovnick, Marianna. *Gone Primitive: Savage Intellects, Modern Lives*. University of Chicago Press, 1991.

Torgovnick, Marianna. *Primitive Passions: Men, Women, and the Quest for Ecstasy*. University of Chicago Press, 1998.

Wicks, Stephen. *Warriors and Wildmen: Men, Masculinity, and Gender*. Westport, CT: Bergin & Garvey, 1996.

NOTES

1. Anthony Rotundo, "Learning About Manhood: Gender Ideals and the Middle-Class Family in 19th-Century America," *Manliness and Morality: Middle-Class Masculinity in Britain & America 1800-1940*, ed. James A. Mangan and James Walvan (Manchester University Press, 1987), 35-55.

2. Sweeney, D. B., Eustace Conway, and Marty Meierotto, "Into The Wild," *Mountain Men*, season 2 episode 1, History, aired June 9, 2013.

3. Ibid.

4. Ibid.

5. Ibid.

6. "Mountain Men: Web Exclusives," *History.com*, accessed July 3, 2013, http://www.history.com/shows/mountain-men/videos

7. Matthew Ferrari, "Primal Giggles: Thoughts on Reality TV's Recent Pieties and Parodies of The 'Masculine Primitive,'" *Flow*, 10, no. 7, September 3, 2009. http://flowtv.org/

8. Anders Hansen, *Environment, Media and Communication* (Routledge, 2010), 136.

9. Kate Soper, *What Is Nature?: Culture, Politics and The Non-Human* (Oxford: Blackwell, 1995), 10.

10. Historical analysis of primitivism's racial implications is arguably more frequently emphasized than its delineation along lines of gender. Primitivism's gender-specific (re)iterations are addressed by a number of scholars, including most prominently: Kurasawa, 2002; Rotundo, 1987; Studlar, 1998; Torgovnik, 1991, 1998.

11. While not within the purview of this essay, it is important to note that some discourses of the "primitive" have served to advance more positive, pro-social, and pro-environmental ideals and movements. Primitivism's generally backward-looking ideological project has been mobilized (most notably in the 1960s) as inspiration for expanding eco-critical awareness, and combating notions of "alienation" symptomatic of industrial modernity. For more on this see Torgovnik, 1998.

12. Robert W. Connell and Raewyn Connell, *Masculinities* (University of California Press, 2005), 185.

13. Rotundo, *Manliness and Morality*, 36. The other two defining masculine ideals of the era Rotundo labeled the "Masculine Achiever" and the "Christian Gentleman."

14. Ibid, 40.

15. Ibid, 46-48.

16. Ibid, 40.

17. Ibid, 42.

18. Leo Braudy, *From Chivalry to Terrorism: War and The Changing Nature of Masculinity* (Random House Digital, Inc., 2010), xv.

19. Johannes Fabian, *Time and the Other: How Anthropology Makes Its Object* (Columbia University Press, 2002),13, 82.

20. Arthur O. Lovejoy and George Boas, *Primitivism and Related Ideas in Antiquity: Contributions to the History of Primitivism* (Octagon Books, 1965), 7.

21. . Stanley Diamond, *In Search of The Primitive: A Critique of Civilization* (New Brunswick, NJ: Transaction Books, 1963), 119.

22. Ibid, 121.

23. Braudy, *From Chivalry to Terrorism*, xv.

24. Ibid, 6.

25. Connell, *Masculinities*, 45.

26. Michael S. Kimmel, *Manhood in America* (New York: Free Press, 1996), 232.

27. Braudy, *From Chivalry to Terrorism*, 86.

28. Ibid, 87.

29. Hansen, *Environment, Media and Communication*, 145.

30. Tom Kelly and Sam Greenhill, "How Bear Grylls The Born Survivor Roughed it—in Hotels," *The Daily Mail*, last modified July 23, 2007, http://www.dailymail.co.uk/news/article-470155/How-Bear-Grylls-Born-Survivor-roughed--hotels.html

31. Bear Grylls, "Moab Desert," *Man Vs. Wild*, season 1 episode 2 (Chatsworth, CA: Distributed by Image Entertainment, 2007), DVD.

32. Ibid.

33. Ibid.

34. "Bear Grylls 'Faked Toxic Volcano Fumes With a Smoke Machine' in new Born Survivor fake row," *Daily Mail Online*, last modified August 12 2007, http://www.dailymail.co.uk/news/article-474866/Bear-Grylls-faked-toxic-volcanic-fumes-smoke-machine-new-Born-Survivor-fake-row.html

35. Kelly and Greenhill, *The Daily Mail*.

36. Stone Martindale, "Discovery 'Man vs. Wild' Not so Rough After All?" *Monsters and Critics*, last modified July 24, 2007, http://www.monstersandcritics.com/smallscreen/news/article_1334235.php/Discovery_Man_vs._Wild_not_so_rough_after_all

37. "Survival Show Faces 'Fake' Claim," *BBC News*, last modified July 23 2007, http://news.bbc.co.uk/2/hi/entertainment/6911748.stm

38. Bear Grylls, *Man Vs. Wild: Season 3* (Chatsworth, CA: Distributed by Image Entertainment, 2009), DVD.

39. Kimmel, *Manhood in America*, 47.

40. SirThrivalist, "A 'Real' Survival Show," *SurvivalistBoards.com*, last modified September 30, 2012, www.survivalistboards.com/showthread.php?t=260374#XKJEZrlVXWzBY4R3.99

41. Les Stroud, Interview on "Fox and Friends," *Fox News*, February 9, 2011. http://www.youtube.com/watch?v=bsp1pUut9h4

42. Justin Lewis, "The Meaning of Real Life," In *Reality TV: Remaking Television Culture*, edited by Susan Murray and Laurie Ouellette (New York: NYU Press, 2004), 288.

43. John Corner, "Performing the Real: Documentary Diversions," *Television and New Media* 3, no. 3 (August 2002): 255-270, quoted in Justin Lewis, "The Meaning of Real Life," In *Reality TV: Remaking Television Culture*, edited by Susan Murray and Laurie Ouellette (New York: NYU Press, 2004), 288.

44. Lewis, "The Meaning of Real Life," 288.

45. Ibid, 290.

46. Dave Canterbury and Cody Lundin, "Shipwrecked," *Dual Survival*, season 1 episode 1, Discovery Channel, Aired June 11, 2010.

47. Ibid.

48. Ibid.

49. Ibid.

50. Kimmel, *Manhood*, 234.

51. Hawke, Myke, and Ruth England. "Amazon," *Man Woman Wild*, season 1 episode 1 Discovery Channel, Aired July 16, 2010.

52. Hawke, Myke, and Ruth England. "Mexico," *Man Woman Wild*, season 1 episode 5 Discovery Channel, Aired August, 20, 2010.

53. Ibid.

54. Ibid.

55. Michael T. Taussig, *Mimesis and Alterity: A Particular History of the Senses* (New York: Routledge, 1993), 68.

56. Roger Horrocks, *Male Myths and Icons: Masculinity in Popular Culture* (New York: St. Martins Press, 1995) 173.

57. Simon Dentith, *Parody* (London: Routledge, 2000), 9.

58. Jonathan Gray, *Watching with The Simpsons: Television, Parody, and Intertextuality* (Taylor & Francis US, 2006), 4.

59. Sarah Berry-Flint, "Genre," in *A Companion to Film Theory*, ed. Robert Stam and Toby Miller (Blackwell, 1999), 7.

60. Steve-O, Chris Pontius, and Manny Puig, Season 4, Episode 2, "Thailand," *Wildboyz*, Complete Seasons 3 & 4 (United States: MTV Networks, 2006), DVD.

61. Ibid.

62. Steve-O, Chris Pontius, and Manny Puig, Season 1, Episode 8, "Belize," *Wildboyz: The Complete First Season.* (Hollywood, CA: Paramount Home Entertainment, 2004), DVD.

63. Mark Moss, *The Media and the Models of Masculinity* (Lexington Books, 2011), 142.

64. David Buchbinder, *Studying Men and Masculinities* (Routledge, 2012), 130.

65. Cynthia Chris, *Watching Wildlife*, (University of Minnesota Press, 2006), 120.

66. Steve-O, Chris Pontius, and Manny Puig, *Wildboyz: The Complete First Season.* (Hollywood, CA: Paramount Home Entertainment, 2004), DVD.

67. Stephen Wicks, *Warriors and Wildmen: Men, Masculinity, and Gender.* (Westport, CT: Bergin & Garvey, 1996), 72-73.

68. Aaron Kipnis, *Knights Without Armor: A Practical Guide for Men in Quest of Masculine Soul*, (Los Angeles, CA: Jeremy P. Tarcher, 1991), 144-45, quoted in Stephen Wicks, *Warriors and Wildmen: Men, Masculinity, and Gender.* (Westport, CT: Bergin & Garvey, 1996), 72-73.

69. Kimmel, *Manhood*, 232.

70. Ibid.

71. Ibid.

72. Bear Grylls and Will Ferrell, *Man Vs. Wild*, season 4, disc 1 (Louisville, CO: Distributed by Gaiam Americas, Inc, 2010), DVD.

73. *Old Spice*, "Double Impact," television advertisement, Epoch Films and Digital Domain, directed by Phil Morrison, 2008. Retrieved from: http://www.youtube.com/watch?v=YtN9CW01QDM.

74. *Old Spice*, "Rocker, Smell Better Than Yourself" advertising campaign, 2011. Retrieved from: http://theinspirationroom.com/daily/2011/old-spice-smell-better-than-yourself/.

75. *Dr. Pepper*, "Dr. Pepper Ten: Mountain Man Commercial," Retrieved from: http://www.youtube.com/watch?v=YDCY56azew8

76. Ibid.

77. Steve Carell, "Survivorman," *The Office*, Season 4 episode 11, directed by Paul Feig, NBC, aired November 8, 2007.

78. Ibid.

79. Ibid.

80. Marianna Torgovnick, *Gone Primitive: Savage Intellects, Modern Lives* (University of Chicago Press, 1991), 37.

81. Ibid.

82. Gaylyn Studlar, "Wider Horizons: Douglas Fairbanks and Nostalgic Primitivism," In *Back in the Saddle Again: New Essays on the Western,* edited by Edward Buscombe and Roberta E. Pearson, 63-76, (London: BFI Publishing, 1998).

83. Dean MacCannell, "Cannibalism Today," *Empty Meeting Grounds: The Tourist Papers* (Psychology Press, 1992), 19.

84. Haraway, Donna, *Simians, Cyborgs, and Women: The Reinvention of Nature* (New York: Routledge, 1991), 169.

85. Les Stroud, Interview by Gary Strauss, "Survival Shows are now the Fittingest on Television," *USA Today*, last modified August 27, 2010. http://usatoday30.usatoday.com/life/television/news/2010-08-27-survivaltv27_ST_N.htm

86. Gary Strauss, "Survival Shows are now the Fittingest on Television," *USA Today*, last modified August 27, 2010. http://usatoday30.usatoday.com/life/television/news/2010-08-27-survivaltv27_ST_N.htm

87. Jan-Christopher Horak, "Wildlife documentaries: From classical forms to reality TV," *Film History: An International Journal* 18, no. 4 (2006): 459-475.

88. Ibid, 473.

89. Michael S. Kimmel, "'Born to run': Nineteenth-century fantasies of masculine retreat and re-creation (or the historical rust on Iron John)," *The Politics of Manhood: Profeminist Men Respond to the Mythopoetic Men's Movement (and the Mythopoetic Leader's Answer)*, ed. Michael S. Kimel (Philadelphia: Temple University Press, 1995), 119.

90. Kimmel, *The Politics of Manhood*, 115.

91. Ibid.

92. Kimmel, *The Politics of Manhood*, 120.

Chapter Thirteen

Catfished: Exploring Viewer Perceptions of Online Relationships

Leslie Rasmussen

The Internet changed the way people communicate and has provided outlets to facilitate seemingly realistic relationships, albeit without physical contact. MTV's new hit show *Catfish: The TV Show*, follows the stories of people who have developed strong intimate relationships via the Internet and aims to bring two parties together for the first time. Creator Nev Schulman dubbed "catfish" as persons who create fake Internet profiles, complete with pictures and other personal information. *Catfish* pulls back the proverbial curtain on Internet relationships and reveals the true identity behind the computer screen. The show addresses the reasons people create fake profiles and engage in long-term communication, and ultimately form bonds based on deception. Schulman and his filmmaker friend, Max Joseph, work to bring participants together face-to-face for the first time.

Several profiled participants have had some characteristic that makes them unique. For example, Trina is a stripper who longs for love, while Kim became overweight after losing her fiancé to suicide. Others have seemingly average backgrounds, but have been caught up in an Internet romance, much to the surprise of friends and family. In one episode, Sonny and her younger sister argue over which of them will begin a relationship with Jamison—a male model the sisters met online. Unfortunately for Sonny, Jamison turns out to be a female named Chelsea. It is later revealed that Chelsea has struggled with her sexual identity and used the Internet as an outlet to engage with other females. While the majority of the episodes seem to yield similar results, there have been some happy endings. In episode six, Kya comes face-to-face with Alyx, whom she met on a vampire Website. Alyx is really Dani, who is a transgendered person struggling with self-identity. Kya spends time with Dani and decides that she fell in love with the person she spoke to—not with his appearance or biological sex. The two have continued a relationship, though this time Dani can be himself. The show has quickly become a hit for MTV, averaging 2.7 million viewers among 12-34 year-olds, ahead of the popular series *Teen Mom 2*. Viewers regularly tune in to see the macabre unfold.

Catfish gained more notoriety in early 2013 when Norte Dame football player and Heisman Trophy candidate, Manti Te'o, revealed he was the victim of a similar Internet hoax. In fall 2012, Te'o spoke candidly to media about the loss of his grandmother and his girlfriend, Lennay Kekua, who tragically died in a car accident while also battling Leukemia. The story naturally garnered sympathy, placing Te'o in the national spotlight. Reporters at the sports blog, Deadspin, investigated Kekau's identity and discovered Kekau was actually a man named Ronaiah Tuiasosopo. Te'o was forced to reveal that he had never met Kekau; rather, they had an intimate relationship that formed online and eventually via telephone conversations. Media outlets buzzed that Te'o had been catfished. *Catfish* creator Shulman was viewed as the resident expert on such cases and garnered more publicity for his show, proclaiming that this could happen to anyone—even a high-profile athlete. Te'o and Notre Dame were forced to address the hoax. Many speculated that Te'o might be a homosexual because he had spoken with Tuiasosopo. In an interview with Katie Couric, Te'o defended his sexuality and explained why he was so drawn to the Internet relationship with who he believed was Kekau.

As proven by the television series, Te'o is not alone. Countless people engage in Internet relationships and grow to trust strangers. The Internet and outlets like social media have made it easy for users to fabricate profiles, which have essentially become the new fake I.D. Te'o explained his embarrassment, but as the show illustrates, many people enter into similar relationship. Several years ago, online dating was considered taboo, but as with anything, times do change. With online dating, however, there is usually some physical interaction at some point. People may meet online, but eventually go on a date. The new trend of removing physical interaction and relying on trust appears to be a shift, perhaps related to changing Internet culture. The popularity of *Catfish* brought Internet relationships to the forefront of popular culture by highlighting individuals and the deeper issues surrounding the desire to enter into a relationship, perhaps altering previous perceptions. The purpose of this chapter is to serve as an exploratory study into perceptions regarding online romantic relationships and Internet culture.

Network lineups regularly include reality programing. Nielsen reported that reality shows have been the most popular genre for the last several years. During a partial count of the 2010-2011 season reality programing was the most popular genre with a 56.4 percent viewership.[1] The rise in popularity over the last ten years had led researchers to question the appeal of the genre. Nabi, and associates, found that viewers reported enjoying interactions among participants in reality shows, while indicating an interest in the lives of others and their interpersonal interactions.[2] Similarly, Hall noted viewers might feel they can obtain a "better understanding of human nature and behavior by viewing reality programing when there is perceived learning.[3] Hall found that the unpredictable nature of reality show was also an appeal for viewers.[4] Hall investigated perceptions of authenticity of reality programs as related to involvement, enjoyment, and perceived learning among viewers.[5] Ultimately, Hall discovered that when reality show participants are perceived as relatable, there is increased enjoyment and engagement among viewers.

Reality programing covers a broad range of topics ranging from competitions, interpersonal observations, and dating. Several television networks run successful reality dating programs. For example, the ABC series *The Bachelor* and its spinoff, *The Bachelorette*, have a combined 25 seasons. Many dating shows like *The Bachelor* franchise are competition-based. For example, *The Dating Game, Temptation Island, Farmer Wants a Wife,* and *Who Wants to Marry a Millionaire* were all based on some form of competition. Ferris et al. used content analysis and survey research to investigate viewer perceptions of dating. Referencing Bandura's Social Cognitive Theory, the researchers explored the ways dating programs may reinforce or shape cultural norms[6] . Ultimately, they reported that perceived realism influenced the acceptance of behaviors shown in the programs among those who had high viewing scores. Previous research regarding perceptions and dating shows is primarily focused on competitive programing.

Several studies have explored online relationships and engagement intent.[7] [8] [9]

In 1998, when many homes still operated with dial-up Internet and chat rooms and instant messaging platforms grew in popularity, Wysocki surveyed people who engaged in online relationships and reported that 50 percent of surveyed participants primarily engaged in online communication for sexual purposes.[10] Two years later, Schwartz and Southern found that the majority of those engaging in online relationships were actually married or in committed relationships.[11] Underwood and Findlay reported that while relationships may begin online, many ultimately evolve to other forms of communication, such as telephones or email.[12] A 2006 study by the Pew Research foundation found that 11 percent of Americans have used online dating sites to meet people. A notable 57 percent of participants felt many people lie when participating on online dating sites. Despite the perception that people lie when engaged in online dating, Katz and Rice found that perceived acceptability of meeting online had improved.[13] Miller similarly found that attitudes are changing when exploring the social perceptions of online relationships among college students. While findings revealed that nearly 75 percent would not participate in online dating, most commonly citing lack of trust and face-to-face communication as the driving reason, open-ended questions revealed a broad range of perceptions regarding Internet dating.[14] While these studies provide insight into online relationships, some do not consider or specify social media as a method for meeting people. However, social media did not see a rise in popularity and growth until early to mid-2000s with the launch of Myspace, followed by Facebook in 2004. The MTV series *Catfish* dominantly chronicles participants who have met on Facebook, though there are some who have met on Internet sites for people with similar interests, which supports previous findings that similarity stimulates attraction.

One area of concern regarding online relationships is deception. Studies have explored the self-presentation and deception among users of online dating sites. Toma and Hancock used experiments to examine the physical attractiveness in the profile presentations of online daters.[15] Results revealed that self-presentation of attractiveness and deception was not confined to an image; rather, the choice to use deception was much more strategic. On the contrary, Fiore argued that online dating has shed its "stigma as the refuge of the awkward," and posits that most deception may be attributed to the perception that others are exaggerating or perhaps that users is subconsciously attempting to present the best version of themselves, while unwittingly being deceptive.[16]

Recent studies have explored perceived emotional support gained from social networks like Facebook.[17] While perceptions of similarity or attraction are factors for developing relationships in traditional settings, computer-mediated contexts are more complex. Wright examined the emotional support college students perceive from using Facebook and found, "Some college students may find it difficult to establish a supportive network of friends and acquaintances in the face-to-face world, but social networking sites, such as Facebook, may help to extend access to a wider support network."[18] Wright found that the perception of similarity among online partners was a notable predictor of perceived emotional support, while Stefanone et al. explained social support as a resource obtained through social media sites.[19] However, Lim and Larose used experiments to explore attraction and similarities and discovered that females were more trusting and attracted to people with dissimilar attitudes, though the same was not true for males.[20] The authors suggest that the elimination of face-to-face confrontations in computer-mediated environments may provide a comfort that allows females to engage with those who have dissimilar attitudes. McGlynn examined the perceived effects of computer-mediated communication on relationships. Results indicated a desire to increase connections and reduce distance among those separated geographically.[21]

Though perceived similarities and attraction are factors in developing relationships,[22] Antheunis, Valkenburg, and Peter[23] explored why the absence of nonverbal communication leads to enhanced attraction for those engaged in online relationships by examining the following variables: amount of self-disclosure, depth of self-disclosure, direct questioning, and reciprocity of self-disclosure. Results indicated that a low level of uncertainty led to social attraction, though it was found to be contingent on the perceived level of information one individual had about another. In 2009, Antheunis, and associates, explained that computer-mediated communication requires greater amounts of self-disclosure, thus stimulates attraction.[24] Notably, they discovered that visual interaction was not a key factor in determining attraction when comparing it against text-based interaction.

MTV's *Catfish* program explores dating via the Internet and the lingering question of whether the person on the other side of the screen is actually who they say they are. Previous research explored online dating perceptions and reality television dating but *Catfish* transcends both areas by exploring the concerns that may arise from the formation of online relationships. Viewer perceptions are likely different from the findings of previous research because of the differences between *Catfish* and other reality dating programs. *Catfish* cast members have formed a bond before the cameras roll. Instead of meeting on a reality show, participants are brought together for the first time. As a result, the show must address the reasons people create false profiles and engage in long-term communication via the Internet. To explore perceptions about participants and online relationships, the following research questions are posited:

RQ1: What perceptions do viewers form about the profiled participants?

RQ2: What perceptions do viewers form about online relationships?

RQ3: What narratives are learned about Internet culture?

Online focus groups comprised of prescreened college-aged viewers were held to investigate the research questions. College-aged students are the core of *Catfish's* viewership and provide a realistic sample. Online groups are typically limited to 8-10 participants; thus two groups were held. Each group was shown a randomly selected episode of *Catfish* from its first season. Following the episode, participants were given a survey to explore their perceptions regarding online relationships and Internet culture. The online focus group method allows viewers to freely express views and perceptions regarding the presentation of online relationships, without fear of criticism from others. The formation of online romantic relationships can be viewed as taboo, thus removing the other group members from the immediate focus group allowed users to share their experiences and perceptions in a safe environment.

A total of 30 participants, 7 males and 23 females, answered questions regarding *Catfish*. The majority of participants were college seniors ($n=22$), while 8 were college juniors, which is an accurate representation of the show's targeted age group. All participants were prescreened to determine that they were viewers of *Catfish*. Because the first season was comprised of 12 episodes, a regular viewer was operationalized as one who viewed a minimum of 9 episodes during the first season. A somewhat regular viewer was operationalized as one who viewed 6 to 8 episodes during the first season. Overall, 10 participants were identified as regular viewers, while the remaining 20 were identified as somewhat regular viewers.

To explore viewer perceptions about the profiled participants on *Catfish*, participants were asked whether or not they felt sympathetic toward the persons who were deceived on the series. The majority ($n=22$) felt sympathy for what the profiled participants had been through. Several participants noted the same sentiment, as indicated by one focus group participant, "I felt sorry for the person because it seemed like they really feel hard for the other person." Seven were not sure whether they felt sympathy, though one participant indicated, "I don't feel bad for the person. We live in a world with FaceTime and Skype, so they should have wondered why the person didn't want to meet them, even virtually." Another participant mentioned technology by stating, "DO YOUR RESEARCH! And use Skype so you can at least SEE who you are dealing with." While the majority felt sympathy for those profiled, it seems there is an expectation for users to take charge of the situation by requesting a meeting, virtual or otherwise, or to exercise a reasonable distance.

When it came to viewer perceptions toward the person who created a fake profile, the majority ($n=22$) felt no sympathy toward the person. One participant said, "Why would I feel bad for a person who lied?" Of the 8 participants who indicated they were sympathetic, one said, "You start to feel bad when you realize that they're having some serious issue or have been bullied . . . but it still doesn't make it okay to deceive someone." Another participant said, "The participants are portrayed as naïve and desperate."

The majority ($n=17$) felt the characters portrayed on *Catfish* were extreme representations of people who would enter into an online relationship. One noted, "The catfished is portrayed as a somewhat normal person who just wasn't careful. The catfisher is portrayed as an abnormal person who has odd ways of looking for attention." Eight participants did not believe the show portrayed an extreme representation, as one noted, "This could happen to ANYONE. MTV does a good job of showing that." Five participants were not sure; some noted an inability to decide because they have not engaged in an online relationship.

To explore viewer perceptions about online relationships, participants were asked how common, they believe people engage in online relationships. The majority ($n=25$) indicated that nowadays, online relationships are common, while a mere 5 indicated online relationships as somewhat common. More than half ($n=19$) felt it is acceptable to enter into an online relationship. Similarly, the majority ($n=24$) felt it is very possible to develop real feelings for a person without meeting them. Four were not sure if it was possible, while two felt it could not happen. Despite the perceived acceptability by the majority, only 7 participants said they would engage in an online relationship, while 19 said they probably would not.

To explore the narratives about Internet culture, participants were asked to identify the messages regarding Internet relationships on *Catfish*. One participant noted that the taboo nature has recently changed by stating, "The relationships are much more acceptable now than they were even 5 years ago." Similarly, a participant indicated, "Online relationships are more common than people acknowledge." While it seems the relationships are more common, there is still some lingering feeling regarding acknowledgement. Another participant claimed there is no difference between online and typical relationships, "Everyone dates online and the relationship formed online is just like relationships formed in person." Another participant echoed the sentiment with, "Online dating works in this society." Despite the acceptance, many participants still said they still would not enter into an online relationship. Many relayed messages of caution. For example, one said, "Parties should be highly suspicious and people should meet in person before they pursue a full-blown relationship." Another said, "The show conveyed that online relationships can be dangerous because you never know who is on the other side of the computer." Others simply stated, "Manage with caution," "The Internet is not always a safe place," "Always be cautious," and "Don't believe everything you read." Ultimately, the majority felt Internet culture and online relationships had shifted to a place of acceptance, yet acknowledged the need to proceed with greater caution because of the potential for deception. Nearly half of the participants felt the show highlighted extreme characters, though several expressed that this could happen to anyone.

While it seems the general perception of the sample is that it is acceptable to enter into a relationship without the physical contact, the majority expressed a need to remain alert to possible deception. Despite the acceptance of online relationships, the majority said they still would not enter into an online relationship, though they did believe it is possible develop deep feelings for a person in computer-mediated environments. This somewhat supports Hall's notion that viewers of reality television may feel programming allows them to learn about human nature.[25] It is also possible that those who view *Catfish* are simply more cautious because of what they have seen on the program, as many participants expressed. The notion that online dating or entering into online relationships is taboo seems to be moot nowadays; perhaps this has resulted from the integral role technology now plays in day-to-day lives. For example, it is not uncommon to send a happy birthday message via a text message or email instead of calling, nor is it uncommon to follow strangers on Twitter. The ease of communication made capable by the Internet may have desensitized the desire for interpersonal interactions while simultaneously making users more trusting.

Overall, it appears the overarching perception of online relationships is acceptance. Participants expressed acceptance regarding the commonality of online relationships and appeared somewhat sympathetic to those who were deceived. A few noted that no one is immune to being deceived online. As *Catfish* illustrates, the persons who create fake or misleading profiles often go to great lengths to deceive others. Some profiles have scores of photographs stolen from another profile or the Internet, while others have detailed descriptions about themselves and expansive friends lists. However, the show also does an excellent job of showing how easy it is to uncover potential deception. A simple Google image search for profile photos often uncovers matches from other online locations. Schulman and Joseph also view and contact people in the friends list of those with questionable profiles. Again, it is a simple method to uncover potential issues of deception. As participants noted, it is important to research before becoming emotionally involved with a person online.

This exploratory study scratches the surface of perceptions regarding online relationships. The small sample of regular viewers posed a limitation, though provided a base for future research. For example, using an online method to allow viewers to freely express perceptions regarding a taboo subject may not be necessary, as many participants expressed acceptance of the topic. Future research should expand the sample size. In addition, it should obtain a sample of those who are not familiar with the show and compare their perceptions to those of regular viewers of the show.

When the Manti Te'o story broke, media outlets claimed he was catfished—the term is embedded in popular culture. As the show's second season premier approaches, it is clear *Catfish* has claimed its stake in popular culture. It has shed light onto a formerly taboo topic and shown that no one is immune to online deception. *Catfish* provides a lesson in practicing responsibility and caution when operating online. The lessons drawn from the show can certainly be transferred to any form of media.

REFERENCES

Antheunis, M., Valkenburg, P., Peter, J., and Schouten, A. "Computer-Mediated Communication and Interpersonal Attraction." Presentation at International Communication Association, Chicago, IL, 2007.

Antheunis, M., Valkenburg, P., Peter, J., and Schouten, A. "Getting Acquainted through Social Network Sites: Testing a Model of Online Uncertainty Reduction and Social Attraction." Presentation at International Communication Association, Montreal, 2009.

Ferris, Amber L., Smith, Sandi W., Greenberg, Bradley S. and Smith, Stacy L. "The Content of Reality Dating Shows and Viewer Perceptions of Dating." *Journal of Communication*, 57, (2007): 490-510.

Fiore, Andrew T. "Self-Presentation and Deception in Online Dating." 2008. Accessed May 5, 2013. http://people.ischool.berkeley.edu/~atf/papers/fiore_secrets_lies.pdf

Hall, Alice. "Viewers' Perceptions of Reality Programs." *Communication Quarterly*, 54, no. 2 (2006): 191–214.

Hall, Alice. "Perceptions of the Authenticity of Reality Programs and Their Relationships to Audience Involvement, Enjoyment, and Perceived Learning." *Journal of Broadcasting & Electronic Media,* 53 no. 4 (2009): 515–533.

Katz, James E. and Rice, Ronald E. *Social Consequences of Internet Use: Access, Involvement, and Interaction.* Cambridge, Mass.: MIT Press, 2002.

Lim, Lynette and Larose, Robert. "Interpersonal Attraction Online: Do Trust and Gender Differences Play a Part in Determining Attraction to Attitudinal Similarity?" Presentation at International Communication Association, San Diego, CA, 2003.

Madden, Mary and Lenhart, Amanda. "Online Dating: PEW Internet and American Life Project." *Pew Internet*. March 5, 2006. http://www.pewinternet.org/Reports/2006/Online-Dating.aspx

McGlynn III, Joseph. "More Connections, Less Connection: An Examination of Computer-Mediated Communication as Relationship Maintenance." Presentation at National Communication Association, Chicago, IL, November 2007.

Miller, Corey T. (2011). "The Cultural Adaptation of Internet Dating: Attitudes Towards Online Relationship Formation." Doctoral Dissertation, University of New Orleans, 2011. http://scholarworks.uno.edu/td/1332

Nabi, Robin, Biely, Erica N., Morgan, Sara J., and Stitt, Carmen R. "Reality-Based Television Programming and the Psychology of its Appeal." *Media Psychology* 5, no. 4 (2003): 303–330.

Nielsen. "10 years of primetime, the rise of reality and sports programming." Last modified September 21, 2011. http://www.nielsen.com/us/en/newswire/2011/10-years-of-primetime-the-rise-of-reality-and-sports-programming.html

Schwartz, Mark and Southern, Stephen. (2000). Compulsive Cybersex: "The New Tea Room." *Sexual Addiction & Compulsivity: The Journal of Treatment & Prevention*, 7, no. 1 (2000):127–144. DOI: 10.1080/10720160008400211

Stefanone, Michael, Kwon, Kyounghee Hazel, and Lackaff, Derek. "Exploring the Relationship Between Perceptions of Social Capital and Enacted Support Online." *Journal of Computer-Mediated Communication*, 17, (2012): 451-466.

Toma, Catalina and Hancock, Jeffery. "Looks and lies: The role of physical attractiveness in online dating self-presentation and deception," *Communication Research, 37* (2010), 335-351.

Underwood, Heather and Findlay, Bruce. "Internet Relationships and Their Impact on Primary Relationships." *Behaviour Change*, 21 no. 2 (2004): 127-140.

Wysoki, Diane. "Let Your Fingers do the Talking." *Sexualities, 1*, (1998).

NOTES

1. Nielsen, "10 years of primetime, the rise of reality and sports programming," last modified April 10, 2013, http://www.nielsen.com/us/en/newswire/2011/10-years-of-primetime-the-rise-of-reality-and-sports-programming.html

2. Robin L. Nabi, Erica N. Biely, Sara J. Morgan, and Carmen R. Stitt, "Reality-based television programming and the psychology of its appeal," *Media Psychology*, 5 (2003): 303–330.

3. Alice Hall, "Perceptions of the authenticity of reality programs and their relationships to audience involvement, enjoyment, and perceived learning," *Journal of Broadcasting & Electronic Media, 53* (2009), 528.

4. Alice Hall, "Viewers' perceptions of reality programs," *Communication Quarterly*, *54* (2006), 191–214.

5. Hall, *Journal of Broadcasting & Electronic Media, 528.*

6. Amber L. Ferris, Sandi W. Smith, Bradley S. Greenberg, and Stacy L. Smith, "The content of reality dating shows and viewer perceptions of dating," *Journal of Communication, 57* (2007), 490-510.

7. Diane K. Wysoki, "Let Your Fingers do the Talking," *Sexualities, 1* (1998).

8. Mark Schwartz and Stephen Southern, "Compulsive cybersex: The new tea room," *Sexual Addiction & Compulsivity: The Journal of Treatment & Prevention, 7* (2000), 127–144.

9. Heather Underwood, H. and Bruce Findlay., "Internet relationships and their impact on primary relationships," *Behaviour Change, 21* (2004), 127-140.

10. Wysoki, *Sexualities.*

11. Mark Schwartz and Stephen Southern, "Compulsive Cybersex: The New Tea Room," *Sexual Addiction & Compulsivity: The Journal of Treatment & Prevention, 7* (2000), 127–144.

12. Underwood and Findlay, 127.

13. James E. Katz and Ronald E. Rice, *Social consequences of Internet Use: Access, Involvement, and Interaction* (Cambridge, Mass.: MIT, 2002).

14. Corey T. Miller, "The cultural adaptation of Internet dating: Attitudes towards online relationship formation," (*University of New Orleans Theses and Dissertations*, 2011).

15. C. Toma, and J. Hancock, "Looks and lies: The role of physical attractiveness in online dating self-presentation and deception," *Communication Research, 37* (2010), 335-351.

16. Andrew T. Fiore, "Self-presentation and deception in online dating," *Berkley,* April 5, 2008, http://people.ischool.berkeley.edu/~atf/papers/fiore_secrets_lies.pdf

17. Michael Stefanone, Kyounghee Hazel Kwon, and Derek Lackaff, "Exploring the relationship between perceptions of social capital and enacted support online," *Journal of Computer-Mediated Communication, 17* (2012), 451-466.

18. Kevin B. Wright, "Emotional support and perceived stress among college students using Facebook.com: An exploration of the relationship between source perceptions and emotional support," *Communication Research Reports, 29* (2012), p. 181.

19. Michael Stefanone, Kyounghee Hazel Kwon, and Derek Lackaff, "Exploring the relationship between perceptions of social capital and enacted support online," *Journal of Computer-Mediated Communication, 17* (2012), 451-466.

20. Lynette Lim and Robert Larose, "Interpersonal attraction online: Do trust and gender differences play a part in determining attraction to do attitudinal similarity?" (International Communication Association, San Diego, 2003).

21. Joseph McGlynn III, "More Connections, Less Connection: An Examination of Computer-Mediated Communication as Relationship Maintenance," (National Communication Association, Chicago, 2007).

22. Kevin Wright, *Communication Research Reports*, 175-184.

23. M. Antheunis, P. Valkenburg, J. Peter, and A. Schouten, "Computer-mediated communication and interpersonal attraction," (International Communication Association, Chicago, 2007) p. 2.

24. M. Antheunis, P. Valkenburg, J. Peter, and A. Schouten, "Getting Acquainted through Social Network Sites: Testing a Model of Online Uncertainty Reduction and Social Attraction, (International Communication Association, Montreal, 2009).

25. Alice Hall, *Journal of Broadcasting & Electronic Media,* 528.

Chapter Fourteen

"I See Swamp People": Swamp People, Southern Horrors, and Reality Television

Julie Haynes

For roughly twenty dollars, internet browsers can purchase a dark green t-shirt with the caption, "I See Swamp People," scrawled around the image of an alligator's head peering above the water's surface. This trademarked phrase belongs to the History Channel, home network of the reality television series, *Swamp People*, and plays upon the memorable line of M. Night Shyamalan's horror film, *The Sixth Sense*. In the film, eight year-old Cole whispers to his psychologist, "*I see dead people.*" This play on words is one of the many nods to the horror genre evident in the reality television series. Indeed, the title of the reality series itself references classical Hollywood horror films such as *Creature of the Black Lagoon* (1954)*, Strangler of the Swamp* (1946)*, Swamp Thing* (1982) and *Return of the Swamp Thing* (1989). Although the intended focus of *Swamp People* is an introduction to Cajun culture and alligator hunting,[1] the series repeatedly invokes horror. In this essay, I argue that *Swamp People*'s various explicit and implicit invocations of horror ultimately link the characterization of Southern culture, generally, and Cajun culture, specifically, to the horrific. Reality television's illusion of authenticity further complicates a critical reading of this connection, reinforcing the "truth" behind these Southern horrors.

Since its inception in the early 1990s, the genre of reality television has evolved into a number of different, albeit overlapping, subgenres.[2] Series cluster around themes of competition (both game show-like and talent-based), makeovers, dating, "docusoaps," court or legal television, and behind-the-scenes views of occupations or lifestyles.[3] As the genre of reality television matures, even more specific subgenres have developed. For example, one subgenre specifically explores themes of horror and the paranormal, with shows investigating haunted places and/or attempting to document supernatural phenomena on video. Such shows include the SyFy Network's *Ghost Hunters,* A&E Network's *Paranormal State,* MTV's *Fear,* and the Travel Channel's *Ghost Adventures* and *Most Haunted,* among others. Additional series feature haunted objects, such as SyFy's *Haunted Collector,* or the sale of spooky collectibles on the Discovery Channel's *Oddities.* Another subgenre provides viewers with a type of "cultural tourism," introducing them to individuals and customs of certain regions. Many of these focus on U.S. regions, such as Alaska (*Ice Road Truckers, Sarah Palin's Alaska*), New Jersey (*Jersey Shore, Jerseylicious*), Los Angeles, (*Selling LA, The Real Housewives of Beverly Hills*), and Miami (*Miami Ink, South Beach Tow*).

An increasingly popular portion of this cultural tourism subgenre documents the lives and activities of rural U.S. Southerners. Series follow individuals from Louisiana, Kentucky, Texas, Georgia, and other Southern states as they participate in events, both mundane and extraordinary. A small sampling of these shows include, The Learning Channel's (TLC's) *Here Comes Honey Boo Boo*, Art and Entertainment's (A&E's) *Duck Dynasty, Billy the Exterminator,* and *American Hoggers,* the Discovery Channel's *Moonshiners,* Animal Planet's *Call of the Wildman, Gator Boys,* and *Hillbilly Handfishin'*, and The History Channel's *Mountain Men* and *The Legend of Shelby the Swamp Man.* These shows typically construct and reinforce a regional identity that is based upon common Southern stereotypes, particularly as they relate to race, class, and gender.[4] This "redneck reality" subgenre also includes the popular History Channel series, *Swamp People.*

Swamp People debuted in 2010 and documents the thirty-day alligator hunting season in the Atchafalaya swamp basin of Louisiana. The series highlights individual hunters or hunting families and follows them as they track, bait, kill, and sell alligators. While much of the camera work focuses on the actual alligator hunt (with special emphasis on the capture and kill of the alligators), the series also explores Cajun or Native Houma customs and interpersonal relationships of the hunters and their families. In short, the show depicts the life of a Louisiana swamper, leading to its title "Swamp People." Viewers are invited to see the series as a true reflection of this "way of life."

Despite its behind-the-scenes focus on alligator hunting and the lives of swampers, *Swamp People*'s allusion to the horror genre remains an undercurrent throughout the series. From the haunting iconography of the swamp itself to the show's title and cinematography, *Swamp People*'s appeal lies, in part, in its reliance on horror. Specifically, the series employs eerie images of the swamp, references classical Hollywood horror films, and incorporates camerawork typically associated with the horror genre. Such devices are applied to the landscape, animals, supernatural phenomena, and people of the Southern swamp.

WELCOME TO THE SWAMP: LANDSCAPE AS HORROR

Occupying the space between land and water, the swamp functions as a liminal, interstitial place—both a border and in-between location—that scholars such as Levi-Strauss have argued can take on either lauded or de-monized positions in myths and cultures.[5] In the case of the swamp, transcendentalists Whitman and Thoreau, for example, hail the swamp as a place of unspoiled beauty.[6] In contrast, however, and more popularly, the swamp has a long association with dread and horror. The murky waters and seemingly impenetrable landscape create a mysterious habitat, a labyrinth inhabited by dangerous animals and equally dangerous people. Indeed, the swamp has been linked with the concept of Hell itself. According to Rod Giblett, references to the swamp as Hell are evident as early as the 14th century, with Dante and later Milton using swamp imagery in their famous descriptions of Hell: "Dante by figuring one circle of hell as a slimy stygian marsh, and Milton by troping Satan as a monstrous swamp serpent who is generated out of the slime of Hell."[7] Anthony Wilson explains that swamps are further horrific in their "unwillingness" to be tamed or developed by Europeans and through their connection with Native Americans. He writes, "The practical presence of Native Americans in the swamps only under-scored their wicked association for Europeans who viewed the Indian as the embodiment of savagery. . . Demonized in figures and intractable in practice, swamps have represented a challenge to imposed order since well before the colonization of American."[8] The swamp continues to be framed as a loath-some place in public memory, literature, and popular culture. As noted, the swamp is the landscape of numerous Hollywood horror films and represents well what Carol Clover calls the requisite "Terrible Place" in horror cinema: "The Terrible Place, most often a house or tunnel in which the victims sooner or later find themselves, is a venerable element of horror. . . dark, labyrin-thine, exitless, usually underground and palpably damp."[9]

The horror symbolized by the swamp is also a distinctly Southern horror. Wilson argues that the swamp is "a feature of the landscape that has been linked profoundly and uniquely to the American South."[10] Thus elements of the swamp deemed horrific in general are extended to the Southern swamp and amplified through Southern history and culture. While swamps and wet-lands exist elsewhere in the United States, the South is home to most of them.[11] The unique landscape and history of the South further fosters a negative, dangerous view of the swamp. For example, in the Antebellum South, the swamp threatens the agrarian economy of the region as a land difficult to develop and farm. Moreover, it symbolizes a forbidden space as a refuge for "Others," including poor whites, Acadians, Native Americans, and runaway slaves:

> As Southern culture evolves into the plantation system in the first half of the nineteenth century, the swamp becomes more clearly opposed, both figurative-ly and practically, to prevailing ideals of white Southern society, which em-phasized racial and cultural purity and ironclad class distinctions. The swamp's status as haven for civilization's exiles gives its threatening signifi-cance for the white South a new and more powerful dimension. [12]

Like the symbol of the swamp, in general, the Southern swamp as a forebod-ing, forbidden landscape remains in literature and popular culture, from com-ic books to television to film.

In *Swamp People,* the characterization of the swamp as a frightening place is established throughout its four seasons and specific episodes. Some of the most explicit references to the landscape as horror come in the show's introduction. Before each show begins, the television screen is completely black, followed by the written statement: "THE WAY OF LIFE DEPICTED IN THIS PROGRAM DATES BACK 300 YEARS." This sentence fades, replaced by "HUNTING, ESPECIALLY ALLIGATOR HUNTING, LIES AT ITS CORE." Viewers are then warned, "SOME IMAGES MAY BE DISTURBING." After a brief, dramatic pause, "VIEWER DISCRETION IS ADVISED" occupies the center of the screen. Thus from its beginning, the producers position the program as scary and potentially graphic, so much so that a viewer advisory must be issued. The source of this fear is quickly connected to the swamp. The warning itself is accompanied by ominous music, mysterious bird cries, the sound of crickets, and the call of an owl—audible cues for the wilderness at night. Visual reinforcement of this comes with a juxtaposition of horror images associated with the swamp: a spotlight shining on cypress knees, a full moon, spiders, snakes, alligators, and hang-ing Spanish moss. Non-linear sounds like those in horror films punctuate these images. [13]

Swamp People's introduction continues by establishing both the danger and the Southern location of this swamp. Narrator and Tennessee native Pat Duke speaks in a deep, Southern accent: "In the farthest corner of America lies the nation's largest swamp. . . A hidden world where nature rules. . . And man fights back. . . Welcome to the Swamp." His narration, in accent, tone, and content, solidify Duke as an "insider" who is warning viewers of the menacing nature of this landscape. Character commentary in the introduction further links the swamp to horror. For example, in the introductions to sea-sons one and three, hunter Troy Landry confesses (in Cajun accent), "You hear noises out here at night that you don't know what they are. You don't want to know what they are." In season one, a hunter calls, "Hey, little birdie," as he grabs a heron by the throat—an impressive feat that is simultaneously surprising and savage. In season two, Terral Evans (famous for always capturing alligators by hand) remarks, "Somethin' about a full moon in the swamp. Everything likes to come out and mess around."

The final section of the episodes' introduction highlights the season's line-up of participants. Horror music is replaced with a banjo soundtrack and sounds of cocking shotguns, once again connecting the series to a stereotypical South. As stoic portraits of the hunters and their names flash by, the horror imagery continues with visions of burning cemeteries, bloody boats and boots, and the final introductory image of a dying alligator with its outstretched claw.

TERROR IN THE SWAMP: CREATURES OF THE NIGHT

Swamp People's introduction establishes the swamp as horror and foretells of possible terror lurking in the swamp. This terror is depicted as both natural and supernatural throughout the series. Natural terrors sometimes include dangerous weather conditions, such as hurricanes, but most frequently focus on threatening animals that inhabit the swamp. These "creatures of the night" include frogs, spiders, insects, and a variety of birds, who take on a menacing quality, especially when viewed from a boat with a spotlight or through night-vision cameras. Indeed many of these nocturnal animals' eyes glow, creating an eerie, horrific atmosphere.

Snakes are an especially present threat, during the day and the night, slithering through vegetation, sunning on trees, or skimming the water's surface. *Swamp People* reinforces the negative cultural associations attached to the snake. Snakes are often shown in close-ups that highlight their scowling eyes, to generate fear and loathing. The snakes' flattened heads and hooded eyes hint that they are poisonous and pose an ever-present threat to the hunters. In several episodes, alligator hunters discuss the poisonous snakes of the Atchafalaya swamp and explain how a hunter might die from certain snake bites before reaching a hospital. In season one, episode seven, "Swamp Wars," swamper Willie Edwards specifically hunts snakes to supplement his alligator income. He relates how he was hospitalized for eight days as a child from a Copperhead snake bite. During his midnight hunt, Willie pulls snakes from the water by hand, not knowing if the snakes are venomous.[14] In season two, episode nine, "Full Moon Fever," Willie once again hunts for snakes at night. He is repeatedly bitten, and although by nonvenomous snakes, becomes increasingly sicker with each bite, until finally he vomits over the side of the boat. In voiceover, Duke explains that even nonvenomous snakes' saliva contains toxins, so that multiple bites still cause negative side effects.

Of course the greatest natural threat of the swamp in *Swamp People* is the alligator. Like the swamp itself, the alligator is a creature of reality and myth who, with its cousin the crocodile, has been associated with dread for centuries.[15] The reptile's ancient existence, its ability to quickly disappear beneath the water's surface, invisible yet still present, its potentially massive size, and its powerful jaws make it mysterious and dangerous. An alpha predator, the alligator poses real, albeit uncommon, risks to humans. This risk is highlighted in *Swamp People.* Throughout the series, hunters and/or the narrator emphasize the very real risk faced by hunters who, confronting the animals in their natural habitat, may easily be bitten, attacked, or pulled overboard by a ferocious gator. The power of the alligator to injure a hunter with a powerful tail swipe or bite off a finger or hand are recurrent reminders to viewers. Justifying the hunting season, hunters are quick to point out how alligators (especially if their numbers are not kept in check) pose a threat to innocent people and their pets. In season one, episode one, Troy Landry discusses how a particularly large "nuisance" alligator has been frequenting a popular boating and recreation spot. He explains how such a gator could easily kill a child playing in the water. His warning is juxtaposed with an eye-level image of a child treading water and then a bird's eye view of an enormous alligator swimming at a rapid pace. This editing sequence mimics film techniques used to frighten audiences as a predator stalks and hunts down its prey. This technique is perhaps most famous in shark attack scenes, particularly like those in *Jaws*.

Like sharks, alligators star as the primary monsters in horror cinema. These usually B horror movies include *Alligator* (1980), which incorporates the urban legend of a giant alligator living in city sewer systems and attacking unsuspecting citizens. Other alligator/crocodile horror films include *Black Water* (2007), *Lake Placid* (1999), *Eaten Alive* (1977), *The Alligator People* (1959), and *The Great Alligator* (1979). In *Swamp People*, alligators are explicitly framed as monstrous. In nearly every episode of the series, the phrase "monster gator" is used by either a hunter of the narrator. This term designates an extremely large alligator, one that will be difficult to trap, kill, and, once dead, get inside the boat. These monster gators pose the most risk to hunters, but also offer the biggest reward if the hunters are successful. Some monster gators are especially vicious, "cannibal gators" that are given nicknames that pay homage to Hollywood monsters, such as "Godzilla," "Loch Ness Monster," and "T-Rex." Like Hollywood monsters, these animals are extremely difficult to kill and much of the show's narrative tension involves the battle between hunter(s) and gator. Also like Hollywood killers or monsters, sometimes alligators are believed to be dead, only to reanimate inside the boat. In these cases, viewers may see movement or signs of life before the hunter, creating a horror-movie-like suspense as audiences wait for the victim to recognize the imminent danger.

Swamp People's camerawork reinforces the concept of the alligator as monster. As noted, sometimes viewers see the alligator from above. Other times alligators are at the horizon line, and viewers see the alligators through the eyes of the hunters. Interestingly, however, *Swamp People* frequently incorporates a point of view (POV) from below. In this case, viewers witness events as if from the alligator's perspective. Such a perspective seems unusual given the inability of directors to truly know what the alligator is seeing (a plausible motivation for reality television) and given the clearly established role of hunter as protagonist in the series. However, the angle is consistent with horror cinema. Horror films frequently utilize the first person camera or "I-camera" with the killer/monster. That is, viewers see actions through the eyes of the monster. Carol Clover cites *Friday the 13th* as an exemplar:

> *Friday the 13th* (1980) locates the I-camera with the killer in pursuit of a victim; the camera is hand-held, producing a jerky image, and the frame includes in-and-out-of-focus foreground objects (trees, bushes, window frames) behind which the killer (I-camera), is lurking—all accompanied by the sound of heartbeats and heavy breathing.[16]

Clover's description is remarkably similar to the POV of the alligator during capture and kill sequences of *Swamp People*. Viewers/cameras are underwater while hunters reel in the baited alligator. The camera gradually surfaces as viewers see a blurry image of the hunter in his or her boat. As the alligator/camera/viewer breaks the surface, chaos follows, with sweeping, unfocused images, thrashing movements, splashing, and yelling (and when the Landrys are hunting, Troy's famous and incessant line, "Choot 'em! Choot 'em!") Before the kill shot is fired, a frequent camera technique is to again shoot from the alligator's POV. Viewers see the hunter looking down the barrel of his/her shotgun, and the movements follow in slow motion as the hunter fires. The scene then becomes still and quiet because the alligator/monster is dead.

THE HAUNTED SWAMP: SUPERNATURAL HORRORS

In addition to the myriad of natural terrors hidden in the Southern swamp, *Swamp People* explores its rumored supernatural terrors as well. References to ghosts and cryptids once again connect the show to the horror genre. In several episodes, swampers tell stories of seeing something unexplainable at night. One of these legends is the story of "Old One Eye," of the "One-Eyed Swamp Monster." In season two, episode nine, three generation of Landrys go frog hunting late at night. At the encouragement of his son, the patriarch, Duffy, shares stories of a one-eyed creature that roamed the swamp of his youth. Duffy explains that he and his brother went rabbit hunting, only to come across something that only had one eye. When the boys shot at the creature, it simply disappeared, only to return seconds later in a different location. Troy explains that numerous others have seen the one-eyed creature, and that grown men have come home scared and shaken from seeing it.

Swamper Terral Evans also shares tales of the supernatural. He recounts the legend of a bigfoot-like creature called the "Honey Island Swamp Monster." This creature haunts the Atchafalaya swamp basin. Like Bigfoot, it is a large humanoid figure, covered in hair and smelling of sulfur. Its cries can be heard late at night, and witnesses have seen large footprints in the swamp, too large to belong to a human being. Terral's wife Dana grew up with tales of this Swamp Monster, and her father claimed to have captured video evidence of the beast. Viewers see this footage, as Terral and Dana explain the legend. In one episode, Terral and Dana take friends out camping to look for the monster. They camp deep within the swamp and set up motion-sensored video equipment. Like scenes from several horror films, the campers sit around the campfire, recounting stories of the Honey Island Swamp Monster. Several times they think they have heard something suspicious and go to investigate. In the morning, haggard from little sleep, the campers head back to civilization. When reviewing their video, they see unexplainable fur and blurred images in one shot. Viewers are invited to speculate whether this is sufficient evidence to suggest the existence of the monster in the swamp. This investigative format follows closely those of the supernatural reality television series. In this way, *Swamp People* also references contemporary horror television.

In season two, episode eleven, "Beat the Clock," alligator hunter Bruce Mitchell and his apprentice Nick are desperate to fill tags (or reach their quota of alligators for the season). They decide to hunt an area called by Cajuns "The Devil's Swamp." According to Cajun lore, a giant alligator named "Lucifer" lives in the swamp, but the natives warn against trying to hunt this alligator or in this area. Bruce explains, "You hear about this and that, and people say, well, don't go back in here 'cause it's bad and stuff happens back there. It's hard to get in, hard to get out. Trees fall on you and stuff like that. But it's just certain parts of the swamp you just don't go in." Despite his own misgivings and the warnings of others, Bruce enters the swamp. Camerawork creates a disorienting feeling for viewers, with angles that shoot up to show tall, dying cypress trees and then quickly cut to flocks of egrets fleeing en masse. Horror music and non-linear sounds punctuate such images. Bruce and Nick soon learn that this area lives up to its reputation. They cannot find the lines they set, Bruce's dog falls in the water, and their boat motor gets stuck in the mud. These problems are attributed, not to poor hunting or luck, but to the supernatural—to the curse that accompanies anyone who dares hunt in Devil's Swamp.

SWAMP PEOPLE AS SOUTHERN HORRORS

In addition to the horrors of the landscape, animals, and the supernatural, the people of the swamp themselves are frequently portrayed as horrific. Like the threat of their ancestors (French Acadians, Native Americans, and runaway slaves), the appeal of *Swamp People* lies, in part, in the horror of the swamp's inhabitants, "Others," who do not look, act, or sound like mainstream America. The show plays upon Southern and Cajun stereotypes and links them to the horrific. This Othering is done through voice, appearance, customs, and hunting techniques.

The series highlights the Southern and Cajun accents and dialect of the swampers, positioning the participants as somehow foreign. The producers explain how the dialect is the result of the Cajuns' French Acadian ancestry. Such ancestry is framed against the standard of the English-speaking colonists. *Swamp People* even uses subtitles when many of the swampers are speaking, suggesting that the language is so incomprehensible and foreign to viewers that they need subtitles to understand what the person is saying.

The image or appearance of the swamper in *Swamp People* also establishes him as an Other. The (male) Southerner as an icon of horror is a common character in horror fiction and film. Films such as *Macon County Line* (1974), *The Texas Chainsaw Massacre* (1974), *Wrong Turn* (2003), and *Hatchet* (2007) show deranged killers in rural, Southern locations. These individuals are sometimes cannibals or engage in incest, "inbreds" who are ignorant and, most notably, violent. The most famous of these films, of course, is *Deliverance* (1972). The film arguably functions as short-hand for the terror of backwoods Southern natives, so much so that banjo music in general, and the signature music of the film, "Duelin' Banjos," signify horror for some. *Swamp People* implicitly references *Deliverance*, both in its use of a banjo soundtrack and its depiction of some of the show's characters. In the introduction to season two, for example, Willie Edwards issues what seems like a warning to outsiders who want to visit or live in the swamp. Edwards looks into the camera, shakes his head, and warns, "If you think you can come out here and do it, good luck to ya." Willie's direct eye contact and doubting expression are intimidating. Moreover, his slight smile reveals a missing front tooth, which links him to the frightening, smiling characters of *Deliverance*.

Other swampers' images are stereotypically backwoods and Southern. Glenn and Mitchell Guist, the Guist brothers, are swampers who have long gray beards and unkempt hair. They, too, are missing teeth and wear haggard leathery faces from living and working in the sun. In several introductions, they are seen in close-up, framed by the light of an old, hand-held lantern. [17] The Guist brothers, along with other swamp people, eat a variety of unusual cuisine that also sets them apart from mainstream America. Food consists of frogs, crayfish, turtles, alligator gar, nutria (also known as a swamp rat), snakes, and of course, alligators. *Swamp People* shows the swampers as they hunt, capture, clean, and cook such animals.

Finally, the people of the swamp are seen as horrific in their primitive hunting techniques. Although hunters do use shotguns, they also incorporate what Clover calls "pretechnical" weapons to catch their prey.[18] Some hunters use their bare hands to capture alligators. Terral Evans almost always captures alligators this way, often so he can capture them alive for scientists. In one particularly gruesome scene, Willie Edwards is bitten by an alligator while using his hands. Willie and his father Junior also use a special hook, known as a treble hook, in their hunts. The men throw the hook attached to a rope in the vicinity of an alligator and hope to hook it. If successful, they pull the alligator (weighing hundreds of pounds) to the boat. In season four, episode one, "Swamp Invaders," Houma hunter Jay Paul Roulinere actually jumps into the water with an alligator in order to subdue it. These dangerous techniques frame the hunters as not only crazy, but as primitive as well, demonstrating the horrific, other-worldly nature of people who live in the swamp.

CONCLUSION: THE REAL REALITY IN SWAMP PEOPLE

The History Channel does not market *Swamp People* as a paranormal or horror-based reality show. Viewers are explicitly invited to discover the world of alligator hunters and the Louisianan Cajun lifestyle. However, as this chapter has demonstrated, the series repeatedly relies on horror references and conventions. Part of the appeal of *Swamp People* lies in the underlying horror of the swamp, its creatures, myths and inhabitants. The show highlights these connections and reinforces their authenticity. What is problematic about such an approach is that it reinforces stereotypes of Southern and Cajun culture through its editing, selection of cast members, and filming choices. Reality television, like all media representations, is never actually "real," but filtered through selections of what to include, what not to include, and how to use the material filmed. Such choices are rendered invisible, however, so that the final show appears to be what really happened in the real life of these real people. *Swamp People*'s home network of the History Channel reinforces this illusion of authenticity even further, as a reputable channel known for presenting historical information to its audiences. In the end, *Swamp People* perpetuates an understanding of the South, especially the Cajun South, as a place of horror.

REFERENCES

Blumstein, Daniel T., Richard Davitian, and Peter D. Kaye. "Do Film Soundtracks Contain Nonlinear Analogues to Influence Emotion?" *Biology Letters* 6 (2010): 751-754.

Bresciani, Edda. "Sobek, Lord of the Land of the Lake." In *Divine Creatures: Animal Mummies in Ancient Egypt.* Edited by Salima Ikram, 199-206. Cairo: The American University in Cairo Press, 2005.

Clissold, Bradley D. *"Candid Camera* and the Origins of Reality TV: Contextualizing a Historical Precedent." In *Understanding Reality Television,* edited by Su Holmes and Deborah Jermyn, 33-53, London: Routledge, 2004.

Clover, Carol. "Her Body, Himself: Gender in the Slasher Film." In *The Dread of Difference: Gender and the Horror Film.* Edited by Barry Keith Grant, 66-116. Austin: University of Texas Press, 1996.

Friedman, James."Introduction." In *Reality Squared: Televisual Discourse on the Real.* Edited by James Friedman, 2-12, New Brunswick, NJ: Rutgers University Press, 2002.

Giblett, Rod. *Postmodern Wetlands: Culture, History, Ecology.* Edinburgh: Edinburgh University Press, 1996.

Haynes. Julie. "Gators, Beavers, and Roaches: Whiteness and Regional Identity in Reality Television." *Images of Whiteness.* Edited by Clarissa Behar and Anastasia Chung, 79-88, Oxford: Inter-Disciplinary Press, 2013.

Huff, Richard. *Reality Television.* Westport, CT: Praeger, 2006.

Levi-Strauss, Claude. *The Raw and the Cooked: Mythologiques, Volume 1.* Chicago: University of Chicago Press, 1969.

McCarthy, Kevin M. *Alligator Tales.* Sarasota, Florida: Pineapple Press, 1998.

Nabi, Robin L. "Determining Dimensions of Reality: A Concept Mapping of the Reality TV Landscape." *Journal of Broadcasting and Electronic Media* 51 (2007): 371-390.

Ouellette, Lauri and Susan Murray. "Introduction." In *Reality Television: Remaking Television Culture.* Edited by Laurie Oeullette and Susan Murray, 1-5, New York: New York University Press, 2004.

Slade, Alison F., Dedria Givens-Carroll, and Amber J. Narro, eds. *Mediated Images of the South: The Portrayal of Dixie in Popular Culture.* Lanham, Maryland: Lexington Books, 2012.

The History Channel. *"Swamp People:* About the Show." A&E Television Networks, 2013, http://www.history.com/shows/swamp-people/about

Thoreau, Henry David. *Walking.* New York: HaperCollins, 1994.

Vileisis Anne. *Discovering the Unknown Landscape: A History of America's Wetlands.* Washington, DC: Island Press, 1997.

Whitman, Walt. *Leaves of Grass and Other Writings.* Edited by Michael Moon. New York: W.W. Norton, 2002.

Wilson, Anthony. *Shadow and Shelter: The Swamp in Southern Culture.* Jackson: University of Mississippi Press, 2006.

NOTES

1. In its "About the Show" section, The History Channel's website explains that *Swamp People* documents the lives of Cajun "swampers through a time of year that is crucial to their survival: the 30-day alligator hunting season. At its core, this is a uniquely American story of a proud and skillful people fighting to maintain an ancient way of life in a rapidly modernizing world, despite the many perils and trials that stand in their way" The History Channel, *"Swamp People:* About the Show," A&E Television Networks, 2013, http://www.history.com/shows/swamp-people/about

2. Debate exists about the actual beginnings of reality television. While roots of the genre are evident prior to the 1990s, some television scholars cite the debut of the MTV series, *Real World,* in 1992 as the starting point for reality television. Others argue that the CBS series,

Survivor, in 2000 marks the true emergence of the genre. For a discussion of the emergence of reality tv and its precursors, see, for example, Richard Huff, *Reality Television,* (Westport, CT: Praeger, 2006), 1-18; Laurie Ouellette and Susan Murray, "Introduction," in *Reality Television: Remaking Television Culture,* ed. Laurie Oeullette and Susan Murray (New York: New York University Press, 2004), 1-5; Bradley D. Clissold, "*Candid Camera* and the Origins of Reality TV: Contextualizing a Historical Precedent," in *Understanding Reality Television,* ed. Su Holmes and Deborah Jermyn (London: Routledge, 2004), 33-53; James Friedman, "Introduction," in *Reality Squared: Televisual Discourse on the Real,* ed. James Friedman (New Brunswick, NJ: Rutgers University Press, 2002), 2-12.

3. For a discussion of reality television subgenres, see, for example, Ouelette and Murray, Introduction," 3-5, and Robin L. Nabi, "Determining Dimensions of Reality: A Concept Mapping of the Reality TV Landscape," *Journal of Broadcasting and Electronic Media* 51 (2007): 371-390.

4. For a discussion of images of Southerners in popular culture, see essays in Alison F. Slade, Dedria Givens-Carroll, and Amber J. Narro, eds., *Mediated Images of the South: The Portrayal of Dixie in Popular Culture* (Lanham, Maryland: Lexington Books, 2012). For essays on reality television's depiction of the South and gender, race, and class issues, see, for example, Julie Haynes, "Gators, Beavers, and Roaches: Whiteness and Regional Identity in Reality Television," *Images of Whiteness,* ed. by Clarissa Behar and Anastasia Chung (Oxford: Inter-Disciplinary Press, 2013), 79-88, and Hernandez's *Duck Dynasty* chapter in this volume.

5. See, for example, Claude Levi-Strauss, *The Raw and the Cooked: Mythologiques, Volume 1* (Chicago: University of Chicago Press, 1969).

6. See Walt Whitman, *Leaves of Grass and Other Writings,* ed. by Michael Moon (New York: W.W. Norton, 2002); Henry David Thoreau, *Walking* (New York: HaperCollins, 1994). For discussions of this position on the swamp and the cultural history of the swamp, see, for example, Rod Giblett, *Postmodern Wetlands: Culture, History, Ecology* (Edinburgh: Edinburgh University Press, 1996), and Anthony Wilson, *Shadow and Shelter: The Swamp in Southern Culture* (Jackson: University of Mississippi Press, 2006.

7. Giblett, 5.

8. Wilson, xv.

9. Carol Clover, "Her Body, Himself: Gender in the Slasher Film," *The Dread of Difference: Gender and the Horror Film,* ed. by Barry Keith Grant (Austin: University of Texas Press, 1996), 78.

10. Wilson, ix.

11. Wilson, xiii; Anne Vileisis, *Discovering the Unknown Landscape: A History of America's Wetlands* (Washington, DC: Island Press, 1997).

12. Wilson, xvii-xviii. It is important to note that Wilson acknowledges the contradictory nature of the Southern swamp described in literature and culture as both a negative and positive place. For this portion of the chapter, I focus on the horrific elements he discusses.

13. Non-linear sounds are used most famously in the soundtracks of *Psycho* and *Jaws.* Such sounds are thought to replicate animals in distress, causing them to be effective means to audibly invoke fear in audiences. See Daniel T. Blumstein, Richard Davitian, and Peter D. Kaye, "Do Film Soundtracks Contain Nonlinear Analogues to Influence Emotion?" *Biology Letters* 6 (2010): 751-754.

14. Willie wears tube socks to cover his arms in this episode. In others, he sometimes wears long sleeves, and sometimes gloves. He does not, however, use any sort of stick or tool to retrieve the snakes.

15. Evidence exists that the Ancient Egyptians and Greeks had at least one deity based on the alligator or crocodile. The Egyptian Sobek took the form of a crocodile or part human-part crocodile creature. See for example, Edda Bresciani, "Sobek, Lord of the Land of the Lake," *Divine Creatures: Animal Mummies in Ancient Egypt,* ed. by Salima Ikram (Cairo: The American University in Cairo Press, 2005), 199-206. The danger of alligators is a common trope in literature and popular culture (comics, films, television shows, and sports mascots) and the source of several urban legends. See, Kevin M. McCarthy, *Alligator Tales,* (Sarasota, Florida: Pineapple Press, 1998).

16. Clover, 69-70.

17. Mitchell Guist died while working in the swamp on May 14, 2012.
18. Clover, 79.

Conclusion

Amber J. Narro

It is reality television that gives us a glimpse into the lives of our neighbors and an opportunity to also look at ourselves. With television dedicating large amounts of time to programming involving Southerners, it is no wonder that there is such intrigue surrounding the swamps, bayous, pageantry and even the accent.

The interest has encouraged viewers to consult with friends on social media and seek out the socialization of those reality television stars. Direct messages, Website comments and tweeting are only the beginning of the outreach as "outsiders" are flocking to the South just to see what all this talk is about—and why in fact Southerners don't pay no mind to ending phrases and sentences with prepositions.

Reality television further presses the stereotypes long associated with the South. While most Southerners don't actually ride everywhere on pirogues or invite alligators to the back door, they are laughing all the way to the bank as they cash in on their "reality." Shows such as Duck Dynasty and Swamp People have a cult-like following and are merchandising the Southern way of life, and tourism associated with that way of life is skyrocketing as well. T-shirts, key rings and coffee cups depict famous jargon, logos and pictures of the "real" South. Reality television stars are pulled in every direction for appearances and endorsements, and many of them have embraced the celebrity following.

Whether it's the manly game of alligator hunting or the real housewives of, well, whatever, Southerners can depend on their charm to invite an audience willing to pay big to soak up the culture. While reality television may be exploiting a mysterious and unwavering population of perceived undereducated underachievers, those who have long been ignored from the outside world may actually enjoy this newfound spotlight as they demonstrate talent, strength, family, love, devotion and, dare we admit, intelligence.

Y'all come back now, ya' hear? And bring your wallets. This show is for sale . . . and the South is cashing in!

Index

265

About the Contributors

Gordon Alley-Young, PhD, is a Professor of Speech Communication in the Department of Communications & Performing Arts at Kingsborough Community College—City University of New York (CUNY). His research focuses on intercultural communication within popular culture and critical perspectives on identity and education. His most recent book chapter is *Whose Niqab is This? Challenging, Creating and Communicating Female Muslim Identity via Social Media* in the Turkish language book *Medya Eleştirileri 2013: Sosyal Medya Ağ Toplumu 2: Kültür, Kimlik, Siyaset* (Beslenme Saati: Reklam Yaratıcıları Derneği, 2013). His most recent journal article is *Writing for Their Futures: High vs. Low-Stakes Assignments and Students' Reflections on Writing Attraction* (*Talking About Learning: The South East European University Language Center Journal of Teaching and Learning*, 2013). He is a former book review co-editor for *American Communication Journal* and has published book reviews in over twenty-five regional, national, and international journals. He is the Immediate Past President of *CLASP: The CUNY League of Active Speech Professors*.

Burt Buchanan (PhD, The University of Southern Mississippi) is an assistant professor of mass communication at Auburn University at Montgomery. Before entering into his current academic position, he had a successful career in television production and public relations with both private and governmental organizations. He has worked as a news photographer, television news reporter, editor, director and producer. He has taught full time at the university level since 2003. His research interests include media portrayals and media history.

Andre Cavalcante is an Assistant Professor at the University of Virginia jointly appointed in the Department of Media Studies and the Program in Women, Gender and Sexuality. Dr. Cavalcante's research explores the dynamic intersection of media culture, everyday life, and identity formation along the axes of gender, sexuality, race and class. His work has appeared in *Critical Studies in Media Communication* and *Watching While Black: Centering the Television of Black Audiences*.

Elizabeth Barfoot Christian is an assistant professor of communication at the University of New Haven. She earned her PhD in mass communication from The University of Southern Mississippi. She is the editor of the award-winning *Rock Brands: Selling Sound in a Media-Saturated Culture* (Lexington, 2011) and the author of a companion yearlong nationally awarded blog on music marketing published by Rowman & Littlefield. Her professional research includes work in prison communication, popular culture and journalism history. She also hosts a weekly radio program, Rock & Rhetoric, on WNHU 88.7 West Haven.

Nicole B. Cox, (PhD, Florida State University) is Assistant Professor of Mass Media at Valdosta State University. Nicole's research interests include feminist political economy, political economy of media, gender studies, reality TV, and online fandom. Her publications include: "Taking the FCC to Church: The United Church of Christ's Activism in Broadcast Regulation," published in *First Amendment Studies;* "Kicking ass . . . With lip gloss: Mediating gender on TLC's 'Police Women of Broward County'," published in *Critical Studies in Media Communication*; "A Little Sex Appeal Goes a Long Way: Feminist Political Economy, Commodification, and TLC's 'What Not to Wear'," published in *Kaleidoscope*; and a co-authored piece with Jennifer M. Proffitt, titled, "The Housewives' Guide to Better Living: Promoting Consumption on Bravo's 'The Real Housewives'," published in *Communication, Culture & Critique*.

Rebecca M. L. Curnalia (PhD, Kent State University) is an associate professor in the Department of Communication at Youngstown State University in Youngstown, Ohio. Her published research has explored learning from the news and the emotional appeals used in political campaigns. Her current research interests explore the myriad media content that influences political opinions, including entertainment media, traditional news media, social media, and fake news. She is lead author of the forthcoming book, *Becoming a Critic: An Introduction to Analyzing Media Content* (2013) published by Kendall-Hunt.

Matthew P. Ferrari is a doctoral candidate in the Department of Communication at The University of Massachusetts, Amherst. He earned a B.A. in Art History and Visual Culture from Bates College, and an M.A. in Film and Media studies from Ohio University. Matthew has published numerous columns in *Flow Journal*, the edited collections *Storytelling in World Cinemas* and *Fighting: Intellectualizing Combat Sports* (forthcoming), and in the journal *Environmental Communication: A Journal of Nature and Culture*. He has presented his work at ICA, NCA, NEPCA, and the Flow Conference, among other venues. Matthew recently received a UMass Graduate School Fellowship to complete work on his dissertation, *Signs of Wildness: Primitivism, Nature, and Performance in Contemporary Media Culture*.

Julie Haynes (PhD, Penn State University) is Associate Dean of the College of Communication and Creative Arts at Rowan University, where she also teaches in the Communication Studies and Women's & Gender Studies departments. Her research interests include rhetoric of media and popular culture, constructions of gender and feminist resistance rhetoric, and regional identity. Her recent work has been included in *Local Violence, Global Media: Feminist Analyses of Gendered Representations*, edited by Lisa Cuklanz and Sujata Moorti (New York: Peter Lang, 2009) and as part of the 2nd Global Conference on Whiteness, Mansfield College, Oxford University, 2012.

Leandra H. Hernandez received her master's degree in communication from the University of Houston and is a PhD candidate and instructor at the Department of Communication at Texas A&M University—College Station. Leandra is a Women's & Gender Studies Graduate Certificate recipient, and her research interests fall under two main categories: health communication with a focus on women's health, and media representations of gender. Thus, she enjoys researching reproductive politics, minority health issues, patient-provider communication, women's pregnancy experiences, media coverage of gender, and media representations of masculinities and femininities, particularly in reality television shows. An award-winning instructor, she enjoys teaching a variety of classes including but not limited to Gender & the Media, Health Communication, Interpersonal Communication, and Interviewing Practices & Principles.

Christopher Mapp (PhD, Louisiana State University) is the holder of the Vernon McCory 1st Amendment Professorship in Mass Communication at the University of Louisiana at Monroe. Mapp joined the faculty of ULM in July 2010, where he teaches journalism and graduate quantitative research methods. He is also director of student publications, overseeing the production of *The Hawkeye* student newspaper and its companion Web site, the

Chacahoula yearbook, and the *Helicon*, a literary magazine. Mapp has published book chapters and articles in academic journals and has presented both at national and regional conferences. Mapp has worked as a reporter, sportswriter and editor for daily and weekly newspapers and has freelanced for national publications and for the Associated Press. Currently, in addition to his faculty position at ULM, he is a scriptwriter for Hollywood Casting & Film in Los Angeles, California, and sits on the company's advisory board. His research interests are varied, including conflict and forgiveness among deployed military couples, imagined interactions and loneliness, deceptive uses of social media, crisis communication and news coverage of hurricanes, and newsprint recycling and the environmental "green" movement.

Pamela L. Morris is currently an Assistant Professor of Communication Studies at the University of Wisconsin–La Crosse where she specializes in media studies. She received her Ph.D. in Communication from Purdue University. Prior to her studies at Purdue, Pamela studied computer science and worked at IBM for 12 years as a programmer and project manager. Her primary research interests are virtual work and technology adoption in organizations, and uses and effects of technology in the media and in the classroom. Most recently, Pamela completed a large grant that involved training supervisors of virtual employees in a government organization. Her current research projects include investigating reality television, legal issues surrounding Facebook's "Like" button, and the use of social media between instructors and students. Pamela thoroughly enjoys her teaching duties, whether on campus or in the virtual classroom.

Amber J. Narro (PhD, The University of Southern Mississippi) is an associate professor of communication and obtained her doctorate of mass communication from the University of Southern Mississippi. She specializes in multi-platform journalism and researches political news coverage, journalism trends and communication for non-profit organizations. With professional experience in both journalism and public relations, she has practical knowledge to add to her courses in journalism, public relations and public communication. Dr. Narro is the coordinator for the England study abroad program at Southeastern, and she has published articles in national and international journals. She has a bachelor's degree in mass communication and journalism and a master's degree in organizational communication, both of which she obtained from Southeastern Louisiana University.

Charissa (Cheri) K. Niedzwiecki is currently an associate professor at the University of Wisconsin–La Crosse where she has taught for the past 19 years. She previously taught at the University of Nebraska–Lincoln, where she also received her Ph.D., and the University of Alaska–Fairbanks. Dr.

Niedzwiecki's primary research interest is in the area of family communication where she did her dissertation on conflict with parents and adolescents and later studied college students, siblings and grandparents. In addition, she has done research with gendered identities and family gender roles. She created new classes in Family, Gender and Intercultural Communication and an online class on Sexuality and Romance in the Mass Media at UW-L. She has published articles in the *Journal of the Wisconsin Communication Association* and *Speech Teacher*. Currently, she is doing research with reality TV (one of her favorite pastimes).

Leslie Rasmussen (PhD, The University of Southern Mississippi) is an Assistant Professor in the Communication Department at Utah Valley University. Her work has been published in *PR Review* and she has presented at academic conferences, including Association for Education in Journalism and Mass Communication, National Communication Association, International Communication Association and Southern States Communication Association.

Alison F. Slade (PhD, The University of Southern Mississippi) is currently a stay-at-home mom with five children. In her spare time, she continues with her academic research interests, which include reality television, social media, and fan culture. For the past three years, Dr. Slade has hosted the nationally syndicated radio program *The Alison Slade Show*, focusing on political discourse from an independent conservative view. Dr. Slade has appeared as a media expert on *The Redding News Review* and *America's Morning News*. She was also a contributor in the award-winning book *Rock Brands: Selling Sound in a Media Saturated Culture* (Dr. Elizabeth Christian, Ed.) and co-editor of *Mediated Images of the South: The Portrayal of Dixie in Popular Culture*.

William C. Trapani (PhD University of Iowa) is an Assistant Professor in the School of Communication and Multimedia Studies at Florida Atlantic University. His research and teaching interests include rhetorical theory and criticism, visual rhetoric, and discourses of national identity. His published work considers the rhetorical manufacture of American national character, and addresses the ways in which that persona is constructed in discursive relation to subjects figured as dangerous to national ideals.

Laura L. Winn (PhD University of Georgia) is an Instructor in the School of Communication and Multimedia Studies at Florida Atlantic University. Her research and teaching interests include interpersonal and family communication with a particular emphasis on gender and culture. Her published work ranges from an examination of gendered language forms to media representations of gender and relational communication dynamics.